The Architecture of William Nichols

Paul Hardin Kapp with Todd Sanders

Foreword by William Seale

University Press of Mississippi / Jackson

ARKANSAS

TENNESSEE

FLORENCE

MUSCLE
SHOALS

OXFORD
UNIV. OF MISSISSIPPI
NICHOLS LIVES HERE
FROM 1846-1848

LEXINGTON
NICHOLS DIES
IN 1853

TUSCALOOSA
NICHOLS ARRIVES IN
1827, LEAVES IN 1834
UNIV. OF ALABAMA
STATE CAPITAL STATE
ARCHITECT

YAZOO CITY
NICHOLS LIVES
HERE IN 1850

FORKLAND

VICKSBURG

JACKSON
NICHOLS ARRIVES IN
1836, LEAVES IN 1848
STATE ARCHITECT
1836 - 1847

MONTGOMERY
NICHOLS STAYS HERE
IN 1834

RAYMOND

MISSISSIPPI

ALABAMA

LOUISIANA

NEW ORLEANS
NICHOLS LIVES HERE FROM
1834 - 1836
ASSISTANT STATE ENGINEER

The Architecture of
WILLIAM NICHOLS

Building the Antebellum South in
North Carolina, Alabama, and Mississippi

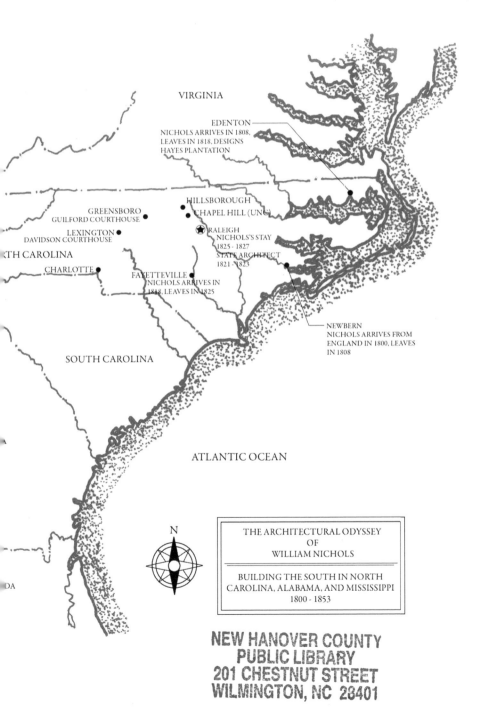

VIRGINIA

EDENTON
NICHOLS ARRIVES IN 1808,
LEAVES IN 1818, DESIGNS
HAYES PLANTATION

HILLSBOROUGH
GREENSBORO
GUILFORD COURTHOUSE
CHAPEL HILL (UNC)
LEXINGTON
DAVIDSON COURTHOUSE
RALEIGH
NICHOLS'S STAY
1825 - 1827
TH CAROLINA
STATE ARCHITECT
1821 - 1823
CHARLOTTE
FAYETTEVILLE
NICHOLS ARRIVES IN
1818, LEAVES IN 1825

NEWBERN
NICHOLS ARRIVES FROM
ENGLAND IN 1800, LEAVES
IN 1808

SOUTH CAROLINA

ATLANTIC OCEAN

N

THE ARCHITECTURAL ODYSSEY
OF
WILLIAM NICHOLS

BUILDING THE SOUTH IN NORTH
CAROLINA, ALABAMA, AND MISSISSIPPI
1800 - 1853

DA

www.upress.state.ms.us

The University Press of Mississippi is a member of the Association of
American University Presses.

Pages ii and iii: Drawing by author and Michelle Zupancic

First printing 2015

∞

Library of Congress Cataloging-in-Publication Data

Kapp, Paul Hardin.
    The architecture of William Nichols : building the antebellum South in North
Carolina, Alabama, and Mississippi / Paul Hardin Kapp with Todd Sanders ; foreword
by William Seale.
        pages cm
    Summary: "The Architecture of William Nichols is the first comprehensive biography
and monograph of a significant yet over-looked architect in the American South.
William Nichols designed three major university campuses—the University of North
Carolina, the University of Alabama, and the University of Mississippi. He also
designed the first state capitols of North Carolina, Alabama, and Mississippi. Nichols's
architecture profoundly influenced the built landscape of the South but due to fire,
neglect, and demolition, much of his work was lost and history has nearly forgotten
his tremendous legacy. In his research onsite and through archives in North Carolina,
Alabama, Louisiana, and Mississippi, Paul Hardin Kapp has produced a narrative of
the life and times of William Nichols that weaves together the elegant work of this
architect with the aspirations and challenges of the antebellum South. It is richly
illustrated with over two hundred archival photographs and drawings from the
Historic American Building Survey"— Provided by publisher.
    Includes bibliographical references and index.
    ISBN 978-1-62846-138-1 (hardback) — ISBN 978-1-62846-139-8 (ebook) 1. Nichols,
William, approximately 1777–1853—Criticism and interpretation. 2. Architecture—
Southern States. 3. Southern States—History—1775–1865. I. Sanders, Todd (Joseph
Todd) II. Title.
    NA737.N45K37 2015

    720.92—dc23   2014024117

British Library Cataloging-in-Publication Data available

Contents

Foreword

Building men mark the rise and flow of civilization. Their buildings are milestones through time. This book takes place in the first half of the nineteenth century, when its character, William Nichols, was setting down many such milestones. History books pay little attention to builders such as he was, compared to judges, doctors, military heroes, elected officials, and the like, who left words that determined their ruling presence.

Paul Hardin Kapp has absorbed all the usual handicaps of research and through hard digging has unearthed the story of William Nichols. He has been heretofore a nearly forgotten architect, when in fact he gave early nineteenth-century America some of its most distinctive buildings. He worked in the South. Most of his buildings are gone today, victims of fire. Dismissed often as a "vernacular" builder, Nichols, in *The Architecture of William Nichols*, emerges full-bodied as a classicist who understood both formal architectural design and regional practicalities. With meticulous research and thoughtful, critical analysis, the author has painted a portrait of a determined man, entrepreneur, land owner, engineer, and most of all a self-proclaimed architect, in a time when the title meant little in the broader context of building.

Architectural historians recall Nichols in localities of the South for what he built there, but little else has been known about him. He was a British subject who arrived in the United States, in North Carolina, cherishing memories of his hometown, the stylish resort of Bath. The neoclassicism and elegant restraint of Bath's new architecture was to influence Nichols's own designs for the rest of his life. From a family involved in building and cabinetmaking, he turned his own ambitions in that direction, beginning an American career of over fifty years moving across the South, building. He knew that for an architect to grow and flower in his work, he needed to be where there was money and the desire to spend it, be it with individuals or governments. He pursued these green pastures from the tobacco of North Carolina to the cotton fields of the flush times in Alabama and Mississippi.

Through the public buildings and private houses he built, Nichols became the most notably prolific architect and builder in the South. The author builds his character from every angle, exhausting every possible avenue of research. Beyond the day-to-day of the architect's career, Kapp explores significantly Nichols's likely sources of design, the architecture and building books he obviously carried with him that inspired his work. His study of these books of the late eighteenth and early nineteenth centuries produces rich results. He builds a context of Nichols's taste, bearing in mind the customs Nichols had known in England. Nichols's admiration, for example, of stone construction made him push his clients to build in stone. Most clients refused, living as they did in a country rich in clay for brick and virgin forests filled with pine, walnut, cypress, and oak. "Captain" Nichols thus built usually in wood.

Kapp's research extends beyond the written and printed page to the actual buildings that prevail. He compares moldings on surviving Nichols buildings to moldings in the early architecture books, and likewise judges details of door surrounds and windows, mantels, cornices, stairs, and the other elements of his houses. The physical sources are few and none escape the author's magnifying glass. One of his sources is from a house still standing only in part, a bow-end ballroom very elaborately detailed inside, that was pulled off a house in Fayetteville, North Carolina, when the rest of the house was demolished. The room preserves Nichols's design skill at its most delicate.

Architecture then and now is not an easy field for making a living. There has to be some more compelling reason than money to venture there. Like many another architect Nichols made every effort to buoy his income from architecture with side-line endeavors. In his case, it was feast or famine. His tenaciousness in holding on revealed the love he held for the profession. In good times he was so busy he was selling drawings to others, for he had no time to build their buildings. Hard times saw his lands advertised for sale.

Nichols was an aggressive and successful job-getter. He built three state capitols (and designed another for Louisiana not built), the latest of them (1838) still standing in a pristine state of preservation in use as the Old Capitol Museum in Jackson, Mississippi. The refined, lofty building mingles Nichols's early exposure to neoclassicism in Bath, simplified American-style, and flavored with the later Greek Revival. In this building he even got his "stone construction" by facing the brick walls, above the basement level, with mastic or stucco, scored to resemble dressed stone.

The two other capitols he built, which the author has reconstructed with great care, were highly successful stage sets upon which state government might perform. To read about them is to wish they had survived. Nichols remodeled the rectangular North Carolina Capitol in Raleigh (1824) in great theatrical splendor to house a statue of George Washington in Roman uniform which had been ordered by the legislature from the celebrated sculptor Antonio Canova in Rome. The architect reconfigured the building with right-angle additions into a Greek cross shape, cutting a lofty rotunda up through the crossing—one of the first rotundas ever in a state capitol—that shed natural light from a shallow dome, also famously including moon glow, on the marble statue. The effect was sublime.

In Tuscaloosa, Alabama (1831), the capitol he built was in the Grecian "plain style" of England and of Bath, again touched firmly with Greek Revival, the interiors cautiously detailed with Roman and Greek motifs. Executed in red brick with wood trim painted white, it was crowned by a shallow dome. A building of remarkable beauty, its interior was thoughtfully devised to take advantage of natural light in colonnaded rotunda and rooms arranged to insure the enchanting effect of enfilade through long-distance interior views.

His other known works included churches, state offices, private houses, and universities. The latter were the campuses of the University of North Carolina, the University of Alabama, and the University of Mississippi. In these projects he addressed master planning, which has survived today in the campuses at Tuscaloosa, Oxford, and Chapel Hill. What was to be his major residential project still stands in Edenton, North Carolina, a wooden structure called Hayes that he completed in 1818, when the architect was thirty-four and America had weathered the war with Britain and stood feasting on the eve of a disastrous depression. One stands before Hayes today and wonders if in its details of heroic wooden columns, heavy louvered blinds, and classical window surrounds it is not a mansion from some tropical romance. It is surely high among the most remarkable American houses of the early nineteenth century, although there is little about it one might actually label "American."

William Nichols was a man of significant architectural gifts. His work in a number of important buildings can stand up to almost any of his contemporaries. Never hampered by being entirely a copyist, he toyed with style, still loyal to neoclassicism, but easily mingling other elements as necessary to please his clients. He is emblematic of an age, yet he stands out distinctly among building men of his time. *The Architecture of William Nichols* is a monumental work and provides a fascinating journey with the protagonist through half a century of building in the South.

—WILLIAM SEALE

Acknowledgments

Researching and writing the story of William Nichols and his architecture has been a wonderful experience and I have been very fortunate to receive generous support and encouragement from a wide variety of people and institutions throughout this journey. I want to first thank Chancellor Emeritus James Moeser for introducing me to Gerrard Hall on the campus of the University of North Carolina at Chapel Hill. It was with him, in the silence of that venerable hall, where my adventure with Nichols began. I want to thank my friend and mentor John Sanders for his guidance and for allowing me to examine his impressive papers on William Nichols in North Carolina. I want to thank Catherine Bishir for her encouragement early on in the project. I am especially grateful to the Campanella brothers, Tom and Rich. Tom gave me a lot of encouragement early on in the project when we were both teaching and working at the University of North Carolina at Chapel Hill. Rich provided me valuable insights on the history of New Orleans during the 1830s. In Alabama, I want to thank Robert Mellown, Professor Emeritus at the University of Alabama, and Robert Gamble, Senior Architectural Historian at the Alabama Historical Commission, for providing me information on Nichols's life and work in Alabama. In Mississippi, I want to thank my editor, Craig Gill, for introducing me to Todd Sanders and I want to thank Richard Cawthon for providing me important insights on the Old Mississippi Capitol. Finally, I want to thank my old friend Louis Watson and his family for their gracious hospitality during my visits to Jackson.

I am grateful to the Athenaeum of Philadelphia for their support through a Charles Peterson Fellowship. This grant provided me the much-needed financial resources to travel to eastern North Carolina and Mississippi for my research. I am also grateful to the University of Illinois School of Architecture and the University of Illinois Research Board for providing the financial support to publish this book.

But I really want to thank my wonderful wife, Wendy. This one is for you, hon!

Chronology

1805
New Bern Academy Portico
New Bern, NC
Client: New Bern Academy Board of Trustees

1806
Judge Donnell Law Office
New Bern, NC
Client: John Robert Donnell

1808
Saint Paul's Episcopal Church (interior carpentry and steeple ornamentation only)
Edenton, NC
Client: Saint Paul's Episcopal Church

1808
Chowan County Courthouse (alteration and remodeling)
Edenton, NC
Client: County of Chowan, NC

1814
Joseph Blount Skinner Office (Old East Customs House, altered in the early
    twentieth century)
Edenton, NC
Client: Joseph Blount Skinner

1816

James Iredell House (mantle and door entries to 1815 addition)

Edenton, NC

Client: James Iredell, Jr.

1816–1818

Hayes Plantation

Chowan Co., NC

Client: James Cathcart Johnston

1818

Bank of the Cape Fear (destroyed by fire in 1831)

Fayetteville, NC

Client: State of North Carolina

1818

Branch of the Bank of the United States (Sandford House)

Fayetteville, NC

Client: Bank of the United States

1819

Cameron-Halliday House (Oval Ballroom, surviving)

Fayetteville, NC

Client: James Cameron

1820

Saint John's Episcopal Church (destroyed by fire in 1831)

Fayetteville, NC

Client: Saint John's Episcopal Church

1823–1827

University of North Carolina

Chapel Hill, NC

    Campus Plan (north quadrangle, now known as McCorkle Place)

    Old West (expanded to the north by A. J. Davis in 1847)

    Expansion of Old East (expanded to the north by A. J. Davis in 1847)

    Belfry (destroyed by fire in 1856)

    Renovations to the South Building (gutted by Arthur Nash in 1926)

    Renovations to Steward's Hall (demolished)

    Renovations to the President's House (destroyed by fire in 1886)

Client: University of North Carolina

1822–1837

University of North Carolina

Chapel Hill, NC

Gerrard Hall (Portico removed in 1892 and reconstructed in 2007. Interior gutted
    except for the balcony and trim in 1930.)
Client: University of North Carolina

1823
Governor's Palace (William Nichols added portico; building demolished in 1885)
Raleigh, NC
Client: State of North Carolina

1823
Ingleside (portico attributed to William Nichols)
Lincoln Co., NC
Client: David Forney

1824
Fayetteville Water Works (demolished)
Adam Street, Haymount Section
Fayetteville, NC
Client: William Nichols, President

1824
North Carolina State House (destroyed by fire in 1831)
Raleigh, NC
Client: State of North Carolina

1825
Saint Matthew's Episcopal Church (substantially remodeled in late 1800s)
Hillsborough, NC
Client: Saint Matthew's Episcopal Church

1825
Eagle Lodge (damaged by fire; portico damaged by wind storm in 1990)
Hillsborough, NC
Client: N.C. F. & A.M. Chapter 19

1825
Archibald Henderson Monument
Old Lutheran Cemetery
Salisbury, NC
Client: Archibald Henderson Family

1825
State Treasurer's Office (demolished in 1840)
Union Square

Raleigh, NC
Client: State of North Carolina

1825
Governor's Palace Outbuildings (demolished in 1885)
Raleigh, NC
Client: State of North Carolina

1825
Wake County Jail (demolished)
Fayetteville Street
Raleigh, NC
Client: County of Wake, NC

1826
Mordecai House (southern addition)
Raleigh, NC
Client: Moses Mordecai

1826
Guilford County Courthouse (attributed to William Nichols, demolished)
Greensboro, NC
Client: County of Guilford, NC

1826–1827
Davidson County Courthouse (attributed to William Nichols, demolished)
Lexington, NC
Client: County of Davidson, NC

1826–1829
Christ Episcopal Church (demolished)
Raleigh, NC
Client: Christ Episcopal Church

1827
Badger House (demolished)
West Edenton Street
Raleigh, NC
Client: George E. Badger

Ca. 1828
State Bank of Alabama (attributed to William Nichols, demolished)
Corner of University Ave. and Greensboro Ave.
Tuscaloosa, AL
Client: State Bank of Alabama

1830

The Forks of Cypress (Nichols remodeled the house, added colossal colonnade;
     destroyed by fire in 1966, stabilized as a ruin)
Florence, AL
Client: James Jackson

1831

Alabama State Capitol (destroyed by fire in 1923, stabilized as a ruin)
Tuscaloosa, AL
Client: State of Alabama

1830–1832

University of Alabama
Tuscaloosa, AL
     Campus Plan Rotunda (destroyed by fire, 1865)
     Lyceum (destroyed by fire, 1865)
     Faculty Residences (two buildings, destroyed by fire, 1865)
     Franklin Hall (destroyed by fire, 1865)
     Washington Hall (destroyed by fire, 1865)
     Jefferson Hall (destroyed by fire, 1865)
     Madison Hall (built in 1854, based on Nichols's design, destroyed by fire, 1865)
     Gorgas House (the only surviving building designed by Nichols on campus)
Client: University of Alabama

1831

Christ Episcopal Church (substantially remodeled in the Gothic Revival style in 1880)
Lurleen Wallace Boulevard
Tuscaloosa, AL
Client: Christ Episcopal Church

1832

Thornhill
Greene County, AL
Client: James Innes Thornton

1832

Rosemount (front section designed by Nichols)
Greene County, AL
Client: Williamson Allen Glover

1834

James Hunter Dearing House
Queen City Avenue
Tuscaloosa, AL
Client: James Hunter Dearing

1835

Louisiana State House (originally Charity Hospital, built in 1815; remodeled by
    Nichols, demolished in 1850)
New Orleans, LA
Client: State of Louisiana

1835

Louisiana State Penitentiary (Nichols supervised construction; demolished in 1917)
Florida Street
Baton Rouge, LA
Client: State of Louisiana

1836–1840

Old Mississippi State Capitol
State Street
Jackson, MS
Client: State of Mississippi

1837–1839

Brandon Male and Female Academy (demolished in 1923)
Brandon, MS
Client: Brandon Male and Female Academy

1839

First Methodist Episcopal Church (demolished in 1882)
North Congress Street
Jackson, MS
Client: First Methodist Episcopal Church

1839–1840

Rankin County Courthouse and Jail (demolished in 1853; Nichols known to have
    administered the construction bid for this building)
Brandon, MS
Client: County of Rankin, MS

1840

Mississippi State Penitentiary (demolished in 1900)
Congress Street
Jackson, MS
Client: State of Mississippi

1842

Mississippi Governor's Mansion
Capitol Street

Jackson, MS
Client: State of Mississippi

1842
Sedgewood
Vernon, MS
Client: John H. Thomas

1843–1846
First Presbyterian Church (demolished in 1891)
Corner of North State Street and Yazoo Street
Jackson, MS
Client: First Presbyterian Church

1843
C. K. Marshall House (Nichols designed front colonnade; demolished in 1962)
Grove Street
Vicksburg, MS
Client: Charles Kendall Marshall

1843
Office for Sharon Female College (office moved to Canton, Mississippi, from Sharon,
    Mississippi, in 1870)
Madison County, MS
Client: Sharon Female College

1845–1849
John J. Poindexter House (demolished in 1960)
Originally on West Capitol Street, moved to Robinson Street
Jackson, MS
Client: Perry Cohea

1846
Mississippi Capitol Iron Fence (removed in late nineteenth century, reconstructed in
    2009)
Jackson, MS
Client: State of Mississippi

1846–1848
University of Mississippi
Oxford, MS
    Campus Plan (Circle)
    Lyceum (expanded 1856, wings added 1905 by Theodore Link; interior gutted by
        fire in 1916; westside portico added in 1927; building substantially rehabilitated
        in 2001)

Jefferson, Lafayette, and Rittenhouse Dormitories (demolished ca. 1925)

Steward's Hall (demolished ca. 1925)

Chapel (completed in 1853, now the Croft Institute for International Studies)

Client: University of Mississippi

1849–1850

Yazoo County Courthouse (destroyed by fire in 1864)

Corner of Broadway Street and Washington Street

Yazoo City, MS

Client: County of Yazoo, MS

1851

Shamrock (demolished in 1936)

Oak Street

Vicksburg, MS

Client: William Porterfield

1852

Hilzheim-Ledbetter House (demolished in 1960)

North State Street

Jackson, MS

Client: William R. Miles

1853

Lexington Female Academy (demolished in 1904)

Lexington, MS

Client: Lexington Female Academy

1853–1856

Chickasaw Female College (design attributed to Nichols, building attributed to
    William Turner; demolished in 1938)

Pontotoc, MS

Client: Presbyterian Female Collegiate Institution of Pontotoc, MS

The Architecture of William Nichols

Introduction

Throughout most of my life, I have been influenced by William Nichols even though I never knew of him. He was one of many important architects who designed the backdrop of my boyhood in the American South. In the southern states of North Carolina, Alabama, and Mississippi, Nichols designed state capitols, governors' mansions, and the campuses of each of these states' most important universities. He designed numerous courthouses, churches, schools, houses, penitentiaries, and prisons. Sadly, most of these buildings have been lost through fires, demolition, or decay; yet, the buildings and places that did survive became a compelling part of the scenery for history, from the Civil War to the Civil Rights Movement to Hurricane Katrina (figure 1).

As a teenager, and later as an adult, I admired the beauty and architecture of these buildings as I passed them, but knew nothing of their builder. The Old Mississippi State Capitol, the Mississippi Governor's Mansion, and the Lyceum at the University of Mississippi were buildings that I passed frequently as a boy; they were, in my mind, the landmarks that defined Mississippi. When I finally researched these impressive buildings as an academic scholar, their designs, their histories, and their architect captivated me.

William Nichols was an exceptional individual. He was someone whose story is impressive on multiple levels, as an architect and as a figure in American history. Armed with a fierce belief in his own talent and some popular architectural books of the day, Nichols would help define the built landscape of the South and articulate the aspirations of a rising class on the American "frontier." Yet, few people are aware of him, and, for others, he is an afterthought. At first, I simply wanted

Figure 1. Hayes Plantation, Edenton, NC, 1818. William Nichols's first significant building, overlooking Edenton Bay. He designed and built Hayes for James Johnston, who would later introduce Nichols to the influential ruling class in North Carolina that became his main client base. (Courtesy of Thomas J. Campanella)

to know why such "dogged anonymity [had] attached itself to a man whose talents were widely acclaimed during fifty years of active practice," but as I learned more about Nichols and his buildings, it was clear that the story of this man—a truly talented architect, an audacious promoter of himself, and an unscrupulous businessman—should be the subject of a comprehensive monograph (figure 2).

My "formal" introduction to William Nichols occurred in 2002 when I began my tenure as historical architect and campus historic preservation manager at the University of North Carolina at Chapel Hill. I was in charge of renovating Gerrard Hall—Nichols's most prominent work on the Carolina campus—and became intimately involved with both the building and its noteworthy history. Upon its completion in 1837, Gerrard Hall was the first assembly building on campus and was used as a chapel throughout the 1800s (figure 3). George Moses Horton, a North Carolina slave who published a book of poems while still in bondage, lectured there in 1859. Famed Harlem Renaissance writer Langston Hughes read poetry there in 1931. Three United States presidents—James K. Polk, William Howard Taft, and Woodrow Wilson—gave speeches from its octagonal wooden platform. A pivotal scene for a major motion picture was filmed there.[1] Interestingly, it was the only building remaining on campus without indoor plumbing in 2002, even though it had been structurally retrofitted in 1930 and again renovated before my arrival (figures 4–7).

The renovation of Gerrard Hall included the reconstruction of an Ionic portico on the south side of the building that was so rotten the UNC Board of Trustees had it removed in 1892. While I was conducting research for the reconstruction of the portico, my interest in Nichols's work was piqued. I applied for, and was awarded, a Charles Peterson Fellowship from the Athenaeum of Philadelphia to study his work in more detail. I spent three years examining and reexamining Nichols's surviving buildings. I read primary and secondary sources of his life and work. I conducted interviews, sketched wood moldings, and stroked the angled curves of his signature Greek-inspired details. I retraced his journey beginning in New Bern, then to Edenton, Fayetteville, Raleigh, and Hillsborough in North Carolina, exploring his early work. Next, I traveled to Jackson, Mississippi, where I studied his masterpieces, the Old Capitol and the Governor's Mansion. I drove for two hours toward the Mississippi Delta to an Odd Fellows Cemetery in Lexington, where Nichols lies in repose among strangers. Working with experts, I examined his prolific amount of work in the

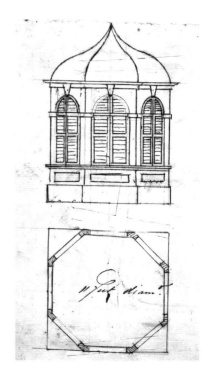

Figure 2. North Carolina State House (first building), Raleigh, NC. Detail drawing of the cupola drawn by William Nichols, dated August 28, 1818. It is the only known drawing attributed to Nichols. (Courtesy of the State Archives of North Carolina)

Figure 3. Gerrard Hall, University of North Carolina, Chapel Hill, NC, 1822–1837. Nichols's first significant building; he would later design the campuses of the University of Alabama and the University of Mississippi. (Courtesy of the North Carolina Collection, University of North Carolina at Chapel Hill Library)

Figure 5. Gerrard Hall, photograph taken during the reconstruction of its Ionic portico, March 2007. (Photograph by author)

Figure 4. Gerrard Hall, 2002, University of North Carolina at Chapel Hill. (Photograph by author)

Figure 6. Erected columns at Gerrard Hall, May 2007. (Photograph by author)

Figure 7. Gerrard Hall with its reconstructed portico. The University of North Carolina's iconic Old Well is to the right. (Courtesy of Dan Sears)

Tuscaloosa, Alabama, vicinity and in New Orleans, Louisiana. I visited buildings that Nichols was associated with either as the builder or as the documented designer. While tracing Nichols's path through the Southeast, I discovered more than the architectural maturity of this carpenter-turned-architect; I became conscious of the parallels between Nichols's rising fame and the emergence of what would later be called the Old South.

Along the way, through an introduction from my editor at the University Press of Mississippi, Craig Gill, I had the pleasure of collaborating on this book with Todd Sanders of the Mississippi Department of Archives and History. Todd also shared my passion for Nichols's work and, like me, wondered why so little had been written or discussed about him. He spent hours performing vital research and contemplating the architectural history of Nichols, and he was an important and effective sounding board for my ideas.

In the span of Nichols's life (1780–1853), the United States went from being a series of colonies to a rapidly industrialized nation. When he arrived on the shores of New Bern, North Carolina, in 1800, the United States was merely twenty-four years old and the South was entrenched in an agrarian economy influenced by the ideas of Thomas Jefferson, and later, Andrew Jackson. It is no accident that Nichols first came to the shores of eastern North Carolina. It was here, from Wilmington to Edenton, that a significant number of English immigrants from the county of Somerset settled during the eighteenth century. Throughout the first half of the nineteenth century, the children of these original English immigrants migrated south and west, bringing with them their ancestors' English sensibilities along with their own American aesthetic. Nichols, a native of Bath, England, understood their taste in homes and architecture; after all, he was one of them. He made a living designing and constructing homes and buildings for these "Carolina colonists" as they were called. As they and their descendants settled farther south and west to shape the societies of Alabama and Mississippi, Nichols went with them. This region of the emerging United States was wild, fluid, and somewhat forgotten by the established and constantly evolving industrialized Northeast where architects such as Benjamin Henry Latrobe, Alexander Jackson Davis and, later, Thomas Ustick Walter flourished, making Nichols the right man at the right time.

Nichols's architecture reflects his own transition from being an Englishman to an American. Unlike other immigrant architects such as Pierre L'Enfant[2] who never conformed to the American environment, Nichols understood his new surroundings. He addressed the environmental challenges of building in the hot, humid South with his English propensities of proportion, scale, and classical detail. He

Figure 8. North Carolina State House, Raleigh, NC, engraving by W. Goodacre. Built in 1824 and destroyed by a fire in 1831, the State House was the first of three state capitol buildings that Nichols designed. (Courtesy of John Sanders)

helped introduce the idea of campus planning to universities in the South, combining the accepted colonial campus prototypes such as Harvard, Princeton, and the College of William and Mary with the more visionary ideas of Jefferson's "Academical Village" at the University of Virginia. He most likely introduced Gothic Revival design to North Carolina. His work, especially in the design of government buildings, expressed the ideals of democracy and society. Most notably, he expressed the idea of the bicameral legislature in American government and designed state capitols in North Carolina (figure 8), Alabama, and Mississippi, which incorporated ideas based on the design of the United States Capitol. Nichols understood the vital role of ornament and iconography in architecture, whether it was a simple Greek motif on a door transom in Edenton, North Carolina, or the design of an Ionic portico on Gerrard Hall at the University of North Carolina. He showed that he understood the role of hierarchy in both architecture and planning by placing buildings in settings that gave a larger meaning not only to their immediate surroundings but also to the entire urban context. This can be seen in his design of the dominant Library Rotunda at the University of Alabama and his design to "remodel" the North Carolina State House in Raleigh. While Nichols did not choose the site for the Mississippi State Capitol (that decision having been determined by the city's planners), his monumental design made an impact on the nascent community as this new building was not only the largest public building in the new town but also in the entire state. His taste for classical architecture combined with innate discernment made William Nichols's legacy not only one of grandeur, but also of resourcefulness, which makes his architecture inventive, autochthonous, and vital (figure 9).

Unfortunately, most of Nichols's buildings have been destroyed by fire, demolished, or rotted from owner neglect. Of the buildings that do survive most of them have been greatly altered by successive generations of owners and occupants. There are approximately seventy-seven buildings, features, and additions documented as or attributed to William Nichols, and there are undoubtedly many more that will remain unknown. Nichols's work was largely forgotten as many of his buildings were replaced to meet changing needs as the South rebuilt itself after the Civil War. Many of those that survived the birth of the New South lost their connection with their designer.

Nichols and his work were rediscovered when architectural historian Thomas Tileston Waterman and photographer Frances Benjamin Johnston documented the work of eighteenth- and nineteenth-century architecture in the South, both for the Historic American Buildings Survey (HABS) and for their book *The Early Architecture of North Carolina* (1941). Talbot Hamlin, the noted Columbia University architectural historian, discussed Nichols, albeit in a side note, in his landmark book, *Greek Revival Architecture in America*, in 1944. In the 1970s, C. Ford Peatross and Robert O. Mellown (at the time, two doctoral candidates in the art history department of the University of North Carolina at Chapel Hill) began researching Nichols while studying under noted architectural and art historian John Allcott. Peatross made Nichols

Figure 9. Mississippi Governor's Mansion, Jackson, MS, 1842. It is the second-oldest continuously used governor's mansion in the nation and an enduring symbol of the Old South. (Courtesy of Wendy Kapp)

the subject of his Ph.D. dissertation, the first comprehensive presentation of Nichols's work.[3] Peatross and Mellown assembled an exhibit of Nichols's work called *William Nichols, Architect*, first shown at the University of Alabama Art Gallery in 1979.[4] The accompanying publication, a fifty-page photographic catalogue and essay, was as complete as any body of research thus far on Nichols. Mellown, now professor emeritus of art history at the University of Alabama, continued to document Nichols's work but only in Alabama, specifically in Tuscaloosa, where Nichols designed the University of Alabama and the first Alabama state capitol.

In the last forty years, historic preservation became a professional endeavor, and preservationists, working for state historic preservation offices and private consulting firms, helped save Nichols's remaining buildings from demolition. Many have been renovated. In 1984, the University of Alabama undertook a comprehensive archaeological project and uncovered the ruined foundations of the campus, long thought lost, that Nichols designed. In 2001, Nichols's main building at the University of Mississippi, the Lyceum, was restored. From 2005 to 2008 the state of Mississippi restored Nichols's Old Capitol to its nineteenth-century appearance, most notably re-covering the building with stucco treated to look like stone along with correcting the damage incurred by Hurricane Katrina.

Not only architectural historians have studied his work; scholars of both American history and political science have studied how his designs influenced the legislative process. John Sanders, former director of the Institute of Government at the University of North Carolina at Chapel Hill and a former UNC system vice president, spent three decades researching Nichols's contributions to North Carolina; he even authored the entry for William Nichols in the *Dictionary of North Carolina Biography*, edited by William S. Powell in 1988. Sanders was particularly interested in how Nichols's architecture was influenced by the workings of state government. He gathered considerable documentation of Nichols's work on the first North Carolina State House, the first Alabama and Mississippi state capitols, and the third North Carolina State Capitol, initially designed by Nichols but later completed by the New York architects Ithiel Town, Alexander Jackson Davis, and David Paton. Richard Cawthon, former chief architectural historian in the Mississippi Department of Archives and History, and Robert Gamble, senior architectural historian for the Alabama Historical Commission, have documented Nichols's work in their respective states and made speculative attributions for additional properties. Cawthon produced an intensive architectural history component of the historic structures report for the Old Mississippi Capitol restoration. John Ray Skates, a professor of history at the University of

Southern Mississippi, wrote *Mississippi's Old Capitol: Biography of a Building* (1990), which not only documented Nichols's involvement with the building but also its long life, first as the state capitol building, then as a state office building, and, finally, as the state history museum. Michael Fazio, a professor of architecture at Mississippi State University, produced a historic structures report in 1996 on the University of Mississippi's landmark building, the Lyceum, which was designed by Nichols. Architect Robert Parker Adams of Jackson researched and analyzed the Old Mississippi Capitol when he was the lead architect in charge of its restoration. In 1990, Catherine Bishir, former architectural historian at the North Carolina Department of Archives and History and senior architectural historian at Preservation North Carolina, placed Nichols in the context of the overall history of North Carolina architecture and building in her landmark book, *Architects and Builders in North Carolina: A History of the Practice of Building*, co-written by Charlotte Brown, Carl Lounsbury, and Ernest Wood. She would later elaborate on Nichols's work in North Carolina in her award-winning book *North Carolina Architecture*, also published that year. The work of these scholars has provided valuable, new information about Nichols and his buildings, allowing for a more complete evaluation of his work as an architect.

During the last fifty years, Nichols has steadily regained prominence within the scholarship of American architectural history and the history of the American South. As the identity of the South has been reexamined, both the real and perceived icons of what is "southern" have been discussed. No matter the point of view in examining southern culture, the impact of William Nichols cannot be ignored. Within the context of American architecture and decorative arts, his accomplishments are impressive. His work is among the best architecture of the antebellum period.

Nichols was a primary architectural chronicler of a rising entrepreneurial class, the aspirations of a civilization to the advent of the Civil War. Although classical precedents published in books by the leading architects of his day influenced him, he responded impressively to the southern environment of hot, humid summers and the limitations of building materials and a skilled labor force. The result was a distinctive and original architecture that was built literally at the edge of the American frontier, an architecture that would help define the look and character of the American South.

Despite his impressive accomplishments, it is important to remember that William Nichols was not a theorist like other architects or builders of his day such as Alexander Jackson Davis, Asher Benjamin, and Minard Lafever. He never published a "builder's guide" or a set of plans or printed material to attract clients. Instead, he was a practicing

Figure 10. William Nichols's tombstone, Lexington, MS. Nichols was proud of being English and also of being a native of Bath, famous for its neoclassical architecture. His tumultuous life led him to the edge of the Mississippi Delta on the eve of the Civil War. (Courtesy of Wendy Kapp)

architect with a set of building principles who would, over time, experiment with and incorporate ideas from other architects and builders in his work. His ability to incorporate the latest ideas found in more urban areas of the country is all the more remarkable since he was practicing architecture in an era when, and an area where, ideas did not travel freely. He went to the cosmopolitan and architectural hub of New York in 1818, made another trip up the East Coast in 1822, and lived in New Orleans between 1834 and 1836. But, by and large, he was completely isolated from recognized centers of architecture and building arts. Despite this isolation, his work reflects the ideas of the leading architectural movements of the time. Nichols's ability to learn and interpret these new stylistic traits by simply reading publications and observing architectural marvels is both intriguing and inspiring.

This book represents the latest examination of William Nichols by assessing and documenting his evolution as an architect. It will demonstrate how Nichols learned from the work of other architects and theorists and how he adapted those ideas to the regional environment and context in which he lived. Its structure reflects Nichols's odyssey throughout the South. The first and second chapters discuss his beginnings in America. Chapter one begins in the water inlets and sounds of North Carolina, featuring his work as a young carpenter who aspired to become a master builder and later an architect. Chapter two focuses solely on his most impressive earliest work, Hayes Plantation in Edenton. Chapters three and four concentrate on his work as the first state architect of North Carolina during which he designed the North Carolina State House, the Governor's Palace, and the campus of the University of North Carolina. Chapter five is the story of his brief, yet most productive period during his time in Alabama. It was there that he designed the state capitol, the campus of the University of Alabama, Christ Episcopal Church, and four notable residences. Chapter six explores the influential architecture he encountered during his very brief tenure in Louisiana, specifically New Orleans. It was in New Orleans that he completely changed his outlook on architectural design, from English-based to distinctively American. Chapters seven and eight examine his mature and later work in Mississippi. Chapter seven highlights the Mississippi State Capitol, the Governor's

Mansion, and the state penitentiary, all of which were simultaneously designed and built by Nichols. These three important buildings visually established the town of Jackson as Mississippi's capital in the nineteenth century. Chapter eight focuses on Nichols's final years and work in Oxford, where he designed the campus of the University of Mississippi and, most notably, the university's Lyceum. It ends with his work in Vicksburg and Yazoo City and his final resting place at the edge of the Mississippi Delta in Lexington, Mississippi. In the epilogue, I assess Nichols's place in American architectural history and the impact of his work on the architecture of North Carolina, Alabama, and, most notably, Mississippi.

Due to the limited amount of research, writing, or analysis that has been done on Nichols's work in over thirty years, the timing is right to reexamine his work and his role in developing the distinctive architecture of the antebellum South. During his career, Nichols evolved from an English-born and trained carpenter/master builder into an American architect of significant stature who accepted the latest styles and trends while maintaining a builder's knowledge of the qualities that constitute a good, solid building.

Nichols did not leave a legacy of writings or renderings. Only one drawing, a design of a cupola for the first North Carolina State House, is attributed to him and preserved in the North Carolina Department of Archives and History (figure 2). Very few letters remain from his hand; his buildings are the only tangible evidence that validates his existence. The course that took this young British carpenter from Bath, England, to Lexington, Mississippi, is truly an American adventure (figure 10).

—PAUL HARDIN KAPP
Urbana, Illinois

Chapter One

THE AMBITIOUS YOUNG CARPENTER

W hen William Nichols arrived in New Bern, North Carolina, in 1800, he came to a new state that was sparsely populated with an agrarian economy and little, if any, transportation infrastructure. These conditions resulted in a shortage of skilled tradesmen and craftsmen and a nonexistent architectural tradition. Difficult terrain and the lack of navigable rivers into the heart of the Piedmont and western frontier restricted both commerce and the exchange of ideas, producing a society in North Carolina that was both frugal and pragmatic. During the eighteenth century, settlement in North Carolina predominantly occurred along the coastal plain in towns such as New Bern. Immigrant groups consisting of Swiss and German settlers initially settled in North Carolina, with English immigrants joining them shortly after. Quakers from both England and Germany, who travelled south from the Wilderness Road in Virginia, settled in the North Carolina Piedmont, while the Scots-Irish settled throughout North Carolina. Each ethnic group endured the harsh reality of an agricultural economy crippled by a limited transportation system of primitive roads and very few navigable rivers. These factors caused the North Carolinians of the eighteenth century to live simply and created a mindset that was reflected in their pragmatic buildings as well.

Before the Revolution, both government and society in North Carolina were fragmented and stifled. This was due mainly to the geographic conditions of the region but also because North Carolina was still a royal colony. Representative government had not yet developed in colonial North Carolina as it had in the neighboring colonies of Virginia, Maryland, and South Carolina. The colonial capitol rotated through several towns before Governor William Tryon built his residence in New Bern, a building that accommodated the governor and not the representative body of the North Carolina colony. Royal governments became isolated from inhabitants living in the North Carolina Piedmont and on the western frontier, a scenario that led to a disastrous ending for royal government during the American Revolution.

At the dawn of the nineteenth century, North Carolina was recovering from the brutality of the American Revolution. The Revolutionary War (1775–1783) had been fought viciously in North Carolina. The British army attacked not just patriots but neutral inhabitants as well. They burned fledgling villages such as Brunswick along the Cape Fear River and countless Carolina farmsteads in their attempt to break the will of the southern colonists through the use of brute force.

Change was rapidly under way when Nichols arrived in New Bern in 1800. The seat of the new state government had been moved to a new capital, Raleigh, in 1792. Under the administration of Richard Caswell, Samuel Johnston,[1] Alexander Martin, Richard Dobbs Spaight, and William Richardson Davie, new ideas were being proposed—first Federalist and then Jeffersonian—transforming North Carolina. North Carolinians built roads and canals; they settled the Piedmont, and established a representative state government similar to what was occurring in Virginia, South Carolina, and the nation as a whole. Industry was developing throughout the state, from the first paper mill in Hillsborough to a shipbuilding industry in Wilmington. North Carolinians established the first public state-owned university in the United States, the University of North Carolina, in 1789 in Chapel Hill. It was given the laudable mission to educate the future leaders of the new state. Old economic and trading practices, such as commerce with the West Indies, gave way to agricultural and, later, industrial trade with neighboring states along the eastern seaboard. All the while, the new prospering generation of North Carolinians became more conscious of their place in society, venturing to fulfill their want for comfort and giving suitable form to their institutions of society and government. William Nichols understood this well and marketed himself as the only architect capable enough to fulfill the aspirations held by North Carolinians for high-style architecture.[2]

There is little doubt that twenty-year-old William Nichols determined his destiny when he first arrived in New Bern; he wanted to be an architect and a successful one. Born in Bath circa 1780[3] into a family of carpenters, joiners, and cabinetmakers that included Samuel Nichols,[4] a surveyor for the city of Bath who became a carpenter and builder, he followed a family tradition[5] (figure 11). Father Samuel probably taught his craft to young William, as apprenticeships were common among acquaintances and relatives in the building trades of eighteenth-century

Figure 11. Photograph of the Dinder House, Somerset, England. Samuel Nichols, a relative of William Nichols, is believed to have designed and built this residence. It was completed in 1802. (Peatross Collection, Courtesy of the North Carolina Collection, Wilson Library, University of North Carolina at Chapel Hill)

Europe. Under Samuel's tutelage, William learned timber joinery and, more importantly, finish carpentry. Young William most likely learned the rudimentary facets of joinery and molding work. As he progressed through his apprenticeship, he became a journeyman builder. In this position, it is entirely likely that William gained knowledge of other building trades such as masonry, plastering, and roofing.

Nichols presented himself as more than simply a builder or skilled carpenter; rather, he was a purveyor of sophisticated living. He aspired to be the expert of a "cultured craft" that he brought with him from England.[6] During the first six years he lived in New Bern, he presented himself as a surveyor, a builder, and a carpenter. Before he was thirty years old, he brazenly called himself an architect with nothing more than a journeyman's knowledge of carpentry and a compendium of pattern and builders' books of his era. Through a careful study of his early buildings, it can be deduced that Nichols relied on several guidebooks for his inspiration to design his earliest buildings. His collection most probably included *The Antiquities of Athens* by James Stuart and Nicholas Revett, and, most notably, William Pain's *Practical House Carpenter*.[7] These books, his skills, and his English heritage allowed Nichols to give the new entrepreneurial, affluent upper class of North Carolinian tobacco planters sophisticated architectural features for their residences and public buildings. In port cities such as New Bern, Wilmington, and Edenton, they learned secondhand of the styles coming from England. These North Carolinians, who wished to emulate the English upper class, provided the type of clients Nichols wished to attract for his building and architectural practice.[8]

From the outset, Nichols's sheer force of personality set him apart from his peers in acquiring and later executing work. In her book *Architects and Builders of North Carolina*, Bishir states: "Like Hawks [John Hawks, the architect of Tryon Palace], Nichols enjoyed a relationship with his merchant and planter clientele different from that of the artisan. If not socially, at least in terms of taste, he was his clients' equal or superior."[9] By linking Hawks with Nichols, Bishir is suggesting that being English had a distinct advantage with the merchant planter clientele over American builders.

Charm and confidence in his ability never left Nichols during his entire career and indeed set him apart from similar aspiring builders who, like him, began as tradesman and tried to make the leap from artisan to architect only to fail. Although historians celebrate the accomplished architects of the time such as Charles Bulfinch and Thomas Jefferson, most of the building done in the first half of the nineteenth century was by builders who learned their craft during rigorous periods as apprentices, laborers, and journeymen. After a number of years working in the fields, these men eventually became builders (or contractors) and designed what they built. Rarely did these men attempt to make the final transition to learn building precedents, and the construction, engineering, and surveying skills necessary to call themselves architects.[10] A builder such as Nichols undertook an arduous apprenticeship, whereas young men from the privileged classes who had the opportunity to learn principles and theories from respected architects and engineers, he learned how to design and build by actually designing and building noteworthy buildings. These fortunate young men also had the means to travel extensively throughout England, France, and Germany to learn, on site, the great buildings of Europe that served as valuable precedents for their own work.[11] A working-class tradesman such as Nichols learned his craft through building trades, builders' guides, architectural pattern books, and the school of hard knocks.

In order for Nichols to have the confidence and audacity to call himself an architect at such an early age, he must have completed a regimented self-study in building techniques and trades and had a firm understanding of timber trades and an astute knowledge of masonry. He had to have learned the basic recipes of mortar mixes, typically alchemistic concoctions that varied from region to region. Moreover, he would have had to understand how to site a building, move earth, and install different types of roof coverings and structures. Architecturally, it was expected that he studied the great works of the day including those of Robert Adam and Christopher Wren, and he would have to understand the latest tastes and styles of popular Georgian design in order to attract clients and convince them he was a true purveyor of "good living." But most importantly, he would have had to gain a comprehensive knowledge of the great icons of the classical past—the documented examples of Roman and Greek antiquity. For an aspiring architect, there were great examples documented by Italian renaissance masters such as Vignola and Palladio, but the works of architecture that Nichols would have had to commit to memory were the series of Greek and Roman temples documented by European architects and archaeologists such as James Stuart and Nicholas Revett who published the landmark book *The Antiquities of Athens* in 1762. This series of Greek temples eventually became accepted as the canons of the classical era and were adapted by builders through the entire eighteenth century and into the first third of the nineteenth century by both English and American architects and builders.

Like most builders and architects of his day in England and America, Nichols was armed with several "how to" pattern books that documented the architectural giants of his day. Pattern books gave the builder/architect a foundation of classical precedents, practical techniques, and pointers that became the basis for the design and construction of buildings. Moreover, these books provided rudimentary lessons in simple carpentry, design, and even how to price built work. The most important books that young Nichols referenced were the works of William Pain.

Pain was the leading writer of guidebooks for builders in the Adam era in England[12]; his books specifically focused on how the stone construction of the classical orders could be transformed into wood construction. Pain was born in 1730 and was a prolific writer of carpentry guidebooks throughout the middle and late eighteenth century. He wrote *The Builder's Companion and Workman's General Assistant* (1758), *The Builder's Pocket Treasure: or Palladio Delineated and Explained* (1763), *The Practical Builder* (1774), *The British Palladio* (1786) and *The Practical House Carpenter; or the Youth's Instructor* (1792; it was published posthumously, for Pain had died around 1790). Pain's books were written explicitly for carpenters; in them were tables for charging service rates, methods to estimate materials, and simple formulas to solve basic geometric problems a carpenter would encounter in the field. In writing his books, Pain was assisted by his sons, James and Henry, who had worked for John Nash[13] and learned valuable ideas about British Palladianism, all of which were accepted and used by American builders in the late eighteenth century.

Based on the moldings Nichols used early in his career as a builder/carpenter and then as an architect, it is evident that *The Practical House Carpenter* heavily influenced him. Published when Nichols was twelve years old and in the last stages of his apprenticeship with his family in Bath, *The Practical House Carpenter* was the simplest and most basic of Pain's books on carpentry. It gave many helpful pointers in building classical elements for buildings; more importantly, it clearly addressed how classicism could be translated into wood construction. This point cannot be overstated either in the evaluation of Nichols's early career or in the overall evaluation of American architecture and construction at the eve of the nineteenth century. Nichols, who was trained as a cabinetmaker and carpenter, gravitated toward this particular resource. The ease of fabricating building columns from timber was something young Nichols must have understood. Furthermore, eastern North Carolina had plenty of timber, making it the logical building material of choice. As for the architecture of the newly christened American republic, Pain's influence was widespread and easily integrated into the somewhat primitive building trades on the eastern seaboard. Finally, it cannot be overstated that nineteenth-century America made extensive use of wood in its architecture. Masonry construction was dominant only in America's urban centers. Owners and builders in dense cities were attracted to masonry construction for its obvious fireproofing quality. In the South, a region of the country with only a few urban centers such as Savannah and Charleston, the fireproofing of masonry buildings was not a primary objective.[14] In North Carolina fabricating buildings out of the more affordable timber was a much more attractive option, making the ability to design and build out of wood a valuable skill. The widespread availability and affordability of wood, along with the scarcity of good building stone and skilled masons, made wood the obvious building material choice. Most professional architects of the nineteenth century in the United States first began as carpenters and wood carvers. These men had an extensive knowledge of construction but a rudimentary knowledge of architecture and planning. Through their mastery of wood, architect-builders such as Samuel McIntire of Salem, Massachusetts,[15] carved and fabricated elongated columns, cut deeper moldings, and stretched reeded moldings taut. Part of this was the fascination of Pompeian details,[16] the fashion of the age spurred by the works of English architects Robert Adam and Isaac Ware and English furniture makers Thomas Sheraton and George Hepplewhite. However, by and large this extensive manipulation of wood was the result of a desire by American builders to show off their skill and mastery over the material.[17] Although there were many skilled builders such as Uriah Sandy and Asa King[18] in New Bern at the beginning of the nineteenth century, there was definitely not a craftsman-architect of the stature of McIntire in North Carolina for two probable reasons: 1) the isolated North Carolina society and its economy could not support such a highly skilled artisan, and 2) the preference of North Carolinians for a plainer and more austere lifestyle. This was perfectly suitable for the young Nichols, whose skill would improve as the taste of the local gentry evolved.[19]

Figure 12. The Royal Crescent (view from Brock Street), Bath, England. Designed by John Wood the Younger, built 1767–1775. (Photograph by author)

A review of Nichols's entire body of work makes it evident that he aspired to design and construct buildings featuring architectural elements inspired by his native England. Both his humble work and his most audacious buildings exhibit a desire to build in the chaste, refined, and classically correct architecture found in his native Bath, a city that he often stated was where he was a native throughout his life and which was even listed on his tombstone. Bath is the city where John Wood the Elder and John Wood the Younger[20] designed and built two of Britain's prime examples of Georgian architecture—The Circus and Royal Crescent (figure 12). Nichols sought to become a great architect in this tradition. Throughout his entire career he attempted to replicate the architectural magnificence of Bath.

Nichols's Earliest Work in New Bern

Nichols's arrival in New Bern, North Carolina, in 1800 was not accidental; his economic and educational limitations and the fact that a significant portion of the population was from Somerset most likely compelled him to choose to go to North Carolina. Given his options of places to immigrate to in the United States, which were provided to him to insure the best chance of success, eastern North Carolina most likely presented him the best opportunity.[21] At the beginning of

Figure 13. Front façade of the Judge Donnell Law Office, New Bern, NC. It is believed to be the earliest building designed and built by William Nichols, ca. 1806. (Courtesy of Wendy Kapp)

the nineteenth century, over 55 percent of North Carolina's population had ethnic ties to England or Wales.[22] Initially, William Nichols relied on the common bond he had with his fellow countrymen in order to acquire work in New Bern. At the time of his arrival, North Carolina was attracting a significant number of immigrants from his native county of Somerset. Through hard work and enterprise, these immigrants soon became the wealthy elite of the state. They developed plantations and mercantile businesses and began to sell goods and products that they produced in eastern North Carolina along the East Coast and in Europe.[23] They produced the wealth necessary to fund the grand buildings that Nichols envisioned. He sought and cultivated friendships with his fellow Englishmen from Bath. These men

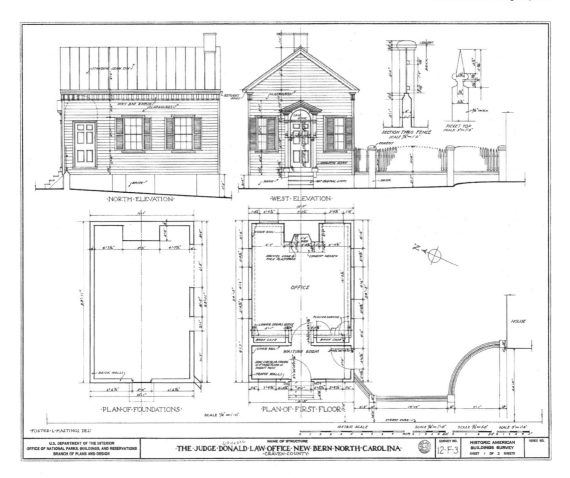

·NORTH·ELEVATION·   ·WEST·ELEVATION·

·PLAN·OF·FOUNDATIONS·   ·PLAN·OF·FIRST·FLOOR·

| U.S. DEPARTMENT OF THE INTERIOR OFFICE OF NATIONAL PARKS, BUILDINGS, AND RESERVATIONS BRANCH OF PLANS AND DESIGN | NAME OF STRUCTURE ·THE·JUDGE·DONALD·LAW·OFFICE·NEW·BERN·NORTH·CAROLINA· ·CRAVEN·COUNTY· | SURVEY NO. 12-F-3 | HISTORIC AMERICAN BUILDINGS SURVEY SHEET 1 OF 2 SHEETS | INDEX NO. |

Figure 14. Plans and elevations of the Judge Donnell Law Office, New Bern, NC. (Historic American Buildings Survey, Library of Congress, Washington, DC)

took firm control of the reins of power, both politically and socially. Nichols's friendships allowed him to enter into social circles that helped his practice flourish. He relied on his British ancestry as he continued to be the architect of choice for the children of the original Somerset colonists, who would later leave North Carolina for the opportunities of fortune out west in Alabama and Mississippi.[24]

The first record of Nichols in New Bern is found in the correspondence of William Tatham, a surveying supervisor for the federal government's first coastal survey. Tatham hired Nichols as an assistant. In a letter to his director, Albert Gallatin, in June 1806, Tatham wrote that

Figure 15. Doric entry (plate 29) from William Pain's *Practical House Carpenter*. (Courtesy of the University of Wisconsin Fine Arts Library Collection)

he found in Nichols "a Clerk, Draftsman, Surveyor, Architect and reg-
ular bred (Bath, in England) Workman of considerable talents, ingenu-
ity, and merit."[25] Interestingly, Tatham was from Somerset as well.[26] It
is unclear how long Nichols worked on the coastal survey, but it is evident that the first building he designed and built was the Judge Donnell Law Office in New Bern, completed in 1806 (figure 13). The small
building was a suitable debut for Nichols; he worked on it alone due
to its small scale and provided proof of his capabilities. The Donnell
Law Office is a typical law office for this period; it is a small detached
timber-frame one-room building with a medium- to high-pitched
roof. Nichols placed double-hung windows on each of the four-framed
walls, which he covered with clapboard. A Doric-inspired tympanum
crowns a prominent doorway capped with a faux fanlight (figure 14).
The door is flanked with stylized pilasters, which are fluted. A Roman
Doric entablature with mutules is featured in the door surround of
the law office. This entablature is scaled somewhat small when compared to the height of the cornice line and suggests an elongation of
the height of the building. The stretching of the building's height and
proportion suggests an Adamesque influence (the fashion in Georgian England) at that time to make the architectural articulation of
the building more delicate in appearance. Similar to the works of Isaiah Rogers[27] in Massachusetts and Samuel McIntire, the Donnell Law
Office suggests that Nichols was trying to convey his skill as a carpenter. However, the final result is more primitive and awkward; if this was
indeed the intent then young Nichols failed. He still had a lot to learn
before calling himself an architect. Even so, the Donnell Law Office
gives us the first indications of the architectural and constructional
ideas of Nichols. His limited understanding and expression of classical orders and details can clearly be seen, specifically in the articulation of moldings. The Donnell Law Office also demonstrates Nichols's
reliance on the knowledge that he gained from Pain's *Practical House
Carpenter*. The Palladian entry is clearly based on Pain's Plate 29 and
reflects both Nichols's skill and limitations (figure 15).

A striking difference between the Pain precedent and the Donnell
Law Office entry is the use of the denticular Doric order instead of the
mutulary order that Pain proposes in his plate. This may have been
a preference of the owner, but it may well have been a decision by
Nichols to show off his skills. If it was indeed the latter, the crude rope-
like molding surrounding the entire door also exposes Nichols's lack
of skill and sophistication at this initial point in his career. The entry of
the small office with its crudely attached rope molding and its simple
blocked keystones is indeed a humble beginning for Nichols's long and
distinguished career.

Despite his crude execution of details at the Donnell Law Office,
Nichols's work immediately stands out as something distinct and

Figure 16. Tryon Palace, New Bern, NC. Designed by John Hawks and built in 1770 (reconstructed in 1959) as the residence for Royal Governor William Tryon. (Courtesy of the North Carolina State Historic Preservation Office)

new, especially when compared to other buildings of the era in New Bern. Only two hundred yards from the small office were the remains of Tryon Palace,[28] a Georgian-styled residence built 1767–1770 for the Royal Governor of North Carolina, and the John Wright Stanly House, a prime example of Georgian architecture in the South, built in the early 1780s. John Hawks, who travelled to New Bern in 1769 with Governor William Tryon from London for the purpose of constructing a residence befitting a royal appointment, designed Tryon Palace.[29] Hawks's work at Tryon Palace demonstrates strict adherence to classical orders and precedents as well as to planning in the quintessential English manor of the English Georgian period[30] (figure 16).

The entablatures were "correctly" proportioned Doric columns that retained their bulky proportion appropriate for the weighty loads Hawks intended for them to convey.[31] The plan layout for the palace shows Hawks's adherence to English manor planning, which is suitable for the damp and temperate climate of England but not for the hot, humid summers of eastern North Carolina. The Stanly House (figure 17) displays fewer adherences to the English manor house in plan but reflects the Adam-based influence of the times in which it was built:

Figure 17. The John Wright Stanly House, New Bern, NC (photograph taken in 1936). (Historic American Buildings Survey, Library of Congress, Washington, DC)

the quoining at the corners of the building, the elaborate entablature, and the tympanum over each of its first-floor windows, all of which convey the image of a cut-stone house rather than a wood frame one. In his first building, Nichols's work differentiated from these two buildings; he clearly worked within the parameters of wood as a construction material, designing and building the office as a carpenter would. His respect for wood as a building material set the small office apart from the regal Stanly House whose wood exterior attempted to imitate stone. Today, with the reconstructed Tryon Palace, the restored Stanly House, and Donnell House and Law Office, South Front Street in New Bern is an interesting visual essay of the transition between the final expressions of the British Empire in North Carolina and the beginning of new architectural expressions for an emerging republic. It is fitting that Nichols's first documented work, albeit humble, is found here.[32]

During this period of his life, Nichols developed roots in his adopted homeland. In 1805, he married Mary Rew of New Bern.[33] It is assumed that she died before 1815 when he married Sarah Simons in Edenton, North Carolina, with whom he had at least two known children, William Nichols, Jr., and Samuel Nichols (possibly named after William's relative in Bath).[34] Due to an ever-growing family to feed, Nichols continued to promote himself as a master carpenter.

While in New Bern, Nichols worked on the largest and most prominent buildings being built, and he gained valuable experience learning how to manage the construction of large buildings, especially managing various tradesmen such as roofers, masons, and carpenters. He was a carpenter for the construction of Saint John's Masonic Lodge in New Bern, built and designed by John Dewey, likely because he was a member of the lodge, which he joined in 1806.[35] The lodge, which was significantly compromised by alterations in the early twentieth century, still retains an English, Georgian influence. Its compact massing, recessed blind center arch, and denticular Doric cornice show the influence of mid-eighteenth-century architecture pattern books by William Chambers[36] and Abraham Swan.[37] Nichols may have fabricated some of the exterior trim work under Dewey.[38] If this is indeed the case, it may have been Nichols's first exposure to stuccoed masonry in North Carolina. Later in his career, Nichols used stucco on his more significant buildings; however, at the beginning of the nineteenth century, it was not a material widely used in North Carolina. As a member of the lodge, he established important contacts within the community that helped him either acquire new work or find much-needed skilled labor to carry out his projects.

The first breakthrough for Nichols came with the building of the New Bern Academy's front portico; he designed and built it around 1806 (figures 18 and 19). Construction of the academy began shortly after Nichols arrived in New Bern in 1800 but work was sporadic because donations and a lottery funded the project. The compact, sturdy two-story brick structure with a pedimented façade suggests that someone quite familiar with the English precedents had designed it. The building's original Federal architecture clearly can stand alone without the portico, as was the case in numerous colonial and early republic buildings.[39] Nichols's semicircular portico was a clear and deliberate departure from the architectural character of the building; it is a composition by itself. The columns suggest a particular type of Doric column that is an individual expression of Nichols as both an architect and a builder. The bases are attic bases (figure 20), a typical feature in a Roman Doric column. However, the scotia molding of the base is taller while the torus moldings are shorter than those described in books by Vignola or Palladio, all of which gives the bases an appearance of being taller and lighter (figure 21). This design was based on John Soane's west elevation of Sydney Lodge, the home of William Yorke in Hampshire, which was featured in Richardson's *New Vitruvius Britannicus*.[40] Here, Nichols is able to show off his abilities in woodcarving, joinery, and carpentry.

It is clear that young Nichols relied on Plate 22 of Pain's *Practical House Carpenter* in his vernacular interpretation of the neoclassical

Figure 18. New Bern Academy, New Bern, NC. (Courtesy of Wendy Kapp)

Figure 19. Front entry portico, New Bern Academy. (Courtesy of Wendy Kapp)

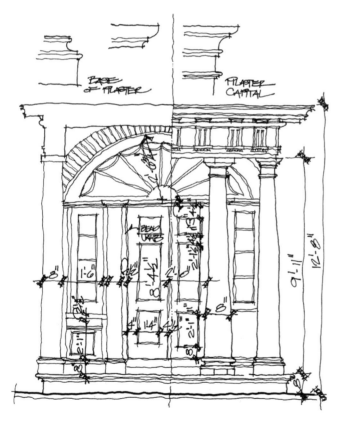

Figure 21. Analysis of the New Bern Academy portico. (Sketch by author)

Figure 20. Column base of the New Bern Academy portico. (Courtesy of Wendy Kapp)

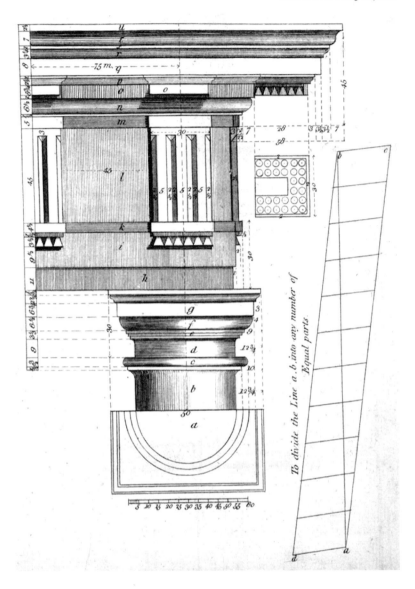

Figure 22. The Doric order (plate 22) by William Pain in *Practical House Carpenter*. (Courtesy of the University of Wisconsin Fine Arts Library Collection)

detailing that he constructed at New Bern Academy (figure 22). The plain and deliberate massing and fenestration of the original academy juxtaposed with the small delicate porch is striking. Clearly the design shows young Nichols's attempt to update the original building with the fashionable architecture and design ideas of late eighteenth-century England.

The New Bern Academy portico illustrates Nichols's level of architectural expertise at this early stage of his career, which was rudimentary and focused entirely on the wood material rather than the entire composition. Nichols was not alone; other carpenter-architects such as Samuel McIntire[41] of Salem, Massachusetts, stylized the classical orders to display their mastery of wood as a material. McIntire would become so preoccupied with the detailing of his building that he neglected the overall composition. Nichols was not as skillful in his work in New Bern but, as with the Donnell Law Office, he was beginning to consider the overall composition of the building design. This is something McIntire never considered in his work. (McIntire and others in New England would eventually create an entirely new style of architecture based completely on building detailing rather than building composition.)[42] Nichols would eventually design with the entire composition in mind, using Stuart and Revett's plates along with the work of William Chambers for ideas on building composition.

The delicately accentuated portico attached to the heavy and rigid massing of the main academy building is admittedly an awkward composition; it is somewhat out of scale and not in harmony with the entire building. However, the portico does have a presence and must have been perceived as new and fresh to a decidedly conservative New Bern, which could be defined by its pragmatic, undecorated buildings. The portico awkwardly clips the arch slightly. It appears that Nichols changed the fanlight, making the mullions and swags more slender and delicate; the panels below the sidelights are flat with only a hint of a bead-delineating panel from stile and rail. The double doors are more precise with no raised panels and small beads.

In six years, he had been very productive as a carpenter in New Bern, earning a reputation as an accomplished builder who could produce small, elegant architectural features for larger buildings. Perhaps Nichols wanted to rebrand himself as a master builder/architect to new clientele. Possibly, the economy of New Bern had peaked and business had slowed, or perhaps the competition with other builders such as John Dewey and Uriah Sandy was daunting. Whatever the reason, Nichols left New Bern, and with it, his humble beginnings.

Historians have associated Nichols with numerous other Federal-era buildings in New Bern. While he may have contributed to them, the lack of images and documentation makes his participation inconclusive. To verify a building as "a Nichols," we analyzed the architectural features of the building in question, then compared them to buildings that are conclusively attributed to him. (Even in the beginning of his fifty-year career, Nichols always had a distinctive signature.) We also examined whether or not Nichols had an association with the client/owner and established a timeline between Nichols's whereabouts and the building's construction date. Based on these considerations, we developed a three-criteria approach—triangulation—to determine whether or not Nichols had indeed designed the building in question: 1) Does the building embody specific and particular architectural features commonly used by Nichols throughout his career? 2) Can a compelling argument be made that the client/owner knew or worked with Nichols on previous building projects or business ventures? 3) Was Nichols living in the vicinity when it was built? We have used this method of triangulation throughout the text to determine whether or not a building was indeed "a Nichols."

In 1806, Nichols moved north along the North Carolina sounds to Edenton in Chowan County, North Carolina. There he presented himself first as a builder and later as an architect. In Edenton, Nichols not only developed his reputation as an architect, but as an expensive one who had difficulties working within a set budget. By the time he left Edenton in 1818, he was considered the first resident architect in North Carolina since John Hawks.[43]

Edenton

In 1806, Nichols moved up the coast to Edenton, a town at the head of the Albemarle Sound near the Virginia border. Edenton was established early in the eighteenth century and had been a colonial capital for North Carolina. The small but enterprising town flourished as both a mercantile center and an agricultural one. As Nichols continued to expand his building practice, he soon began to apprentice young boys for the carpenter trades. Before moving to Edenton, he took Nimrod West, age fifteen, as an apprentice. In 1807, his first year in Edenton, he employed Benjamin Boulton as a house carpenter apprentice. As Nichols's business began to flourish, he apprenticed Cornelus Leary (an orphan of John Leary) and James Reed, a free mulatto who was twelve years old. It is unknown how long these young men stayed with Nichols, but it is clear that he was training men to carry out his designs. He would continue training apprentices throughout his career in North Carolina.[44]

He also transferred his Masonic membership from the St. John's Lodge, No. 3, in New Bern to the Unanimity Lodge, No. 7, in Edenton. On August 27, 1808, Nichols was initiated into the Unanimity Lodge; but on November 17, 1808, he was expelled from the lodge and from the Freemasons all together. The reasons for his expulsion were never mentioned in the Unanimity Lodge records. Although he continued to be associated with Freemasons, and later on designed Eagle Lodge No. 19, in Hillsborough, North Carolina, in 1825, Nichols would never be a member of the Freemasons after 1808 in any of the states he lived and worked in.[45]

Shortly after Nichols arrived in Edenton, he was given a significant design and construction project that would enable him to begin defining himself as an architect—the interior renovation of Saint Paul's

Figure 23. Saint Paul's Episcopal Church, Edenton, NC. (Courtesy of Wendy Kapp)

Church. Saint Paul's Church was originally an Anglican church (later becoming Episcopalian) founded when Edenton was established in 1712 (figure 23). The brick masonry shell of the church was begun in 1736 but it was not fully enclosed until 1760.[46] Similar to many brick Anglican churches in the region, it was a one-story simple gable-ended brick building with large Roman arches. The interior was as simple as the exterior, consisting of a large two-story volume of plastered walls and a flat ceiling.[47] The slow pace of construction reflected the meager means of the congregation. By the end of the eighteenth century, the congregation had saved enough money to renovate the interior of the church. In early 1806 the congregation hired Nichols to design and build a new interior to the church consisting of a balcony, new pews, and an altar.[48]

Nichols proposed an interior renovation and a new spire for Saint
Paul's Episcopal Church (figure 24). The proposal and the following
deliberations regarding the price are worth noting because they shed
light on Nichols's audacious character. In *Architects and Builders in
North Carolina*, Catherine Bishir conveys the struggle that the client
(Saint Paul's Church) and the architect (Nichols) had in achieving what
they wanted in the final design and building.

> He proposed a program of neoclassical interior woodwork, plus a spire
> flanked by urns to finish the ancient tower. His price for workmanship
> alone, not including materials or masonry repairs, was $3,300. The star-
> tled building committee urged a cheaper and plainer scheme. But Nichols
> refused any such "abridgement of the work," for, as he explained with
> remarkable candor, "it would procure me no credit which is an object
> with me." A compromise contract of $2,150 omitted steeple and vases.
> But by the time he finished, he had his spire and vases, plus other refine-
> ments, to a total of $522 extra.[49]

Throughout his career, Nichols never lost confidence in himself as
either an architect or a businessman. He was audacious, aggressive, and

boastful. In short, he was a bit of a cad. He was never shy in exaggerating his abilities or experiences and often persuaded the unsuspecting client to undertake an elaborate and costly design. This persistent arm-twisting may have accomplished high-styled designs, but it also resulted in resentment from misled clients. In *Architects and Builders*, Bishir conveys the disappointment and anger of University of North Carolina President Joseph Caldwell after enduring the building campaigns of Old East, Gerrard Hall, and Old West in which Nichols allegedly designed these three buildings with little, if any, regard of the precarious finances of the fledgling university. In fact, Gerrard Hall took fifteen years to complete due to the university's financial hardships. Bishir quotes this warning by Caldwell:

> He (Caldwell) believed that too many architects acted "upon the principle that people ought not to be informed at first of all the amount of expense, and all the difficulties of a public undertaking, lest they can be deferred by an apprehension that they are insurmountable." [Architects], he claimed, gave underestimations knowingly, so that the "people once induced to commence" would continue until the work was well advanced, and then be forced to find additional money for the rest, "that what has been already expended may not be wholly lost. This differs little, if anything, from absolute knavery."

Bishir surmises that Nichols was the "knave" that Caldwell was referring to in his warning about architects. But she also notes that at the dawn of the nineteenth century, when North Carolina was being redefined as a republic, leaders such as Caldwell, William Richardson Davie, and Calvin Jones[50] all complained about the limitations of local builders and the precedents for buildings, specifically historic landmarks, they used, yet they objected to the cost of "higher" style building. Despite their reservations, in the end, they wanted better-designed buildings. Nichols was the right man, at the right time, at the right place, and he was eager to provide them with this stylish architecture. Although Nichols did not help his case by not being completely honest about all of his business affairs, there were many factors that could lead to cost overruns. In examining Nichols's work, it is not clear whether he was blamed for cost overruns during the construction of buildings or whether he was digging for more money from a client.[51] This issue followed Nichols throughout his fifty-year career. In the first decade of the nineteenth century in Edenton, if people with means wanted better, more refined buildings, then they had to pay dearly for them. Fortunately for the ambitious young Nichols, they did.[52]

The congregation of Saint Paul's Church perhaps had no idea that Nichols wished to completely transform the interior of the church.

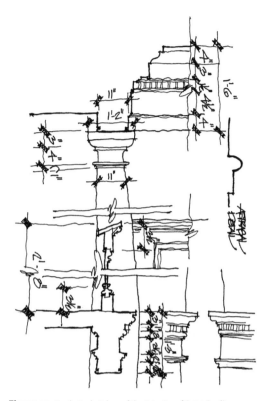

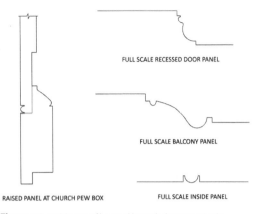

FULL SCALE RECESSED DOOR PANEL

FULL SCALE BALCONY PANEL

RAISED PANEL AT CHURCH PEW BOX   FULL SCALE INSIDE PANEL

Figure 26. Molding profiles used by Nichols at Saint Paul's Episcopal Church. (Sketched by author and drawn by Tim Penich)

Figure 25. Analysis sketches of the interior of Saint Paul's Episcopal Church. (Sketch by author)

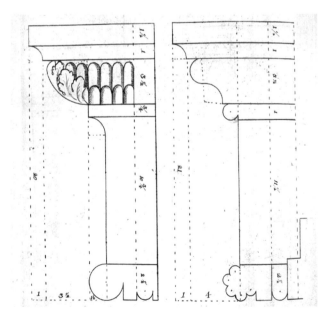

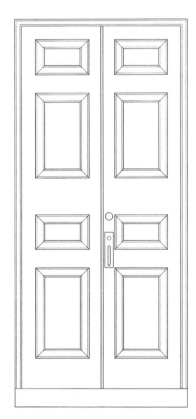

Figure 28. Double doors at Saint Paul's Episcopal Church. (Sketched by author and drawn by Tim Penich)

Figure 27. Typical moldings found in William Pain's *Practical House Carpenter*. (Courtesy of the University of Wisconsin Fine Arts Library Collection)

His interior renovation of Saint Paul's in Edenton included a new balcony, pews, altar, railing, and a spire with flanking urns which are now gone.[53] Nichols's ideas about detailing, proportion and finished carpentry, all of which were based on Pain's *Practical House Carpenter*, are clearly seen. As was the case with the New Bern Academy, Nichols was working with an existing building, a massive shell of brick masonry in which he gracefully inserted a Pain-Adamesque–inspired interior. At Saint Paul's, Nichols was able to display his craftsmanship and knowledge of the English-inspired classical orders. The Saint Paul's balcony is supported by eight colossal Doric columns, with all the moldings and proportions following Pain's instructions (figures 25, 26, 27, and 28).

The entablature he designed for the interior is smaller and more delicate than the entablature typically found in English Georgian architecture. Nichols discarded the heavy and more formal details found in Georgian architecture and embraced a mannerist expression of the classical idiom that is commonly referred to as the Federal style. The church's entablature is denticular Doric, but cannot be considered Doric in the strictest sense. Nichols began to shift away from Pain's pattern book and to express his own ideas of how a Doric entablature is composed; this was not a radical shift, rather a gradual one. As a carpenter, Nichols attempted to display his skill and talent with wood and utilized the material to its maximum: columns are stretched, moldings are flatter and elongated, and the dentils within the entablature are delicate and small. All of this stands in stark juxtaposition to the heavy masonry of the church's shell.

Intersecting the columns midway up the shaft is the main beam that supports the balcony. It is similar in composition to the main entablature of the columns except for one distinct difference: a prominent cyma reversa molding, two inches in height of the entablature and terminates the architrave below the frieze. What is interesting to note about the Saint Paul's balcony is that the overall design and construction are straightforward. Its most prominent visual feature is the railing, composed of recessed panels, small cyma reversa moldings, and flat boards. The panel is simply, but deliberately, built; each element is carefully placed both functionally and aesthetically. The overall effect of the balcony is a delicate one of slender proportions, all the while respecting the nature of the wood. This is totally different from what we see in Hawks's design ideas, which rarely addressed the materiality of design. Instead, his focus was more on composition and less on building. At Saint Paul's, moldings and architectural elements such as columns are clearly based on Pain's pattern books and are designed with fabrication of the wood in mind. Whether this is a reflection of Nichols's ability as a carpenter or his own expression of the classical

Figure 29. Interior of the Chowan County Courthouse, Edenton, NC. Nichols worked on an early renovation of the courthouse and installed the Pain-influenced Doric columns. This photograph was taken in 2000 during the latest renovation. (Courtesy of Hager Smith Design, PA)

ideal, distinctive detailing of what would become his "signature" begin to appear.

After finishing Saint Paul's in 1808, Nichols began to get other work, first as a specialty (finish) carpenter and later as an architect-builder. His work at Saint Paul's is as much the work of a master carpenter as it is of a developing architect. He began to undertake projects that were more complicated than those in New Bern. At Saint Paul's, he had tackled the most complex building in his career thus far. His work there is an example of precision; all of the components fit together, much better than his works in New Bern. In this small church, Nichols developed a building vocabulary or language of columns and moldings that would become his signature for the next ten years.

William Nichols continued to work as a carpenter from 1809 to 1817. Examples of his craft from this period can be found in homes and houses throughout Edenton. It is entirely likely that in the nineteenth and twentieth centuries, small pieces of his work such as an entry here or a mantle there, could be found in houses up and down the streets of Edenton; but time and changes in fashion have most likely destroyed many of these small creations. Some, however, did survive and stand out when compared to the vernacular buildings in which they were installed. A good example of the Nichols "touch" is found on the front door of the James Iredell House on East Church Street in Edenton (figure 30). Circa 1810, Hannah Johnston Iredell, James Iredell, Sr.'s widow, built a two-story wing to the west of the original 1759 and 1776 structure. In 1816, James Iredell, Jr., remodeled the two-story west wing and, based on these improvements, hired Nichols to fabricate a new door entry and new mantles.[54] The house is simple in plan and form with a wing that has a two-story porch, typical for a large late eighteenth-century house in eastern North Carolina. However, the front door makes a decidedly different statement from the rest of the simple detailing of the house (figures 31 and 32). The door casings are noticeably more defined with stretched cyma reversa back band moldings. The door itself has tighter beaded moldings at the stiles and rails than the doors in other parts of the house. But what truly stands out is the transom railing, which separates the transom from the front door. This component is embellished with reeded carvings and, in its center, is a carved Greek key, all of which appear to be influenced by the work of John Soane, who originally developed these details in his work in the last two decades of the eighteenth century in England.

Nichols also designed the living room mantle, which incorporates the same cyma reversa moldings found at Saint Paul's. Two archways with fluted casings and thin elongated pilasters, all of which are capped with a fluted keystone, flank the mantle. He would use these elements in numerous houses and public buildings in North Carolina.

Nichols's work can also be found in the old Chowan County Courthouse in Edenton, one of the most important architectural works in Colonial America. The courthouse was designed in 1767 and has been attributed to both John Hawks and master builder Gilbert Leigh of Williamsburg, Virginia.[55] Based on the detailing found in the courthouse, it appears that Nichols was involved in the building's 1808 interior renovation. The six elongated Doric capitals placed in the main courtroom to support the second floor are identical to the ones found in Saint Paul's and are remarkably similar to the portico columns at New Bern Academy. All of these columns conform, both in proportion and geometry, to the specifications found in William Pain's *Practical House Carpenter*[56] (figure 29).

Figure 30. James Iredell House, Edenton, NC, 1936. (Historic American Buildings Survey, Library of Congress, Washington, DC)

Figure 31. The entry at the James Iredell House, Edenton, NC. (Courtesy of Wendy Kapp)

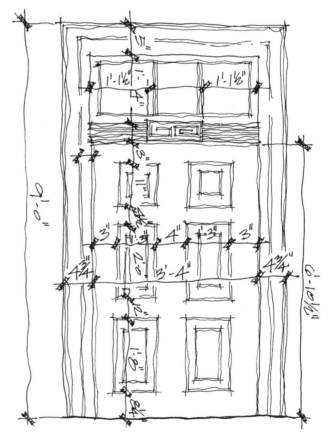

Figure 32. Detail sketch of the main entry of the James Iredell House. Nichols redesigned and built the entry. (Sketch by author)

In 1814, Nichols designed and constructed the building across from the courthouse on Colonial Avenue known as the Old East Customs House, or the Joseph Blount Skinner Law Office (figure 33). With its compact cube-like massing, it appears to be the first architectural composition by Nichols and reveals his preference for pure geometric form. Despite significant early twentieth-century additions and alterations, the small one-story wood frame structure retains a considerable amount of Nichols's Grecian-inspired design. It is a compact square hipped roof building with a heavy Doric entablature, which projects a full column diameter from the frieze. The heavy cornice is fully supported by large mutules and is capped by a large cyma reversa molding, conforming to classical canon. This time the columns adhere to the 1:8 diameter to height ratio, as prescribed in classical canons of architecture, but Nichols built the columns square, not round.

The simple elegant two-columned entrance portico faces the courthouse. The top two-thirds of the square columns are fluted. The echinus is much more pronounced with a thumb-shaped ovolo molding. The bases are much simpler, consisting of splayed moldings and square plinths (figures 34 and 35). At the corners of the simple pavilion are pilasters matching the size and detail of the front columns. While reflecting Pain's ideas of geometry and proportion, the building has a heavier appearance due to the large moldings, a clear departure from the light, elongated designs of New Bern Academy and Saint Paul's Church.

Figure 33. The Joseph Blount Skinner House (also known as the Old East Customs House), Edenton, NC. This is the earliest known residence designed and built by Nichols, ca. 1814. (Courtesy of Wendy Kapp)

Figure 34. The entry of the Joseph Blount Skinner House, Edenton, NC. (Courtesy of Wendy Kapp)

Figure 35. Detail of the entry at the Joseph Blount Skinner House (Old East Customs House). (Sketch by author)

The front door is prominently Grecian and echoes not only the work of John Soane but also that of John Nash, who first began working in this straightforward, geometric manner when he designed the villa known as Llanerchaeron in 1795 in Wales.[57] Within the small Grecian portico, the door surround is composed of a heavy Grecian Doric entablature, which is also mutulary in design. The architrave is small and defined by a simple raised fillet or square molding; the frieze is much deeper than that at Saint Paul's. The cornice consists of mutules and moldings that match the main cornice. The most prominent feature of the door entablature is a carved plaque inserted in the middle of the frieze. The front door is also very distinctive, flanked by pilasters that match the square columns with identical capitals and fluting; the door has a transom over it with a Roman lattice design. More importantly, the transom rail is reeded with a prominent Greek key motif in its center and matches exactly the front door of the James Iredell House only two blocks north (figure 36). The Old East Customs House must have had a striking presence in Edenton when it was completed. With its simple compact geometry, bold use of the Doric order, clean and bold wood construction, the Old East Customs House was a new fresh architectural expression, especially when likened to comparable houses near

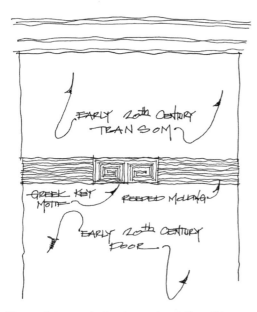

Figure 36. Transom detail, main entry, Joseph Blount Skinner House (Old East Customs House). (Sketch by author)

Figure 37. Corner board and pilaster condition at the Joseph Blount Skinner House (Old East Customs House), Edenton, NC. (Courtesy of Wendy Kapp)

Figure 38. Corner pilaster condition, Joseph Blount Skinner House, Edenton, NC. (Sketch by author)

it in Edenton and most notably, the very Georgian Chowan County Courthouse (figures 37 and 38).

As is the case in New Bern, historians have attributed a number of other notable buildings to Nichols in Edenton. He is credited for designing and building the Baptist Meeting House in 1810 along with two other structures circa 1810. The first is the Chowan County Jail, a simple wooden structure, and a house built for Mrs. Harriss. All of these buildings have been demolished and there is no known record of their descriptions. As with New Bern, the full breadth of Nichols's work in Edenton will forever remain open to speculation.[58] By 1815, Nichols had reached the first of several crossroads in his life and career. He had become a U.S. citizen in 1813 and subsequently lost his first wife due to unknown causes and married his second one, Sarah Simons of Chowan County. He also received the breakthrough he had been longing for: the design of a new house for James Cathcart Johnston, called Hayes Plantation.

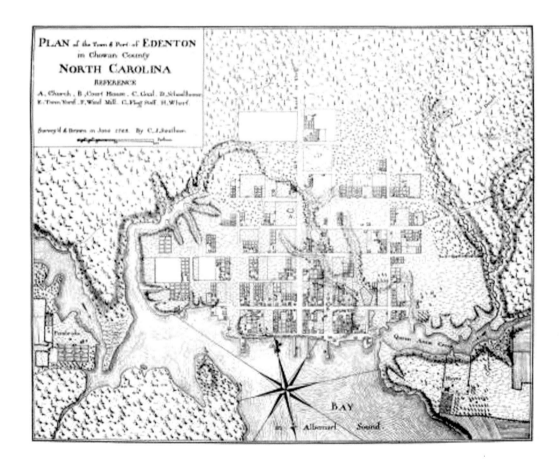

PLAN of the Town & Port of EDENTON
in Chowan County
NORTH CAROLINA
REFERENCE
A, Church. B, Court House. C, Gaol. D, Schoolhouse
E, Town Yard. F, Wind Mill. G, Flag Staff. H, Wharf

Survey'd & Drawn in June 1769. By C. J. Sauthier.

BAY
in ye Albemarl Sound.

Hayes

On the C. J. Sauthier Map of Edenton drawn in 1769, Hayes Plantation is shown as a modest farm across Queen Anne Creek, east of the bustling little town (figure 39). Even today, it sits in splendid isolation from the town, retaining its agrarian sense, a stark contrast to the civic nature of Colonial Avenue a few hundred yards away. With its spectacular views of Edenton Bay, Hayes Plantation was the home of patriot Samuel Johnston, a gentleman planter who pursued the business of agriculture in a grand manner.

Samuel Johnston was one of the most influential and successful North Carolinians of his day. Born in 1733, Johnston was a native of Dundee, Scotland. He came to North Carolina as a child in 1736. His uncle was Gabriel Johnston, royal governor of the North Carolina colony in 1734. Gabriel Johnston brought Samuel and his parents to North Carolina where they resided on a plantation between New Bern and Wilmington called Poplar Spring. It was here that Samuel spent his youth. He studied at Yale College but did not graduate from there; instead, he came to Edenton and read the law under the guidance of Thomas Barker. He became a successful attorney and planter, leader of the American Revolution in North Carolina, governor of the new state from 1787 to 1789, and one of North Carolina's first U.S. senators from 1789 to 1793. He had several plantations, Hayes (665 acres in size) being one of them, which he purchased in 1765. The Sauthier map[1] shows the footprint of a house he built on the property, which appears to have been a wood frame "I" house with small wings attached to both the north and south sides. Historian Mills Lane has a different perspective on the original Hayes. In his book *Architecture of the Old South—North Carolina*, Lane suggests that Samuel Johnson

Figure 39. Map of Edenton, NC, by C. J. Sauthier, 1769. An earlier manor house is shown at Hayes Plantation, which lies southeast of the town of Edenton, on the opposite banks of Queen Anne Creek. (North Carolina Collection, University of North Carolina at Chapel Hill Library)

built a tripartite Palladian house, which Lane bases on a family map showing a simple sketch of a two-story gable house with one-story dependencies attached by a colonnade.[2] Lane also states that Johnston received some architectural renderings from Tryon Palace architect John Hawks in 1773 and that the first house was built between 1790 (the year Hawks died) and 1801. It is unknown whether or not the initial home was based on Hawks's renderings.[3]

His son, James Johnston, was both well educated and industrious. He received a classical education in New York while his father was serving in the U.S. Senate; he then studied at the Woodbury School in Philadelphia (1792–1796) and graduated in 1799 from the College of New Jersey (now Princeton University). Before returning to Chowan County, he briefly studied French at the University of North Carolina. After reading the law, he received his law license in 1804. However, he never enjoyed being a lawyer and became much more interested in agriculture. By 1806, Johnston had devoted himself to the full-time operations of his father's plantations.[4]

In 1814, Samuel Johnston gave Hayes to James and urged him to build a new, albeit simple, house in which to live and manage the plantation. According to a letter written by James Johnston, the "dwelling house and out-house [were] out of repair and uninhabitable."[5] Echoing the prevailing attitude of his generation—that of simplicity and frugality—Samuel Johnston bestows the following advice to his son: ". . . I hope you will always prefer a plain and simple stile of living to a gaudy and tinsel appearance, a passion to which there are no bounds and which too often leads to the want of solid comforts and a wretched state of dependence."[6] Ignoring his father's advice on frugality and modest living, the younger Johnston set out to build one of the most unique and grandest houses in North Carolina.

At some point in 1814, Johnston approached Nichols about designing and building the Hayes Plantation residence. In a letter written late that year, Nichols responds to Johnston by offering his services:

> Sir: I take the opportunity by your Boys to inform you that what time could be spared from the attention required by a very sick family has been entirely taken up by the business of my shop, the only [th]ing I have to depend on for subsistenc[e]. Your plans consequently been [neglected?] if however Sir I can be of service to you after the first day of January you may command me—having arranged my business in such a manner as to be able to attend to you. Yr. obdt and hbl servt, Wm Nichols.[7]

It is interesting to note that by hiring Nichols as an architect and a master carpenter, James Johnston broke away from the convention of the landowner acting as the "gentleman architect" for the project and instead sought the services of a "professional" one. Johnston was, however, intimately involved in the everyday affairs of the construction, acting as contractor and keeping detailed financial and work logs. According to his diaries and ledgers, Johnston purchased one hundred thousand units of locally made brick and hundreds of feet of feather-edged clapboard. He secured tradesmen, brick masons from Virginia, slave tradesmen for sawing timber, local carpenters (some of which were either free blacks or slaves) and a painter.[8]

After over a year of planning and nearly three years of building, the large wood frame home at Hayes Plantation was completed in the fall of 1818. As with his other projects, no designs, sketches, or notes by William Nichols exist. The house itself—a conglomeration of Federal, Greek, Palladian, British, and American influences—is testament enough. Hayes is quite large, approximately eleven thousand square feet, comparable in size to the grand brick mansions in neighboring states, including Mount Vernon in Virginia and Drayton Hall in South Carolina.[9] The timber-framed Hayes is nevertheless a house of rich complexity and elegant detailing, a wonderful mix of on-site craftsmanship and imported components that relate very well to each other. It demonstrates the sophisticated tastes and sensibilities of the owner and the talents of a hardworking, highly skilled craftsman.

If James Johnston's desire was to have a Palladian-style house similar to the grand plantations of Virginia, such as John Tayloe's Mount Airy and Robert Beverly's Blandfield or even Washington's Mount Vernon, then he was evidently influenced by the many interpretations of Andrea Palladio's Villa Badoer, a sixteenth-century Renaissance tripartite in northern Italy. The villa consists of a large center block with flanking smaller pavilions and provided inspiration for many grander homes in Europe and the mid-Atlantic region of the United States, including Tryon Palace in New Bern and Monticello and Mount Vernon in Virginia. Johnston also may have had books containing designs similar to the Villa Badoer, most notably William Adam's *Vitruvius Scoticus*. The conceptual design of Hayes encompasses three features of Palladian design and the interpretation of it in the mid-Atlantic region: 1) the main house cubic massing, 2) the design of the rectangular dependencies, and 3) the colonnade "connectors" that contained small rooms (figures 40 and 41). There were other precedents that influenced Nichols's design, most notably the Temple of Delos in Stuart and Revett's *The Antiquities of Athens* evident in the creation of specific details found on the exterior of the house such as the northeast portico (figures 42 and 43). He interpreted and fabricated these ideas using his understanding of Pain-Adamesque detailing (figures 44–47). Nichols also relied heavily on William Pain's *Practical House Carpenter* for inspirations in detailing the house.

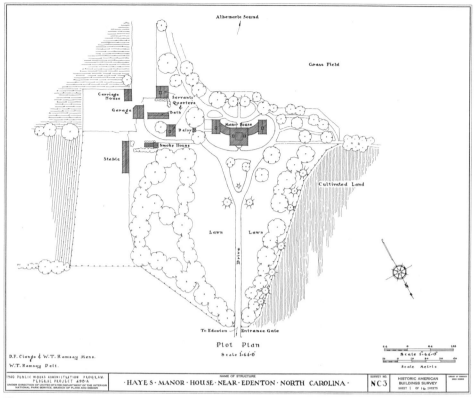

Figure 40. Site plan of Hayes Plantation, Chowan County, NC. (Historic American Buildings Survey, Library of Congress, Washington, DC)

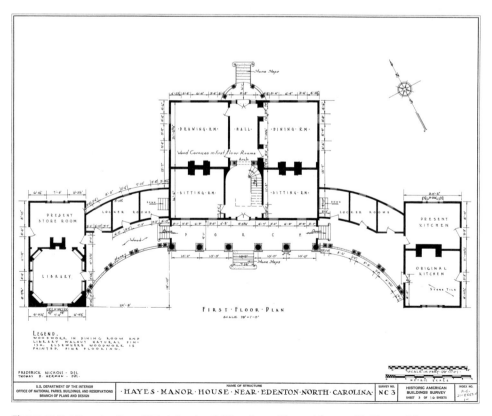

Figure 41. First-floor plan, Hayes. (Historic American Buildings Survey, Library of Congress, Washington, DC)

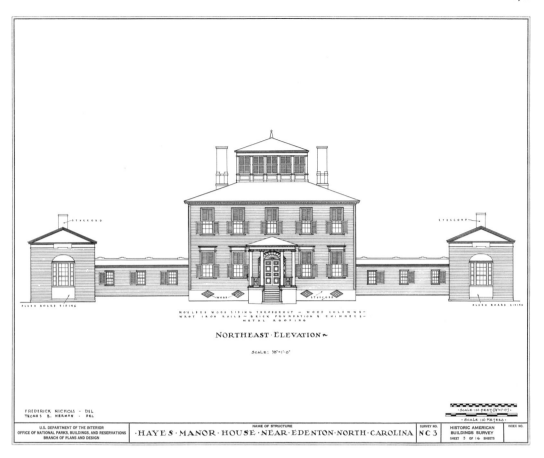

NORTHEAST ·ELEVATION~

SCALE: ⅛"=1'·0"

FREDERICK NICHOLS - DEL
THOMAS B. HERMAN - DEL

U.S. DEPARTMENT OF THE INTERIOR
OFFICE OF NATIONAL PARKS, BUILDINGS, AND RESERVATIONS
BRANCH OF PLANS AND DESIGN

NAME OF STRUCTURE
·HAYES·MANOR·HOUSE·NEAR·EDENTON·NORTH·CAROLINA·

SURVEY NO.
NC 3

HISTORIC AMERICAN
BUILDINGS SURVEY
SHEET 5 OF 16 SHEETS

INDEX NO.

Figure 42. North elevation, facing road entry, Hayes. (Historic American Buildings Survey, Library of Congress, Washington, DC)

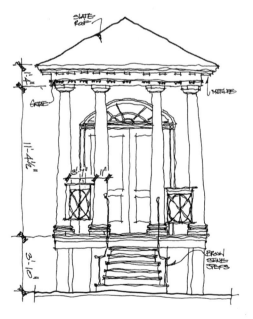

Figure 43. Entry porch, Hayes. (Sketch by author)

During the construction of Hayes, Nichols was able to travel north to purchase items for the house that were not readily available in Edenton. It has been documented through letter correspondence that Johnston sent Nichols to New York in 1817 to purchase items such as iron railings, brownstone steps, stone for surrounding the fireboxes, and mantles. Nichols expressed disappointment to Johnston in the quality of mantles that he found in New York and stated that he would rather fabricate mantles to his liking out of wood and on site.[10] It is not known where else

Nichols traveled when he went to New York. Nevertheless, he was able to incorporate ideas that he experienced in the architecture being built in the Northeast with what he had designed and nearly completed in Edenton.

Hayes's tripartite design follows the tradition well established by many earlier mid-Atlantic plantation manor houses. The center block, cubic in form, is a two-story building with a hipped roof capped by a large hipped belvedere supported by twenty-four square columns. The main mass is a double-pile center hallway house with two front parlors, a dining room, and a sitting room. The center hallway is divided by an arched opening that leads to a winding stairway. The front (north) façade is a six bay composition of large double-hung sash windows with operable swinging louvered shutters for the bottom window sash and awning louvered shutters for the top window sash. The north façade boasts a semicircular small one-story Doric portico with a half-cone shaped roof covered in slate. The front door welcomes guests with a low half-circular fanlight window flanked by multilight sidelight windows (figure 43).

Hayes's semicircular portico is Nichols's further elaboration of the New Bern Academy portico that he built some twelve years earlier. The Doric columns are once again the elongated, flat disc-shaped capital columns that he designed and fabricated at Saint Paul's Church and the Chowan County Courthouse. The proportions of the columns and the entablature are similar to those at the New Bern Academy. In the overall composition of the entablature, all of these elements align with corresponding elements of the cornice. While deductive composition of classical porticos was not an uncommon practice in America in the early nineteenth century, Nichols's creation demonstrates his command of this idiom using his carpentry skills, knowledge of neoclassical design, and sheer audacity. The portico shares similar detailing of the corona and the mutules as found in the New Bern Academy portico and the Skinner Law Office, all of which reflect the influence of the ideas found in the plates in Nichols's copy of the *Practical House Carpenter*.

On Hayes's south façade (figures 44 and 45) facing Edenton Bay, Nichols designed a two-story colossal Doric portico similar in elongation and proportion to his earlier and smaller porticos but, as found at the Skinner Law Office, he was influenced by the Temple of Apollo at Delos depicted by Stuart and Revett (figure 46). The shafts of the portico are fluted but the fluting begins after the entasis of the column starts, similar to what is shown in the Delos precedent. Once again the entablature is smaller in proportion than actual Greek and Roman examples. Nichols also introduced a new motif to the entablature, a simple square plaque over each column capital. The mutules

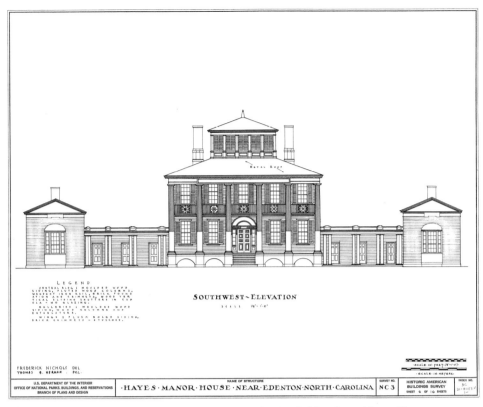

Figure 44. South elevation, facing Edenton Bay, Hayes. (Historic American Buildings Survey, Library of Congress, Washington, DC)

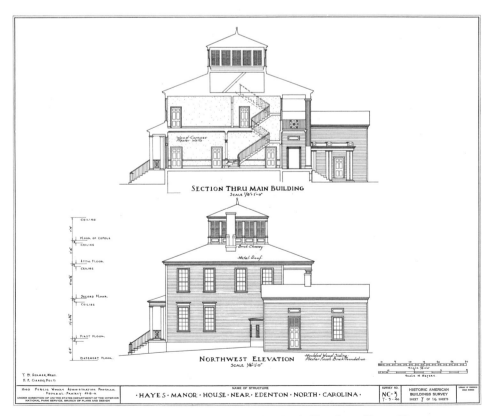

Figure 45. Building section and side elevations, Hayes. (Historic American Buildings Survey, Library of Congress, Washington, DC)

Figure 46. Temple of Apollo at Delos by Stuart and Revett. (Ricker Library of Art and Architecture, University of Illinois at Urbana–Champaign)

are doubled, setting a rhythm of triglyphs similar to what is found on the north portico, a Nichols trademark detail that began at Hayes[11] (figure 47). The double rhythm of the cornice and entablature is also found in the intercolumniation of the one-story colonnades that connects the dependencies to the main house. For these colonnades, Nichols used the Doric column that he developed at New Bern Academy. He then compressed the frieze and made the entablature denticular, very similar in form to the entablature at Saint Paul's Church. Above the cornice, Nichols installed a simple wood-paneled parapet.

Figure 47. Exterior molding details, Hayes. (Historic American Buildings Survey, Library of Congress, Washington, DC)

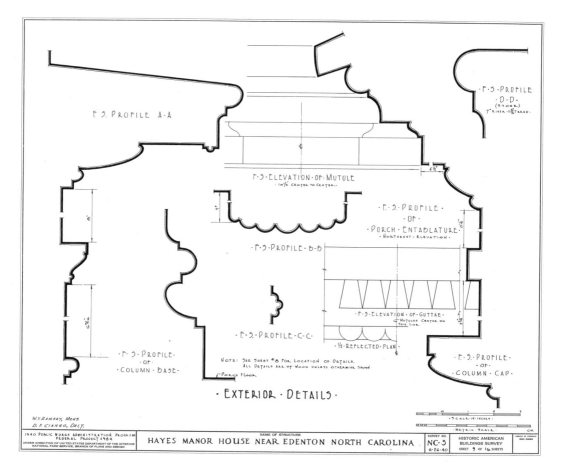

While the composition is simple, it allowed the colonnades' porticos to achieve the appearance of being both light and prominent to the rest of the house while making a graceful statement towards Edenton Bay. With the massing and composition, as well as the construction out of wood, one can see similarities between Hayes and George Washington's Mount Vernon; however, it is safe to say that these similarities are coincidental. Unlike Hawks's Royal Palace at New Bern, both Hayes and Mount Vernon are manor houses built in a way that responds to available affordable materials, wood, and the skill sets of the local labor and building trades of the time. Moreover, both manor houses were designed to respond to the environmental conditions of the mid-Atlantic region. They both have colossal porticos facing the breezes of waterways (Albemarle Sound at Hayes, the Potomac River at Mount Vernon), and they are designed with central halls and cupolas or observatories, which provide passive cooling throughout their interior rooms.

The interior of the main section of the house continues with the Pain-influenced style of classicism. Greek keys and frets, Nichols's Edenton-inspired trademark, are used throughout the house.[12] The center hall and main parlor both have an elaborate cornice-ceiling treatment of frets punctuated with rosettes; the wall terminates with shallow coveto moldings, all of which define the ceilings in an elegant manner. Rosettes, prevalent throughout the house, are used to terminate the corners of the fretted casings of all of the doors and windows. The mantles, which Nichols designed and built on-site, demonstrate his grasp of the most current architectural and decorative styles in England (figures 48–50). The main mantles consist of fretted pilasters and frieze boards; large rosettes accent the corners while a flat and elongated cyma-reversa molding supports the mantle shelf. Also a flat, large plaque is centered in the middle of the mantle. The mantles throughout the main section of the residence are simple and elegant and seamlessly fit within the overall design of the house.

What is definitely the most striking Pain-influenced feature in the interior of Hayes is the archway between the front and rear of the central hall. Here, Nichols introduced the most ambitious carpentry work of his young career—a grand archway. Two "Temple of the Winds" columns with matching pilasters at the walls support the archway. The flatness of the acanthus leaves and the severity of both the proportion along with the lip at the top of the capital of the columns clearly show that Nichols was following Pain's Plate 28 of *Practical House Carpenter*. The column shafts also show less of a tapered entasis similar to all of the columns Nichols designed and fabricated (figures 51–54).

The connected dependencies at Hayes are simple gable-ended one-story structures that gracefully receive the colonnades and the small storage rooms set behind them. Each dependency has a specific

Figure 48. Main parlor fireplace at Hayes. (Courtesy of Thomas J. Campanella)

Figure 49. Detail of mantle. (Courtesy of Thomas J. Campanella)

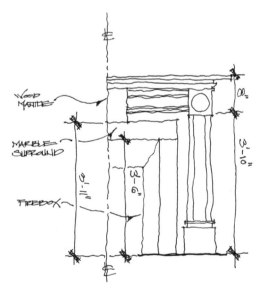

Figure 50. Detail sketch of the parlor mantle at Hayes. (Sketch by author)

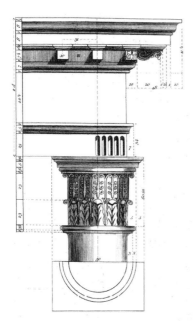

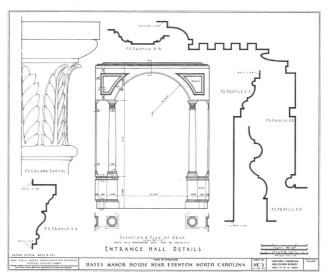

Figure 51. William Pain's plate 28, "Temple of the Winds." Nichols used this precedent for the entry arch in center hall of Hayes. (Courtesy of the University of Wisconsin Fine Arts Library Collection)

Figure 52. Entrance hall details at Hayes based on William Pain's "Temple of the Winds" plate. (Historic American Buildings Survey, Library of Congress, Washington, DC)

Figure 53. Entry arch at Hayes. (Courtesy of Thomas J. Campanella)

Figure 54. Column detail of the entry arch at Hayes. Nichols based the column details on the "Temple of the Winds" plate found in William Pain's *Practical House Carpenter*. (Courtesy of Thomas J. Campanella)

Figure 55. Hayes looking west. (Courtesy of Thomas J. Campanella)

Figure 56. Hayes, entrance façade facing south. (Courtesy of Thomas J. Campanella)

function: the east dependency is the kitchen and the west dependency is James Johnston's library. At the south façades of these matching dependencies, Nichols inserted a blind arch with a large double-hung sash window flanked by two narrow double-hung windows. The window element on the gable ends are treated in the same manner as the front door; they are cut into the weatherboard surface of the mass with each board precisely cut to match the radius curve of the arch and the window jambs. Shutters then flank the large window. Inside the kitchen dependency, the kitchen and storerooms are spartan and

Figure 57. Hayes, south-facing façade facing Edenton Bay. (Courtesy of Thomas J. Campanella)

Figure 58. Detail of the east pavilion at Hayes. (Courtesy of Thomas J. Campanella)

utilitarian, with no ornamentation applied to the walls or the ceiling (figures 55–58).

However, the interior of the west or library dependency greatly differs from the east dependency. With its octagonal room with several "Gothick" details, it is one of the most famous rooms in North Carolina. Its inspiration is Strawberry Hill, Earl Horace Walpole's eighteenth-century Gothic villa in London. Images of Strawberry Hill appear in Johnston's copy of Horace Walpole's *A description of the villa of Horace Walpole, youngest son of Sir Robert Walpole Earl of Oxford,*

at Strawberry-Hill, near Twickenham: With an inventory of the furniture, pictures and curiosities[13] with one startling difference: Walpole's plan was square in design (figure 59). The ceiling in the library at Hayes is vaulted, with a fresco of faux ribs in aquamarine, white, and golden brown. Pointed arched bookcases and pointed window casings articulate the architecture of the room while plaster busts of George Washington and Samuel Johnston, James's father, look down on the simple library table centered in the room. The bookcases and paneling are heart pine, stained a chocolate color (figures 60–62). The applied panels are beveled, giving a hint of pilasters and friezes. Stylized crosses accent the corners and center of the mantle face while a simple cyma-reversa molding supports the mantle shelf. Pointed gothic arches spring from both the mantlepiece and two side doors (one of which is false) that flank the fireplace. A simple beveled board divides the wall space and allows a faux finish of red marble to contrast with the wood paneling. Even though Nichols would continue to practice and build in four states for the next thirty-six years, he would never replicate the brilliance and beauty of the Hayes library. With its magnificent architecture, exquisite furnishings, and dramatic views of Edenton Bay, the Hayes library is a magnificent space and one of the greatest works of architecture in North Carolina history.

The entire house is capped with a sizable observatory, defined by twenty-four stylized Doric columns that support a pyramidal roof.

Figure 59. Walpole's library at Strawberry Hill, Surrey, England, 1754, etching by Edward Edwards, 1781. John Chute designed the library; it was the inspiration for Johnston's library at Hayes that Nichols designed. (Courtesy of the Lewis Walpole Library, Yale University)

Figure 61. Detail of the mantlepiece in the library at Hayes. (Courtesy of Thomas J. Campanella)

Figure 60. The Gothic-inspired library at Hayes. (Photograph by author)

Figure 62. Dome ceiling of the Hayes library. (Courtesy of Thomas J. Campanella)

Louvered shutters provide privacy and shelter from the rain. The observatory performed two important functions pertaining to the creature comforts of the house's occupants. First, it gave Johnston and his guests a place to enjoy the bay breezes. Secondly, working with the large center hall and the grand stair and when the roof hatches were opened, the observatory worked like a large chimney, which drew hot air from the interior. With the windows open, cooler air flowed throughout the house, making the observatory an excellent example of a passive cooling system in architecture.

Clearly, Nichols employed sound and responsive ideas for comfortable living in the southern environment. Early in his career, he designed buildings that maximized the prevailing breezes and with deep overhangs shaded the occupants from the hot summer sun. In today's modern era of air conditioning and electricity, architects have largely discarded ideas that Nichols successfully employed at Hayes. Passive cooling was a part of the conceptual design, an important and highly successful aspect of his architecture. This attentiveness to the southern climate, combined with English influences and classical building ideas, made Hayes the Classical Revival precedent setter for the Greek Revival movement in the southern backcountry some twenty years later. The beauty of Hayes is a result of more than Johnston's taste and Nichols's influences; it is that, plus the culmination of William Nichols's skill as an architect and craftsman that allowed him to create a home that was both Federal and Classical Revival in style. It was a resounding success for Nichols.

The architectural magnificence of Hayes and Nichols's association with Johnston created the unique opportunity for him to become the first resident architect in North Carolina since John Hawks. According to Bishir, Nichols's "success at Hayes served as an important springboard. The house itself presented his abilities in no uncertain terms. And by satisfying Johnston, he had gained a generous and influential patron."[14] Patronage, from a stable client base (something all architects aspire to obtain), was something Nichols had desperately sought throughout the first third of his career; he finally earned it in Johnston, who favorably recommended him to friends and influential family members. In 1816, Johnston wrote a letter to his cousin, James Iredell, Jr.,[15] who at the time was serving in the North Carolina General Assembly, and Iredell hired Nichols to remodel his home in Edenton two years earlier and advocated that Nichols be contracted as the architect of a proposed state penitentiary:

> I observed a long report of the Committee on the Penitentiary. Should the legislature do anything on that subject I must beg the favor of you to remember Nichols—if anything can be done for him in his line—I know of no man so well qualified to superintend of that kind and I think you might venture to recommend him in that way. . . It would be of infinite advantage to the public to have such a man to superintend their buildings instead of trusting the business to a committee, as is usual who know nothing about it.[16]

Johnston's endorsement of Nichols is also his indirect endorsement of the use of an architect to design and execute complex building projects. Although the bill for a penitentiary failed in 1817, the committee did receive "an elegant plan from William Nichols, an architect from Edenton." Nichols's maturity and mastery of architecture and building would coincide with the maturity and establishment of the state of North Carolina. As the state's institutions, specifically the state government and the state university, would become more established, they would require an architecture befitting them. With Johnston's endorsement, Nichols would, one year later, secure the coveted position of superintendent of state buildings for North Carolina.

The Hayes experience was the last one for Nichols in eastern North Carolina. By 1818, the coastal region of North Carolina began to decline as the eighteenth-century economic and agricultural practices were beginning to take their toll on farmlands, specifically the over-cultivation of tobacco, which removed essential nutrients in the soil. Moreover, opportunity was waiting for North Carolinians west of the coastal plains, first in the Piedmont and then in the south and west. As the center of governmental power moved from New Bern to Raleigh, the economic center moved from New Bern to Fayetteville, where the Cape Fear River becomes navigable. It is here that Nichols, a shrewd opportunist, began his career-long practice of "following the money."

Nichols left Edenton shortly after he finished Hayes, bound for Fayetteville. Once in Fayetteville, he continued to work for patrons and eventually the state of North Carolina. He also became an entrepreneur and a land speculator in both Cumberland and Wake counties in central North Carolina.[17] When Nichols left eastern North Carolina, he also left his reliance on the precedents and guidance of William Pain's pattern books. His work after Edenton had less resemblance to Pain's details as he began using architectural precedent books. More of his work would emulate or actually be constructed of stone and brick masonry rather than wood. This departure from one set of design ideas to another would become a common trait of Nichols's fifty-year career.

And what about James C. Johnston? How did he fare working so intensely for four years on such a grand house that was a monument to his aspirations? Hayes would be his main residence for the next forty-seven years of his life, first with his sisters, Penelope and Helen, and then with his nephew, also named James C. Johnston (who later added "Jr." to his name) and his family. Johnston never altered the house and did not spend very much time at home; he traveled extensively to his other plantations in Pasquotank and Northampton counties and also vacationed near Hot Springs, Virginia, and in New York.[18] Johnston died in 1865 and, with no offspring, left Hayes Plantation to Edward Wood, an Edenton attorney and business colleague.[19] The Wood family has lived at Hayes since 1866. Careful stewards of the house, they have made minimal alterations in order to provide a small kitchen and bathrooms.[20] Hayes Plantation is a rare example of Nichols's residential work that has survived fire, federal occupation during the Civil War, and alterations from succeeding generations.

Chapter Three

CAPTAIN WILLIAM NICHOLS,
STATE ARCHITECT OF NORTH CAROLINA

Wuilliam Nichols is listed in the U.S. Census of 1820 as a resident of Fayetteville. Nichols's census entry states that his family consisted of one white male between the ages of twenty-six and forty-five (Nichols), a white female between the ages of sixteen and twenty-six (his wife, Sarah), and two sons under the age of ten (William, Jr., and Samuel). The census listing also stated that Nichols was engaged in commerce and manufacturing and that he owned three slaves—a couple with one child.[1]

In the early part of the nineteenth century, Fayetteville was one of the largest and most prosperous cities in North Carolina. Located at the fall line of the Cape Fear River, it had served briefly as the state capital until Raleigh was designated as such in 1792. Nevertheless, it still served as the primary market center for the upland settlers. It had a population of four thousand people and was laid out in an orderly gridiron around a central courthouse square.[2] From 1820 until 1860, North Carolina continued to develop to the west, and Fayetteville was experiencing rapid growth and prosperity. Nichols sought building commissions in this bustling city. As early as 1816, while Nichols was still in Edenton, he was able to persuade Representative James Winslow of Fayetteville to sponsor his design for a new North Carolina penitentiary. In June 1818, Nichols wrote Senator Archibald Murphey[3] regarding the Cape Fear River opening for navigation at Fayetteville. (Naturally, Nichols knew the opening of this water transportation would bring business—and building—there.) Murphey's answer is unknown, but shortly thereafter, Nichols moved his family to Fayetteville later that year.[4] When he arrived, Nichols began marketing his services as an architect to the upper middle class in the North

Carolina Piedmont using Johnston as a reference to extol his talents and capabilities.[5]

The state government hired Nichols to do various architectural and building work shortly after his arrival. James Iredell, Jr., a former client from Edenton and chair of the "Committee Appointed to Examine the State of the Public Buildings" in the North Carolina State House of Commons, helped Nichols secure a consulting position for the state of North Carolina on individual projects.[6] Later that year, Nichols was appointed superintendent of public buildings.[7] In 1821, an opportunity that significantly helped Nichols flourish as an architect was his appointment to the position of state architect in North Carolina. He held this position until 1822. Not only did the position of state architect carry with it a lofty, impressive title; it also included a salary of four hundred dollars per month, a very respectable sum of money in the early decades of the nineteenth century. Holding this position made Nichols's establishment as an architect complete; he now had financial stability for the first time in his career. It also gave him the opportunity to work on some of the state's most important building projects, specifically the first North Carolina State House and the campus of the University of North Carolina. Lastly, it gave Nichols the social stature that would enable him to market his talents and business to the wealthiest North Carolinians of the period. While committed to his work for the state of North Carolina, he had also developed a prosperous and productive private practice designing churches, public buildings (such as Masonic halls and courthouses), and fine residences throughout the North Carolina Piedmont.

The state architect appointment may have saved Nichols's career. Without it, it is entirely likely that Nichols might have floundered and remained a talented local builder rather than an influential regional architect. This stroke of good luck and fortune did not happen often. In *Greek Revival Architecture in America*, Talbot Hamlin discusses the fates of European-born architects who were contemporaries of Nichols, all of whom began with ambitions and great expectations only to end their careers as bitter and disappointed men. Hamlin cites several foreign-born talented architects such as the French-born architects Joseph Francois Mangin and Joseph-Jacque Ramée, who came to America and worked hard but failed miserably.[8] Ramée, the architect who designed the campus and the original buildings of Union College in Schenectady, New York, enjoyed initial success but later fell out of popular favor and could not attract any new clients or work even though his Union College design is still considered a breakthrough in campus design.[9] He later moved to Hamburg, Germany, and practiced there until his death. Mangin simply disappeared after his initial successes designing the New York City Hall.[10]

The most glaring example of a foreign-born architect failing to succeed in America was Benjamin Henry Latrobe. Although he is now considered one of the greatest architects of the early nineteenth century in America, the last years of his life and practice were marked with disappointment. Latrobe lacked the ability to adjust to customs and practice standards in America. He quarreled with his collaborators and clients; he remained suspicious of contractors and tradesmen who worked on his buildings, often accusing them of stealing his ideas. At the end of his career, he was employed as a civil engineer in New Orleans, not an architect. He died unexpectedly of yellow fever in New Orleans in 1820.[11] Like most brilliant and talented artists and architects, Latrobe was misunderstood and underappreciated during his life and career. He was only recognized for his architectural accomplishments long after his death.

Residential Work and the Waterworks in Fayetteville

Unlike his time in Edenton and New Bern, Nichols expanded his practice from a local to a regional one while in Fayetteville. He spent extended periods in Raleigh and worked in Hillsborough and in Chapel Hill. By the end of his tenure in North Carolina, he had branched out as far west as Greensboro in Guilford County and as far south and west as Lexington in Davidson County.[12] He worked as an architect who, at times, only produced the design and the drawings, but on other projects, he worked as both architect and master builder. He continued to have a fondness for pure cubic geometry in his overall compositions of buildings but was practical enough to be flexible in his design ideas. He worked with the local clientele's prevailing attitudes of building at the time in the Piedmont, which had a simple vernacular building tradition. If a client's ideas or tastes differed from his, he worked to meet those needs while adding his typical flair and style.

Clients looked upon his designs as both bold and new but not something impossible to build. His pragmatism is clearly seen in his domestic works in Fayetteville, Hillsborough, and Raleigh. Most of this work was built only a few years after the remarkable Hayes, and few of the houses he designed and built resemble it; instead, the houses Nichols designed in the Piedmont contain the typical massing and plan layouts found in most North Carolina Piedmont houses, a predominantly Quaker plan probably with a side hall and flanking parlors, suggesting that Nichols may have had a limited role as an architect in both designing and building these houses. This is not to say that Nichols abandoned his ideals for the Piedmont vernacular building traditions; rather he simply made the most of his limitations while

Figure 63. The Oval Ballroom in Heritage Square, Fayetteville, NC, 1819. This small pavilion was originally one of two wings designed and built by Nichols for James Cameron and his young bride, Catherine McQueen Halliday. (Photograph by author)

slowly evolving the forms and spaces of his designs from one project to the next. While Hayes was a revolutionary breakthrough in design resulting from a successful creative collaboration with James Johnston, Nichols's design work in Fayetteville and other parts of central North Carolina was deliberate and cautious.

Unfortunately most of Nichols's work in Fayetteville was lost due to a devastating fire in 1831.[13] What does survive is very telling of what he wanted to do and how he continued to evolve as an architect. Shortly after the completion of Hayes in Edenton, a gentleman named James A. Cameron called upon Nichols. Cameron had just married the wealthy Catherine McQueen Halliday, the widow of prosperous Fayetteville merchant Robert Halliday. In 1819, Nichols designed and built two one-story octagonal wings as additions to their existing residence. Unfortunately, the Cameron-Halliday House burned in the Great Fire of 1831. Out of the entire complex only the small "Oval Ballroom" (figure 63) remains. The Oval Ballroom was moved from its original location early in the twentieth century to the area of Fayetteville called Heritage Square. It is adjacent to the only other surviving Nichols building in Fayetteville, the Sandford House, which was originally built as the Branch Bank of the United States.[14] His position as architect and

Figure 64. Interior of the Oval Ballroom, Heritage Square, Fayetteville, NC. (Frances Benjamin Johnston Collection, Library of Congress, Washington, DC)

builder is evident through a letter from James Iredell, Jr., to James C. Johnston stating that Nichols received the commission to design the Branch Bank of the United States and the Bank of the Cape Fear in Fayetteville. Along with the Cameron-Halliday House, the Bank of the Cape Fear was lost during the 1831 fire. There are no existing images of their appearance.[15]

The original layout of the Cameron-Halliday House is not known. The existing Oval Ballroom suggests that it was built adjoining the main block of the original house. How the small Oval Ballroom survived the fire is unknown but based on the completeness of its design as a stand-alone structure, it is entirely likely that it was connected by a colonnade similar in design to the colonnade connections at Hayes. From the outside, the Oval Ballroom is quite ordinary and vernacular in its appearance. It is a wood framed octagonal building sheathed with pine clapboard and supported by brick piers with pierced brick "skirts" that were most likely added in the early twentieth century when it was moved to its current location.[16] The hipped roof is also basic in form and detailing with box fascia cornices and simple moldings. Along the long end of the octagonal shaped building is a very simple brick chimney. The exterior of the Oval Ballroom can easily be dismissed as a utilitarian outbuilding, nondescript and inauspicious, all of which is very misleading when compared to the building's interior—a richly detailed grand room, considered one of the finest interiors in the South (figure 64). Hamlin states in *Greek Revival Architecture in America* that "the delicate Ionic pilasters, with their lovely wreathed entablature, and the exquisite trim of the entrance door have sophisticated 'Greek' character one would expect to find in New York rather than in North Carolina." Hamlin also dated the construction of the Oval Ballroom to 1830, eleven years later than when Nichols actually built it.[17] This is a revealing mistake by an architectural historian of the early part of the twentieth century, which indicates that Nichols was already quite ahead of the times in the design of the Oval Ballroom.

A "sophisticated Greek character" is not what one would naturally expect to see in central North Carolina during the early decades of the nineteenth century. The Oval Ballroom was decidedly Greek in nature, and it is worth noting that it was designed at the height of the neoclassical period in American architecture. What motivated Nichols in designing such an elaborate room is not known; perhaps the clients' taste and means may have given Nichols another opportunity to utilize his knowledge and talents to their greatest potential. It will also remain unknown how or if Nichols altered the existing Cameron-Halliday House to reflect this refinement since the building was lost to fire. Nichols may have been emulating building interiors he saw in New York and other eastern seaboard cities during his purchasing trip for Johnston two years earlier. If that were the case, it would explain Hamlin's comparison of the Oval Ballroom to similar interiors found in New York and Philadelphia. What is significant is that in less than fifteen years after his design and construction of the slightly awkward portico for the New Bern Academy, Nichols had designed an interior that was as fashionable and exquisite as any built in the United States in the first half of the nineteenth century, all apparently based on his own work and experience without benefit of any formal training or oversight by an older, more experienced architect.

Although called a "ballroom," the Oval Ballroom is actually rather small. Oval in shape and set in the octagonal wood frame exterior structure, the ballroom's walls are an exquisite composition of plaster ornamentation. Fourteen fluted Ionic pilasters mark the room with capitals containing accurate egg and dart ornamentation and tight volutes. The attic bases of the pilasters are also accurate in their proportion; these bases set the height of the wall base, which is the dado for the façade composition of the room. Set in between the pilasters on the east and west ends are large double-hung sash windows, three of them on each end. The windows distinctly stand out with reeded casings terminated by plain blocks. Below each window are recessed panels that rest from the base molding. The cornice of the room is particularly distinctive and is its most dominant feature. Here Nichols's entablature is composed of a reeded frieze and an elaborate dental cornice capped by an egg and dart and gilded leaf ornament. The Oval Ballroom is not the typical Federal (or neoclassical) style interior;

it was something much more elaborate and shows that Nichols was evolving away from his counterparts (like McIntire of New England) and showcasing his interest in the latest and greatest design trends.

The other surviving building that Nichols designed in Fayetteville, the Branch Bank of the United States, is also found at Heritage Square at 225 Dick Street.[18] It is also referred to as the Sandford House (figure 65). The Sandford House is a double-pile house with a two-story portico that was popular with North Carolinians of this period. It appears that Nichols remodeled the existing building adding on the two-story portico which Peatross stated attempted to make "the residence nearly equal in dignity to Nichols's handsome [Cape Fear] State Bank on neighboring Gillespie Street." The massing and plan of the Sandford House appear quite ordinary, but the detailing of the exterior of the portico is quite sophisticated. The portico is designed so that the columns superposition over each other, with Doric order columns on the first floor and Ionic columns on the second (figures 66–68). The Doric columns are noticeably different from any of the columns fabricated for his buildings in either New Bern or Edenton. Here at the Sandford House, the column capitals are much more refined. The echinus looks less like a saucer and has a more pronounced curvature. There is no astragal, and the necking curves outwardly to support the echinus (figure 69). What is most noticeable about these columns is that the shafts are fluted but with no bases, suggesting they are Greek, not Roman, Doric columns. With the refined detailing this is a noticeable departure from the work in Edenton. More importantly, this leads one to assume that Nichols is relying on Greek precedents described in Stuart and Revett and less from the precedents described by William Pain. In central North Carolina, Nichols was able to secure better tradesmen for his designs, or his tradesmen were now becoming more skilled. At the Sandford House and the Oval Ballroom, Nichols was beginning yet another evolutionary stage in his design thinking; this transitional period was not immune to awkward design decisions, some of which were based on his Edenton work. An example of this can be found with the crown molding on the cornice of the Sandford House. The form of this molding is curiously incongruent with the rest of the Greek-influenced composition, suggesting the only Pain-like influence on the entire building. The portico's composition is less impressive at the second floor where Nichols uses the Ionic order; the columns do not follow ancient precedents as closely as the first-floor Doric section of the portico. This may not have been Nichols's fault; he most likely had difficulty finding a craftsman who possessed the skill to make an Ionic column that matched the ancient precedents found in *The Antiquities of Athens*. Despite the limitations of craft and execution, both the Sandford House and the Oval Ballroom suggest a significant

Figure 65. The McLeran/Adam/Sandford House in Heritage Square, Fayetteville, NC. Nichols elaborated on the typical "I" house plan and embellished it with his own sense of Greek-inspired ornament. (Photograph by author)

improvement in his ability to detail a building. It is clearly obvious that much improvement had been made in the fifteen years since he built the New Bern Academy portico. His use of classical orders and classical compositions gave his surviving Fayetteville work a decisively Greek character (figure 70). Nichols evidently learned quite a bit in his experience at Hayes in Edenton. As reflected in his work in Fayetteville, he was now more confident in his abilities to build grander work. As Nichols would receive larger and larger commissions, the details of his buildings would become more and more sophisticated. He began to explore richer and more complicated precedents in his work. It appears that Nichols lived in Fayetteville from 1818 to 1821.

Figure 66. Partial elevation sketch of the Sandford House, Fayetteville, NC. (Sketch by author)

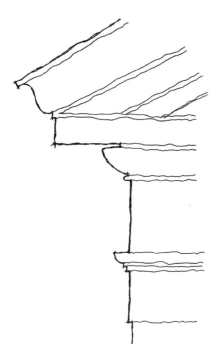

Figure 67. Cornice detail sketch, Sandford House, Fayetteville, NC. (Sketch by author)

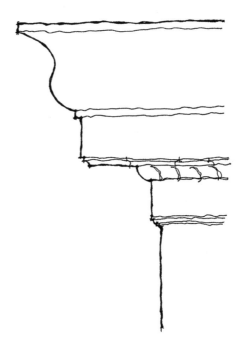

Figure 68. Main cornice detail, Sandford House, Fayetteville, NC. (Sketch by author)

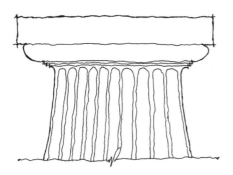

Figure 69. Column capital, front porch, Sandford House, Fayetteville, NC. (Sketch by author)

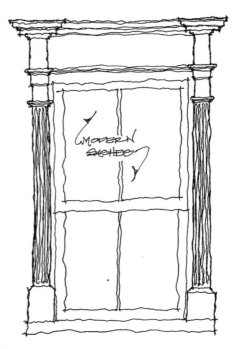

Figure 70. Typical exterior window at the Sandford House. (Drawing by author)

He most likely designed several other domestic structures, but all of this is lost due to the calamitous fire that burned almost all of Fayetteville in 1831.[19]

During his time in Fayetteville, he engaged in an engineering project both as the designer/engineer and as the owner of Fayetteville's first waterworks.[20] In 1820, the North Carolina General Assembly created the Fayetteville Water Works with William Nichols named as president. The General Assembly stated that the waterworks was charged with "the act for supplying the town of Fayetteville with pure and wholesome drinking water."[21] Nichols proceeded to acquire four lots on the east and west sides of Adam Street in the Haymount section of Fayetteville for the waterworks in 1821 from Hiram Robinson and other owners not listed in the actual deed for two hundred dollars. By this time, Nichols was listed as living in nearby Wake County, which is also where Raleigh and the state capitol are located.[22] In 1822, Nichols bought out one of his investors of the waterworks, Gurdon Robins, for the sum of five hundred dollars. Interestingly, Nichols's sometime business rival, Ithiel Town, was a witness to the deed.[23]

The complex was begun in 1822 and completed in 1824. There are no surviving images that describe the appearance of the facility. The most relevant informative source of pre-1831 Fayetteville, the John MacRae Map of Fayetteville (published in 1825), only gives scant clues of the facility, which may well have been in a state of construction at the time the map was being drafted. The engineering of the waterworks was quite crude compared to today's standards. The water mains were constructed out of bored pine logs, and a pump apparatus located within the North Eccles dam propelled the water.[24] Another pumping station building was located north of Fayetteville on Blount's Creek.[25] The waterworks continued its operation throughout the pre-Civil War era and it is assumed that it was no longer operational after the Civil War. In 1908, a modern water treatment facility was built in Fayetteville.[26]

Even during this time of intense activity of designing and building expensive residences and starting and building a waterworks for a town with an approximate population of over four thousand people, Nichols was also beginning an important architecture practice building significant public buildings, first, for the state of North Carolina, and second, for the University of North Carolina. Over an eight-year period, Nichols made a profound impression on the city of Raleigh and the campus of the state's university. As state architect of North Carolina, Nichols was involved with building types that were not the typical design opportunities for the average architect/builder of the period. These buildings were very public in their nature and served important state institutions, such as college campuses and buildings for the University of North Carolina, courthouses for counties throughout the North Carolina Piedmont, and a jail. One type in particular that he designed during this period was a state capitol. Through his work, Nichols helped to define in the South the form and spatial articulation of the state capitol building. He designed capitols in three states. His first state capitol was officially considered a "remodeling"—the extensively reconfigured North Carolina capitol. He would then refine his ideas regarding the design of the state capitol with the first Alabama State Capitol of 1831 in Tuscaloosa, and finally the Mississippi State Capitol of 1836 in Jackson. The second architectural type he helped define in the South was the university campus and its buildings, beginning with the University of North Carolina, later with the first campus of the University of Alabama, and finally, at the end of his life and career, the University of Mississippi.

The University of North Carolina

In 1820, Nichols was given the opportunity to design the first master plan of the University of North Carolina at Chapel Hill after its founding. It was the first institutional type of architecture that Nichols designed in his career. The University of North Carolina, which opened its doors in 1795, has been referred to as the "first state university" in the United States[27]; its initial campus planning was by William Richardson Davie, Samuel McCorkle, James Hogg, and Joseph Caldwell.[28] It could easily be considered the last colonial college campus plan in the United States. The first buildings at the University of North Carolina resembled the brick pile buildings—"built for their business and nothing else"—similar to the early buildings at Harvard[29] or the "brick piles" that Jefferson despised at his alma mater, the College of William and Mary.[30] The University of North Carolina's campus initially started as one large building, which later became known as Old East (figure 71).

Here both student and teacher resided under one roof. Davie, McCorkle, Hogg, and Caldwell initially envisioned the campus as defined by one grand tree-lined avenue that would run from northeast to southwest along an axis set by the Masonic practice of orientalization.[31] Soon after Old East was completed and classes commenced in 1795, new buildings were almost immediately built that were detached from Old East. Dining services were accommodated in a small wooden structure known as Steward's Hall, located directly east of Old East. To the west, a small brick structure, Person Hall, with large arched windows, was erected as an early chapel. All of this confused the initial intent of the first "master" plan because a fourth building, later to be

Figure 71. Old East, University of North Carolina, Chapel Hill, NC, drawing by John Pettigrew. Built in 1795, Old East was the first building for the first public university in the United States. Nichols designed and built a third-floor addition to it in 1823. (Courtesy of the North Carolina Collection, University of North Carolina at Chapel Hill Library)

called the South Building, was built in a proposed avenue that sat perpendicular to Old East. With its construction, the initial Davie master plan was lost. Construction started in 1798 but took seventeen years to complete due to funding problems that the university encountered in the early days of its existence.

The South Building was practically new, having been finished five years prior to Nichols's arrival on campus in 1820. It was encountering significant structural problems caused by chronic leaks around its cupola. By this time, neither McCorkle nor Davie was involved in the planning of the university; Caldwell, who was serving his second term as the university's president, was the only planning founder that remained at the university. Caldwell struggled to keep the university's buildings in working order. He received very little, if any, funding from the North Carolina General Assembly. Maintenance and expansion of the campus was primarily funded through donations from private individuals. Caldwell welcomed any support he could get from the state government, which sent Nichols to Chapel Hill to repair the existing buildings and plan and build new ones. From 1820 until 1827, Nichols reworked and transformed the University of North Carolina campus, laying the foundation of the university's campus plan.

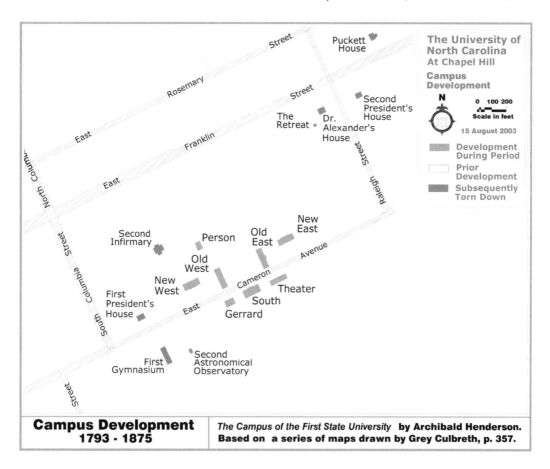

The University of
North Carolina
At Chapel Hill

Campus
Development

0 100 200
Scale in feet

15 August 2003

Development
During Period

Prior
Development

Subsequently
Torn Down

Campus Development
1793 - 1875

The Campus of the First State University by Archibald Henderson.
Based on a series of maps drawn by Grey Culbreth, p. 357.

Figure 72. Diagrammatic map of the University of North Carolina, Chapel Hill, NC. (Courtesy of Paula G. Davis, Engineering Information Services, University of North Carolina at Chapel Hill)

The placement of the South Building was significant because it reflected the increased connection of the university with the new village of Chapel Hill. It was parallel to what was rapidly becoming the main retail street for the village, later to be known as Franklin Street. Although it ended any idea of a "grand avenue" from north to south, it established the idea of a quadrangle form for the campus. Both Nichols and Caldwell understood that a new plan was slowly emerging for the university campus: a quadrangle rather than an avenue (figure 72).

Both men capitalized on the opportunity to determine the physical growth of the campus. Nichols's work in Chapel Hill not only determined how the University of North Carolina's campus would grow and evolve; it also helped define the prototypical college campus in the South. This would essentially be the creation of an exterior room—a quadrangle—that was defined by rectilinear three-story brick buildings with a monumental, primary building defining the orientation of the quadrangle. Nichols's campus plans were somewhat similar to the Princeton campus and the campus at the College of William and Mary, but he would design the buildings and the exterior spaces in such a way that they could be adapted by later generations. He would later apply the ideas he developed in North Carolina on the campuses of Alabama and Mississippi. Architecturally, other campuses in the South would emulate the work he did at Chapel Hill.

Nichols's work in Chapel Hill was the earliest known masonry buildings that he designed and built; it is also where one first encounters Nichols's persistent dogged use of native stone. As with other immigrant architects from Europe, he desperately tried to capture the splendor of buildings of his native Bath but with disappointing results. Nichols's attempt to use the native Orange County sandstone known as "gritstone" was disastrous and necessitated extensive renovations of these buildings during their life span. Ironically, Nichols would move and practice in regions of the country that did not have viable building stone, yet he continued trying to build out of cut, ashlar substandard stone.[32]

At the University of North Carolina, Nichols's challenge was to develop the master plan that had been envisioned by Caldwell. Nichols's earlier idea was to expand the emerging quadrangle east to west and not north to south, as had originally been done with the establishment of Franklin Street and the "grand avenue." Caldwell was keenly interested in providing the university a proud "face" to the old Raleigh Road, which ran south of South Building coming from the east. Providing a good "face" to perspective legislators from the General Assembly had always been high on the priority list for any UNC administrator and Caldwell was no exception. Caldwell proposed adding three new buildings approximately the same size as Old East and the South Building. He was aware of how the campus would grow in the future with Franklin Street defining the campus north boundary, and he wanted to begin planning a southward expansion for the university.[33]

Nichols capitalized on Caldwell's idea of a new south-facing orientation, but he also saw the need to retain and reinforce the already developed north-south axis of the campus. In Caldwell's plan, the newly built "old chapel," Person Hall, was isolated from his proposed east-west quadrangle. Nichols developed the existing campus into a classic tripartite campus quadrangle or "green" with a main building (the South Building) flanked by two other buildings (Old East and a newer west building later called Old West), which he designed and built in 1823. With a tightening of the space in which Caldwell was originally proposing a mirror building of Old East, the quadrangle achieved its own character-defining scale and became a cohesive ensemble of buildings and grounds which enabled the peripheral Person Hall to be brought back and made relevant to the overall campus composition.

With the placement of the West Building and the development of the east-west access and north-south axis, Nichols shaped the overall planning structure of the University of North Carolina and provided a framework of building placement and quadrangle design that defined the physical nature of the university for the rest of the nineteenth century and well into the twentieth century until after the Second World War. His legacy on the campus at Chapel Hill is profound and influenced not only how the northern quadrangle would develop but also how the southern quadrangle would develop as well, though it would not be built for another one hundred years.[34]

Few architects in the first half of the nineteenth century had developed college campuses, even though the concept of a college campus is a peculiarly American architectural invention. Very few colleges planned for a multibuilding campus. Most, in fact, followed the single-building precedent set by Harvard College and the College of William and Mary; with the building of Old East, the University of North Carolina was no exception. Extensive university campuses were not commonly built in the nineteenth century. Colonial colleges and universities that became known as the Ivy League developed in an ad hoc manner in the eighteenth and nineteenth centuries. Campus development was an opportunity that not many architects had the privilege to undertake in the first half of the nineteenth century. Of Nichols's contemporaries, very few designed college campuses. By 1820, Jefferson's University of Virginia was well under way. Before returning to Europe, Rameé had designed Union College in Schenectady, New York (which could have inspired Jefferson's plan for the University of Virginia since it was slightly earlier), and Robert Mills had designed what would become the University of South Carolina at Columbia.[35] Latrobe had peripheral involvement with the University of Virginia. Thomas U. Walter[36] designed Girard College in Philadelphia, and Alexander Jackson Davis designed several—Davidson College near Charlotte, North Carolina; Virginia Military Institute in Lexington, Virginia; and significant parts of the University of Michigan—as well as significantly influencing the architecture of the University of North Carolina after Nichols's period of involvement during the 1840s.[37] Nichols not only made his mark at the University of North Carolina but also carried the lessons he learned to new state universities in the South, first in Alabama and then in Mississippi.

Once Nichols had clearly defined the tripartite arrangement of buildings of the north quadrangle (now known as McCorkle Place), he then recognized the need for it to have a focal point, an object or folly (figures 73 and 74).

While replacing the roof of the Main Building (later known as the South Building), he removed the old rotting cupola and relocated it along with its bell and reworked it into a new ornamental building, the Belfry. Little is known of the design and detailing of the "old" Belfry. There are only two images of it known to exist, one being a paper

Figure 73. Paper cutout of the University of North Carolina campus, ca. 1825 by Helen Hogg Hooper Caldwell. The simple cutout shows Steward's Hall (far left, demolished) and the South Building (far right). Nichols removed the problematic cupola from the South Building and converted it into the Belfry (middle). (Courtesy of the North Carolina Collection, University of North Carolina at Chapel Hill Library)

Figure 74. The University of North Carolina in 1852. This lithograph shows the new additions on Old East and Old West that were designed by Alexander Jackson Davis. In the middle of the image, there is the Belfry, which was destroyed in a fire that was a student prank in 1856. (Courtesy of the North Carolina Collection, University of North Carolina at Chapel Hill Library)

cutout by the wife of a Professor William Hooper, Frances Pollack Jones Hooper,[38] circa 1820, and the other a stylized print of the campus done circa 1850. Both images give tantalizing clues of the nature of the Belfry and the nature of Nichols's detailing. The small structure was round and appeared to have a solid base with a simple door to access the bell. Above the base of the Belfry was a small circular temple with elongated columns supporting a simplified and delicate entablature and a simple metal-covered dome. The images of the Belfry suggest that Nichols was still very much influenced by the Adam-Soane tradition of England and colonial America. One can assume that it resembled the detailing at Hayes, the Old East Custom House in Edenton,

Figure 75. Gerrard Hall at the University of North Carolina. Nichols and university president Joseph Caldwell deliberately built the portico of Gerrard Hall so that it faced south in an attempt to influence campus expansion in that direction. Expansion to the south campus would not occur until one hundred years later. (North Carolina Collection, University of North Carolina at Chapel Hill Library)

and the New Bern Academy portico. There is irrefutable evidence that it was built out of wood because it burned in 1856 when the students set it ablaze as a prank.[39]

Nichols responded to the university's student population expansion by adding a third floor to Old East; he then designed and built Old West, which matched Old East, in 1823. Any distinctive detailing on both Old East and Old West was removed when A. J. Davis later expanded both buildings and reworked the roofs, adding the bracketed Italianate-designed rafter tails to the buildings in 1847. Old West, like Old East, was most likely plain in detailing and similar in massing to Old East, but Old West was divided by party walls, creating two distinct sections. Its multiple entries gave Nichols a prototype of a dormitory design, which he would use in designing the campuses of Alabama and Mississippi. Old West and the expansion of Old East are his first documented work in masonry.

His final and most important design for the University of North Carolina was the "second or new chapel," which was the first assembly building for the university (figure 75). Named Gerrard Hall, after Revolutionary War veteran and university donor Major Charles Gerrard, it was designed by Nichols in 1822. It suffered numerous delays, an all-too-common problem for the antebellum building program at the underfunded university. The budget shortage was exacerbated when Nichols failed to design and build within the university's budget for Gerrard Hall. President Caldwell did not appreciate the cost overruns in the building project and evidently became irate with Nichols and his inability to stay on budget. Their relationship would grow tense, especially since Nichols was also operating as state architect. Nichols probably made the most of his advantageous position over Caldwell, which no doubt caused ill will between Nichols and the cost-conscious and frugal university president.

Gerrard Hall was different in design from anything William Nichols had designed up to this point in his career; this was partly due to its function as an assembly hall on a university campus, but it was also partly due to Nichols's ability to build with masonry. Moreover, the artisans working under him better crafted his elaborate details. Gerrard gave Nichols the opportunity to build a heroic building in the Greco-Roman tradition. This enabled him to borrow more directly from classical precedent. He seized upon an idea that Caldwell had developed in planning for future campus buildings that better utilized the university's available land, most of which lay south of the South Building. He also seized on another idea of Caldwell's: to design a building that would serve as a gateway to the campus facing toward the southeast and, symbolically, the North Carolina State Capitol in Raleigh. From this idea, Nichols designed Gerrard Hall with a prominent colossal portico, which provided both a visual front door face for visitors coming from the east in Raleigh and also a visual anchor for a new south quadrangle of the future. Caldwell accepted the proposal and instructed Nichols to design the front façade of Gerrard to face south; it was the first campus building to do so at the university and it was also the first building of a new quadrangle.

Unfortunately, the university administration misjudged the longevity of the brief economic boom that came after the War of 1812. The economy of the state soured in the last half of the 1820s, and with it, the building of Gerrard. Construction stalled and became a protracted ordeal after work began in 1822; it would not be completed until 1837. During this long construction period, local politics played a negative role in Gerrard's contribution to Nichols's master plan. Caldwell had underestimated the power of the business owners on Franklin Street who feared that southern expansion of the campus would lead to another commercial development south of Franklin Street. They pressured Caldwell to abandon the university's intentions of southern expansion in what would turn out to be one of the earliest town-gown political struggles in Chapel Hill.[40] Soon after the completion of Gerrard Hall, the master plan of the university was returned to its original orientation, which was north. Campus expansion toward the south resumed one hundred years later in 1921. All of this had a negative impact on how Gerrard Hall would be regarded by the university community. The grand portico was never viewed or appreciated as Nichols had intended. Gerrard had lost its role as an anchor building and then appeared to be completely out of place with its portico facing nothing but wilderness. Despite this unfortunate twist of fate, the portico would command enough admiration that it would not be completely forgotten. In 1856, Alexander Jackson Davis proposed an expansion of Gerrard Hall. He proposed expanding it by one third of its length to

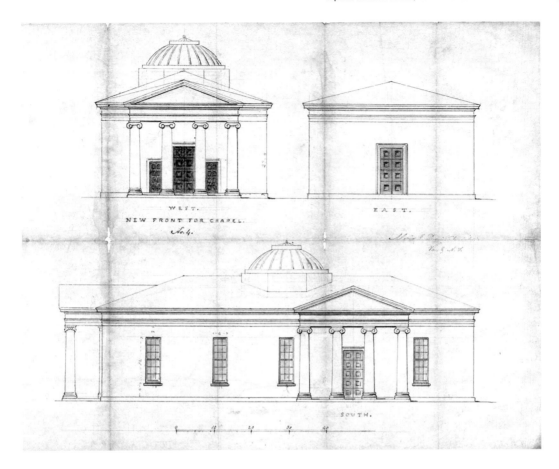

WEST.

NEW FRONT FOR CHAPEL.

No. 4.

EAST.

SOUTH.

Figure 76. Proposed expansion of Gerrard Hall by A. J. Davis in 1856. Davis proposed to keep Nichols's portico and replicate it on the west side of his addition. He also proposed a low-sloped dome for the building. Davis's proposal was never built. (Courtesy of the North Carolina Collection, University of North Carolina at Chapel Hill Library)

the west; he then proposed adding a portico to the west side and a low dome. Despite such a radical change in design, Davis kept the south-facing portico and in his drawings meticulously documented it in his design (figure 76). This expansion was never built. The portico eventually fell into disrepair after the Civil War. By the end of the nineteenth century and after years of neglect, the University of North Carolina's Board of Trustees directed the administration to demolish the portico, leaving Gerrard seriously misshapen and forgotten during the entire twentieth century.[41]

For Nichols, Gerrard Hall exhibits very little of his Pain-influenced designs of eastern North Carolina; here Nichols begins to design in the "Greek style." He indulges freely in the precedents of Greek and Roman antiquity and extensively uses the landmark architectural book *The Antiquities of Athens* by Stuart and Revett. The centerpiece of the Gerrard design is the colossal Ionic order portico; Nichols models this portico directly on the Temple of Illissus[42] of Athens (figures 77-80). From a national perspective, this precedent is not all that uncommon, but from a regional or North Carolina perspective the portico was very

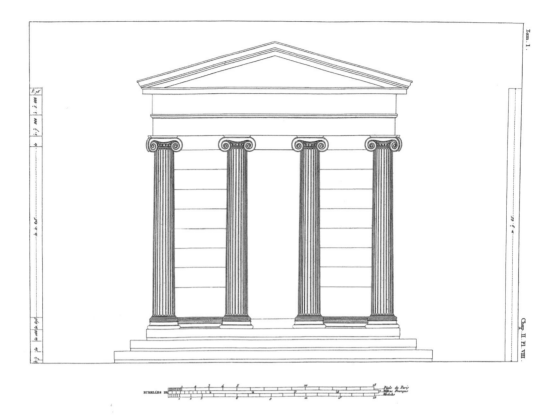

Figure 77. The *Temple of Illissus* in Athens as described by Stuart and Revett in *The Antiquities of Athens*, 1769. Nichols used as inspiration the drawings of Greek Classical architecture that were recorded by Stuart and Revett in their book. He used the Illissus precedent for the portico at Gerrard Hall and several other buildings he designed throughout his career. (Courtesy of the Ricker Library of Art and Architecture, University of Illinois at Urbana–Champaign)

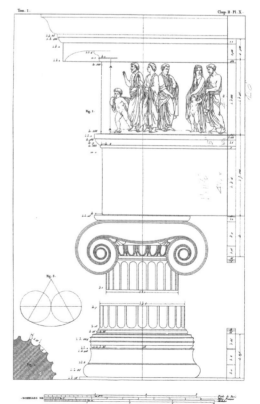

Figure 78. Detail plate of the entablature and column of the *Temple of Illissus* by Stuart and Revett in *The Antiquities of Athens*. (Courtesy of the Ricker Library of Art and Architecture, University of Illinois at Urbana–Champaign)

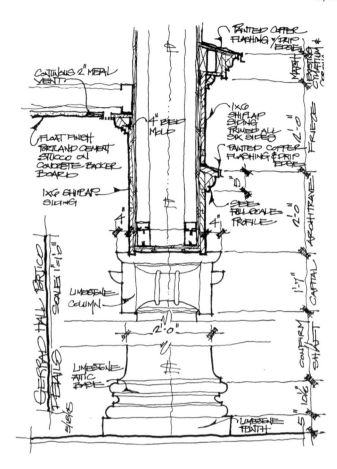

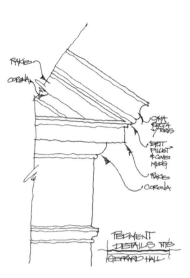

Figure 80. Cornice details for the reconstruction of the Gerrard Hall portico. (Sketch by author)

Figure 79. Study of the reconstruction of the Gerrard Hall portico at the University of North Carolina at Chapel Hill, 2005. The portico was accurately reconstructed after a comparison with the Stuart and Revett plates and a verification of the molding prints on the building and archaeological study of its foundation. (Sketch by author)

significant; it was, in fact, unprecedented. Unlike his domestic buildings, Nichols finally had the opportunity to design something grand at the university. Caldwell and the university's board of trustees decided it would be the first large assembly building on campus and directed Nichols to make Gerrard give the campus a grandeur that it had not yet accomplished.

The portico also reflected the changes of taste and aspirations of the early nineteenth century in America; the idea of embodying the ideals of ancient Greek and Roman democracy was taking hold in North Carolina. As the first public university in the United States and one that was literally an idea born from the aftermath of the Revolution, the University of North Carolina saw itself as being the embodiment of the new democratic republic. For everyone involved in the university, it made logical sense to build in an architectural form that reflected the democratic ideal.[43] Nichols was well aware of the national sentiment that was shared by his fellow North Carolinians of the new American republic; he obviously believed that the classical idiom was the appropriate architecture to distinguish Gerrard Hall as a "heroic building" for the campus. The timing was right for the introduction of Greek classicism on the Chapel Hill campus as well as throughout the state. Although sometimes referred to as the "New Chapel," its exterior has little resemblance to a church or a chapel. Only an Alabama white marble tablet set into the east-facing brick wall between the two entrances hints at its religious program. It reads:

Gerrard Hall
1822
And To do Justly and to Love Mercy, and to Walk
Humbly with Thy God

When it was finally completed, Gerrard Hall was considered the "show place of the State" despite the fact that its setting was somewhat forgotten.[44] For a building with such a grand function and importance on campus, it is rather small. The removal of the south-facing portico in 1892 and the addition of numerous grander buildings of the Beaux Arts age caused Gerrard to appear an unimportant and incidental building.

It is a simple brick masonry two-story building with a six-to-twelve-pitch roof and ten bays of windows on its long-sided façades, the north and south elevations (figures 81–85) Doors were once placed on the north and south sides of the building and two doors remain on both its east and west elevations. It is still used as an auditorium and it still retains its original seating arrangement. During the nineteenth century, there was a space located in the center of the hall, a nave, which was reserved for the seating for the faculty; it was approximately eighteen feet square in size and the students irreverently called it the "bull pen." The original interior layout consisted of a semicircular row of benches with backs that reached to the neck, causing students seated behind the faculty to see only their heads. Distinguished guests (including United States presidents William Howard Taft, Woodrow Wilson, and James K. Polk, member of the UNC class of 1818 and the only UNC alumnus to become president of the U.S.) and speakers were seated also in the "bull pen." This small seating space inside the assembly hall accommodated about forty persons. A narrow passageway connected the "bull pen" with the speaker's stand, located at the west end of the hall. Other hints of its religious purposes included a choir balcony embellished with a gothic cross or cinquefoil motif. On the north, south, and east sides of the interior, a balcony was built that enclosed the interior. The balcony, the choir balcony, and the door and window casings are original and were designed by Nichols. All details of the interior reflect Nichols's English influence. The original moldings, which still remain, are elongated and flat.

It is the Ionic portico that makes Gerrard Hall so noteworthy. Nichols chose the Temple of Illissus for the precedent as described in Stuart

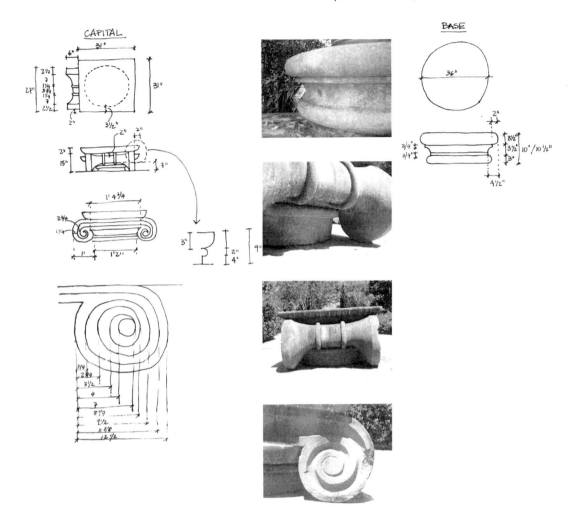

Figure 81. Detailed measurements of the original capital and base from the portico of Gerrard Hall. After the portico was removed in 1892, two members of the community who later used them as garden ornaments salvaged the capitals and bases from two columns. The original column elements were carved out of local North Carolina Triassic sandstone, which proved to be a substandard building stone. John Robb carved the bases and capitals; they were measured and used as templates for the new limestone columns of the reconstructed portico. (Courtesy of Ann Beha Architects)

and Revett. The portico consisted of a simple entablature modeled true to the Illissus precedent with shiplap siding and simple moldings. In 2005, the University of North Carolina decided to reconstruct the portico when it renovated Gerrard Hall for the first time since 1930. During the design phase of the Gerrard Hall renovation in 2005, fragments of the column capital were found; they had been used as lawn and garden ornaments in yards throughout Chapel Hill. This would prove to be a very lucky break for the architectural and historic preservation team who sought to reconstruct the portico. Without these elements, it would have been an exercise in pure conjecture. The team located the foundations of the portico and analyzed digitized photographs that revealed "ghosts impressions" where the entablature met the building. These were carefully measured, then compared in proportion to the original Stuart and Revett plate of the entablature of Illissus.[45]

The columns were simple with the Ionic column capitals somewhat stylized. The abacus is somewhat larger than its ancient precedent; the

Figure 82. Reconstruction of the Gerrard Hall portico, March 2007. (Photograph by author)

Figure 85. Interior of Gerrard Hall, ca. 1890. (Courtesy of the North Carolina Collection, University of North Carolina at Chapel Hill Library)

Figure 83. Erection of the new limestone columns for the Gerrard Hall portico, April 2007. (Photograph by author)

Figure 84. The reconstructed portico for Gerrard Hall during construction, June 2007. (Photograph by author)

cushion runs straight across the capital and the volutes are flatter. The echinus is plain and does not have any egg and dart work integrated into the design. This would become a typical detail found on Ionic columns that were designed by Nichols from 1822 until 1836. The shafts are plain, unfluted, and were originally built out of brick covered with stucco. The columns rest on Roman attic bases, which are incongruent to the entire portico if one looks at the composition from an academic point of view. Records indicate that John Robb[46] carved the capitals and the bases.[47] These columns, along with the base foundation and the windowsills, were carved out of the poor quality local sandstone that was quarried between Chapel Hill and Hillsborough in Orange County. The limited skill of John Robb and the poor quality of the stone material explain the stylized nature of the Ionic columns at Gerrard. While building Gerrard, Nichols introduced a color palette that incorporates the tan lime wash but paints the trim, including the entablature, a dark brown, which makes the building appear heavier than it actually is. This color palette would be used on all of the early campus buildings and it remains unclear to this day who originally initiated it. Records indicate that the noted science professor Elisha Mitchell (for whom Mount Mitchell in western North Carolina is named) may have implemented it when he assumed the post of superintendent of buildings and grounds for the university but this has never been conclusively proven.[48] Nevertheless, when Carolina's most illustrious alumnus, President James K. Polk, came to speak at Gerrard Hall in 1847, the building was painted in these colors.[49]

Nichols worked at Chapel Hill even after his tenure as state architect ended, continuing until 1827, when he left for Alabama. Gerrard Hall was still not completed and would not be for another ten years after he left; it is doubtful that Nichols kept up any correspondence with the university about the status of the building or any other building he designed on the University of North Carolina campus. All of his work on the Carolina campus—the building of Old West, the expansion of Old East, the reworking of South Building, the erection of the Belfry, and the construction of Gerrard Hall—was financed through the sale of valued assets, most notably several thousand acres of land donated by Charles Gerrard, for whom Gerrard Hall was named, as well as the sale of the university's preparatory school. This money totaled over $49,000, a significant amount of money then.

In building Old West, the university's board of trustees agreed to a final contract amount of $26,587.54 with Nichols. This included the construction of the building, his design and contracting fee of $1,000, and the cost of surveying and marking house lots in Chapel Hill. Apparently, this "cost-plus-a-fee" contractual agreement was not to the liking of the board of trustees, who had to pay for Nichols's cost overruns. For the second phase of campus building, they made a new contract with Nichols under which he assumed all of the responsibility and the trustees paid him at their convenience. The university paid Nichols $22,017.88 during 1826 and 1827. In the final statement, the payments were specifically recorded for "Labor and material in repairing the President's House, Stewards Hall, getting timber, making bricks and building the new Chapel, taking down the cupola from the South Building along with the roof repair, and for building the belfry."[50]

The cost overruns for the buildings Nichols designed and supervised, coupled with the fact that he would later abandon Gerrard Hall before it was completed, did not endear him to President Joseph Caldwell. Caldwell expressed his frustration in working with Nichols in a series of scathing correspondences, which never directly called him out specifically but instead generalized him as a "knave," an undesirable character who would deceive a client.[51] Unhappy clients like Caldwell proved to be a liability that would haunt Nichols for the rest of his life.

The Gerrard portico became a much-used precedent and prototype for Nichols on other buildings. After 1822, he used it for a variety of buildings from university to governmental buildings and fine residences. As state architect, Nichols had the luxury of a baseline of work and a steady salary. He used this to help expand his private practice and used his salary to invest in land and business ventures. Along with having a very laudable practice working as the state architect of North Carolina, Nichols developed an impressive private practice constructing significant buildings within a one-hundred-mile diameter from Fayetteville.

Hillsborough and Raleigh

From 1823 to 1827, Nichols's career and business interests boomed. He was considered a desirable and fashionable architect, one who had carried the respectable title of state architect. He had also trained a group of tradesmen to execute his work. His two sons, William, Jr., and Samuel, were old enough to work in the family business, and they helped to manage his numerous building commissions as well as business ventures. Business was indeed good for Nichols, and it appears that he overextended himself by taking on too many projects. During this period, he began a practice of rehashing or recycling his designs for other clients. From a business standpoint this made a lot of sense. At this point in his career, Nichols had developed a personal and perfected architectural style, and he had trained his tradesmen and laborers to construct it. It became evident at this time that he started a practice of retracing his older drawings, sketching and marketing them as novel designs to unknowing clients.

William Nichols's involvement in various private houses and institutions will always remain a point of speculation by many historians who are familiar with his work. Some buildings can definitely be attributed to Nichols through documentation, while others are generally assumed to be Nichols's designs. It is reasonable to assume that Nichols may have had a loose involvement in the design of several buildings,

Figure 86. Ingleside, Lincoln County, NC (photograph taken in 1938). This residence has been attributed to Nichols; the portico is similar in detail to Gerrard Hall. (Historic American Buildings Survey, Library of Congress, Washington, DC)

most likely in the conceptual design. An owner may have hired him to develop a design and then hired a separate builder to construct it. Nevertheless, several buildings, built between 1822 and 1827, share striking similarities to Gerrard Hall, which proves two theories: that Nichols frequently recycled his designs for various uses and functions, and that Nichols's designs were quite popular. It is fair to say that by this time in his career, clients throughout eastern and central North Carolina who were aware of his style came to expect a "Nichols" building when they hired him to design either a public building or private residence. At the time he was designing buildings in nearby Raleigh (the North Carolina state capital) and Hillsborough (the Orange County seat), he had developed the design for Gerrard Hall and its Ionic portico. These buildings imitate the Illissus-inspired Ionic portico and, to a certain extent, the overall massing of Gerrard Hall.

One example of Nichols's influence is evident in the design of a house known as Ingleside (figure 86), the residence of John Forney in Lincoln County, located in the southwestern part of North Carolina just north of Charlotte. Ingleside is a good example of conjecture of any association by William Nichols. The two-story brick house was built in 1817 and was most likely Federal in its original overall design. Soon after completion, a colossal Ionic portico was added that bears a striking similarity in its appearance to the one at Gerrard, except that the Ionic columns did not have bases. In his book on the architecture of North Carolina, Mills Lane links Nichols's name to the Ingleside portico although there is no documentation such as drawings or correspondence to support the claim, and he does not document his source. One could assume that Forney may have requested a design

Figure 87. North Carolina Governor's Palace, Fayetteville Street, Raleigh, NC. Built in 1814, the original house was a seven-bay Federal-style residence; Nichols designed the portico addition that was based on the Temple of Illissus. (Peatross Collection, Courtesy of the North Carolina Collection, Wilson Library, University of North Carolina at Chapel Hill)

from Nichols that would improve and update his home similar to what had been done at the Sandford House in Fayetteville.[52] A building project that was definitely designed by Nichols and built at the same time as Gerrard Hall was the remodeling project for the governor's house or "palace." Demolished ca. 1885, it was located at the end of Fayetteville Street opposite the State House in Raleigh (figure 87). The Governor's Palace was also distinctly Federal in its overall design and appearance, and Nichols updated the building with the Gerrard Illissus Ionic portico. The result has a striking similarity to Gerrard Hall in its massing, material selection, and molding profiles. The main difference between the Governor's Palace and Gerrard porticoes is the simplified, crude attic bases of the Governor's Palace's columns.

The overall appearance of these three buildings—Gerrard, Ingleside, and the Governor's Palace—echoes the Illissus precedent, both in size and proportion. Nichols's use of the ancient Greek precedent is an added layer to an existing building or in the design that has been accepted through the vernacular tradition. With buildings such as the Governor's Palace, what was behind the portico was decidedly late Colonial or Federal. Nichols was not reinventing typology with his buildings at this point in his career; these elements were only additional features that could be easily removed without compromising the function of the building, as was clearly seen when Gerrard lost its portico in 1892. Historians such as Hamlin and Lane consider these buildings by Nichols as transitional works that helped evolve American architecture, specifically North Carolina architecture, from the simple vernacular structures with late Georgian details into the Greek Revival.

Figure 88. Eagle Lodge, Hillsborough, NC, 1825. This photograph was taken before the original portico was severely damaged by a windstorm. (Historic American Buildings Survey, Library of Congress, Washington, DC)

Figure 89. Double doors at Eagle Lodge, Hillsborough, NC. (Sketched by author and drawn by Tim Penich)

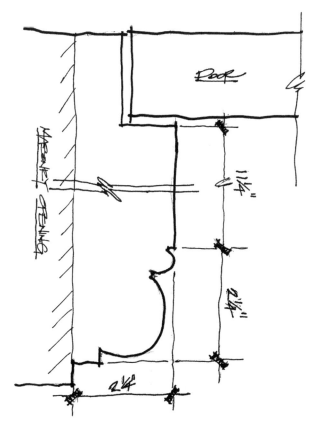

Figure 90. Doorjamb condition, Eagle Lodge. (Sketch by author)

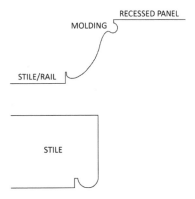

Figure 91. Door detail drawings from the front doors at Eagle Lodge, Hillsborough, NC. (Sketched by author and drawn by Tim Penich)

While there is merit in these summations of Nichols's work, one must take into account that his work in North Carolina reflects a gradual move from Federal to Greek Revival in North Carolina. Innovation in design was something that William Nichols wanted to accomplish but so was his desire to develop a profitable business. He apparently had no problem recycling and reusing tried and true designs that proved to have a satisfactory result with his clients.

Nichols's tendency to rehash earlier designs, such as Gerrard Hall, can be seen in his design and construction of Eagle Lodge No. 19, the Masonic lodge for Hillsborough, North Carolina (figures 88–91). The Masons of Eagle Lodge funded the construction of the building through several lotteries, which were empowered by an act of the North Carolina General Assembly in 1820, for an amount not to exceed four thousand dollars; this was to include both the purchase of the lot on King Street in Hillsborough and the construction of the building.[53] As mentioned in chapter 1, Nichols was a Freemason for a very short time and was expelled from the Unanimity Lodge in 1808 in Edenton. He most likely earned this commission because he was doing a significant amount of work in nearby Chapel Hill (twelve miles south of Hillsborough) at the time that the members of Eagle Lodge were planning to build their building. The first mention in the lodge's minutes of the planning of the building occurs in an entry dated May 15, 1823.[54] At this time, Nichols was building his Governor's Palace and Gerrard Hall. An entry dated September 4, 1823, announced that "Captain Nichols is appointed as superintendent for the construction and that $4,000 is appropriated for the purchase of the lot and the construction of the building."[55] The building was completed and dedicated in January 1825.[56]

Eagle Lodge is severe in its overall composition with Nichols's use of pure geometry rather than applied ornamentation. This institutional building is a brick cube mass, forty feet in height, width, and length, with a small Ionic portico at its entry; it is capped with a pyramid-hipped roof. Today, its plain walls laid in an English bond pattern, sandstone sills, and jack arches do not reveal its earlier more striking appearance. When the lodge was first built, the building included an observatory or belvedere that, according to local history, was used by the town's academies as a classroom. The occupants, in order to escape the oppressive heat of summer in Hillsborough and catch the summer breezes, certainly would have used it. It was removed in 1862, most likely because it had fallen into disrepair. Images of the belvedere or observatory have yet to be found but, based on the framing of the roof which is original to the building and written descriptions found in the records of the lodge, it was fifteen feet square in plan with a hipped pyramid-shaped roof.[57] An argument can be made that Nichols reused his design of Hayes Plantation for Eagle Lodge. Built only five years earlier, Hayes and the lodge share some common characteristics. Both buildings are cubic in overall form; Eagle Lodge is a perfect cube of forty feet by forty feet by forty feet, while Hayes is approximately fifty-two feet by thirty-nine feet. The small porticoes are virtually the same in dimension and both had observatories or belvederes on their roofs. Another striking similarity between the two buildings and others by Nichols throughout Edenton and New Bern can be found in the pilasters, which are splayed and fabricated in a stylized Doric order. Based on the detailing of the portico at the lodge, it could be assumed that the belvedere was detailed in a similar manner as the one at Hayes.[58] However, that is where the similarities end between the wood-framed residence, Hayes, and the brick masonry–built Masonic hall.

Eagle Lodge is one of a several buildings Nichols designed that share the popular Illissus Ionic portico. He used this precedent as at Gerrard, the Governor's Palace, and Ingleside. However, the difference in the Eagle Lodge portico from the other three porticos is its reduced scale; it is much smaller in scale than Gerrard but identical in size to the one at Hayes.

The years 1818 to 1827 were a period in Nichols's career in which he developed his architecture for a larger scale of building; by doing this, he freely explored new uses for classical precedents and embraced the ancient Greek aesthetic in architecture. He continued in one form or another exploring the use of ancient Greek architecture and ideas in new American building typologies for the rest of his life. But his works were evolutionary, not revolutionary, and in 1823 certain detailing traits remained in his work. In the latter half of the 1820s, his earlier training and work as a carpenter influenced Nichols's work. This can clearly be seen in his design of openings, specifically doors. Window and door trim remained flat, elongated, and delicate, very much in the English neoclassical tradition employed by Latrobe or Soane. Doors, both at Gerrard Hall and Eagle Lodge, were tall double leafed with flat recessed panels accented by simple beads and jambs. They were precise in detailing, almost minimalist in nature, and strikingly similar to those at Hayes, Saint Paul's, Chowan Courthouse in Edenton, and the New Bern Academy.

In this period of flourishing activity, it is obvious that Nichols could not have been designing everything attributed to him. There simply was not enough time, considering that he was designing and supervising the first major expansion of a state university, multiple residences, a church in Fayetteville, the Wake County Jail, and the North Carolina State House expansion. Some houses built during this time and attributed to Nichols, such as Fairntosh in Durham County, bear little similarity to works such as Hayes or the Sandford House in Fayetteville and were most likely built by someone else. Other work attributed to Nichols in central North Carolina such as the Mary Read Anderson House in Raleigh remain sketchy in written description or documentation for an understanding of Nichols's involvement or even a description of the house. When assessing architecture built in this period in North Carolina, one must also consider the influence of Nichols in the building profession. Because Nichols trained builders through the old apprentice tradition and also cultivated business relationships with other subcontractors, they were trained in Nichols's tastes and sensibilities. He continued to employ boys as apprentices and he even took on some who were quite young, including James Riggs who was only five years old when Nichols apprenticed him in Hillsborough on April 16, 1819.[59] As was the case with Jefferson and his builders, Dinsmore and Nielson,[60] Nichols's ideas were perpetuated by his apprentices or his subcontractors; their buildings or designs were not necessarily Nichols "knockoffs," but because they fabricated what Nichols had taught them, they were essentially peddling his ideas to their own clients. Furthermore, property owners were becoming more and more enamored with "Greek," and these associates of Nichols were more than happy to provide their clients with designs that originally came from the "great" architect William Nichols. In the end, these Nichols followers and his work broadened his influence throughout central North Carolina.

An example of work built by a colleague and collaborator of Nichols is the Hassel-Nash House, also known as Pilgrim's Rest, in Hillsborough (figure 92). Although it shares some features that are strikingly similar to Nichols's work at Hayes, Pilgrim's Rest, built in 1822, is very unlikely to have been designed or built by Nichols. It is different in its overall design from any documented work by him. With its raised foundation, it is essentially a two-story Palladian-inspired house with a center block and two flanking pavilions, a form rather common in the area made popular by English eighteenth-century pattern books. While similar to the arrangement found at Hayes, but with the wings awkwardly attached to the center mass, it has a geometrically awkward manner. Similar to Hayes, the pavilions are accented by a distinctive triple double-hung sash window, an architectural feature that was only used at Pilgrim's Rest and no other building in Hillsborough. The house's porch also shows a Nichols influence; it is a one-story porch nearly spanning the entire façade with wood carved Ionic columns. But that is where the similarities to Nichols's work end. The center mass of Pilgrim's Rest is distinctively flat in its massing. It consists of a prominent, shallow, one-room center mass that tends to accent its façade qualities rather than the building's massing. The tympanum has a Gothic-influenced, pointed arched window that is incongruous to

Figure 92. Hassell-Nash House, also known as Pilgrim's Rest, Hillsborough, NC. Although the Ionic columns and the tripartite massing have led historians such as Roger Kennedy to speculate that Nichols designed this residence, it does not have similar massing or detailing found in other works done by Nichols. Nichols's craftsman and colleague John Robb most likely designed and built it. (Historic American Buildings Survey, Library of Congress, Washington, DC)

the Pain-influenced qualities found in the rest of the detailing. The house plan is a "Quaker plan," a popular house layout in the North Carolina Piedmont, with a side entry and flanking windows. A hall is on the east side and a parlor on the west. The flanking wings abut directly to the east and west sides of the center mass and relate awkwardly to the center parlor. In North Carolina, it is called the Quaker plan house layout because it was used predominantly in Quaker communities in Guilford and Alamance counties.[61] Based on the entirety of his work, it is very evident that Nichols did not design Pilgrim's Rest. His interest in pure geometry and his desire to remain true to his English-inspired Grecian architecture precluded him from designing and building a residence that mixed stylish elements, awkwardly assembles the overall massing of the residences, and, finally, it does not have a center entry.

When compared to Hayes and the Sandford House, Pilgrim's Rest cannot be considered a Nichols design. The building lacks the cubic massing found at Hayes, the Old East Custom House in Edenton, Gerrard Hall, the Governor's Palace, and Eagle Lodge, all of which were designed by Nichols at the same time it is assumed Pilgrim's Rest was built, in 1822. The window detailing, especially the precise shiplap siding and cut openings, found at Hayes and the bank in Fayetteville, is not found at Pilgrim's Rest. However, the Nichols touch is found in its Ionic columns and the flanking wings' fenestration. These details suggest that the owner, Eliza Hassell, originally of Charleston, South Carolina, either could not obtain or afford the services of Nichols and instead hired one of his associates, perhaps Nichols's collaborator John Robb who carved the columns at Gerrard Hall, or more likely, designed the house with Robb and based her ideas from plates found in pattern books or what she saw or remembered from Charleston.

Since drawings or letter correspondence from Nichols or Robb or Hassell regarding the design and construction does not exist, we will never
know for certain who actually designed Pilgrim's Rest. However, in a
comparison of the columns, the workmanship appears very similar to
the wood Ionic columns found on the Eagle Lodge, located two blocks
to the south of Pilgrim's Rest, and the stone capitals found at Gerrard.
The columns make a compelling argument that Robb designed and
built this landmark and that any involvement by Nichols was peripheral at most.

The sphere of Nichols's influence on other builders is well documented by both Bishir and Peatross, most notably his involvement
with John Berry, a young aspiring builder who later became a prominent regional architect. Berry, along with brick mason Henry Richards, built Eagle Lodge when they were young men under the guidance
of Nichols. Berry later gained prominence and fame in Hillsborough
designing its primary landmark, the Orange County Courthouse.[62]
He later went on to build the library and ballroom at the University
of North Carolina, Smith Hall (now Playmakers Theatre). Berry also
designed and built the Methodist Church in Hillsborough in 1850 and
built the Hillsborough Baptist Church (designed by William Percival
in 1855).

It is entirely likely that Berry and Richards had a hand in building another of Nichols's landmarks in Hillsborough: Saint Matthew's
Episcopal Church. Built in 1825, it is one of the earliest examples of
Gothic revival architecture in North Carolina (figure 93). Saint Matthew's is one of the oldest surviving Gothic-inspired buildings in
North Carolina. It is unclear how much involvement Nichols had
with Saint Matthew's; he most likely presented a design consisting
of plan and elevations to the church vestry and left the detailing to
the contractor for the project, Samuel Hancock. Its massing is fairly
typical for churches of this period, consisting of a small gable-ended
sanctuary. The building and its prominent steeple (built later in 1869)
are situated on the hill overlooking the town. The brickwork is Flemish bond and the windows are slim lancet arched windows set in a
recessed panel of the wall. The interior, especially the altar area, was
significantly changed during the latter part of the nineteenth century
(figures 94–96). The large timber trusses supporting the roof appear
to be from the late nineteenth century as well. However, the balcony
remains from the original design and, along with it, two elongated
columns reminiscent of the columns used in Edenton and New Bern,
indicating that Nichols still used Pain-influenced detailing when he felt
it expedient and appropriate. The balcony itself has an elaborate wood
panel consisting of Gothic crosses, very similar in form to the balcony
found at Gerrard Hall that was built at approximately the same time

Figure 93. Saint Matthew's Episcopal Church, Hillsborough, NC, 1825. Saint Matthew's Episcopal Church is one of the earliest Gothic Revival churches in North Carolina. The tower was added in 1869. (Courtesy of Wendy Kapp)

Figure 94. The altar and apse of Saint Matthew's Episcopal Church, Hillsborough, NC. Nichols's arch remains intact but most of the interior was altered late in the nineteenth century. (Courtesy of Wendy Kapp)

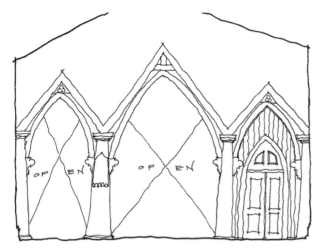

Figure 95. East elevation of the sanctuary, Saint Matthew's Episcopal Church, Hillsborough, NC. (Sketch by author)

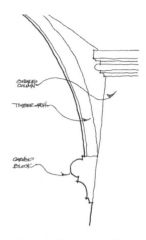

Figure 96. Details of the timber arch in Saint Matthew's Episcopal Church, Hillsborough, NC. (Sketch by author)

Figure 97. Arch and column condition, Saint Matthew's Episcopal Church, Hillsborough, NC. (Sketch by author)

Figure 98. Balcony condition in Saint Matthew's Episcopal Church, Hillsborough, NC. The detailing of the Doric columns reflects William Pain's influence on Nichols. Similar columns can be found on Nichols's buildings in Edenton and New Bern. (Courtesy of Wendy Kapp)

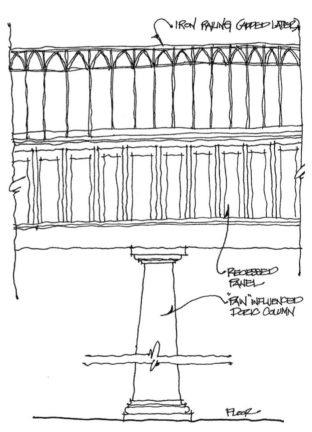

Figure 99. Balcony details, Saint Matthew's Episcopal Church, Hillsborough, NC. (Sketch by author)

Figure 100. Moses Mordecai House, Raleigh, NC. (Photograph by author)

(figures 97–99). While it is possible that Hancock made the columns and the balcony, it is conceivable that Robb was subcontracting for both Nichols and Berry and fabricating columns and other architectural elements in 1826, three years after the building of Pilgrim's Rest. The fact that Robb was building in Orange County for Nichols and that Pilgrim's Rest is built using some of Nichols's detailing but none of his design ideas convincingly suggests that Robb designed or built Pilgrim's Rest and Nichols had little, if any, involvement with its design and construction.

At the same time, thirty-five miles away, Nichols was designing and building one of the more significant additions and renovations of any house in Raleigh—the Mordecai House (figure 100). The home of Moses Mordecai, a prominent planter and citizen in Raleigh, was a simple one-and-a-half-story timber-frame house with a side hall plan layout. His large family had outgrown the house by the end of the eighteenth century, and Mordecai hired Nichols, who transformed the interior plan of the original house and then added a large two-story addition to the south of the original building, which faced the small but growing town of Raleigh.

Nichols added a single-pile, two-story addition with a center hall massing to the south end of the original residence. The house, which exhibited a low-pitched hipped roof and was somewhat similar in form to the Sandford House in Fayetteville, was clearly a departure from the cubic massing of Hayes. The massing of the transformed Mordecai House is accented by a two-story portico that was also similar to the

Figure 101. Lower porch condition and column capital, Mordecai House, Raleigh, NC. (Photograph by author)

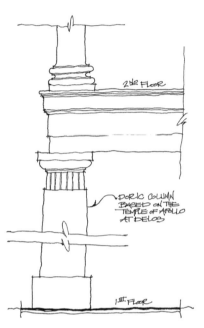

Figure 102. Sketch of the lower porch at Mordecai House, Raleigh, NC. Nichols based the column design on the *Temple of Apollo at Delos* by Stuart and Revett. (Sketch by author)

Figure 103. Upper porch, Mordecai House, Raleigh, NC. (Photograph by author)

Bank of the United States Branch in Fayetteville in both massing and composition but strikingly different in its detailing. Nichols adapted the lower level of the portico from Stuart and Revett's plate of the Temple of Apollo at Delos. The columns have plain shafts for almost all of their length except for the twelve inches (or so) immediately below the column's capital, which is fluted (figures 101 and 102). Interestingly, he departed from the Delos precedent at the lower entablature, which carries a plain, three-band architrave with no hint of a frieze or cornice. The upper columns and portico follow the Illissus model of the Ionic

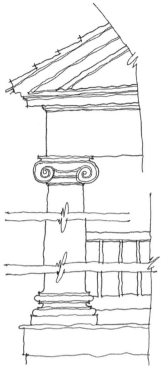

Figure 104. Details of the second-floor portico, Mordecai House. (Sketch by author)

Figure 105. Front door details, Mordecai House. (Sketch by author)

Figure 106. Front door of the Mordecai House, Raleigh, NC. (Photograph by author)

order similar to what was built for Gerrard Hall in Chapel Hill, the Governor's Palace, and Eagle Lodge in Hillsborough (figures 88 and 89). The front doorway reflects Nichols's English tendencies in detailing and perhaps even an influence from structures he saw firsthand during his out-of-state trips. Similar to the entry at Hayes, the siding changes from weatherboard or clapboard to shiplap siding, which is smooth and precise, conveying a more finished appearance within the porch as if an outdoor room. The doorway is "cut" and "inserted" into the siding, which allowed Nichols to delete large casings to join the entry into the wall. The entry itself consists of a low arched fanlight with flanking sidelights and a multipaneled door. The new addition presented an imposing presence to all who were traveling from Raleigh (figures 103–106).

The interior of the Mordecai House is a continuation of the refined English-inspired neoclassical architecture found in the Oval Ballroom, the Sandford House, and at Hayes. Cornerblocks and reeded casings surround all of the openings; fireplaces are accented by mantles with Ionic pilasters and simple frieze blocks reminiscent of the entries at the Old East Custom House in Edenton and at Hayes. The central passage stairway is also distinctively delicate with simple turned newels, square pickets, or balusters, and a winding railing similar to the Sandford House in Fayetteville.

During this relatively short period of his career from 1818 to 1827, Nichols was incredibly prolific not only as an architect, but also as an engineer and entrepreneur with his establishment of the first waterworks in Fayetteville. Along with the buildings clearly documented as his work in Fayetteville, Chapel Hill, Hillsborough, and Raleigh, he also designed new courthouses for Guilford and Davidson counties in North Carolina.[63] In addition, he designed the first sanctuary for Christ Episcopal Church in Raleigh on the corner of North Wilmington Street and Edenton Street.[64] It was described as a wood-frame Gothic Revival church, although no image survives. He began the construction of the church in 1826, the year before he left North Carolina, and he did not see it completed in 1829. Apparently, it was well received by both the church members and the public. It was mentioned in the November 1, 1826, edition of the *Raleigh Register*, which stated: "[From] the acknowledged talents of the architect, we have no doubt this church will be an ornament to the city."[65] He also continued to design remodeling projects for existing residences during his last year in North Carolina. Sadly, these buildings are long gone, having either burned or been torn down to make way for bigger, more modern buildings. The most influential and significant of these lost buildings designed by William Nichols was the extensively remodeled North Carolina State House.

Chapter Four

THE STATE HOUSE IN RALEIGH

Throughout the first part of his career, William Nichols always sought the fame and recognition he felt was his due. The breakthrough project that allowed him to receive his long-sought recognition was the design and construction of Hayes. When he arrived in Fayetteville in 1818, he sought to benefit from his success at Hayes and the economic boom that the state was experiencing after the War of 1812. Along with designing numerous private commissions, he was appointed first superintendent of state buildings and then state architect of North Carolina, a position that he held until 1823 and which gave him a salary of four hundred dollars per month. During this tenure as state architect, Nichols utilized his talents, both as an architect and as a salesman, and designed a new capitol building that became a model for at least two other state capitols in the Deep South. He developed his own ideas about how a capitol building should look and work. He expressed democratic ideas in architectural space and form. His design of the new state house in Raleigh was the beginning of his essay on American democracy that he would later elaborate in designs for new state capitols for Alabama and Mississippi. In getting what he wanted—to build a grand edifice—Nichols would downplay an existing State House, which was, in fact, a rather newly constructed building, for a grander and more appropriate capitol building for the state of North Carolina. The original State House building was a modest structure designed and built by Rodham Atkins. He began when Raleigh was first established in 1792 and completed the building in 1794. It was built in the same manner as courthouses found throughout the state and its common, simple form reflected the sensible, no-nonsense approach to building found in North Carolina throughout the eighteenth century (figure 107).

Figure 107. State House, Raleigh, NC. It was originally built by Rhodham Atkins in 1794; Nichols substantially altered it in 1824. Watercolor sketch by J. S. Glennie in 1811. (Courtesy of Princeton University Library)

By 1818, many of North Carolina's leaders had grown weary of the plain nature of the Atkins State House and wanted both the hall of state government and the capital city to look more elegant and appropriate for its function as the formal seat of state government. Once again, Nichols was the right man at the right place to accomplish both. Due to its placement within the capital city and its function as the seat of government, Nichols knew it was paramount for this symbolically important building to be a significant piece of architecture in Raleigh, which at the time was young and struggling. He understood that a state capitol should embody key architectural elements that symbolize democratic governmental representation, thus defining the capitol as different from other buildings. This realization of the symbolic nature of architecture in capitol buildings is the main reason the State House was a success. Nichols understood that democratic government required an imposing and distinctive edifice.

It is unclear exactly when Nichols was first appointed state superintendent of public buildings but, by 1818, soon after he had moved his family from Edenton to Fayetteville, he was consulting for the state government and managing repair and renovation projects for state buildings. In a May 27, 1818, advertisement in the *Raleigh Register*, Nichols placed the following notice for cypress shingles on behalf of the state of North Carolina:

> Shingles Wanted, for the repairs of the Government Buildings of the City of Raleigh, one hundred thousand well cressed 18 inch, 20 inch and two feet Juniper or Cypress Shingles of the best quality. Persons disposed to deliver the whole, or a part only will please forward their terms to the subscriber in Fayetteville.
> Wm. Nichols, Superintendent of Public Buildings.[1]

Nichols's role with the state soon expanded tenfold with the arrival of an unconventional statue from Italy that catapulted him into the role of state architect. In 1815, the North Carolina General Assembly had commissioned the renowned neoclassical sculptor Antonio Canova to produce a marble statue of George Washington. Once it was delivered to the General Assembly, it became apparent that the Roman version of Washington, seated and in a toga, would clearly overwhelm the modest State House; it was at this point that the statue committee turned to Nichols for some "professional assistance."[2] He was asked by a legislative subcommittee to prepare a report on the state of disrepair found at the State House and the Governor's Palace. Sensing a major commission, Nichols was eager to help the statue committee and began his campaign to reconstruct the Atkins-designed State House with a new one of his design. Nichols responded to the committee's concerns in the following statement:

> Had it been equestrian a space in centre of the west front it would have been suitable, or had it been pedestrian, then a kind of Monopteros Temple or Canopy supported by twelve columns and open all round might have been a sufficient appendage and protection. But from its being formed in a sitting posture an enclosed building either a circular or parallelogram with a dome and portico would be proper.[3]

He quickly dismissed the idea of a separate, smaller building and immediately proposed either a complete remodeling or a completely new State House to accommodate the grand Roman version of Washington. Nichols wanted, as he wrote in a letter to state officials, to "give the house a respectable appearance worthy of the capitol of the State of North Carolina."[4] Nichols then stated that a significant amount of repair was needed at the governor's house as well.

The subcommittee, chaired by Nichols's former client James Iredell, Jr., of Edenton, concurred with Nichols and submitted the following report to the General Assembly:

> The Committee who were appointed to examine the state of the public buildings report that in company with Mr. Nichols, the Superintendent of the Public Buildings; they have examined the Governor's House and the State House and found each in a state of dilapidation, and requiring the immediate attention of the Legislature. They requested Mr. Nichols to draw up a report on the state of the buildings, and the repairs necessary to be made. They have examined his report and entirely concur with him in opinion as to the present condition of the buildings and of the repairs which ought to be made.

Iredell continues in his report:

> Your committee are of opinion that as the State House requires thorough repair, this is a proper time for making these improvements to it, which the convenience of the General Assembly and the appearance of the building require. They think that another Story should be added, for the purpose of making suitable committee rooms; and that there should be projections on the north and south side for offices. The two Halls be enlarged by removing partitions which separate them from the rooms now occupied by the Clerks and decent galleries should be constructed. The Cupola should be converted into a simple Dome, and the present Bell be recast or another one procured. Arrangements are also necessary for placing the Statue of General Washington in an eligible situation within the building. All these improvements and arrangements would not cost a larger sum to the State, whilst they would add much to the convenience of the General Assembly and of their Officers, and be highly ornamental to the building.[5]

Nichols was persuasive in convincing Iredell and other committee members that a newer, remodeled, State House of his own design was desperately needed. He wanted to reinforce his case for a complete transformation of the State House, listing his "specifications" for repairs:

> A specification of repairs necessary to be done on the State House.
> To repair the fractures on the outside walls and prevent their extension by excluding the weather. To remove several large pieces of timber which injudiciously placed on the outside of the walls and to fill the space with bricks. To place arches or some other support under the intersections of the passages where heavy brick walls are built on a mere wood lintel. To repair or replace the present the present [sic] porches at the entrances

and front doors wide frames. Repairs to all the windows and doors throughout the house and a new Stair Case. The roof to have an entire new coat of shingles; the Cupola to be repaired and the Bell to be recast and Sundry repairs to plastering and painting; But as the House Stands in need of many accommodations, as well for the purpose of facilitating the business of the Session as for comfort of the Members, plans accompanying this have been formed for the general improvement of the building; to accommodate the Assembly in all its departments and to give the house a respectable appearance worthy of the capitol of the State of North Carolina, keeping economy strictly in view have been the motives which produced this effort. Should these plans be approved at the present time, when it is deemed necessary for the house to undergo repair, would be most proper. As the time occupied in either operation would be much the same, the difference in expense would not be in material, whilst the difference in appearance and convenience would be immense, and could the timber and stone on the public lands in the vicinity of Raleigh be applied exclusively to the purpose and for the benefit of the State buildings, it is confidently believed that the expense attending the suggested improvements would be considerably lessened.

All of which is respectfully submitted by Your Obt. Servant, Wm. Nichols[6]

So Nichols made his pitch. Not only was the current State House in an advanced state of decay, it also was a safety hazard due to initial faulty construction and design. Moreover, Nichols convinced the General Assembly that North Carolina deserved more of a regal edifice than what the Atkins-designed State House could offer. Additionally, due to the significant amount of work needed just to repair it, he stated that repairing it back to its current form would not be prudent. A complete remodeling of the State House that corrected all of the deficiencies in the Atkins design would not cost significantly more— especially if the state government used resources it had on state lands located near Raleigh. Thus he stated to the North Carolina General Assembly that the construction of a new State House would cost more than renovating and expanding the existing one. Nichols then submitted to the General Assembly his design for a transformed State House, as described by Iredell in his building committee summary. He estimated the cost for all of this at twenty-five thousand dollars.[7] Apparently his persuasive sales pitch worked. The North Carolina General Assembly agreed to Nichols's plan to extensively remodel the State House.[8]

The House of Commons recommended this appropriation for the remodeling of the State House but not without some reservations. In his resolution recommending the appropriation for the remodeling, House Speaker Alfred Moore forcefully expressed his endorsement for a complete remodeling of the State House but also voiced his concern about the expense of remodeling:

> The Committee to whom was referred that part of the Governors Message, which relates to the Statue of the late General Washington, and the necessary preparations to be made for its reception, and the permanent accommodation, having attentively considered the subject beg leave to offer the following Report—aware of the nature of their charge, and the responsibility they incur; your Committee have gladly availed themselves of professional assistance, and with pleasure acknowledge their obligations to the State Architect for his advice, and for the drawings which accompany this report.
>
> After a mature and thorough examination, it was plain to your Committee that no plan could be devised the execution of which would not be Expensive, and it only remained for them, to ascertain and adopt the one, which would combine most usefulness, with that taste and elegance, which the nature of the subject, made so absolutely indispensible.
>
> The first idea, which presented itself, was to erect a separate building for the reception of the Statue; but this was wholly laid aside for the reasons offered by Mr. Nichols the architect, in paper marked A, which is herewith submitted.
>
> Roll marked B contains a drawing of alterations to be made in the State House,[9] and an outside view of the same when completed. It is to this last plan that your Committee would wish particularly to direct the attention of the Legislature, as it meets their undivided approbation, and is respectfully offered for adoption.
>
> It will be perceived by examining the estimate of the Architect, that the expense of accomplishing the plan of the separate building, would be from eleven to twelve thousand dollars, and it is obvious, that the building when finished, can ever be applied to any other than its original purpose, or indeed would it admit of a connection with any other. Your committee therefore thought it most advisable, as a necessity existing for laying out a considerable sum of money, that money should be applied in making such alterations in the State House, as while they furnished an elegant and appropriate site for the Statue of that great and Excellent person, whose memory we intend to perpetuate, in this specimen of art, and tribute of affection, would be an ornament to our Metropolis, and provide proper accommodations for our Supreme Court, the heads of departments; and both houses of the Legislature. All of which may be accomplished at an expense of not more than twenty five thousand dollars, and that too, to be drawn by degrees from the Treasury, in the course of two years.

Moore then adds some personal commentary regarding the attitudes about the remodeling from the Senate:

A proper provision for the expected Statue, obliges us to do something:— but if this cause did not exist, your Committee presumes, that the late debate in the Senate, furnished conclusive evidence of the insufficient accommodation afforded by the Senate Chamber at the least; and the consequent necessity of its enlargement. Those who for hours stood wedged together in mass, and the many who could not penetrate into the room, tho, willing to submit to any inconvenience, will heartily unite with your Committee in the regret, that the accommodations offered by the Senate, has not been equal to the courtesy and politeness, which so distinguished the members of that honorable body, upon the interesting occasion alluded to.[10]

And with that, Moore recommended the House of Commons approve the expenditures to remodel the State House. He ended his resolution by saying, "To fail, is to become ridiculous."

Through the clever manipulation of placement of a statue, Nichols began an essay in the architecture of democracy and bicameral government. He received approval for the twenty-five-thousand-dollar remodeling appropriation at the end of December 1819.[11] The General Assembly authorized that land be sold to help fund the remodeling project and that Nichols, acting as the state's architect, select a tract of land for a quarry for the building stone needed for the remodeling.[12] By the end of 1820, Nichols had persuaded the General Assembly to formally appoint him state architect.[13] With his grand plan for the State House underway, Nichols made the most of the circumstances and made a direct request for a larger salary to Governor Jesse Franklin.

Sir,

I am extremely desirous of gratifying the general wish of our Citizens by having the State House in readiness to receive the next General Assembly. But to the effect this desirable object, on my part will be required, all that industry and method can perform. And it is only by the most unremitting attention I can hope to perform this arduous task, which will oblige me to abandon more lucrative engagements entered into at Fayetteville long before my appointment as Superintendent of Public Buildings. I therefore take the liberty Sir, respectfully to request your Attention to this Subject, hoping that you will make such additional compensation, as will enable me to withdraw my attention from other objects, and as will be somewhat equivalent to the Services required. Under all the circumstances I would hope that a Salary of Sixteen hundred dollars per annum in quarterly payments will not be deemed unreasonable.

I am Sir
Very respectfully
Your Obedt. humbl. Servt.
William Nichols[14]

Franklin gave Nichols his requested annual salary of sixteen hundred dollars, making him the most important architect in North Carolina.

It is important to remember that two types of precedents for American government buildings had been established at the early part of the nineteenth century. One type was the legislative house in the form of a Roman temple, established by Thomas Jefferson, architect of the Virginia State Capitol (started in 1785).[15] Jefferson viewed government as sacrosanct, a virtuous and respectful institution. Even though the Romans used temples for their ancient religion and not politics, Jefferson thought it the perfect architectural symbol for the newly formed republic. The design of both legislative branches under one Roman temple would also echo the overthrow of the Roman monarchy and the formation of the great Roman republic, just as America had dethroned the English monarchy for its own republican government.

The second type of American design precedent was the design of the United States Capitol, originally conceived by Dr. William Thornton, significantly improved upon and refined by Benjamin Henry Latrobe, and completed by Charles Bulfinch.[16] Their capitol placed emphasis on a meeting place for two separate, but equal, legislative branches with a communal ceremonial space in the middle. Unlike Jefferson's temple, both houses of government are as architecturally prominent on the exterior as the interior. Thornton, Latrobe, and Bulfinch transformed Jefferson's shrine to the republic into something uniquely American: a classically inspired modern governmental building that combined the practicality and symbolism of a democratic, representative government.

It is unclear whether Nichols saw the U.S. Capitol during his trip to New York in 1818, and it is doubtful that he ever met Latrobe, who was then at the zenith of his career, associating himself with the most influential people in the nation such as Jefferson and President James Madison. Nichols was, however, influenced by Latrobe's career path and was likely aware of his notable work including the Virginia State Penitentiary, the Baltimore Cathedral, and his various works in Philadelphia. But what Latrobe had done on Capitol Hill was to introduce figurative spaces to monumental government buildings through his remodeling and reworking of the chambers of the two separate houses, the House of Representatives and the Senate. The final result would be the architectural manifestation of bicameral government. By doing this, Latrobe transformed Jefferson's Roman temple into something more unique and fitting to the American experiment in democratic government: two chambers, equal in prominence, unified by a central and ceremonial rotunda and dome, clearly visible in the building's exterior.[17] More importantly, Latrobe designed the chambers as great halls reminiscent of the classical world's outdoor theatres and

Figure 108. The U.S. Capitol, ca. 1820, by Benjamin Henry Latrobe. (The Benjamin Henry Latrobe Archives, Library of Congress, Washington, DC)

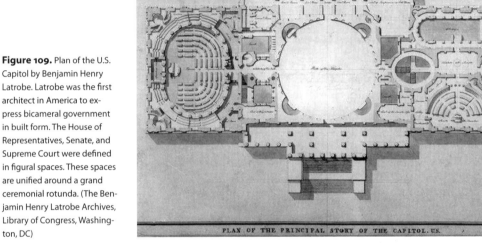

Figure 109. Plan of the U.S. Capitol by Benjamin Henry Latrobe. Latrobe was the first architect in America to express bicameral government in built form. The House of Representatives, Senate, and Supreme Court were defined in figural spaces. These spaces are unified around a grand ceremonial rotunda. (The Benjamin Henry Latrobe Archives, Library of Congress, Washington, DC)

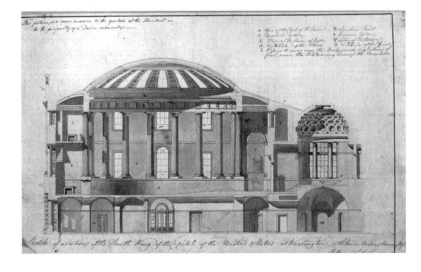

Figure 110. Section of the chamber for the House of Representatives by Benjamin Henry Latrobe. (The Benjamin Latrobe Archives, Library of Congress, Washington, DC)

the classical basilicas, creating beautiful assembly rooms rather than generic and conventional rooms. This simple twist of precedent transformed not only the architecture of legislative government but also how governing bodies interacted with and were presented to the general public. Assembly seating was oriented in a semicircle that faced the bench of the House speaker or the Senate president. A visitor gallery supported by a grand colonnade separates the public, theoretically allowing observations without interrupting the business of the governing body.[18]

Thornton's original design idea for a capitol building was hardly new. Colonial capitols, such as the capitol of Colonial Williamsburg (which was re-created in the 1920s) with its twin apsidal ends, were designed with this conceptual layout scheme. Latrobe inherited this initial design and developed it into a uniquely American building type.

Latrobe's most brilliant feature in the U.S. Capitol was clearly his inventive use of domes and half domes throughout the Capitol, albeit not the towering and massive dome of today (figures 108 and 109). His use of the half dome in the Old Supreme Court in the Capitol inspired more than just an interesting and articulated ceiling. By juxtaposing the Doric entablature with the half dome, Latrobe was able to convey the illusion of a greater and larger space in what is a rather small room (figure 110). All of this had caught the attention of Nichols: the articulation of the governing bodies in the form of the building, the rigorous use of the classical orders, the manipulation of ceiling planes and vaults, and the use of grand rotundas and domes. This was on his mind as Nichols made his pitch to the Committee on Public Buildings.

The Canova statue of Washington (figures 111 and 112) was a very convenient device for Nichols to use to transform the humble Atkins version of the North Carolina State House to a more Latrobe-like capitol building. To say that the old State House was remodeled is a gross understatement; Nichols completely obliterated any semblance of the old building with his new and ambitious design. Inspired by Latrobe's capitol, Nichols built the new North Carolina capitol on a cruciform plan that completely transformed Atkins's humble capitol. This allowed him to build a new Senate Chamber and a new House of Commons Chamber. The House Chamber was semicircular in plan and surrounded by Ionic columns that supported a visitors' gallery; above, a vaulted ceiling was supported by another set of Ionic columns. The Senate Chamber was circular in design with a half-domed ceiling; colossal Greek Doric columns upheld the visitors' gallery. Nichols also used Latrobe's revolutionary idea of designing chambers based on classical amphitheaters. He was able to fully maximize the House and Senate chambers through his extensive knowledge of space, classical order, and structure in designing the interiors of the State House.

Figure 111. Statue of a seated George Washington by Antonio Canova placed within the North Carolina State House Rotunda designed by William Nichols. Nichols used the statue as the primary reason to radically alter the original State House. (Courtesy of the State Archives of North Carolina)

Figure 112. Statue of George Washington seated and in Roman attire by Antonio Canova, 1815. (Courtesy of the State Archives of North Carolina)

Nichols transformed the North Carolina State House from a simple cubic block into a Greek cruciform plan; in the center of the Greek cruciform plan was, of course, the raison d'etre for the endeavor—the domed rotunda space for the Canova statue of George Washington. Shallow recessed arches and flattened pilasters articulated the wall surfaces of the rotunda of the State House, and a delicate stylized entablature demarcated a two-story light well culminated by the dome. The entire ensemble provided a pleasing sense of light and air befitting this grand statue.

Nichols completely changed the exterior of the State House as well; he added a third floor to the Atkins building, hipped the roof, then protruded the middle section front and back to define the entry as well as the front façade. The middle section of the tripartite composition consisted of a rusticated base with arched window and door openings on top of which rested a pseudo-portico of Ionic pilasters and large double-hung sash windows with smaller sash windows on the third floor. The entablature was stylized and the fenestration was similar to the center section, all of which was defined with heavy window

Figure 113. The North Carolina State House, Raleigh, NC. Engraving by W. Goodacre. (Courtesy of John Sanders)

Figure 114. The North Carolina State House, ca. 1830. Painting by Jacob Marly. (Courtesy of the North Carolina Museum of History)

surround moldings and entablatures. The shallow dome capped the entire composition along with a delicate lantern that allowed natural light to fill the rotunda[19] (figures 113 and 114).

What is also interesting to note about Nichols's North Carolina State House was its exterior finish. Here Nichols applied a smooth stucco finish and scored the surface of the building's exterior to resemble ashlar stone. As Nichols's commissions became larger and more complex, so did his taste for elegant building materials. He wanted to build in stone, but finding good, solid stone and skilled tradesmen in the South was difficult. This proved to be a source of frustration for Nichols for the rest of his career.

With the engaged columns and pseudo-portico, Nichols's North Carolina State House has both classical and English influences. However, on a planning and conceptual level, it was the influence of Latrobe and the U.S. Capitol that formed Nichols's design of the State House. In his book about the work of Alexander Jackson Davis, John Sanders credits Nichols with creating the archetype for state capitols: "In the remodeled State House, Nichols combined the architectural features that henceforth would characterize American state capitols: central portico(es) on the long dimension(s) and an external dome expressing a central rotunda, flanked by balanced wings housing the two legislative chambers—only the second structure to do so."[20]

As the State House neared completion in 1821, the Committee on Public Buildings sent Nichols to New York to purchase furnishings and draperies for the chambers. The trip to New York allowed Nichols the opportunity to view and experience the latest tastes in architecture emerging from the Northeast. As he had done for James Johnston four years earlier, Nichols spared no expense in decorating the remodeled State House; he purchased large chandeliers, red damask silk draperies, and fine furniture.[21]

Nichols's State House was grand and audacious; it helped usher neoclassicism into North Carolina on a grand scale but it was not built at the budget he had proposed. Nichols's original estimate for the State House was twenty-five thousand dollars. By the time the building was finished in 1822, it cost sixty-five thousand dollars, more than double Nichols's original estimate. Just as his work on Saint Paul's Church in Edenton nearly bankrupted the parish coffers, he wantonly ran up the cost of the building project and blew the budget allocated by the North Carolina General Assembly. This led to his dismissal as state architect by the General Assembly in December 1822.[22] In the December 6, 1822, *Raleigh Register*, Nichols placed the following announcement:

> The Subscriber respectfully informs Gentlemen who may require his Professional services, and whose frequent applications he has been unable to attend to, that his engagement with the present year has been terminated, and that then he will be ready to receive their commands. Letters directed to him at Raleigh until the 1st of January, will be attended to.
> W. Nichols[23]

Even though cost overruns caused Nichols to be dismissed from his position as state architect, the State House could not be considered a failed building project. Quite the contrary, it was a resounding success, and did precisely what the architect and the client wanted it to do: bring elegance and monumentality to what was a very young and provincial capital in Raleigh. One of Nichols's chief rivals, New York architect Ithiel Town, said it was "a more elegant building than any other State has yet erected, it is convenient, appropriate and in good taste."[24] Governor Gabriel Holmes praised the "talents of the Architect" and said "it was evident of such an elegant specimen." He expressed his satisfaction at giving encouragement to genius and attainment in one of the fine arts, which has hitherto been so known, or properly estimated, among us."[25]

Anne Newport Royall, a writer of travels throughout the United States, visited the State House in 1829. In her book *The Black Book; or, A Continuation of Travels in the United States*, she describes Nichols's State House:

> The state house is a very handsome building, of brick, and the exterior painted with a cream color. It is 102 feet in length, 56 wide, and 43 feet high, with a splendid dome, and sky-lights. The state house stands on an elevation, in the centre of the large square, called Union Square, in the midst of a beautiful grove, the natural growth of the soil. The trees are tall and slender, and thinly scattered over the ground. The square is enclosed by a wall, with four handsome gates opening at the end of each street. The whole exterior representing one of the most finished pictures of taste and beauty.

In her description of the State House, Mrs. Royall praises Nichols in his design of the building's interior:

> But the skill of the architect is reserved for the interior. The galleries, chairs of both Speakers, windows, &c are done in *Nichols'* best style, and highly finished. The stucco is much superior to that of the domes on the Capitol in Washington, in color and smoothness, and the seats and galleries are painted of a bright blue. It contains a superb Statue of Gen. Washington, executed in Italy, by the greatly admired Canova . . .
>
> This Statue is placed in the centre of the State House, first story, and cost $10,000. But this proud monument is not satisfied with this extravagance; the Legislative Halls are hung round with the richest damask silk—this is a brilliant red, of the most costly texture, with the richest gold fringe and tassels, and hangs round the windows and chairs of both Houses, in thick folds from the ceiling to the floor. It has also a portrait of Washington, done by Sully, the best likeness extant; and the largest, and most splendid Chandelier I ever saw, not excepting those in Congress Hall; and upon the whole, by far the most splendidly furnished of any public building I ever met with in the United States. It cost $10,070!!![26]

Mrs. Royall was not one to casually praise anything she viewed or experienced in her travels, especially in North Carolina. She was quite critical of the plain and drab quality of the rest of Raleigh and noted in particular the pale complexion of the Raleigh women. She was most critical of Fayetteville; she even referred to the men of that small city as "rednecks."[27]

Mrs. Royall's comparisons of the State House to the U.S. Capitol in Washington were deliberate; other than the Pennsylvania State Capitol designed by Stephen Hills and finished the same year as the North Carolina State House, no other capitol building had followed the precedent set by the U.S. Capitol.[28] By following Thornton's and Latrobe's precedents, the English-born Nichols physically encapsulated the symbolic elements that have come to represent "temples of democracy": 1) the cruciform plan of balanced wings, 2) the rotunda, 3) the dome, and 4) the colossal portico. Unlike either Jefferson's Virginia State Capitol or Gideon Shryock's Kentucky State Capitol,[29] Nichols's North Carolina State House was very deliberate in featuring these elements as symbols to define the state capitol building. The idea of a building to house republican democracy was as new as the idea of modern republican democracy itself, but the architecture of capitols had already developed a group of symbolic elements that defined them. The noted architectural historian of American governmental buildings William Seale elegantly described the architecture of state capitols as symbols in the following passage from an essay published in a 1975 article in *Design Quarterly* from the Walker Art Center:

> The history of state capitols is the history of a group of symbols that were born in colonial times, triumphed during the first decade of the young nation, and survive, altered but un-diminished today. They are the architectural symbols of American democracy. Their beginnings were political; architecture devised by legislatures. They have survived in spite of professional architects who never really understood them and who battled against them quite as vehemently in 1828 as in 1961 in Honolulu, where the most recent state capitol was completed. These American symbols are now in legislative structures all over the world, the accepted legislative architecture of democratic governments. As symbols they are abstract, that is, they are not necessarily specific and uniform in their appearance. Indeed, they are very flexible. As a syndrome they can be rearranged, reshaped, and everybody is satisfied, as long as they are there. In their most familiar form, four symbols can be pointed out as the obvious features of U.S. capitols: the dome, the balanced wings—suggesting a bicameral government—portico and rotunda.[30]

Easily recognized, these symbols immediately set a capitol building apart from other buildings. Nichols understood this well and developed his own method of expressing the symbols of democracy in a capitol building. His understanding was both simple and elegant. Once it was completed, everyone knew the building that stood in the center of what is now known as Union Square in Raleigh was the temple of democracy for North Carolina. Nichols would later elaborate and refine his ideas of state capitols in projects in Alabama and Mississippi.

The state hired him again to design and construct a small brick state treasurer's office on the Union Square in 1825, which cost $2,005. The building was torn down when the third (and still standing) capitol was completed in 1840.[31] Along with adding the portico at the Governor's Palace, he would also design and erect two new outbuildings on the grounds. (These two buildings were demolished along with the Governor's Palace in 1885.) Both of these smaller building projects seem irrelevant when compared to his impressive architectural achievement, the State House.[32]

Though Nichols continued to practice in North Carolina designing private homes, two county courthouses, and a church (as discussed in the previous chapter), his work for the state government of North Carolina was over, and he soon departed to practice architecture in Alabama. Despite leaving a wake of overblown budgets, Nichols had greatly helped the overall image of the state with his twenty-five-year career in North Carolina by adding elegance to many classically inspired buildings throughout the state from New Bern to Edenton, from Fayetteville to Hillsborough, and even as far west as Greensboro and Lexington. It was Nichols who finally defined the campus layout at the University of North Carolina, designing a focal point for its main outdoor space with the Belfry. Finally, he helped define the new capital city of Raleigh, which had originally been planned as a Philadelphia-like gridiron city a little more than twenty-five years earlier, with a new State House on Union Square that forever determined the form of the city, even though it burned to ground nine years later.

If William Nichols had been contemplating leaving North Carolina for the Southwest, he did not show it in regard to his numerous business ventures, specifically in land acquisition in Wake County. From 1825 until weeks before he left North Carolina for Alabama in 1827, Nichols purchased significant tracts of land in western Wake County along one of the main tributaries of the Neuse River, Crabtree Creek. He first purchased a 25-acre tract from Thomas Henderson in June of 1825.[33] Then one year later, he purchased 478 acres from Delia Haywood, who was the executor of her husband's, William Haywood's, estate for $2,200.[34] Nichols continued assembling a larger tract of land along Crabtree Creek. In a tax sale conducted by the Wake County sheriff, John Dunn, Nichols purchased 320 acres for $34.[35] Finally, in April of 1827, at another Wake County land sale, one month before he began his new job as the state architect of Alabama in Tuscaloosa,

Nichols purchased 520 acres along Crabtree Creek for $1,700.[36] In a period of less than two years, Nichols had assembled a tract of over 1,300 acres of land in western Wake County; there is no documentation that he ever leased it out for cultivation or had any intention to develop it for commercial use. Apparently, he assembled this tract as a long-term investment. Today, William Umstead State Park and the Raleigh-Durham International Airport are located roughly on this tract.

The reasons why William Nichols left North Carolina after building up a practice of twenty-five years are both complex and contradictory. On the surface, Nichols appeared to have been well established both professionally and personally. He owned a significant interest in the Fayetteville Water Works, which he helped to build. He also began heavily investing in tracts of land in Wake County.[37] It is possible, however, that by 1827, North Carolinians may have outgrown Nichols's English-inspired classical architecture. Perhaps his business soured due to a lack of prompt professional service, or at least the perception of poor attentiveness to clients' needs. His large workload of building projects was spread over a wide swath of central North Carolina. As he got busier, his attention to clients may have declined, leading to frustration by his client base. In their catalogue *William Nichols, Architect,* Peatross and Mellown allude to an unfinished structure for Christ Church in Raleigh,[38] and to the frustrated documented complaints from Mrs. George E. Badger, a client who complained that Nichols had only told the workman how to finish the arch in the passage, and "did not as he promised give a drawn plan."[39] Perhaps North Carolinians grew tired of his repackaging an earlier scheme for a new client, as is evident in the rehashing of the massing and observatory of Hayes in the Eagle Lodge project in Hillsborough, or his use of the Temple of Illissus scheme simultaneously at Gerrard Hall, the Governor's Palace, and the Eagle Lodge. Since Nichols had always presented himself as a purveyor of high-style living as a marketing ploy, he no doubt attracted a "high maintenance clientele" which may have become frustrated with imitative work and frequent absences from the job site. It is certain that Nichols overextended himself with the work commitments throughout the North Carolina Piedmont. Even with today's technology and ease of transportation, it would be daunting to keep up with and please all of his clients.

A series of overblown budgets on important building projects most likely discouraged future clients in North Carolina from hiring Nichols as well and this probably led him to move to a new place and begin anew. His most significant building projects, the North Carolina State House, finished in 1824, and the buildings he either designed or repaired at the University of North Carolina that he finished in 1825, cost significantly more than what Nichols had estimated. This annoyed several of the most prominent leaders in North Carolina, from Governor Gabriel Holmes to University of North Carolina president Joseph Caldwell.

There may have been personal reasons for his departure from North Carolina in 1827. The Wake County Court Minutes name William Nichols numerous times, for example, in May 1823, when the court assessed him seventy-five dollars and legal costs to be paid to a Jacob Marling. The *Raleigh Register* newspaper published the records of the Wake County Court of Pleas and Quarter Sessions in 1829, which suggested that Nichols failed to make payments for the purchase of several slaves from Delia Haywood (the same person from whom he had purchased the 478-acre Crabtree Creek tract), resulting in civil penalties from Wake County:

> . . . it having been made to appear to the Court that the Defendant has removed himself [Nichols] beyond the limits of this State, or so conceals himself that the ordinary process of law cannot be served on him: It is therefore ordered by the Court, that advertisement be made for six weeks in the Raleigh Register, for the Defendant to come forward on or before the next Term of this Court, to be held at the Court House in Raleigh, on the 3rd Monday of May next; then and there to replevy and plead to issue, otherwise, judgment will be made final, and the property levied on the condemned subject to Plaintiff's recovery. Teste. B. S. King, CC[40]

In the end, Nichols may have left North Carolina simply to expand his business enterprise. It is possible that he may have envisioned developing his business to become much larger and regional, perhaps following the example set by Ithiel Town, who by now was travelling from New York to North Carolina conducting business in municipalities with his patented bridges. Conceivably, Nichols grew disillusioned with his clientele, or they grew disillusioned with him. It is plausible that Nichols was running away from creditors. Maybe he realized that the future of North Carolina was not as favorable as it once was. After all, a younger generation of North Carolinians was moving to Alabama, the nation's new frontier. With the slowing economy in North Carolina, new construction had scaled back significantly. Regardless of the reasons behind his decision, his architectural legacy would remain intact. He had designed numerous stately houses, churches, and courthouses. He built and operated a waterworks, designed a university campus and a state capitol. Nichols had done as much as anyone to transform the idea that buildings could be fashionable, even beautiful, in North Carolina.

Whatever the reason, in 1827, forty-seven-year-old William Nichols left North Carolina for the "frontier" state on the rise, Alabama, in search of greater opportunity and fortune, never to return to North Carolina. He depended on his two sons, Samuel and William, Jr., to carry on the family business there.

It appears that at the time Nichols left North Carolina, his eldest son, Samuel, stayed behind in North Carolina. Samuel managed William, Sr.'s half interest in the Fayetteville Water Works. On October 19, 1827, Nichols conveyed the other half interest in the waterworks to Hugh McLaurin for two thousand dollars. From 1827 until 1832 Samuel managed William, Sr.'s interest in the waterworks, but due to his father's need for an infusion of capital funding for projects in Alabama, Samuel put Nichols's ownership of the waterworks up for auction on October 27, 1832. In the October 2, 1832, *Fayetteville Observer* advertisement leading up to the auction, Samuel stated that the reason for the auction of his father's interest was the following: "that the property is now offered, in consequence of the proprietor having made extensive contracts in Alabama, which require large investments of money." On November 12, 1832, William Nichols, Sr., gave his son Samuel power of attorney to sell and make title to the Fayetteville Water Works and other property he possessed in Cumberland County. On December 7, 1832, Samuel Nichols sold his father's interest in the Fayetteville Water Works to Williamson Whitehead for $1,950. There is no other record of Samuel found in Fayetteville after the land transactions that he performed on behalf of his father.[41]

Nichols's other son, William, Jr., initially moved to Alabama with his father but returned to North Carolina after Nichols's State House was destroyed by fire in 1831. In 1832, the North Carolina General Assembly hired Nichols to design a new state capitol building in the same location as the previous one that he remodeled in 1824. Rather than return to North Carolina, Nichols appointed William, Jr., to submit his design for the new state capitol to the North Carolina Commission on Public Buildings and then manage its construction. Armed with a new set of plans designed by his father, William, Jr., presented the plans to the building committee, who approved them and paid William, Jr., $350 as a professional fee on June 26, 1833.[42] It appears, however, that the Commission on Public Buildings was not confident in William, Jr.'s abilities to build the new state capitol and decided to pay the fees he had accrued up to this point, terminate his services, and hire a new architect to complete the design and build the building. William, Jr., was quite bitter about how he was treated by the commission and expressed his feelings in a letter to Governor David Lowry Swain in December 1833. In the letter, William, Jr., stated that he produced and submitted a set of plans for the new capitol building that were approved by the building commissioners, who then voted him a pittance of a fee, which was not sufficient to "defray" his personal expenses. He went on to say that his professional services were rejected by the commissioners, and "confided the execution [of the building] to incompetent hands."[43]

In August 1833, the North Carolina General Assembly commissioned the firm of Ithiel Town and Alexander Jackson Davis[44] to complete the capitol that William Nichols, Sr., had designed and William Nichols, Jr., had begun to build. William, Jr., did not return to Alabama and resume his work with his father; instead, he chose to remain in North Carolina and designed the Fayetteville Academy building in Fayetteville in 1833, the same year he was working on the new state capitol project.[45] In a letter to George W. Haywood, an attorney in Raleigh, William, Jr., claimed that he had been the state engineer for the states of Georgia, Alabama, and Louisiana.[46] In 1839, William, Jr., married Nancy Dunn of Wake County and began a family in Fayetteville.[47] He then encountered some profoundly bad fortune in 1841 and was incarcerated in the Wake County Jail (which, ironically, his father had designed) for allegedly stealing a slave.[48] William, Jr., pleaded not guilty to this charge and another for horse stealing.[49] Slave stealing was a serious charge in antebellum North Carolina; it also appears to have been a federal offence due to appeals that he sent directly to Washington, D.C. If convicted, William Nichols, Jr., could have been put to death. Incarcerated, he was not only frightened for his life but also deeply insulted that his reputation was tarnished. He wrote two letters while in jail that have survived; in the first letter, he appeals to Governor John Motley Morehead to release him from jail and allow him to defend himself. In it, he states the following to Morehead:

> I would invite your Excellency to call on that I might explain myself more at length; but my audience chamber is not fitted for one of your rank and official dignity. It has been a great while since I was entertained and comforted in the regal palaces, gilded saloons and courtly halls of the old world. My present apartments would compare more favorably with the dungeons of the Inquisition or the black hole of Calcutta than with them.[50]

In his second letter, Nichols, Jr., wrote to Haywood requesting legal representation from him. Nichols, Jr., states the following:

> Saturday, 24 March 1841
> Dear Sir,
>   Circumstances of a painful and incomprehensible character to me have placed me in most disturbing situation, which will perhaps render it necessary for me to avail myself the services of legal counsel, tho I hardly know for what . . .

Will you do me the favor to drop me a line as soon as you receive this and inform me with regards to Judge Badger's intentions and also whether you will lend me your aid. I can satisfy you with regard to my ability at how to pay you a liberal fee and if I were not my father's purse is as attainable to me as it is to himself. The heavy affiliation under which I have labored heavily during the winter have prevented me from supplying the means of doing so at the present moment. With regard to the charge brought against me, so revolting to every principle of my nature, I can give you no information. All I know is that I find myself in a most perplexing dilemma; but I cannot tell how I got into it nor can I see my way out of it. I see nothing around me but loath and hear language mucked and disgusting to my ears, yet I cannot realize that I am in prison; I doubt my own identity and all appear to be in a dream. Confinement is torturing enough to my feelings; but it is in the nature of the charge that disturbs me the most. If I thought myself capable of such an act I would not live another moment. I would rather at this moment be a convicted murderer than even be suspect of dishonesty. My mind is bewildered when I think of it. The iron had sunk deep into my soul and my heart bleeds at every pore.

I came to Raleigh last fall some time intending to remain only a week but I have been loitering around about somewhere ever since without object motive or bruising very much to the injury of my affairs at home, the distress of my family and the prejudice of my reputation. I stopped first with Col. Gasborough but how or when I left there I do not know (Perhaps he can tell for I have no distinct recollection of anything that has happened since about the first of Dec.)

Nichols, Jr., concludes his letter:

This is the great crisis of my life. Death itself in its most appalling form would be preferable to longer confinement in this horrible and loathsome place. My brain is becoming deranged and the feelings of my aged father whose existence is more wrapped up in mine and of a young, proud and high-spirited wife are kept upon this rack. My situation is truly a deplorable one. Here I am at the home of my childhood, and yet I am a stranger in a strange land, far distant from home, alone, helpless and friendless.

I would like to know how or why it is and who is persecuting me. This personal enemy is malicious and vindictive yet I cannot see what he has to do with this matter. Please let me hear from you on the receipt of this letter.

Your obd't servant,
W. Nichols[51]

Haywood did not respond to William, Jr.'s plea for help, and he did not receive any financial support from Nichols, Sr. By July 1841, the situation appeared very bleak for William, Jr.; Weston R. Gales, a prominent member of the Whig Party and a member of the North Carolina General Assembly,[52] summarized William, Jr.'s prospects in a letter to a colleague in Washington, D.C., discussing the need for professional engineering services in North Carolina:

> Professionals to lend, such as yourself, is very rare here, and the demand is about to increase very much. The only civil engineer that we have had for some years is Nichols, who furnished a draft of our capitol and whom you must know. For six months, or more, he has been immersed within the walls of our dungeon, on a charge of stealing a negro. The punishment is death, but he has not had his trial.[53]

In October 1841, William Nichols, Jr., was tried in Wake County Superior Court on the charge of slave stealing. He was unable to employ counsel for his defense and R. M. Saunders was assigned by the court to defend him. On October 7, 1841, the jury found William Nichols, Jr., not guilty of slave stealing; however, he still had to stand trial for stealing a horse. He somehow raised five hundred dollars through securities bonds and was released on bail.[54] By the end of 1841, William, Jr., was unable to pay his debts and declared bankruptcy.[55] In April 1842, he was found not guilty of horse stealing but by now the entire ordeal had left him penniless. He took an oath of insolvency and was absolved for costs incurred from both the Superior Court and the Wake County Jail.[56] There is no record of William Nichols, Jr., after his felony cases in either Wake County or Cumberland County. His father, William, Sr., never returned to North Carolina to aid his jailed and impoverished son; no correspondence has been found written by Nichols on his son's behalf. He was now hundreds of miles away in the Deep South, faring quite well, with a new bride and the completion of two Greek Revival masterpieces that not only capped his career, but defined Jackson and antebellum Mississippi—the Old State Capitol and the Governor's Mansion. Before these final achievements, though, he would put his architectural stamp on yet another emergent state—Alabama—by designing her public face and transforming her private one.

Chapter Five

Alabama

I n 1827, William Nichols left North Carolina and his twenty-seven-year architectural and building practice to seek fortune (or perhaps a new life) on what was considered the western frontier in the newly established state of Alabama.[1] While the circumstances that compelled Nichols to leave North Carolina are conjectural, this does not appear to have been a spontaneous or impulsive decision. The children of Nichols's client base in North Carolina were now leaving their family farms and plantations for the virgin land of Alabama and Mississippi, a compulsion North Carolinians called "Alabama fever."[2] Fifty years of overcultivation of tobacco left much of North Carolina barren. The railroad, which would allow successful transportation and commerce to the western part of the state, was still decades away. From 1815 to 1840, North Carolina experienced a serious decline in its population as most of the future generations moved south and west. By 1850, it would earn the unflattering nickname of "the Rip Van Winkle State," referring to the state's sleepy economy while neighboring states experienced economic booms. This economic downturn limited Nichols's architectural opportunities. It was time for him to look elsewhere for work.

The 1820s became an age of transformative change in the United States, most notably in the South. By 1825, the last of the Revolutionary War generation and Virginia dynasty[3] presidents had left office. The Louisiana Purchase in 1803 had doubled the size of the United States and allowed numerous Virginians and North Carolinians to seek their fortunes in the "Old Southwest." Treaties between the United States and the Cherokee and Creek Nations of American Indians, such as the Treaty of Fort Jackson and the Treaty of Doak's Stand, also significantly increased the southwestern territories that eventually became the northern sections of Georgia, Alabama, and Mississippi. The Adams-Onis Treaty of 1819 between the United States and Spain allowed the United States to acquire Florida in 1821.[4] All of these political accomplishments generated significant migration of Americans from the Atlantic seaboard to the Deep South.[5] The second war for independence, the War of 1812, had decisively made the United States independent from Great Britain. It had also cleared the path for westward expansion of the United States by expelling the allies of the British: the Spanish colonial government and the Creek and Choctaw Indian Nations. During the 1820s, Americans were reaping the benefits of the outcome of the war by migrating and settling west of the Appalachian Mountains. The hotly contested election of 1824 allowed the existing political establishment to remain in power as the House of Representatives elected John Quincy Adams president over Andrew Jackson but, since Andrew Jackson had won the popular vote, it was clearly evident that change was under way throughout the country.

This new generation that would define the South were merely children (or not yet born) when the American colonies had been under British rule. They came of age when the predominantly agrarian culture was still ruled by the provincial elite in both the North and the South. But in the first three decades of the nineteenth century, this new generation transformed the country in every way imaginable. They developed new cities like Chicago and Cincinnati, spurred industrialization, and developed new transportation systems such as canals and, later, railroads into the heartland. They developed new cash crops, specifically cotton, to market in Europe. Their main focus, the source of their livelihoods and fortunes, was land. They grew fortunes by both developing the wilderness into productive cropland and speculating in land development. As they acquired wealth, they sought to redefine the cultural and political structures of their lives and as they prospered, they challenged the status quo and demanded a seat at the political table. They insisted on being heard in the political arena—both in Washington and in their own state capitals—and built a new government that gave more citizens (albeit all white men) the right to vote. Men like Henry Clay of Kentucky, John Calhoun of South Carolina, and Thomas Hart Benton of Missouri represented them. They championed their ideas and causes—westward expansion, the lowering of tariffs of imported goods from England, and the right to own slaves.[6]

This new generation of Americans built towns along with state and political governments that embodied their ideas and values; they built churches, schools, and colleges. Finally, they built houses, sometimes mansions, which conveyed their fortunes, their sense of importance, and their ideals. Likewise, someone who embodied their

Figure 115. Andrew Jackson, seventh president of the United States. Engraving by Thomas Phillibrowne after a painting by Alonzo Chapel, ca. 1858. (Library of Congress, Washington, DC)

values—Andrew Jackson—would lead them (figure 115). From 1812 to 1840, Jackson would lead the first generational transformation in American history. In the North, his followers ushered in the industrial age of America. In the South, his followers expanded an agriculturally based economy that thrived on the lands that Jackson either conquered or negotiated through treaties with the Spanish or the Creek and Choctaw Nations.

Nichols, too, caught Alabama fever and moved to this booming region where a state was literally being built and fortunes were being made. The right man at the right time, his considerable talents and skills would become the architectural form of this vision that defined this new state. Even so, Nichols spent only seven years in Alabama, arriving in the newly established capital city of Tuscaloosa in 1827 and leaving it in 1832. He spent another two years in the northern part of the state, in and around Muscle Shoals, and in the central Alabama town of Montgomery. He was first hired as the state architect, a position similar to that he held in North Carolina, and was named state engineer in 1831. His time in Alabama was the most productive period in what was already a prolific career. He was forty-seven years old, which many consider one's creative prime age. Nichols explored ideas and principles for urban design that he no doubt learned in Bath as a young man. In Tuscaloosa, he designed the state capitol, the University of Alabama, the Episcopal Church, and some of the state's grandest residences. Although colonial coastal cities such as Mobile continued to benefit architecturally from European-trained architects such as the French-born Claude Beroujon,[7] Nichols influenced inland Alabama, from Forkland to Florence,[8] architecturally defining the region as we know it today: the Old South.

Had just a small portion of this impressive work survived in Tuscaloosa, Nichols would have been recognized and celebrated by the likes of Hamlin and other noted architectural historians in the twentieth and twenty-first centuries. Unfortunately, Union cavalry led by General John Croxton in the last days of the Civil War burned Tuscaloosa and, most notably, the University of Alabama. The University of Alabama was considered a prime target for the torch; it had been converted into a military institute by university president Landon Garland in 1860. During the Civil War, the University of Alabama became the

predominant training institution for junior officers for the Confederate army.[9] His Alabama capitol burned to the ground from an electri-
cal wiring fire in 1923.[10]

Nichols arrived in Alabama at the same time Andrew Jackson was
establishing himself as a prominent national figure. In 1829 Jackson
became the seventh president of the United States. Jackson was a new
kind of national leader; he believed in the advantages of a "meritoc-
racy" and not a nation ruled by an "aristocracy." He envisioned the
American republic as a "middling landscape" between the savagery of
the Indian wilderness (which he took steps as a military general and
later on as a president to obliterate) and the decadence of Old World
Europe. This vision resonated with the new American generation who
sought to make their fortunes in the "Old Southwest." It was a vision
based on a belief in a nation of small property owners who enjoyed
freedom from monopolists and men of privilege. It was rooted in Jefferson's ideals of a country ruled by a "natural aristocracy among men
determined not by birth but virtue and talents."[11]

When Jacksonian democracy swept across both Alabama and Mississippi, it came with a detrimental price. In 1833, after Nichols had
built the state capitol and the University of Alabama, Jackson dissolved
the Bank of the United States by withdrawing federal funding. This
led to a national credit crisis spurred on by real estate speculation in
states such as Alabama and Mississippi, which culminated with the
Great Depression of 1837.[12] This depression posed serious challenges
to Nichols's career in Mississippi.

Nichols in Frontier Alabama and the Alabama State Capitol

Despite the fact that younger North Carolinians fled the state for
greater opportunities in Alabama and Mississippi, they still clung to
the traditions and practices that had been developed in North Carolina. Up to the onset of the Civil War, transplanted North Carolinians
continued to send their sons back to the University of North Carolina
for their education. Although North Carolina continued to shrink in
population, the University of North Carolina grew and flourished during this period. With the exception of Yale, it was the second largest
university in student population in the United States. Largely out-of-
state students who were children of transplanted North Carolinians
supported it.[13] Governmental, religious, and farmstead practices were
transplanted by these new settlers as well. On the one hand, the new
citizens of Alabama wanted to reinvent themselves; but on the other
hand, they wanted to transfer the old systems and customs from "the
Old North State" to the newly developed farmlands of Alabama. This

included an establishment of a predominantly county form of government, which supported agriculture, the Episcopal Church, and a plantation-based society. However, they were not interested in continuing the subsistence agriculture practices or the cultivation of tobacco. Instead, they planted a more lucrative cash crop—cotton.

The 1819 Alabama constitution established a small central Alabama town called Cahawba as the state capital. Cahawba was not an ideal site; its hot and humid summer climate made it susceptible to yellow fever. It was also vulnerable to flooding; in fact, the statehouse itself was flooded in 1819. The drafters of the constitution stipulated that the legislature "should have the power to designate by law the permanent seat of government, which shall not thereafter be changed," which must be decided by the 1825 session of the Alabama legislature. It also stipulates that the legislature could allow the capital to remain in Cahawba. In 1825, after a fierce political debate between sectional factions already growing in the state, the Alabama legislature relocated the state capital to Tuscaloosa, which sat high on the bluffs of the Black Warrior River in the northwest section of the state. The legislature convened in Tuscaloosa in 1826.[14]

At first, the Alabama legislature met in the Bell Tavern, a popular hotel in Tuscaloosa, which was hastily enlarged and outfitted until a new capitol could be built or at least a larger temporary capitol could be fabricated. On December 14, 1826, the legislature appointed a committee of five building commissioners (none of whom were architects) to select several potential sites for the state capitol and to develop a building design. Three weeks later on January 10, 1827, they recommended Childress Hill, which fronted Broad Street (Tuscaloosa's main street) and was adjacent to the Black Warrior River, the primary mode of transportation for the town. It also reviewed and tentatively approved a design for the capitol building that was developed by the five commissioners. Apparently, the committee's design was not warmly received; one critic described it as "having more appearance of a Dutch barn or a cotton factory than a State Capitol." No drawings of the proposed capitol building have survived, only the specifications, which stated that the building was "to be a large rectangular two-story brick building 150 feet by 130 feet. The basement story was to be constructed of 'dressed stone in square blocks' with an eighty foot by seventy foot room for the House and an eighty foot by sixty foot room for the Senate." In addition to the legislative chambers, the building would also house the Supreme Court, the state bank, secretary of state, governor, comptroller, and treasurer. The design was debated on several political levels: the southern faction of the state wanted to do everything it could to prevent Tuscaloosa from becoming the capital while the northern faction was embarrassed by the aesthetics of the current state house. One Huntsville legislator even referred to it as a "gin-house."[15]

However, both the legislature and the Capitol Commission could agree on one thing: they needed an architect to design and build the new capitol building. On February 3, 1827, the state of Alabama advertised in the Tuscaloosa, Huntsville, and Mobile newspapers for a building superintendent and state architect. Interested architects were to apply as soon as possible since the legislature would approve the recommendation of the architect from the commission on May 20, 1827. Nichols no doubt found out about the advertisement and applied. With his impressive experience of having finished designing and building the North Carolina State House, at forty-seven years old and with over thirty years of building experience, he was obviously a very strong candidate. He arrived in Tuscaloosa in May of 1827 and brought with him his younger son, William, Jr., to assist him.[16]

Nichols fit in well with the newly established Alabama society. Not only did he come to the state as an established architect; he was also a living connection for the new Alabamians to North Carolina and to England. He benefited from the distance between Alabama and North Carolina, which obscured his somewhat problematic reputation of being too expensive and unpredictable with his clients and their money. Nichols had a fresh young generation of leaders as clients who were eager to establish the course of their state on Jeffersonian (and later, Jacksonian) principles. This new society built churches, bank buildings, schools, and homes that conveyed their stature in the community. Nichols found himself in a perfect situation to continue his practice with a clientele who not only had money and aspiration, but who respected him as an architect. In 1828, he purchased eighty acres in Tuscaloosa County. It is not known what kind of residence he lived in or built for himself there.[17]

Nichols immediately went to work designing the capitol building. He found the committee's design unsatisfactory and made his opinion widely known. In a June 8, 1827, article published by the Huntsville *Southern Advocate*, Nichols clearly conveyed what he thought of the committee design:

> [He] had serious objections to the plan, which apparent to the eye of
> an experienced and tasty [*sic*] architect, and which, we doubt not, will
> induce the Legislature to alter the plan when properly explained.[18]

After hearing Nichols's opinion, the Capitol Building Commission concurred with the new superintendent and state architect and requested that Nichols develop a new design for the Alabama State Capitol. In the meantime, the commission began procuring bricks and stone for

Figure 116. Alabama State Capitol, Tuscaloosa, AL, ca. 1831. This lithograph shows that the Alabama State Capitol resembled the North Carolina State House. (North Carolina Collection, University of North Carolina at Chapel Hill Library)

the building; this turned out to be a very wise decision for the state government since it allowed the construction period to be both expedient and cost effective. Nichols spent the rest of 1827 designing a new capitol despite the fact that he did not have a contract from the state.

In November 1827, Nichols presented a design for a capitol building based on the legislature's approved budget of forty thousand dollars. It was too small and modest for the legislature, who apparently wanted a grander, larger building. They rejected his lesser design and directed him to design a grander building with a revised estimate for the construction of the building. Nichols wasted little time with their new directive and submitted a new design that would eventually be built. He also submitted a new cost estimate of fifty-four thousand dollars to the Alabama legislature on December 17, 1827. The legislature was quite pleased with Nichols's services up to this point; they approved his contract as state architect and superintendent on January 15, 1828. The contract stated that Nichols would be paid $1,000 for services rendered from May 1827 to January 1, 1828, and that he would receive an annual salary of $1,749 to be paid quarterly. His main responsibilities included designing and building the state capitol and also designing and building the academic buildings and grounds of the new University of Alabama, which would also be located in Tuscaloosa.[19]

In the design of the Alabama State Capitol, Nichols elaborated on his earlier North Carolina State House of 1824 (figure 116). The Alabama State Capitol was cruciform in plan and Palladian in overall style. It had "faux" porticos with engaged Ionic columns that could almost be considered pilasters. The masonry openings were simpler in articulation than the windows at the North Carolina State House. The base/basement of the building was clad in rusticated stone. The entrance to the building was through the central arch of the projected

Figure 117. Alabama State Capitol, Tuscaloosa, AL. The capitol survived the Civil War and later became a women's college, only to burn down in 1923. (Historic American Buildings Survey, Library of Congress, Washington, DC)

gable on the ground floor. The capitol's most prominent feature was a shallow dome, built using de l'Orme's[20] techniques, and surmounted by a lantern which admitted light into the rotunda space below. The second- and third-floor exterior walls were brick[21] (figure 117). The Ionic entablature and a stone balustrade unified the elements of the façades and concealed the low-sloped hipped roof. The flanking wings consisted of plain walls with punched windows supported with carved lintels whose surfaces were articulated with carved Greek keys, swags, and garlands; the corners were accented by stylized pilasters. The short ends of the building, which faced north and south, featured a large Palladian window flanked by double-hung windows. At the ground level, there were small porticos with stone columns. Nichols designed these porticos using the Greek version of the Doric order, the first time Greek Doric order would be used in Alabama.[22]

The interior of the building was even more impressive. The cruciform plan reflected the bicameral nature of state government with its large spacious halls. The plan was composed of the two houses of the legislature at either end—the Senate Chamber at the north end and the House Chamber at the south. The Alabama State Supreme Court was located in the western part of the cruciform plan while the eastern part held the entrance vestibule on the main, *piano nobile*, level and the state library was located on the top floor. In the center of the building was the rotunda, which joined the two wings. Nichols intended it to house a grand statue, similar to the Canova statue of Washington in the North Carolina State House, but apparently the Alabama

Figure 118. House of Representatives Chamber, Alabama State Capitol, Tuscaloosa, AL. (Historic American Buildings Survey, Library of Congress, Washington, DC)

Figure 119. Interior view of the Alabama State Capitol rotunda. The Alabama rotunda was similar in design to the rotunda in the North Carolina State House. (North Carolina Collection, University of North Carolina at Chapel Hill Library)

legislators did not see the need to place a statue in the space. The dome of the rotunda was coffered and the lower section had niches for more statues. Nichols stated that these niches would be used "for statues, which patriotism grant, our infant state may fill in a manner worthy of herself, at some future day. If she should ever fill them at all."[23] The lower space was ornamented with a low relief sculpture of winged sun disks and wreaths located on pedimented impost blocks between the supporting arches (figure 119). Similar to his work in North Carolina, these emblems convey the legislature's Masonic inclinations. On the second floor, eight colossal Corinthian pilasters supported by a band of Greek fretwork and surmounted by a full entablature bolstered the dome. A circular gallery connected the House and Senate chambers. The entrance vestibule consisted of two grand curving flights of stairs leading up to the *piano nobile* floor level.

The chamber of the Alabama House of Representatives was inspired by the chamber in the U.S. House of Representatives. It was rectangular in form but its northern end had a semicircular Ionic colonnade that was semielliptical in plan and contained a spectators' gallery. On the south end of the House Chamber was an elevated rostrum of the speaker flanked on either side by an Ionic column supporting an entablature with the Latin motto *"Pro Patria,"* meaning "For (One's) Country" on its frieze. The floor of the hall was divided into a series of rising elliptical tiers on which the desks for the legislators (also designed by Nichols) were placed (figures 118 and 119). At the north end of the building, the Senate Chamber was located; it was the same size as the House Chamber yet distinctively different in both form and decoration. In the center of the chamber was a shallow dome with a centered chandelier. A Corinthian peristyle of twelve columns in the center of the chamber supported a visitors' gallery above. The president of the Senate's desk was situated between the two northernmost columns with a backdrop of "rich crimson damask curtains" bundled in folds with hanging festoons from the beak of a golden spread eagle. The senators were seated on two rising tiers around the circle of columns.[24]

Essentially, Nichols refined his North Carolina State House design for the Alabama State Capitol. He reworked the design that he understood and, more importantly, it was what the clients wanted. By designing a building that clearly responded to the functional needs and philosophical ideals of bicameral government, Nichols was perpetuating the idea of a "temple of democracy" within the context of Jacksonian democracy.

It is worth noting how different in form both the Alabama and North Carolina capitols were when compared to other capitols built at the same time. For example, in the same year that the Alabama State Capitol was completed (1831) a new capitol building for Kentucky was also built. Gideon Shryock, a young, brilliant architect from Lexington, Kentucky, designed an equally beautiful state capitol by attempting to replicate the Temple of Minerva Polias of Ancient Greece, which resembled, in both form and plan, Jefferson's Virginia State Capitol. This may have been the result of Kentucky[25] having a significant number of Virginians settling in it.[26] In 1827, Ithiel Town designed a temple-inspired state house for the state of Connecticut in New Haven.[27] The capitol also differed from the Georgia State Capitol in Milledgeville, which resembled the Philadelphia State House (Independence Hall) when Jett Thomas first built it in 1807. It would later be transformed into a Gothic-styled building through a series of alterations that culminated in 1837.[28] Nichols's capitol buildings were different from other state capitols perhaps, but very similar to the U. S. Capitol; the cruciform plan that placed the legislative branches on both ends of the building and the Supreme Court in the middle followed the national Capitol precedent. This was a more appropriate design solution than trying to conform an ancient precedent to a new use, as was the case in Shryock's Kentucky capitol and Town's Connecticut capitol. Shryock's capitol design is similar to Jefferson's design; within the interior of the temple form, the House Chamber is located on the north side of the small rotunda while the Senate Chamber is located to its south. Neither Jefferson's nor Shryock's capitol designs became the accepted design solution for state capitols; instead the form of the U.S. Capitol would ultimately become the prototypical capitol building design. Nichols helped promote this idea, first in North Carolina in 1824, and then in Alabama seven years later.

Due to the challenging frontier conditions existing in Tuscaloosa, Nichols had great difficulty building the Alabama State Capitol. He benefited from the Capitol Commission's decision to purchase brick and stone for a capitol while the design was being determined; nevertheless, both materials and craftsmen were scarce in Alabama. Craftsmen were moving into Tuscaloosa seeking construction jobs but not in great numbers. In fact, Nichols brought a number of craftsmen with him from North Carolina, most notably John Robb. Robb served as the foreman on the project and carved the Ionic capitals and bases on the east façade and the Doric columns on the north and south porticos. Two stonecutters named Baker and Swinney were contracted to provide the elaborately carved lintels and sills for the upper windows. But even with these craftsmen busily fabricating elements of the building, it was simply not enough for completion within a reasonable time period. Nichols advertised in newspapers as far afield as Nashville, Tennessee; Lexington, Kentucky; and Cincinnati, Ohio, for skilled stonecutters, brick masons, and even more bricks. Most of the timber was sawn and then joined by either slaves or free blacks. One ex-slave described late in his life how he had "whip-sawn" beams in saw pits on the construction site. James Mallery and William Morton, Jr., created the elaborate joinery for the Supreme Court, vestibule, House, and Senate chambers.[29]

Accomplished carpenters like John Fitch[30] who moved from Connecticut to Tuscaloosa fabricated the elaborate winding twin staircases. Records show numerous slaves sent to apprentice in various building crafts on the capitol building. Even with all this labor thrust on the building project, it was not enough and progress on the building languished. Both the legislature and the town population grew increasingly impatient about the capitol. In June 1829, the town council decided to hold the Fourth of July celebration on "Capitol Hill." Nichols reluctantly agreed and stated to the council that the capitol would be "in as great a state of forwardness as practicable for the accommodation of the ladies and reception of the company generally."[31]

Work continued through 1829 and though it was still unfinished the Alabama legislature met in the building in November. As the legislators met in their chambers, workmen were hurriedly trying to complete the construction of the building. In his November 17 message to the legislature, Governor John Murphy stated his satisfaction with the finished product and added his hope that it would "long remain a monument of the liberal ambition," an enlarged but not "extravagant munificence of the State" and that it would "long remain the council hall and the citadel of liberty." He praised the architect, stating that "the taste, skill, and experience of the Architect, Captain[32] Nichols, deserved the highest commendations. In this edifice's beauty and use have been happily combined while a system of proper economy has been made to pervade the whole arrangement."[33]

The Tuscaloosa *Intelligencer* stated in October 1829 that "to the foreigner the building presented a pleasing evidence of the advance made by our infant state in the arts and general improvement, without at the same time, bearing testimony of extravagant disbursement of public treasure." The reporter further praised Nichols by saying that "from the best information that could be obtained, there never has been one erected in the United States, for the same sum, half so spacious, convenient, durable and imposing. All agree that, as a specimen of architecture, it stands unsurpassed and bespeaks of the extensive acquirements of Capt. Nichols who superintended its construction." What the capitol symbolized also delighted Tuscaloosa citizens, which was the positive progress of Tuscaloosa becoming a city and Alabama becoming a state. Never being modest, Nichols himself described his capitol as "grand, imposing and striking in its proportions, and productive of the most pleasing sensations to the cultivating mind."[34] The presence of the grand refined state capitol set in the new frontier town of Tuscaloosa must have been both jarring and compelling. Most of its building stock consisted of log cabins and wood frame shanties; roads were practically nonexistent.

Despite all the praises Nichols received from the people of Alabama, his work was not without problems and neither was Nichols. Soon after it was completed, the roof leaked badly. The cause of the roof leaks was the flashing, which failed around the copper plate covered dome. The building leaked so badly that in the winter of 1830–1831 Nichols had to place a temporary wood framed structure over the dome. It was dismissively referred to as a "wooden wig" and, by spring

1831, commissioners hired a "skillful barber" to remove the "frightful wooden wig"; the solution to fixing the leak was to remove the flat seam copper roof and replace it with a wood shingle roof. This was certainly disappointing for Nichols. Throughout the project, having been labeled, either fairly or unfairly, as an over-spending architect, he was determined to stay within the fifty-three-thousand-dollar budget from the General Assembly. At the beginning of the construction project, he stated to the General Assembly that "strict attention to expenditure and a scrupulous regard to economy throughout the progress of the building" would be required. By towing the line on the building's budget, Nichols made many enemies with his subcontractors. In December 1829, several of them brought charges against him to the capitol building commissioners citing that Nichols neglected his official duties and mismanaged funds. These charges, along with several additional "murmurings," were dismissed. Nichols weathered these charges, but the accusations hurt his reputation and his workload decreased. It appears that the perpetuated and unfavorable opinions Nichols earned in North Carolina followed him to his new home in Alabama.[35]

It is interesting to note that by the end of the Alabama's capitol construction, its prototype, the North Carolina State House, had burned and the North Carolina General Assembly sent for Nichols to come back to Raleigh and design its replacement. At this time, Nichols must have been feeling overextended or, perhaps, he simply did not want to return to North Carolina. Instead, he sent his son, William Nichols, Jr., to negotiate the contract and represent him in the design of the building, which greatly resembled his original North Carolina State House. However, the project was fraught with problems. After several building delays, the foundation was finally laid and the contract between William Nichols, Jr., and the North Carolina Building Commissioners was terminated. William, Jr., was arrested and imprisoned for stealing a slave as recounted in chapter 4, and Nichols lost his chance to rebuild it.[36] However, Nichols had designed the planning, footprint, and massing of this new North Carolina capitol.[37]

The University of Alabama

It is a terrible tragedy that the original campus of the University of Alabama burned at the end of the Civil War. The Grecian-inspired campus was a union of the founders' ideals, the educational theories of the era, and Nichols's architectural vision of campus design, a perfected ideal of the "academical village" established by Thomas Jefferson at the University of Virginia.[38] Students and teachers lived, taught, and learned together in mid-to-large-sized neoclassical buildings surrounding a university square, its rotunda in the center, creating a campus in the shape of the lower-case Greek letter pi.

The planning of the University of Alabama actually began while Nichols was still a burgeoning architect in Edenton, North Carolina. In 1818, the governor and legislature of Alabama were instructed by the federal government to establish a "seminary for learning" as part of the "Act of Admission for Alabama into the Union." One individual in particular was instrumental in establishing the University of Alabama—Israel Pickens (1780–1827) (figure 120). Pickens was a native of North Carolina and was the same age as Nichols. He began his political career representing Burke County from the western part of North Carolina and later served North Carolina in the U.S. House of Representatives for two terms. During a congressional session in 1816, Pickens met Andrew Jackson in a boardinghouse in Washington, D. C. Jackson, fresh from battle campaigns in the Deep South from the War of 1812 and wars with the Indian nations, sparked Pickens's interest in Alabama. In the following year, Pickens secured a federal appointment as the registrar for the federal land office in St. Stephens, Alabama, in the newly created Alabama Territory, which had been formed from the eastern half of the Mississippi Territory when Mississippi became a state in 1817. There, he became very influential politically, and was influential in forming the state of Alabama, which was admitted into the Union on December 14, 1819. Pickens led one of the two groups fighting for control in the state. His group, committed Jeffersonians, and later Jacksonians, were known as the "North Carolina Faction." They were weary of central banks and concentrated apportionment of political power, and instead embraced Jefferson's ideas of an agrarian-based republic. Their chief rivals, the "Georgia Faction" (who were also referred to, unflatteringly, as the "Royal Party"), were essentially Federalists or Whigs in the tradition of Alexander Hamilton and were viewed as aristocrats by Pickens and his colleagues. Pickens won the gubernatorial election of 1821, securing power for the North Carolina Faction, making them become the prominent power brokers in the state during the antebellum period in Alabama.[39] The establishment of the North Carolina Faction as the power holders in Alabama politics would prove beneficial to Nichols as the young leaders of the "Carolina colony" continued to keep their North Carolina ties.

Pickens significantly influenced Nichols's career in Alabama by setting the initial course for the architecture and planning for the campus of the University of Alabama. Even so, it is doubtful that Pickens ever knew Nichols. Pickens was from the western Piedmont of North Carolina and left for Washington a couple of years before Nichols relocated to Fayetteville and Raleigh from Edenton; he died in 1827 in Cuba,

Figure 120. Israel Pickens, governor of Alabama, 1821. (Courtesy of the Alabama Department of Archives and History)

where he retreated to ease health ailments from tuberculosis that he contracted, only a month before Nichols arrived in Tuscaloosa.

In 1822, as Nichols was expanding the campus of the University of North Carolina, the legislature incorporated the University of Alabama and, although ex officio, Governor Pickens was named president of the board. In that same year, Pickens wrote Thomas Jefferson and requested a copy of the plan of the University of Virginia.[40] By now the seventy-nine-year-old former president and leader of the American Revolution was constructing his academical village at the University of Virginia with several pavilions already built and classes under way. At this time, planning had begun in earnest on the signature building of the complex, the Rotunda, which was set to begin construction two years later in 1824. By 1827, a year after Jefferson's death, the University of Virginia had already captured the imagination of the American people with tourists coming from far distances to see firsthand the ensemble of buildings which Jefferson conceived as a coherent campus.[41]

It is unclear if Jefferson ever responded to Pickens's request, but what is clear is that Alabamians wanted to emulate Jefferson's architectural accomplishment at the University of Virginia. Minutes indicate that during an 1822 meeting of the University of Alabama Board of Trustees, one of Pickens's protégés, William Beene of Cahawba, presented the board with an engraved plan of the University of Virginia. (At this time, an engraved plan of the UVa campus by New York engraver James Maverick was easily attainable.)

The campus as an "academical village" was one of the few issues that the state legislature and university board of trustees would agree on concerning the new college. Beginning in 1818, when the federal government stipulated that the territory of Alabama should have a "seminary of learning," by 1828, the legislature and the university's board of trustees struggled to establish the university. The first challenge for the board of trustees was to raise the funding necessary to purchase a tract of land, then construct buildings for instruction and dormitories, provide faculty housing, and finally, hire faculty and an administration. Funding for all of this was to come from the sale of two townships of land in the state, approximately forty-six thousand acres, which were designated by the federal government during the time Alabama was considered for statehood. From 1822 until 1825, the Alabama legislature argued over how the land was to be sold. Governor John Murphy proposed that the land should be auctioned intact in 1822. In 1823, Israel Pickens (now back in the legislature as a representative) persuaded the legislature to set a fixed price of seventeen dollars an acre for the township land. The prime land in the township did sell for that amount but the less desirable land did not. In 1824, the legislature adjusted the price of university township land based on its desirability. Most desirable land sold for seventeen dollars an acre, less desirable land was priced at twelve dollars an acre, and the least desirable land was priced at eight dollars an acre. By 1825, the university fund had grown to the respectable amount of sixty-seven thousand dollars.

However, determining a site for the university stalled progress for two years while the Alabama legislature and the board of trustees hotly debated its location. Frustrated by these political delays, Governor Murphy demanded the legislature select a site for the University of Alabama on November 20, 1827.[42] The Alabama legislature spent the next month considering thirteen towns throughout northern and central Alabama. The list included: Gage's Greensborough in Greene County, Lagrange in Franklin County, Athens in Limestone County, Montevallo in Shelby County, Honeycomb Springs in Jackson County, Somerville in Morgan County, Moulton in Lawrence County, Davis in Antauga County, and three towns in Tuscaloosa County—Elyton, Village Springs, and Tuscaloosa, which was by now the state capital. Four days after Christmas in 1827, the legislature finally selected Tuscaloosa to be the location for the University of Alabama. The board of trustees was directed to select a site within fifteen miles of Tuscaloosa.[43]

Meanwhile, Nichols, who had been appointed state architect of Alabama earlier that year in May, was busy building the Alabama State Capitol and extensively remodeling an impressive residential home near Florence, Alabama, in Lauderdale County, the Forks of Cypress. In fulfillment of his duties as state architect, Nichols was assigned to be advisor to the university's buildings and grounds committee in January 1828.[44] On March 22, 1828, they presented to the full membership of the board of trustees three tracts of land near Tuscaloosa, each one approximately eighty acres. The board of trustees voted to purchase Marr's Field and an adjacent fifty-acre tract, which buffered the new university campus from the town and "prevent[ed] immoral persons from settling on same land." The adjacent tract also possessed "superior quality of the clay for making bricks for the buildings and the quantity of wood thereon which could be spared there from [sic] for burning."[45]

Interestingly, only two days after the board of trustees approved the purchase of Marr's Field for the campus, Nichols, with the support of the building and grounds committee, submitted a master plan, building plans, elevations, and detailed cost estimates to the board of trustees. The March 24, 1828, board of trustees minutes note that Nichols's master plan and architectural design consisted of "two blocks of dormitories, one block of professors' houses, a chemical laboratory, and lecture rooms." Evidently, Nichols and the buildings and grounds committee were very confident that the entire board would select Marr's Field as the campus site.[46]

Unlike the situation he inherited at the University of North Carolina, Nichols had tabula rasa, virgin land untouched by human hand. He would create his college campus from the beginning. There were very few architects in the American South at this time more qualified for this university commission than Nichols. Perhaps only Robert Mills, who had designed college buildings at the University of South Carolina, could rival him in expertise and talent. Nichols, like Mills, had the unique perspective of having experienced campus design firsthand in Chapel Hill. As of 1828, there were very few state universities started in the South, especially in the Deep South, and even fewer state universities at the level of size, curriculum, and student population as the University of North Carolina (which, incidentally, in 1828, was considered more prestigious in the South than its sister school, the University of Virginia).[47] Through his Chapel Hill experience, Nichols may have had a better understanding of how an early nineteenth-century campus operated than Thomas Jefferson.

Whereas Nichols was more pragmatic with his campus design, Jefferson was making a philosophical statement about the enlightenment and the destiny of the American people. Jefferson's Lawn was closed on the north (northeast) with the Rotunda, which housed the university's library, and open-ended on the west (southwest), which faced the Blue Ridge Mountains and America's frontier destiny. Nichols, under the direction of the University of Alabama Board of Trustees, took Jefferson's inspiration and designed a beautiful, yet pragmatic campus, instead of a philosophical one. Rather than an open-ended lawn, Nichols created a university square.

The genius of Jefferson's plan is that he innately understood that a university was indeed an ensemble of buildings and grounds. He demonstrated that hierarchy and coherence in architecture on a campus were important to its design, and he was one of the first architects to develop the campus as an urban center, which he called the "academical village." Jefferson's campus had ornamental and vegetable gardens, dining halls (that he called hotels), debating chambers, colonnade student rooms, and classrooms and faculty residences in the pavilions, each housed in its own building yet connected by colonnades and arcades. Unfortunately, Jefferson never completely understood the business of pedagogy and remained jaded by his own college experience at the College of William and Mary, which he considered an unfortunate experience. Jefferson abhorred what he dismissively referred to as the "large piles or houses" similar to the Wren Building at the College of William and Mary. He regarded these buildings as being inefficient and as breeding grounds for disease. Jefferson preferred smaller pavilions that were based loosely on his own home, Monticello, and the ones he experienced in Paris during his tenure as ambassador to France. Although conceptually his vision was brilliant, the residential nature of his Lawn would stifle the expansion of the university throughout its history.[48]

Nichols was more pragmatic. He understood his clients' wishes to pay homage to the vision of Thomas Jefferson, but he also had learned from the mistakes and the significant achievements he made in Chapel Hill working with the University of North Carolina's President Joseph Caldwell early in the 1820s. Through his experience designing UNC and the clients' clear direction to pay homage to the University of Virginia, Nichols designed the next evolution of campus planning in America by combining the ideas that made the University of North Carolina and the University of Virginia into a new campus experience.

Nichols's vision for this new Alabama campus came from his understanding that support buildings such as dormitories and classrooms had to be more than simple pavilions. Jefferson intended that each one of his pavilions would be a work of architecture in itself without giving much thought on exactly how they would evolve or exactly how the entire campus and the university would grow and continue to serve the state. The original campus of the University of Virginia would remain forever static. The residential nature of the pavilions and the rigidness of the colonnades and student rooms did not give any room for expansion or adaption of the Virginia campus. In short, the Lawn would be frozen in its evolution with the completion of the Rotunda in 1826. University administrators attempted to expand it and retain the Lawn as an ensemble in 1850 with an expansion of the Rotunda by Robert Mills; it was destroyed by fire in 1898. The university would only expand again in the last years of the nineteenth century when Stanford White closed the Lawn's southwest end with his academic building design now known as Cabell Hall.

As directed by the University of Alabama Board of Trustees, Nichols designed a heroic building, the Rotunda, as the centerpiece for the campus befitting the ideals of Mr. Jefferson and his followers. However, in order to make the campus pragmatic—as well as symbolic—he also planned the Lyceum, a multipurpose building that housed classrooms and laboratories, located north of the Rotunda. Flanking the Lyceum on the east and west sides, Nichols designed four three-story professors' residences. He proposed four medium-sized, three-story

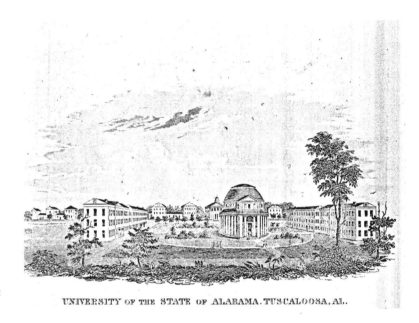

UNIVERSITY OF THE STATE OF ALABAMA. TUSCALOOSA, AL.

Figure 121. Lithograph per-
spective of the University of
Alabama campus before 1865.
(North Carolina Collection,
University of North Carolina at
Chapel Hill Library)

rectangular simple brick dormitories with low-pitched gables, each
accommodating forty-eight students in four-man suites (figure 121).

Nichols laid out the campus at the University of Alabama in the
shape of the Greek lowercase letter π (figure 122), which is similar to
the "U" shape layout of Jefferson's University of Virginia (figure 123).
Nichols designed a campus composed of eleven buildings on a line
north and parallel of the major thoroughfare to town, the Huntsville
Road, which was later renamed University Avenue. An academic
building and the dining hall were placed in this parallel line. The two
rows of dormitories projected southward and were given names of the
founding fathers, Washington and Jefferson, Madison and Franklin.
Washington Hall and Jefferson Hall were built during the first campus
building phase of 1830–1832. Nichols designed and built Franklin Hall
in 1832 and was paid by the board of trustees three hundred dollars for
his services. (Madison Hall was later built in 1854, a year after Nichols
died, but it was based on his design.) He then proposed two steward's
halls or dining halls flanking the dormitories, but only one, located on
the western end of the campus, was ever built.[49] This "hotel" or dining hall, now called the Gorgas House for its most famous resident,
Confederate General Josiah Gorgas,[50] is the only surviving Nichols-
designed building on the campus.

It appears that the Lyceum was the main academic building and
the Rotunda (figures 124 and 125) was designed for the library and cer-
emonies such as dances and commencement exercises. The Alabama
campus was the opposite of Jefferson's colonnade student rooms,
which were punctuated by large "pavilion" faculty residences. Instead,

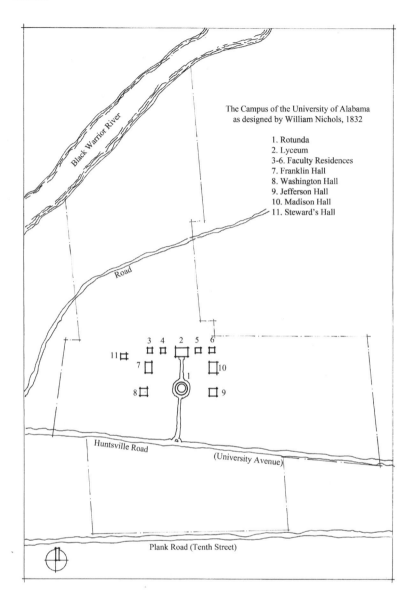

The Campus of the University of Alabama
as designed by William Nichols, 1832

1. Rotunda
2. Lyceum
3-6. Faculty Residences
7. Franklin Hall
8. Washington Hall
9. Jefferson Hall
10. Madison Hall
11. Steward's Hall

Figure 122. Site plan of the University of Alabama, Tusca-loosa, AL. Map is based on the University of Alabama Board of Trustees' minutes of March 24, 1828, and the University Survey by Basil Manley et al., 1852. (Drawing by author)

at the University of Alabama, Nichols made the dormitories the primary buildings and the faculty residences the smaller, secondary buildings. Nichols placed in the center of the entire campus ensemble the Rotunda. The dormitory buildings looked remarkably similar to the reworked Old East and Old West that Nichols designed and built in Chapel Hill only five years earlier. The six simple buildings defined a tightly formed quadrangle, similar to the grounds and buildings found at the University of Virginia.[51] The main campus buildings were masonry in construction, built out of the same brick as the capitol with sandstone foundations that was quarried from the nearby Black

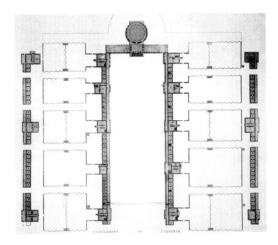

Warrior River. The brick was fired on site, and all of the lumber was cut from the university's own timber tract. The total construction cost to build the University of Alabama campus in 1831 was fifty-six thousand dollars.[52]

A reporter from the *Southern Advocate* submitted a detailed description of how the campus appeared before students entered the new university in April of 1831. The reporter first describes the southern section of the campus from the Huntsville Road, noting the fruit trees in the experimental farm. He writes that the ensemble of university buildings sat

Figure 123. Site plan for the University of Virginia by Peter Maverick (1780–1831), 1825, based on a drawing by John Neilson (d. 1827). (Courtesy of the University of Virginia Library)

Figure 124. The rotunda at the University of Alabama. This is the only known photograph of the rotunda taken prior to 1865 when Croxton's Raiders burned most of the University of Alabama campus. (North Carolina Collection, University of North Carolina at Chapel Hill Library)

Figure 125. Archaeological excavations of the ruins of the rotunda at the University of Alabama, Tuscaloosa, AL, in 1984. (Courtesy of the W. S. Hoole Library, Special Collections Library, University of Alabama)

on high ground overlooking the Black Warrior River and appeared "well enclosed." Referring to the campus as "University Square," the first building he describes is the Lyceum, a two-story building with a hexastyle colossal Ionic portico and approached by "a handsome flight of steps." He notes that the Lyceum was forty-five feet wide and seventy-five feet deep. The interior consisted of six apartments, a theater for chemistry lectures, two smaller rooms on the first floor, with three "splendid" rooms, one of them measuring forty-five feet by thirty feet, on the second floor. Two monumental staircases flanked its entrance lobby.[53]

Just as at the University of Virginia, the focal point of the University of Alabama was the Rotunda, which housed the library. At Jefferson's Lawn at Virginia, the Rotunda is the focal point at the northeast end of the campus; at Alabama, Nichols placed it in the middle of the campus, another example of how he developed an idea at one place and adapted, evolved, and refined it at another. At the University of North Carolina, Nichols saw a need to give the north quadrangle (later to be called McCorkle Place) an object, a focal point to look upon, the Belfry. The Belfry at North Carolina was much smaller than the Rotunda he designed and built at Alabama, but the placement of both objects accomplished two of his objectives as an architect: 1) both buildings establish the architectural hierarchy for the entire campus, and 2) both buildings provided a focal point in the college yard.

Contrary to Jefferson, who wished for viewers to look out northeastward to his temple of knowledge (the Rotunda) and southwestward to opportunity and destiny (the Blue Ridge Mountains), Nichols designed a complex that looked inward and on itself with one main object—his Rotunda. It is clear that Nichols did not wish to copy Jefferson's Rotunda design; he most likely recognized the shortcomings in the design of a circular building that Jefferson could not. Nichols understood that every building, even circular ones, required a front façade and a rear façade, whereas Jefferson struggled with giving the Rotunda a rear façade. Nichols's solution was both direct and simple, and it respected the purity of the round form in both its exterior form and interior layout. Jefferson had designed rooms that were awkward. His successors, architects Robert Mills and later Stanford White, and then in the last half of the twentieth century, architectural historian Fredrick Nichols (no known relation to William Nichols)[54] struggled with the problem of giving Jefferson's Rotunda a front face and a back face. William Nichols's Alabama rotunda was designed with a colossal Ionic portico on its south side and a smaller Ionic colonnade surrounding the entire building, giving this freestanding object building, the Rotunda, many faces and many ways to enter and encounter it.

Interestingly, Peatross believes that Nichols's inspiration was not Jefferson's Rotunda but Henry Holland's Marine Pavilion in Brighton, England. Holland's pavilion is more reminiscent of Bramante's Tempietto, which is smaller than the Alabama rotunda, but since we do not have any documentation from Nichols explaining his intentions (as was the case with the North Carolina State House), this is only speculation. The brick round walls and simple masonry openings with double-hung windows were definitely based on the ideas of Jefferson. The wood framed dome, built using the same French principles of de l'Orme, also inspired comparison to Jefferson, but the plan was quite different. Nichols understood the difficulties of dividing a circle into rooms and chose not to do it; instead, he made the lower level of the building as open as possible for the commencement ball function of the building, and he designed the upper level like Jefferson's with a peristyle of columns, in this case Ionic. The dome had an oculus but it appears to have been flatter than the one found at the Rotunda at the University of Virginia.

The result was one of the most beautiful rooms in the South. It most certainly was something to admire in 1831 in Tuscaloosa, Alabama, and, based on all descriptions, had the Nichols touch in detailing, delicate moldings, and precisely proportioned Grecian columns following English standards of classical detailing. By written accounts from people who experienced Nichols's Alabama campus, it was a resounding success. Many people noted its elegance of both architecture and planning. The *Southern Advocate* proudly stated that "it not only adorned the institution, but also added honor to its architecture, and to the artisans employed in its construction."[55]

Another account of the campus was from Juliet Coleman, a young woman who traveled from Connecticut to the South and journeyed to Tuscaloosa on the Huntsville Road. After days of finding no real settlements and only a scattering of cabins and small dwellings of early Alabamians, she was struck by its beauty and noble presence. "The University of Alabama is as beautiful as any I have ever seen for a college or even any other buildings except for the public buildings at Washington. One of them [the Rotunda] is perfectly round . . ." But then Miss Coleman points out a glaring design flaw in Nichols's Rotunda: "The inside of it is a whispering gallery, which echoes 60 times very loud."[56]

The library may have been artistically pleasing but unfortunately it was an acoustical calamity. While a normal tone of voice was barely audible at close distances within the main reading room, one could hear a whisper anywhere in the library.[57] Students used to drop books on the floor as a joke just to hear a thunderous clamor reverberate

Figure 126. Gorgas House (Steward's Hall), the University of Alabama, Tuscaloosa, AL. Originally built as a hotel in the Jefferson tradition, it is one of only four buildings that survived the burning of the University of Alabama on April 3, 1865, by Croxton's Raiders. (Historic American Buildings Survey, Library of Congress, Washington, DC)

Figure 127. Gorgas House, the University of Alabama, first floor (dining room). (Historic American Buildings Survey, Library of Congress, Washington, DC)

throughout the large, circular, domed reading room. One librarian recalled just how poor the acoustics were:

> A striking characteristic of that room was the immense reverberation of sound, produced by ordinary conversation, or by walking on the floor. The least harshness in the voice of a person speaking reverberated, that could not be heard at the distance of three feet by another person. If a person would stamp his foot upon the floor, the sound produced was like thunder in loudness, and its reverberations would continue with lessening loudness, and finally die after a minute or longer.[58]

Figure 128. Gorgas House elevations, the University of Alabama, Tuscaloosa, AL. (Historic American Buildings Survey, Library of Congress, Washington, DC)

Obviously, Nichols was not aware of the science of acoustics in buildings; however, his work was both well planned and well built.[59] The *Southern Advocate* concluded its review of Nichols's work stating the following: "The simplicity, the justness, and the science of the plans are an unhesitating tribute of admiration for the efforts of taste and genius, which had executed them."[60]

Despite Nichols's remarkable architectural achievement with the University of Alabama, it did not survive the Civil War. Brigadier General John T. Croxton and his raiders torched it days before Appomattox in 1865. Gorgas House, the dining hall, was the only Nichols design spared by the Yankees. It is a simple rectangle building with a hipped roof and a simple small Ionic portico, flanked by two graceful winding stairs with cast-iron newels and railings. When Nichols originally built it, Gorgas House was functionally similar to the hotels at the University of Virginia (figures 126 and 127).

It had large dining halls on both its ground floor and main floors. To make it inhabitable for a faculty member and his family in 1840, the large dining room was divided into a parlor, three bedrooms, and

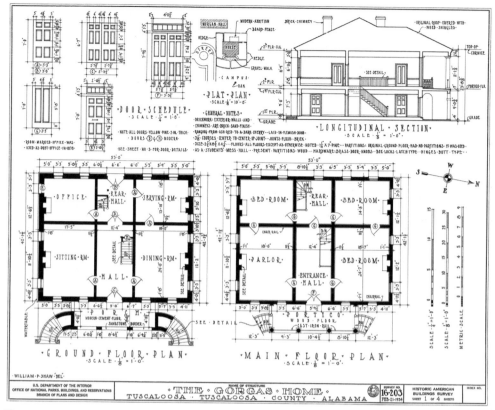

Figure 129. Gorgas House floor plans, University of Alabama, Tuscaloosa, AL. (Historic American Buildings Survey, Library of Congress, Washington, DC)

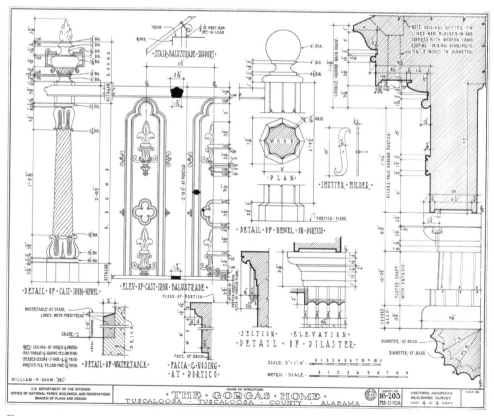

Figure 130. Exterior details of the Gorgas House, the University of Alabama, Tuscaloosa, AL. (Historic American Buildings Survey, Library of Congress, Washington, DC)

an entrance/stair hall.[61] (The striking difference between the Gorgas House and its counterparts at Virginia is the fact that the main floor is set on a *piano nobile* and is, in reality, the second floor.) Nichols designed the main floor to take advantage of the breezes that would roll down the hot farmlands of Alabama. The ceilings were set high, and large double-hung windows were liberally placed on all four sides of the building. Nichols had learned long ago that he needed to provide passive cooling through the architectural design in the hot, humid summers of the South. After all, upholding an architectural theory or ideal was one thing, but being comfortable in the summer was more important to the occupants (figure 128).

Prior to the residential alterations, the first, or ground, floor was originally designed to be one open space for a student and faculty dining hall; the second floor was designed as a residence for the steward, or dining hall master. The lower level was partitioned to form a living parlor, entrance hall, and dining room in order for the house to become a larger residence in 1841.[62] The style of the Gorgas House has been called "Low Country Raised Cottage"; however, the building does not embody any of the characteristics, specifically the lack of wood, which were commonly used in building cottages. With its original first-floor open plan and its eighteen-inch Flemish bond brick walls, the house has a nonresidential presence, making it clearly part of the lost institutional ensemble that was the original Nichols campus of the University of Alabama (figures 129 and 130).

Nichols accomplished a great amount of work in a relatively short period of time at the University of Alabama; it was a remarkable achievement. In its day, it must have been a breathtaking ensemble of buildings to view from the Huntsville Road. The campus stood complete and removed from the rest of the town, and the landscaped fields and the arbors of trees in and around the campus gave it a very impressive, if not noble, appearance along the Black Warrior River. In the last decades of the nineteenth century, the University of Alabama would be rebuilt on the original site but not in the same form as Nichols's design. His unified, harmonious, and innovative campus design was lost.

Residential Work in Alabama

Before Nichols arrived in Alabama in 1827, refined houses for the wealthy were similar in architectural composition to the earlier great houses built in Virginia and North Carolina during the first two decades of the nineteenth century. These houses, such as Belle Mont, built primarily along the Tennessee-Alabama state line, are simple in form, and more modestly articulated through the handling of specific

Figure 131. Christ Episcopal Church, Tuscaloosa, AL, ca. 1830. The only known building Nichols designed with a portico that was recessed between pilasters known as "inmuris." (Historic American Buildings Survey, Library of Congress, Washington, DC)

Figure 132. Side view of Christ Episcopal Church, Tuscaloosa, AL. This view shows the church's cupola; Nichols designed similar churches for the Methodists and Presbyterians in Jackson, Mississippi, a decade later. (Historic American Buildings Survey, Library of Congress, Washington, DC)

details, such as wire-fine reeding on casings and transoms, and delicate mantlepieces. Men who had only recently emigrated from the mid-Atlantic states of Virginia, the Carolinas, and Georgia built them with a secondhand understanding of Jefferson's architectural principles.[63] William Nichols would change this.

While working on the Alabama State Capitol and the University of Alabama, Nichols continued an active residential practice in west central and northwest Alabama, the portion of the state still considered the rapidly developing frontier. He designed the Episcopal Church in Tuscaloosa (figures 131 and 132) and four large houses for the Alabama gentry. He obtained these commissions primarily through business relationships he developed with prominent Alabamians and from his personal relationships with newly transplanted North Carolinians.[64] Sadly, almost all of Nichols's residential and ecclesiastical work in Alabama is long gone, either burned during the Civil War, altered beyond recognition (as is the case with Christ Episcopal Church in Tuscaloosa), or razed in the early decades of the twentieth century.[65]

Unfortunately, there is no documentation that links Nichols to any of these homes or others that have been lost to time; his association with them is based on local tradition, conjecture, and speculation. With all of the work he was involved in Tuscaloosa, it is not probable that he was actively involved in all of the buildings that were attributed to him during his seven-year stay in Alabama. Even so, certain buildings constructed during his Alabama tenure of 1827 to 1835 have (or had) striking similarities, both in detail and proportion, to buildings that have been credited to Nichols in either North Carolina or Alabama. There are two obvious and probable reasons for this: Nichols may have sent sketches to clients who had hired him to design a specific feature for their residence, or, as what happened in North Carolina, artisans and tradesmen in Alabama copied his designs for their clients. In order to identify these constructions as Nichols designs, three factors were triangulated: 1) Is it the architecture of William Nichols? 2) Did the owners of these homes know William Nichols? 3) Was Nichols in Alabama when the house was built? If all three of these questions can be answered in the affirmative, then it is considered a Nichols design. This is the same approach we used in determining Nichols's work in North Carolina (see chapter 1).

The only ecclesiastical design that Nichols did in Alabama was Christ Episcopal Church in Tuscaloosa. Nichols definitely knew the founding members of the vestry, men who were either on the building commission for the Alabama State Capitol or the University of Alabama Board of Trustees. Its architecture, cubic in form, is English Soane-influenced Roman Classical Revival, just as Nichols used in many buildings in North Carolina, including Gerrard Hall, the Governor's Palace, Ingleside, and his newly built Alabama capitol and university buildings. Neither a picture nor description of the interior exists, so no comparisons can be drawn. Nichols was definitely in Tuscaloosa, having just finished the University of Alabama. Christ Episcopal Church is an extremely significant piece of Nichols architecture, since it is the only known building in which he designed the front façade recessed into the massing of the building with columns between pilasters. This is an architectural composition known as "inmuris" (Latin, "set into wall"). In between Nichols's freestanding columns, there was a niche within a solid wall. Since its radical remodeling from Greek Revival to Gothic Revival in 1882, this façade was destroyed. Several alterations and expansions to this church have left it bearing no similarity to the Nichols design.

One of the most brilliant examples of Nichols's residential architecture is the Forks of Cypress, the grand home of James Jackson in Lauderdale County (figure 133). The Forks of Cypress was originally built in 1820, seven years before Nichols arrived in Alabama. James Jackson (1782–1840), a prominent state senator, knew Nichols and his architecture, specifically the Alabama State Capitol, which was completed when Jackson became president of the Alabama State Senate in 1830.[66] In that same year, he hired Nichols to remodel his northern Alabama home in order to follow the current tastes of the time.[67] Nichols designed what originally had been a Virginia-influenced Federal style double-pile residence into a Greek temple–inspired redesigned

Figure 133. The Forks of Cypress, Lauderdale County, AL, 1830. The house burned in 1966 and the Alabama Historical Commission stabilized its ruins. (Frances Benjamin Johnston Collection, Library of Congress, Washington, DC)

Figure 134. Ionic columns, the Forks of Cypress. (Historic American Buildings Survey, Library of Congress, Washington, DC)

manor house. The colossal Ionic portico was based on the Temple of Illissus and the proportion of the entablature and the columns directly correspond to the Stuart and Revett plates that Nichols possessed (figure 134).[68]

It is also interesting to note the craftsmanship and detail of the columns themselves. The Ionic columns at the Forks of Cypress were very similar, nearly identical, to the Ionic columns at Nichols's Gerrard Hall at the University of North Carolina and Eagle Lodge in Hillsborough, North Carolina. The columns themselves suggest the hand of Nichols's colleague John Robb, who had followed Nichols to Alabama.[69] Nichols's remodeling design transformed the Forks of Cypress into one of the earliest Greek Revival temple houses in the United States.[70] Like so

Figure 135. Stair hall, the Forks of Cypress. (Historic American Buildings Survey, Library of Congress, Washington, DC)

Figure 136. The Forks of Cypress, main parlor mantle. (Historic American Buildings Survey, Library of Congress, DC)

Figure 137. The Forks of Cypress, second-floor mantle. (Historic American Buildings Survey, Library of Congress, DC)

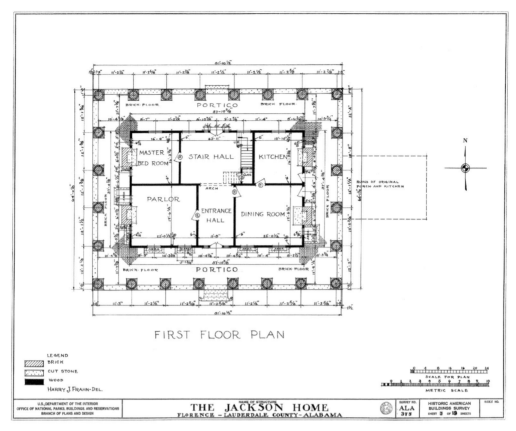

Figure 138. The Forks of Cypress, first-floor plan.(Historic American Buildings Survey, Library of Congress, Washington, DC)

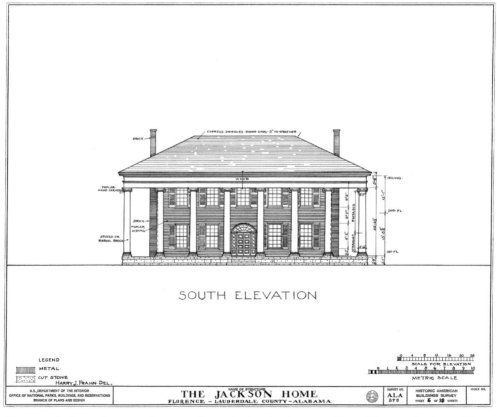

Figure 139. The Forks of Cypress, south elevation. (Historic American Buildings Survey, Library of Congress, Washington, DC)

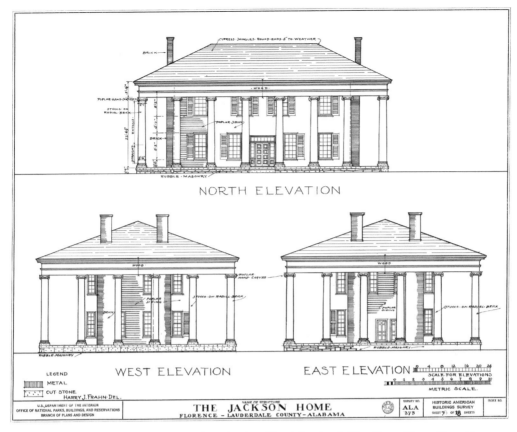

Figure 140. The Forks of Cypress, north, west, and east elevations. (Historic American Buildings Survey, Library of Congress, Washington, DC)

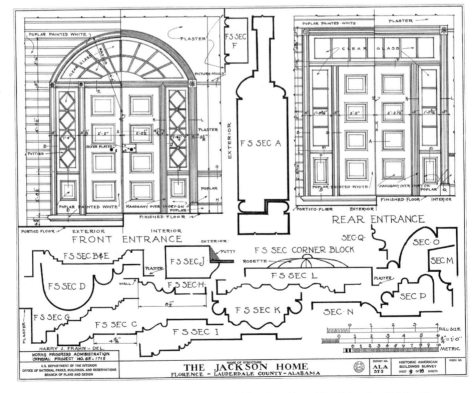

Figure 141. The Forks of Cypress, details of entryways and full-scale moldings. (Historic American Buildings Survey, Library of Congress, Washington, DC)

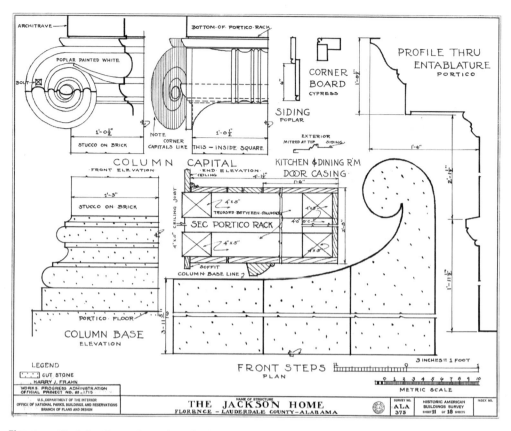

Figure 142. The Forks of Cypress, Ionic column details. (Historic American Buildings Survey, Library of Congress, Washington, DC)

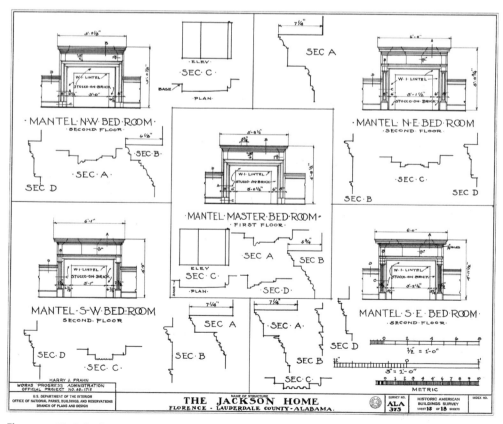

Figure 143. The Forks of Cypress, mantle details. (Historic American Buildings Survey, Library of Congress, Washington, DC)

much of Nichols's work, the Forks of Cypress burned in 1966. The Alabama Historical Commission now preserves it as a ruin. Fortunately, the Historic American Buildings Survey extensively documented it in 1936 (figures 135–143).

In Greene County, located directly southwest from Tuscaloosa, Nichols obtained two large residential commissions through his association with James Innes Thornton (1800–1877). They are Thornton's mansion, Thornhill, and the neighboring mansion, Rosemount. Fortunately, these two grand residences survive, are listed on the National Register of Historic Places, and remain predominantly intact. Thornton, who was secretary of state of Alabama from 1824 until 1834, was well aware of Nichols's work, specifically the Alabama State Capitol. He hired Nichols to design his residence in 1832, and it was completed in 1833. When Thornton, at the age of thirty-three, hired Nichols, he had already built a successful reputation as both a lawyer and a planter. A native of Spotsylvania County, Virginia, he studied at what is now Washington and Lee University and then he immigrated to Huntsville, Alabama, where he studied law and became a lawyer in 1820.[71] In 1825, Thornton moved to Greene County and married Mary Ann Glover, the daughter of prominent Greene County planter Allen Glover. Even though Mary Ann died a few years into the marriage, Thornton remained in Greene County and continued to develop his plantation, composed of nearly two thousand acres of land and tended by one hundred slaves. Throughout the antebellum period, Thornton would be known as an innovative planter. He became an active promoter for using marl[72] as an early fertilizer on his cotton fields and was adamant about soil conservation. He once belittled his overseer for allowing slaves to burn cornstalks in the fields, stating that he had emigrated from Virginia because of its depleted soil.[73] After he married Amelia Smith of Virginia in 1831, he began the planning of his manor house, which he named "Thornhill" after his ancestral home in England "Thorn-on-the-Hill." Nichols designed it that year and it was completed in 1833.[74]

Thornhill (figure 144) is similar in form, construction, and composition to the Forks of Cypress. It is a double-pile two-story wood frame structure, sheathed in clapboard. Its most prominent feature is its full width hexastyle colossal Ionic portico. Thornhill is more refined in detailing than the Forks of Cypress, a result of Thornton's affluence. In building Thornhill, Thornton hired highly skilled carpenters from Virginia to fabricate its most prominent architectural features, most notably the fluted shafts of its Ionic columns. However, it appears that Nichols had his colleague, John Robb, carve the Ionic capitals for the house. Because of their plain echinus, these capitals are very similar to the ones found at the Forks of Cypress and Gerrard Hall. Other

Figure 144. Thornhill, Greene County, AL. (Courtesy of the Greene County, Alabama, Historical Society)

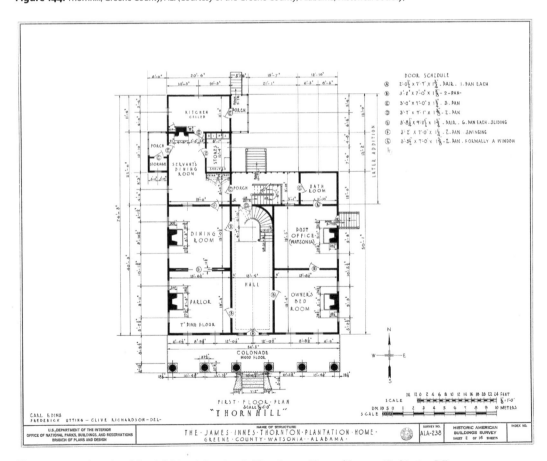

Figure 145. First-floor plan of Thornhill. (Historic American Buildings Survey, Library of Congress, Washington, DC)

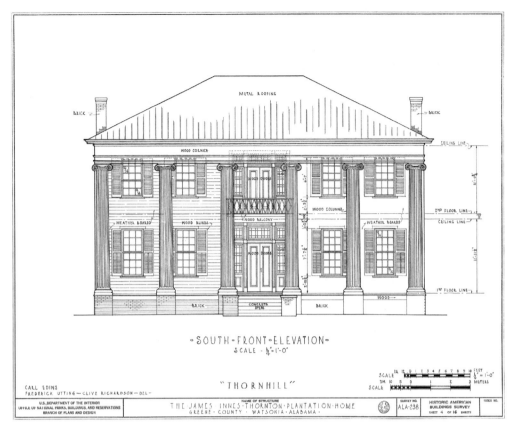

Figure 146. Thornhill, south façade. (Historic American Buildings Survey, Library of Congress, Washington, DC)

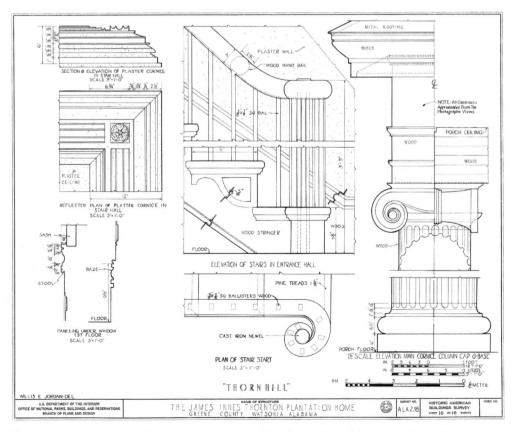

Figure 147. Thornhill, architectural details. (Historic American Buildings Survey, Library of Congress, Washington, DC)

elements that are more refined are the graceful winding staircase and the ornate front
balcony beneath the large portico ceiling.[75]
The fluted colossal Ionic columns support
the hipped roof, slightly broken at the front.
A balcony with a wheatsheaf balustrade is set
over the central main entry of the residence.
Both the main entrance and the entrance
to the balcony have elaborate sidelights and
single-panel doors.[76] Thornton spared no
expense in building Thornhill. Exotic marbles
were used in fabricating the Grecian mantles
for the fireplaces and all of the door hardware
throughout the house is silver plated brass
(figures 145–148).

Through his work on Thornhill, Nichols
received the commission to design the large
residence for Thornton's brother-in-law from
his first marriage, Williamson Allen Glover
(1804–1879).[77] Shortly after Thornton arrived
in Greene County and married Mary Allen
Glover, Williamson Allen Glover's father, Allen Glover of Demopolis,
gave him a three-thousand-acre tract of land in Greene County to start
a plantation and build a manor house. Glover named his plantation
Rosemount and hired Nichols to design the house in 1831, the same
time that Nichols was designing Thornhill. Nichols planned the original residence in 1832 (figure 149). In order to accommodate his large
family, which grew to sixteen children, Glover continued to add on to
the house, specifically at its rear. The last addition occurred in 1855.[78]

Similar to Thornhill, Rosemount is a two-story wood frame house,
cubic in massing with a medium pitched hip roof that is capped or
culminated by a large hipped roof observatory. It has a full length, full
width, hexastyle colossal Ionic portico. The portico structure, in which
the supporting columns or posts rise directly from ground level and
stand free in front of the porch deck itself, is known in Alabama as
a "Carolina Porch." [79] The center doorway is surrounded by ornate
sidelights with a transom. Above it is a balcony with a lattice balustrade. Nichols designed a highly innovative and open floor plan for
Rosemount composed of a large vestibule with flanking reception
rooms, located east and west of the vestibule. Each of the reception
rooms has fireplaces with mantles that were similar to the ones he
designed at the Mordecai House in Raleigh six years earlier. North of
the vestibule, Nichols designed a large "Great Hall," sixty feet long and
twenty feet wide. In it, he placed a simple Federal style straight run

Figure 148. Ionic columns at
Thornhill. (Historic American
Buildings Survey, Library of
Congress, Washington, DC)

Figure 149. Rosemount, the Glover-Legare House, Greene County, AL. (Historic American Buildings Survey, Library of Congress, Washington, DC)

staircase detailed in a manner similar to the stairway he designed at the Mordecai House. (Glover would later divide this room in half with one wall containing a series of large cased openings, perhaps as a way to address sagging ceilings. He made additions to Rosemount from 1835 until 1860.) Unlike at either the Forks of Cypress or Thornhill, Nichols added a large observatory to the hipped roof featuring small Doric columns on three of its four sides and a small outdoor walk around a small, enclosed room, which Glover and his family used as a music room.

The entire design of Rosemount bears a striking resemblance to Nichols's masterpiece in North Carolina, Hayes, which he designed and built fourteen years earlier[80] (figure 150). The two buildings are nearly the same size, Rosemount being slightly larger. The portico column spacing of both Hayes and Rosemount is nearly identical with the base of the Rosemount portico structured in a similar manner as Hayes. Thornhill, Rosemount, and the Forks of Cypress were three new versions of the cubic-formed large house design that Nichols originally developed at Hayes. What is interesting to note about all of these buildings is that passive cooling was definitely considered in their design, making Nichols one of the few architects who actually designed with the climate in mind. Passive cooling features are found

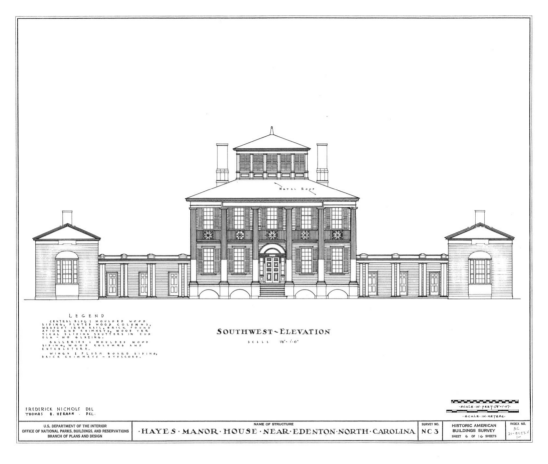

LEGEND
CENTRAL BLDG. MOULDED WOOD
SIDING, FLUTED WOOD COLUMNS,
WROUGHT IRON RAIL, BRICK FOUND-
ATION AND CHIMNEYS, WOOD VER-
TICAL SLIDING SHUTTERS IN CUP-
OLA - NO GLAZING.
GALLERIES: MOULDED WOOD
SIDING, WOOD COLUMNS AND
ENTABLATURE.
WINGS: FLUSH BOARD SIDING,
BRICK CHIMNEYS - STUCCOED.

SOUTHWEST~ELEVATION
SCALE   1/8"=1'-0"

FREDERICK NICHOLS   DEL
THOMAS B. HERMAN   DEL

| U.S. DEPARTMENT OF THE INTERIOR
OFFICE OF NATIONAL PARKS, BUILDINGS, AND RESERVATIONS
BRANCH OF PLANS AND DESIGN | NAME OF STRUCTURE
·HAYES·MANOR·HOUSE·NEAR·EDENTON·NORTH·CAROLINA· | SURVEY NO.
NC 3 | HISTORIC AMERICAN
BUILDINGS SURVEY
SHEET 6 OF 16 SHEETS | INDEX NO.
NC
21-EDET.V
1- |

in much of the vernacular architecture built in the Deep South at this time, but not necessarily in the high-styled residences designed by architects. Unlike architects such as Benjamin Henry Latrobe, Nichols understood the value found in vernacular-inspired passive cooling design features. Spatial configurations comprising open center halls and flanking parlors facilitated cross ventilation of summer breezes throughout the houses. Large, grand staircases were not necessarily designed for ceremonial purposes but rather as thermal "chimneys" that allowed heat to rise up and out through windows, observatories, or roof hatches. While Nichols would design using all of these features, the most useful were the colossal porticos or colonnades, which allowed residents to enjoy outdoor breezes while escaping the summer sun. As Robert Gamble pointed out in his survey book *Historic Architecture in Alabama,* "[T]he monumental colonnade that became so conspicuous a feature of many Alabama dwellings was more than merely an ego-satisfying way in which planter and merchant alike could proclaim their worldly success. It also answered gloriously the need for a broad and lofty 'piazza' against the summer sun," something

Figure 150. Hayes Plantation, Edenton, NC, 1818. Hayes was Nichols's first architectural composition that incorporated cubic massing, colossal columns for the portico, hipped roofs, and an observatory. He continued to explore using these architectural elements in his residential work in Tuscaloosa and Greene County. (Historic American Buildings Survey, Library of Congress, Washington, DC)

Figure 151. Rosemount, Ionic columns details of the front porch. (Historic American Buildings Survey, Library of Congress, Washington, DC)

Figure 152. Rosemount, main stair. (Historic American Buildings Survey, Library of Congress, Washington, DC)

Figure 153. Rosemount, main parlor mantle. (Historic American Buildings Survey, Library of Congress, Washington, DC)

Nichols had learned early in his career at Hayes when designing its colossal portico that faced Edenton Bay and its breezes.[81]

The observatories were built for the owners to enjoy the breezes of higher elevations; although views were also important, they were outweighed by comfort. All of these architectural features, as well as others designed in these houses, illustrate the impressive knowledge of environmental design that Nichols had developed in his work in order to make the hot, humid Alabama summers bearable. Unlike John Hawks, the architect of Tryon Palace from an earlier generation, Nichols conformed English building custom to the climate of the American South and was able to build houses that were accommodating to summer temperatures, a skill that would prove very useful in the

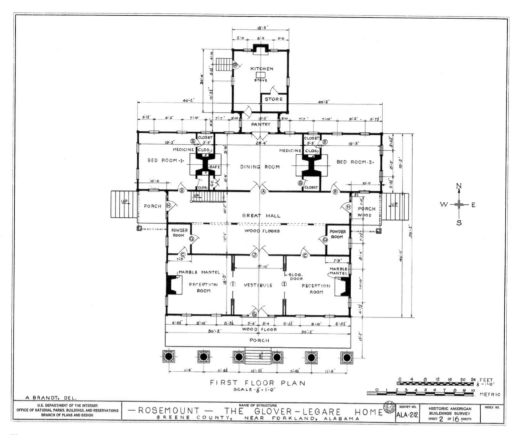

Figure 154. Rosemount, first-floor plan. (Historic American Buildings Survey, Library of Congress, Washington, DC)

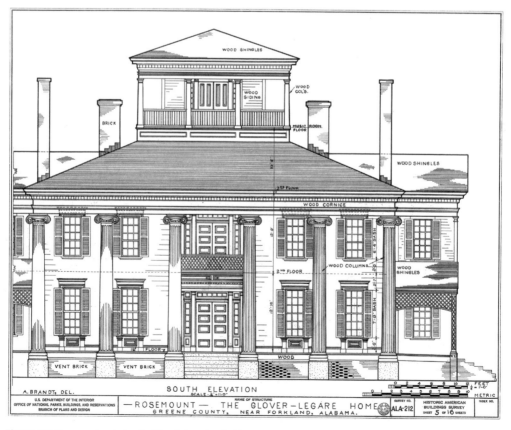

Figure 155. Rosemount, main façade. (Historic American Buildings Survey, Library of Congress, Washington, DC)

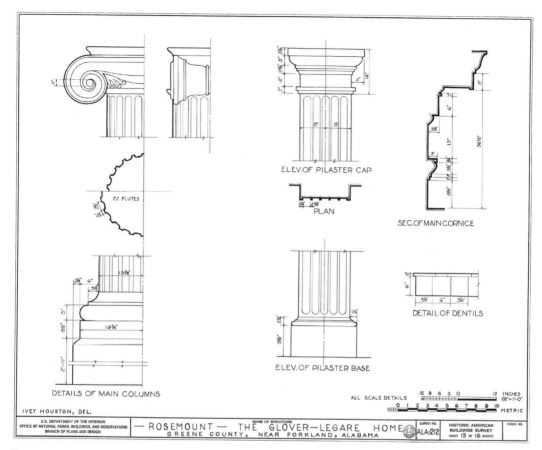

Figure 156. Rosemount, column details. (Historic American Buildings Survey, Library of Congress, Washington, DC)

Deep South. Nichols was indeed first and foremost a pragmatic architect, practical and conscious of his client's need for comfort (figures 151–156).

Before he left Tuscaloosa, Nichols designed a large house for James Hunter Dearing (1787–1861) in 1833; master builder John J. Webster built it in 1834 for fourteen thousand dollars (figure 157). Fortunately, the Dearing House is still standing. Dearing, a successful steamboat captain and Tuscaloosa merchant, held two positions that enabled him to personally know Nichols, serving as a commissioner on the Alabama Capitol Building Commission and as the director of the State Bank.[82] He was a native of North Carolina and his wife, Julia Searcy, was from a prominent Chapel Hill family. He arrived in Tuscaloosa before the town had been incorporated in 1819 and started a successful steamboat service along the Black Warrior River, first using a steamboat he had built called the *Tom Bigbie*. It is said that he made the second successful trip to Tuscaloosa along the Black Warrior River in

Figure 157. James Hunter Dearing House, Tuscaloosa, AL, 1834. (Historic American Buildings Survey, Library of Congress, Washington, DC)

1816. He built his residence on Queen City Avenue, close to Nichols's University of Alabama campus and the Alabama capitol.[83] Dearing and his family only lived in the house for two unhappy years. Rowdy students from the University of Alabama constantly harassed him and his family, stealing chickens from his hen house, trampling the family's flower gardens, and singing obscene songs throughout the nights around the home. The final insult to Dearing was when the students abducted a woman servant from the residence in 1836.[84]

Similar to Thornhill and Rosemount, the Dearing House is a two-story cubic massed residence with a low-sloped hipped roof and a full-length colossal hexastyle Ionic portico spanning its front façade (figure 158). It was the first house built with such an impressive portico in Tuscaloosa. Over the front entrance, there is a balcony with a wheat-sheaf balustrade that resembles the balcony at Thornhill (figure 159). As with Rosemount, Nichols designed a space on the roof in order for the Dearings to enjoy summer breezes. Instead of an observatory, Nichols designed a roof deck surrounded by a turned baluster balustrade. Single chimneys flanked the roof deck.

There are several features in the Dearing House that are different from either Thornhill or Rosemount. The first notable difference in the Dearing House is the overall construction of its exterior: solid brick

Figure 158. Columns, Dearing House. (Historic American Buildings Survey, Library of Congress, Washington, DC)

Figure 159. Dearing House, front entrance and balcony. (Historic American Buildings Survey, Library of Congress, Washington, DC)

masonry walls covered with stucco. The front doorway is also different. It is composed of double wooden doors with a flat fan-shaped transom, rectangular sidelights, and pilasters. On the second floor, the door leading onto the balcony has a rectangular transom and sidelights. These building moldings and details closely resembled comparable details in Nichols's residential designs in North Carolina. The plan is composed of a center hall with flanking parlors. The staircase is simple in detailing with square pickets and Grecian-inspired newel posts, similar to the stairways he designed for Hayes and the Mordecai House in North Carolina and the Forks of Cypress, Thornhill, and Rosemount. The main stairway has a large landing supported by a low archway, buttressed by Temple of Winds columns, all of which resembles the central hall at Hayes. The door casings, along with the upstairs mantles, resemble those at the Mordecai House. After passing through several owners, the Dearing House was purchased by the University of Alabama in 1944 and converted into their University Club.[85]

The Dearing House was most likely the last significant building that Nichols designed in Alabama, even though there have been several buildings erroneously attributed to him. James Hunter Dearing's brother, Alexander Dearing, also built a house that, at first glance, is very similar to both the James Hunter Dearing House and Thornhill. However, upon closer examination, it appears to have been heavily influenced, but not designed, by Nichols. The colossal Ionic columns for the hexastyle portico are not in the same proportion as the Nichols-designed portico at the James Hunter Dearing House. Moreover, the balcony does not share the same proportions as the balconies found on Thornhill, Rosemount, or the James Hunter Dearing House. Finally, Nichols was living in Jackson, Mississippi, when the house was constructed in 1836. Nevertheless, its design was clearly influenced by Nichols's work. It is entirely likely that it was designed and built by John J. Webster, the builder who built James Dearing's house two years earlier.

For several decades, it was believed that Nichols designed the President's House at the University of Alabama. As is the case with the Alexander Dearing House, the President's House shares the residential architecture features that Nichols was designing during his time in Tuscaloosa. However, university records state that Michael Barry designed it; more importantly, it was built in 1842 when Nichols was living in Jackson, Mississippi. However, with its cubic massing, low-hipped roof, and hexastyle colossal Ionic portico, it cannot be denied that Nichols's architecture had influenced this building.[86]

Peatross and Mellown have suggested that the Dr. John R. Drish House, also known as Monroe or Malone Place, in Tuscaloosa could have been designed by Nichols or that he, at the least, submitted design ideas for it. However, along with being a successful physician, Drish was also a successful building contractor who may have designed and built it himself. It was originally built in 1837, three years after Nichols had left Alabama, and altered significantly by Drish throughout the next two decades, including an addition of an Italianate tower on its north side in 1860. Once again the house's composition, one of simple cubic massing, a colossal Ionic columned portico on the north side, and curiously, a colossal Doric ordered portico on the south side, demonstrates Nichols's influence on this house and this city's architecture.[87]

The cubic and volumetric houses of the Forks of Cypress, Thornhill, Rosemount, and the Dearing House help to make the argument that Nichols was slowly evolving a type of dwelling that not only responded to the grand aspirations of its owners but also to the environmental factors of the region, such as the use of innovative architectural features that maximized ventilation, all of which incorporated vernacular design ideas already established in Alabama. These designs included large porticos, halls, and roof features conducive for stack ventilation, and aligning large windows and doors in order to maximize cross ventilation. Nichols's career was not one of invention or revolution, but rather evolution. He chose to change his design ideas gradually, responding to the needs and wants of his clients. Although choices of ornament and materials, most notably the use of stone from quarries near the Black Warrior River, show how Nichols stubbornly clung to the ancient English practices of his roots in the use of building materials, his plans and overall forms illustrate his willingness to adapt to the Deep South climate around him. He learned early on in the swamps and marshes along the sounds of coastal North Carolina that certain features in architectural design respond well to the climate and can provide comfort.

Alabama Legacy

Although Nichols's use of classical order and design became more and more sophisticated over time, it nevertheless remained solidly English during his Alabama years. Up to this point, Nichols had never designed anything using the Corinthian order; this was most probably because he never had the skilled labor to do so. The Corinthian order was not a simple one to fabricate (Jefferson's attempt to have domestic labor carve Corinthian columns was calamitous). Even John Robb, who carved capitals for his buildings in North Carolina and Alabama, was limited in his ability. The Ionic columns produced by Robb are vernacular in overall form and never included any egg and dart detailing in the echinus of the capital.[88]

Having designed and built the state capitol, the University of Alabama campus, Christ Episcopal Church, and four grand residences, Nichols had indisputably left a profound mark on the architecture of Tuscaloosa. He trained numerous craftsmen, builders, and prominent residents of Tuscaloosa about English-inspired Grecian designs. His influence on the city's image would continue for nearly twenty years after he left, as builders and architects would continue to emulate his architecture. The impact that he made on Tuscaloosa and western Alabama cannot be overstated. It is indeed a tragedy that so much of his work, along with the works of architecture he influenced, has been lost in Tuscaloosa.

In surveying Nichols's work in Alabama, historian John Ray Skates stated it best:

> The area was an architectural blank slate. No state buildings had been put up; the University of Alabama, to be located in Tuscaloosa, had to be planned and built; rich Black Belt planters in the surrounding countryside had, as yet, no fine houses.[89]

Nichols helped change that. After his seven-year tenure in Tuscaloosa and neighboring Greene County, the land switched from being architecturally "blank" to architecturally distinctive.

This short period of practice in Alabama was a very prolific period in his career; while building the University of Alabama and Christ Episcopal Church, Nichols also accepted the position of state engineer of Alabama in 1831 and was surveying for a new canal near Muscle Shoals in the northern portion of the state.[90] But, by the later part of 1832, the state's building projects were completed and Nichols was released of his duties by the Alabama Legislature. His career seems to have stalled around 1833, when he relocated to Montgomery, the city that would eventually become the state capital in 1846.[91] There is no indication Nichols completed any architectural work during his year-long stay.

His capitol building in Tuscaloosa would only serve as the seat of state government for ten years. In 1841, the Alabama legislature vacated the Tuscaloosa capitol and gave it to the University of Alabama, who would struggle to maintain the large building with its meager appropriations from the legislature. In 1845, the Board of Trustees of the University of Alabama signed a ninety-nine-year lease to a syndicate dominated by the Alabama Baptist Convention that established Alabama Central Female College in the old capitol building. Although it was not officially affiliated with the Baptist Church, it was locally known as "the Baptist college."[92]

In 1861, the old capitol building nearly became the capitol of the Confederate States of America. After the inauguration of Jefferson Davis, the Provisional Government of the Confederacy considered several cities for its capital. The city fathers of Tuscaloosa proposed making the old Alabama capitol the capitol building for the Confederacy. Tuscaloosa was considered for its centralized location by the Confederate congress, as it was halfway between the easternmost city in the Confederacy, Charleston, South Carolina, and the westernmost city, Austin, Texas; however, the political and economic influence of Virginia compelled the Confederate congress to select Richmond as the capital city over Tuscaloosa. The old capitol was one of the few buildings that survived the Civil War in Tuscaloosa. Shortly before the Civil War, there were several ideas explored for reusing the building, including moving the University of Alabama there. Even though it had survived the Civil War, it tragically burned while undergoing a long-awaited renovation in 1923.[93]

When Nichols came to Alabama in 1827, he was seeking fortune with his fellow North Carolinians, but by 1833, William Nichols was looking simply for employment. He asked for and received a recommendation from his good friend, Governor John Gayle of Alabama, for the position of state architect of Mississippi to design the proposed new state capitol building in Jackson. On October 12, 1833, he personally wrote Mississippi Governor Charles Lynch, stating his credentials and why he should be selected to design the proposed state capitol of Mississippi:

> . . . from the circumstance of having had more experience in the construction of State Capitols than any other individual in the Union—and from being well versed in the various prices and modes in the Southern Country . . . I could bring with me a fund of information which would result in producing an Edifice not surpassed for Elegance, Convenience, Stability, and Economy of Expenditure by any building of similar Character of the Union.[94]

Despite his strong statement of qualifications, Governor Lynch and the Mississippi legislature overlooked Nichols for John Lawrence who was appointed state architect of Mississippi in 1833.

Nichols also had mismanaged key opportunities to solicit work out of Alabama. It is important to note that, by all accounts, Nichols did not leave Alabama once during his seven-year tenure there. Instead he sent his son, William, Jr., to supervise the building of a new North Carolina capitol with disastrous results. It is documented that, during his time in North Carolina, he traveled to New York, Philadelphia, and Washington, D.C., in order to procure materials or architectural components for his clients' buildings such as mantles or stone steps. These were important trips, enabling him to see new and emerging currents in American architecture and to adapt his ideas and style in order to sustain his creative work.[95] But there is no documentation suggesting that he made similar trips to northern cities for his clients during his seven years in Alabama.

Desperate for a job, Nichols, now fifty-four, accepted an offer to become assistant state engineer of Louisiana in 1834, a position beneath his expertise. Going to New Orleans was exactly what he needed to rekindle his creative talent and jumpstart his career. There, Nichols experienced a different aspect of the development of the United States during the antebellum era—the industrialization of America. At this time, New Orleans was rapidly becoming one of the most productive port cities in the United States. Like most port cities, it would become a conduit of the southern region for new ideas in art and culture as well as politics and the economy. His stay in New Orleans was short, lasting only two years, but it would be the most informative and educational experience of his life.

Chapter Six

LOUISIANA

William Nichols and his wife, Sarah, moved from Montgomery, Alabama, to New Orleans, Louisiana, in December 1833 when he accepted the position of assistant state engineer for the state of Louisiana. For the first time in his career, William Nichols was not moving to a place where he had a potential client base to support his private practice. The architect/builder, who had designed two capitol buildings, two university campuses, five churches, two courthouses, a waterworks, and numerous impressive homes in North Carolina and Alabama, was now merely a civil servant of the state of Louisiana.

There were no opportunities for Nichols to design grand homes or buildings here; even so, it was a beneficial period in his career as an architect. Little is known about his work in Louisiana since the few buildings he designed no longer exist. However, Nichols emerged from this period in New Orleans—a booming, burgeoning, cosmopolitan city—a more imaginative and innovative architect; his work in the last period of his life would be fresher and more distinctive than anything he had designed or built since Hayes Plantation. Interestingly, for the first time since he was a young man in Bath, William Nichols was able to experience an urban and sophisticated city. Up to this point in his career, he had lived in the sparsely populated coastal areas of North Carolina. Raleigh and Fayetteville had only been somewhat larger than New Bern and Edenton. Tuscaloosa was a frontier town of the "old Southwest" and the Montgomery he left was barely an outpost on the Alabama River. All the places Nichols had lived and worked before New Orleans lacked sufficient transportation connecting them to the outside world, limiting communication as well. Nichols had been isolated from current architectural ideas and theory; years of this isolation had caused his work to grow stale, especially in regard to its ornamentation. His time in New Orleans, however, rejuvenated his creative talents and his career.

As a young man learning his profession, Nichols, like most architects, relied heavily on precedents found in pattern books and architectural folios, specifically the English ones from the late eighteenth and early nineteenth centuries. Armed with Stuart and Revett's *Antiquities of Athens*, William Pain's carpentry assistance books, a firsthand knowledge of the architecture of John Wood the Elder and John Wood the Younger in Bath, and perhaps other English books on architectural design, he could present himself as a fashionable architect in 1800. Seventeen or eighteen years later, he would greatly benefit from traveling to Baltimore and New York. But from 1819, the time he arrived in Fayetteville, to 1827 when he left Alabama, it can only be verified that he traveled to New York once to purchase furnishing and fixtures for the North Carolina State House in 1824.[1] Now, he was living in New Orleans, a port city that was quickly becoming one of the most important urban centers in the South, if not in the entire nation. Nichols was finally experiencing the visual dialogue of architecture firsthand.

During the third decade of the nineteenth century, the Greek-inspired classical architecture that Nichols learned from Bath and designed in North Carolina and Alabama was now evolving into something more—the Greek Revival. Made popular by the pattern books of Asher Benjamin and Minard Lafever, the Greek Revival was bolder and more decorative than the Soane-influenced Grecian architecture. The third decade of the nineteenth century would also be the first time industry would play a part in architecture. Architectural elements such as columns, entablatures, doors, and windows were now beginning to be fabricated and shipped throughout the world. The rapid industrialization of the North was another aspect of the Jacksonian Age, and the availability of fabricated elements from industrialized American cities would influence the architecture of the antebellum South and Nichols's work for the last two decades of his life.

From a business and practical standpoint, Nichols needed a new look and new ideas for his architectural work; his private practice had ended, temporarily, and he was lacking money to support both himself and his wife, Sarah. In 1834, he sold parcels of land back in Wake County, North Carolina, to his son Samuel.[2] He also sold a tract of his Wake County land to a family member of his wife, Mary Simons, in June of 1835.[3] He reduced the size of his architecture and building business and was no longer accepting young men and boys as apprentices as he had done in North Carolina and when he first arrived in Tuscaloosa.[4]

New Orleans was a good place for Nichols to restart his career as an architect. He is credited with working on two large projects: the state penitentiary in Baton Rouge and the remodeling of the old Charity Hospital into the new Louisiana State House.[5] Although his official title was assistant state engineer, he essentially undertook architectural projects for the state of Louisiana. What was initially a discouraging setback in employment would actually become the rejuvenation of his career and his creativity.

What is important to consider about his brief tenure in New Orleans is not the work he did but what he learned. His time in New Orleans can be best described as a creative, but necessary, sabbatical from his previous work. During this time, he would learn and embrace new ideas in architecture and the decorative arts; he would also learn about ideas being developed in New York, specifically the writings and designs of New Yorker Minard Lafever. Finally, he would learn firsthand the new architecture from Lafever's colleague, James H. Dakin. It was Dakin, his brother Charles Dakin, and his partner James Gallier who transformed New Orleans, beginning with their masterpiece, the Merchants' Exchange. Nichols studied and emulated Dakin's and Gallier's work and incorporated their most innovative ideas into his own work in Mississippi three years later.

The 1830s was a golden decade in the history of New Orleans. At the time, it was considered the unofficial capital of the West; its port rivaled New York in size and business activity. Information and ideas flowed freely in this port city, and highly skilled artisans and craftsmen flocked there to benefit from the construction boom. Of all the craftsmen and architects who came to New Orleans, none was more important or talented than James Dakin. Nichols never worked directly with or for Dakin, but he took part in the same business circles as Dakin and Gallier. Reviewing the work of the Dakin brothers and Gallier is important in evaluating Nichols's architecture after his time in Louisiana. It was this work that influenced Nichols in the last stage of his career. Through his New Orleans experience, Nichols would stop designing in the neoclassical tradition of Soane, Adam, and Pain and become proficient working in the new Greek Revival style of Lafever and Dakin, a younger generation of men who were eighteen and twenty-six years younger, respectively, than Nichols.

Nichols's firsthand encounter with Dakin's work was brief. James Dakin (1806–1852) came to New Orleans in November of 1835 and Nichols would leave for Mississippi in early 1836. It is safe to assume that the two men had only a passing and professional acquaintance. According to Dakin's biographer, Arthur Scully, Dakin's beginnings were similar to Nichols's. They had both experienced an apprenticeship in carpentry, but unlike Nichols, Dakin would complete an important apprenticeship in an architecture firm. He was born near New York City in 1806 and apprenticed for a carpenter relative, Herman Stoddard. In 1829, Dakin became a draftsman and apprentice to Alexander Jackson Davis (1803–1892) in the firm of Town and Davis. Town and Davis quickly became the preeminent architectural firm in the country and a major rival to Nichols in North Carolina. Davis, only three years older than Dakin, was the young new star of what was then the emerging architecture profession. Originally trained as an illustrator and a delineator, Davis's artistic statement was one of building composition, not necessarily of building construction.[6] Dakin, however, was a builder/architect similar to Nichols.

Town and Davis would become a firm known throughout the country as one of innovation and invention. They were one of the architectural leaders in transforming the Adamesque or Pain idiom of the early Greek Revival into something more contemporary for the times. In their buildings one finds what Davis called "pilastrades," a colonnaded wall made out of pilasters, rather than just colonnades, so that more natural light could enter the Greek temple buildings. This new architectural element led to another creation, the elongated window, a design akin to a curtained wall. Davis called it the "Davisean window." These innovations in architectural design made the work of Town and Davis very distinctive. In 1836, Davis joined William Strickland and Thomas U. Walter in establishing the American Institution of Architects, the precursor of the American Institute of Architects.[7]

Dakin greatly benefited from his experience apprenticing under Davis and became a capable and competent architect, combining his carpentry experience with the knowledge he gained from Davis. While working for Town and Davis, Dakin designed an elaborate mansion in Brooklyn for J. W. Perry in 1832, a design that made him full partner in the Town and Davis firm. Along with David Paton (1801–1882), Dakin most likely worked on the North Carolina State Capitol after the commission was taken away from Nichols by the North Carolina General Assembly.[8] By 1835, Scully notes, Dakin had a larger interest in the firm than either Town or Davis.[9] Dakin was quickly rising to the level of Davis's talent, but it was Davis who had the "star" power and commanded the largest amount of credit and respect in the partnership. By 1833, Dakin left the partnership and struck out on his own in New York. His largest built commission was the Doric temple design of the First Presbyterian Church in Troy, New York. This impressive building clearly reflects the Town and Davis influence on Dakin with its heavy dominant pilasters and large windows. The finest building Dakin designed while working independently in New York was the magnificent Greek Revival masterpiece, the Bank of Louisville in Louisville, Kentucky, built in 1834.[10] Perhaps feeling the need to leave

Davis's formidable shadow or perhaps to find better business opportunities, James Dakin left New York and moved to New Orleans to
join his brother, Charles, and the Irish-born Gallier to form a practice
that would dominate the Crescent City during an economic boom
fueled by trade, particularly in cotton. During this time, New Orleans
would be transformed through the work of talented craftsmen and
architects such as the Dakin brothers, Gallier, and the earlier work of
Benjamin Latrobe.[11]

Exposure to the architecture of the Dakin brothers and Gallier
would have a profound influence on Nichols and his work. While in
New Orleans, Nichols would be introduced to Minard Lafever's *The
Modern Builder's Guide*, first published in 1833, and his *Beauties of
Modern Architecture*, first published in 1835. Lafever's *Guide* was
widely acclaimed when it was first published and immediately considered the most significant guide of architecture and construction since
Stuart and Revett's *Antiquities of Athens* and Peter Nicholson's *Vitruvius Britainnicus*. Dakin contributed to the Lafever books with finely
delineated drawings of details and elements. Along with Asher Benjamin's *The Practical House Carpenter*, Lafever's work is considered the
most influential published work on architecture in America before the
Civil War.[12]

Lafever took a more personal and "modern" interpretation of
ancient Greek architecture and ornament; the plates in his books were
not archaeologically influenced so much as they were based on the possibilities for ornamentation in modern, industrial New York. His work
was fresh and inventive. Hamlin considered him the greatest decorator
in American nineteenth-century architecture.[13] But what is important
to note about Lafever and his publications is that he took Greek orders
and decorative ornamental motifs that naturally embody delicacy and
restraint (such as anthemia and rosettes) and transformed them into
an American expression of freedom and energy.

Lafever's books had a profound impact on American architecture
in the first half of the nineteenth century. Before Lafever, Davis, and
other pattern book authors such as Asher Benjamin, American architects (including Nichols) relied heavily on the precedents set by Adam,
Soane, Pain, and the guidebooks of Stuart and Revett. These works
were based on archaeology and interpreted in a distinctly English tradition. After Lafever, everything changed. Part of the reason was that
a distinctively new American generation had taken power in America and this generation was no longer tied to English culture. In 1835,
Andrew Jackson was finishing his second term in the White House and
America was rapidly urbanizing and industrializing. An urban middle
class was emerging and with them came the beginnings of consum-
erism, which Lafever was motivated to express in a new and artistic

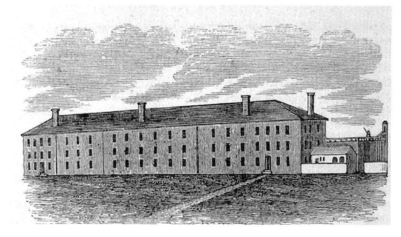

Figure 160. Etching of the Wethersfield Prison, Wethersfield, CT. The Louisiana State Penitentiary in Baton Rouge was based on this prison design. (Courtesy of the Connecticut State Library)

Figure 161. Louisiana State Penitentiary, Baton Rouge, LA, ca. 1862. Nichols supervised its construction in 1834 and 1835. (Courtesy of the Louisiana State University Libraries)

manner. Nowhere was this emerging mercantile class more prevalent than in 1830s New Orleans.

Nichols came to work in New Orleans under Benjamin Buisson, the state engineer for Louisiana in 1834.[14] His first project at his new job would be supervising the construction of the new state penitentiary in Baton Rouge,[15] which began before Nichols arrived in Louisiana. The Louisiana legislature had authorized the building of the Louisiana State Penitentiary two years earlier. A five-member commission was established to oversee the construction and instructed to purchase a suitable lot in what was then the small town of Baton Rouge. The commissioners chose a site on Saint Anthony Street, between what is now Florida and Laurel streets in downtown Baton Rouge. The design was based on the Wethersfield, Connecticut, Prison[16] (figure 160) and, although it is likely that Buisson designed the jail, Nichols probably designed a fair amount through on-site decisions. The penitentiary

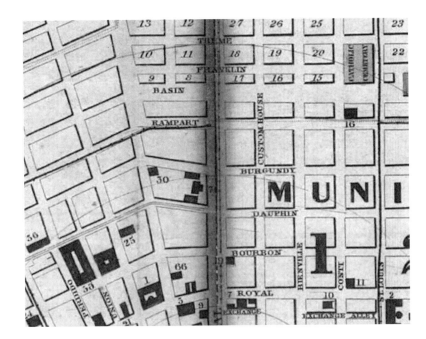

Figure 162. Louisiana State House as shown in *Norman's Plan of New Orleans & Environs, 1845*, New Orleans: B. M. Norman, 1845. Nichols's Hall of Representatives is the rear addition of the building located west of Canal Street and between Burgundy and Dauphine streets. (Library of Congress Digital Maps Collection)

was a 3-story brick masonry building with a hipped roof, 154 feet wide facing north to south and 44 feet deep with a tall wall extending 240 feet from east to west beyond the prison block (figure 161). Convict labor built the penitentiary and the construction of it lasted throughout Nichols's tenure in Louisiana. When it was completed at the end of 1835, it housed 100 convicts and cost $50,000 to build.[17] He was regularly traveling to Baton Rouge from New Orleans, and it appears that Nichols never established a permanent residence in either place, which would explain why he was not listed in the New Orleans directory of 1835.[18]

Nichols was also given the commission to expand and convert the old Charity Hospital in New Orleans into the new State House[19] (figure 162). Henry Sellon Boneval Latrobe, the son of Benjamin Henry Latrobe, designed Charity Hospital in 1815–1816. Henry was a promising young architect who moved to New Orleans in 1810 to manage the construction of the elder Latrobe's waterworks complex for the city. The waterworks project suffered numerous delays, from squabbles over permits with the former French municipal government to delays in transporting equipment from Baltimore to New Orleans during the War of 1812. While waiting for the waterworks project construction to begin, young Henry erected an elaborate funerary monument based on his father's design for the grave of Eliza Lewis, wife of territorial governor William Claiborne, in the St. Louis cemetery. He also designed numerous houses, such as the Jean Baptiste Thierry House on Governor Nicholls Street, two houses for Bernard Marigny in New

Figure 163. Charity Hospital of New Orleans, 1815, as depicted in the *Plan of the city and suburbs of New Orleans* by I. Tanesse; Rollinson, sc New York: Charles Del Veechio, New Orleans: P. Maspero, 1817. (Library of Congress, Washington, DC)

State House of the State of Louisiana. built 1815.

Figure 164. The Louisiana State House as depicted in the *Topographical Map of New Orleans and Its Vicinity* by Charles F. Zimpel (engraver), 1833–1834. (Courtesy of the Historic New Orleans Collection, Williams Research Center, New Orleans, LA)

Orleans, and additions to Ormond Plantation near Destrehan, Louisiana. Sadly, young Henry Latrobe's potential as an architect was not fulfilled; he died in New Orleans of yellow fever in 1817 at the age of twenty-four.[20]

Young Latrobe's Charity Hospital was located between Burgundy and Dauphine streets and occupied the entire city block between Canal and Baronne streets. Embodying several architectural features found in his father's designs, it was a two-story rectangular massed building, gable-ended, with simple parapets that terminated a low-pitched roof.[21] The hospital appears to have been brick construction covered with stucco and had a nine-bay façade composed of tall, arched windows that rested on the main floor or *piano nobile* of the building. The basement (ground floor) had square, simple windows directly beneath the large arched windows; the entry was highlighted by a simple pedimented entry (figure 163). Between 1815 and 1834, two one-story pavilion wings were added to the complex. These wings flanked the original two-story building, forming a forecourt that faced Canal Street. The space was defined by a wrought-iron fence and decorated with orange and lemon trees. Brick piers accentuated two personnel entries and a main carriage entry (figure 164). The Charity Hospital Board of Directors sold this impressive building and grounds for $125,000 in 1832 to the state of Louisiana.[22] Two years later, the Louisiana legislature directed William Nichols to convert it into a new State House.

Once again, Nichols had the opportunity to work on a capitol building, but this would only be a remodeling project. Budget and direction from the Louisiana legislature did not allow him to transform this building as he had done ten years earlier in Raleigh. The best source for the remodeling plans is the construction contract, which stipulates the expansion would include a large rear wing, containing a hall for the House of Representatives. Sixteen fluted Corinthian columns at a height of twenty feet tall were to support a gallery. This appears to have been similar to the House of Representatives Chamber Nichols designed in the Alabama State Capitol five years earlier.[23] Nichols also altered an interior portion of the old hospital to become the Senate Chamber, semicircular in form with "ten turned columns that defined the senators' area from the viewing gallery." Owen Evans was hired as the builder. These alterations took little more than a year to complete.[24]

Opinions varied regarding the State House with its new Hall of Representatives wing. In 1838, New Orleans city newspapers *The Price-Current* and *The Commercial Intelligencer* described it as "handsome, but unfortunately speakers are heard with difficulty . . . It is in contemplation to erect an edifice more worthy of the State, but when this is done is uncertain." As was the case with the library at the University of Alabama, Nichols once again designed a chamber with poor acoustics. Author and later clergyman Joseph Holt Ingraham[25] was very impressed with the State House. He described it in his book *The Southwest by a Yankee*, published in 1835, in the following passage:

> Its snow white front, though plain, is very imposing, and the whole structure, with its handsome, detached wings, and large green, thickly covered with shrubbery in front, luxuriant with orange and lemon trees, presents decidedly, one of the finest views to be met within the city. These two buildings [Christ Church and the State House], with the exception of some elegant private residences, are all that are worth remarking in this street, which is less than a mile from the river, terminates in the swampy commons, everywhere surrounding New Orleans, except on the river side.[26]

During the first half of the nineteenth century, Louisianans were never comfortable with New Orleans as the state capital. It is safe to assume that the hospital–State House building was only meant to be a temporary solution for a home for the Louisiana legislature. Due to high humidity from its proximity to swampland in New Orleans, the building was never a suitable hospital; likewise, it did not make a suitable legislative hall either. Despite the fact that the state government paid a hefty sum to purchase the building from the Charity Hospital

Board of Directors, they neglected to allocate sufficient funding to maintain it. By the early 1840s a consensus was being made that New Orleans should not be the power base of the state. Many legislators from rural parishes considered New Orleans too remote; outspoken citizens believed the city's many pleasures a distraction for the legislators.[27] By 1845, the remodeled Charity Hospital–State House had fallen into an embarrassing state of decay. *The Price-Current* referred to it as "that miserable, old and dilapidated structure known as our State House" and that "rat trap."[28] The fate of Nichols's State House was sealed with the passage of the Louisiana Constitution of 1845, which stipulated that the seat of government be relocated to Baton Rouge. (By then Nichols had been living in Mississippi for years and had completed his own capitol masterpiece there.) The Louisiana state government commissioned premiere architect James Dakin to design a new state capitol building that would become a Gothic masterpiece of public architecture, now known as the Old Louisiana State Capitol. In 1850, the state sold Nichols's State House, and it was soon demolished. The land was subdivided and commercial buildings were constructed on the site.[29]

The Influence of James Dakin, Charles Dakin, and James Gallier on William Nichols

In 1835, the year Nichols completed the remodeling of the Louisiana State House, James Dakin arrived in New Orleans and joined his brother Charles and James Gallier in a firm that would eventually transform the city. The Dakin brothers and James Gallier's most significant work was the New Orleans Merchants' Exchange Building; it would be a stunning masterpiece and would profoundly influence Nichols. The building was massive in scale and much more urban than anything Nichols was accustomed to seeing in the Deep South. The exterior, a simple cladding of granite coursed in an ashlar bond pattern, reflected the influence of Town and Davis on Dakins and Gallier. This façade was typical of an Alexander Jackson Davis design with its stripped stylized pilasters in a rigid rhythm with window openings separated by recessed spandrels. On the ground floor, Town and Davis and the commercialism of New York distinctively influenced the commercial façade with its large storefront windows defined by the rigid order of the pilasters. The central entry was subtly defined with a very severe architrave opening.

While the outside of the Merchants' Exchange was severe, the inside was one of the most ornamental and well-articulated buildings in the South. The auction house and office building consisted of a large

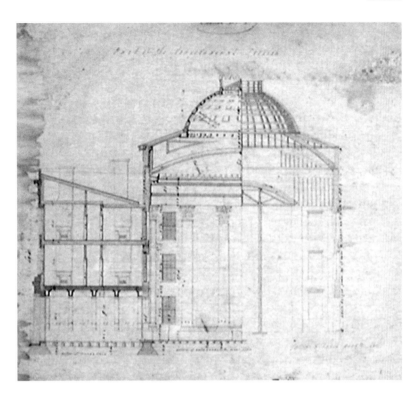

center enclosed court, used not only for auctions but also as a passive cooling "chimney" that allowed air convection to occur, thereby removing the hot, humid air in the surrounding offices and promoting air circulation throughout the building. In the large enclosed court, Gallier and the Dakins used colossal Corinthian pilasters based on the Lafever/Dakin plate of columns from the Choragic Monument of Lysicrates. (The entablature was also based on the same Lafever plates with elaborate cyma pattern moldings and acroterion patterns drawn by Dakin in Lafever's book). The three-story court had a balcony at the second floor defined by a heavy balustrade. A coffered dome capped the space with plaster ornaments terminated by a dome-covered oculus. This exquisite room was painted in light, "transparent colors." Sadly, the building burned in 1960[30] (figure 165).

According to Gallier, Nichols publicly questioned the structural integrity of the great vaulted dome; he obviously failed to understand its structural design. He may have questioned its "firmitas" (strength) but not its "venustas" (beauty). The use of the "new" language of ornament, the richness of color, and the clarity of plan must have greatly impressed Nichols because despite his earlier reservations, he imitated the roof design for his next big project, the Mississippi State Capitol. It is unknown whether Nichols ever saw the finished Exchange Building, but it was certainly close to completion when he left for Jackson,

Mississippi, in 1836. He even cultivated professional relationships with the artisans and craftsmen working on the Exchange, as he would employ several of them later in Mississippi.[31]

Nichols's time in New Orleans was brief; even so, it was a very important one for him as an architect. The discussion of architectural ideas and construction occurring in New Orleans transformed his view on building and ornament. Although he would never become an innovator like James Dakin, it rejuvenated his thought process on design and allowed him to discard the aged and somewhat tired English tendencies he had used in North Carolina and Alabama. Nichols had benefited and suffered from working in the borderland frontier of the South. During the ten years prior to his arrival in New Orleans, he had relied too heavily on a business-as-usual approach to building and design, but, in New Orleans, he witnessed firsthand the new spirit of architecture that was clearly American. Nichols had reengaged into the cultural marketplace of high American architecture long enough to develop transformative ideas before he returned to the upper frontier lands of the South in Mississippi.

Meanwhile in Jackson, Mississippi, John Lawrence, the Tennessean who had won the job of state architect over Nichols, was languishing over a Gothic Revival–styled capitol building. Neither Lawrence nor the building were faring well, and Mississippi Governor Charles Runnels finally fired Lawrence. He hired Nichols, who immediately left New Orleans for Jackson in early 1836 for the final and most impressive stage of his career in Mississippi.

Chapter Seven

THE MISSISSIPPI STATE CAPITOL AND THE OFFICE OF STATE ARCHITECT

"... I could bring with me a fund of information which would result in producing an Edifice not surpassed for Elegance, Convenience, Stability, and Economy of Expenditure by any building of similar Character in the Union."
—**William Nichols** in his letter applying for the position of state architect of Mississippi to Mississippi Governor Charles Lynch

M ississippi was the last state where William Nichols would reside; over the previous thirty-five years, he had lived in three states, serving two as state architect and one as assistant state engineer. He was fifty-eight years old when he came to Jackson, the capital of Mississippi, in January of 1836 to be state architect after Governor Runnels fired John Lawrence. Eight months after his arrival, Nichols remarried for the third and last time. (What happened to Sarah Simons is unknown.) His bride was Lydia Lucinda Smith, a native North Carolinian who was thirty-two years old at the time of their marriage on September 23, 1836.[1]

Nichols's reputation as one of the preeminent architects in the South had been well established with the numerous important public and private buildings that he credited as examples of his design skill. However, his signature design and ideas on architecture were now significantly changed, influenced by what he saw and experienced in New Orleans. He was not the same architect who had designed the North Carolina State House in Raleigh fourteen years earlier or the same architect who built the Alabama State Capitol in Tuscaloosa seven years earlier. William Nichols had experienced a career-changing moment in New Orleans. He had learned new forms and a new, fresh, and distinctively American language of ornament. This all came from an acquaintance with the architecture of James Dakin and exposure to pattern books by Minard Lafever. Nichols met and developed business relationships with skilled tradesmen in New Orleans—craftsmen, stone and wood carvers, and ornamental plasterers—who possessed the necessary skill sets to fabricate and erect his creations. Plus, they were comfortable building the new Lafever-influenced ornaments. In Mississippi, Nichols not only had regained the covetable title of state architect but also the equally impressive annual salary of three thousand dollars.

In Jackson, Nichols built the city's three most significant buildings from the antebellum period: the capitol, the Governor's Mansion, and the state penitentiary. He designed and built two important churches in Jackson, the First Methodist Episcopal (M.E.) Church and the First Presbyterian Church, and two significant houses, the Hilzheim-Ledbetter House and the Poindexter House. He designed buildings for two schools near Jackson, the Brandon Male and Female Academy in Rankin County, and a small office for the Sharon Female Academy in Madison County. Later, he developed a more regional practice in central Mississippi, designing a colonnade portico addition for the home of Charles Kimball Marshall in Vicksburg and a small manor house called Sedgewood for John Thomas in Madison County. Toward the end of his career, Nichols designed the campus of the University of Mississippi and its signature building, the Lyceum; the Yazoo County Courthouse; Shamrock, the home of William Porterfield in Vicksburg; and the Lexington Female Academy[2] in Lexington, Mississippi. Unfortunately, only the capitol and the Governor's Mansion have survived in Jackson. Sedgewood and the small office building for the Sharon Female Academy (now relocated to Canton, Mississippi) are still standing in Madison County. The historic campus plan and the exteriors of the Lyceum and the old chapel are all that survive at the University of Mississippi. All of the other buildings Nichols designed or influenced were demolished in the late nineteenth century and throughout the twentieth century. Images in various collections found in the Mississippi Department of Archives and History in Jackson, the University of Mississippi Archives, and the Historic American Buildings Survey in Washington, D.C., are all that remain of these buildings. They are the basis for verifying that William Nichols designed these now-lost buildings in Mississippi.

Mississippi's Golden Age

Nichols found Mississippi to be more advanced in culture and architecture than the Alabama he had moved to nine years earlier, but from an economic standpoint, it was not as secure. From 1835 to 1840,

Mississippi experienced an economic and political transformation that was brought about through the military accomplishments and presidential policies of Andrew Jackson. The most significant event that Mississippi, along with the rest of the United States, endured was the economic depression caused by the Stock Market Panic of 1837. For the first time, the United States' economy was affected by an economic calamity, one that was caused by rampant speculation in real estate. Speculative investment, based on the purchase of land on credit, was rampant in Mississippi during the first decades of the nineteenth century. It first brought about an era of economic prosperity in the state but later caused a financial catastrophe both within the private sector and in the state government, all of which had a profound impact on Nichols's practice.

From the late eighteenth century to the end of the War of 1812, both political power and culture resided along the Mississippi River, specifically in Natchez. The French had established Natchez early in the eighteenth century, and it became the home of many of the ruling elite who made their fortunes in agriculture, shipping, and land speculation after the upper part of West Florida, the territory later known as the Mississippi territory, was ceded to the United States by Spain in 1798.[3] When Mississippi entered the Union as the twentieth state on December 10, 1817, the state legislature first met in the town of Washington in a tavern owned by Charles de France and soon after in a large town house called Texada in Natchez. The seat of government was relocated to Columbia in 1821 and then to the newly created town of Jackson in 1822.[4] The moving of the state capital from the Natchez area of the state to a more central location was not unprecedented; it was a common pattern in states throughout the South and in the Midwest to relocate their state capitals to the central region of their state. This practice was done in order to make the seat of the state government more accessible to citizens who lived in the backcountry.

Migration into the state by settlers predominantly from Tennessee, Georgia, and the Carolinas began after the Choctaw Indians ceded a large tract of land that is now central Mississippi to the federal government through the Treaty of Doak's Stand in 1821.[5] The various treaties with the native populations had legally opened up settlement from the Tennessee line to the Gulf of Mexico and Louisiana, and from the Alabama line to the Mississippi River. The Treaty of Dancing Rabbit Creek with the Choctaw Indians in 1830 and Treaty of Pontotoc with the Chickasaw Indians in 1832 opened up east-central and north Mississippi, respectively. This resulted in a significant land rush by settlers into the northern two-thirds of the state. In 1833, the Dancing Rabbit territory was organized into sixteen counties and in 1836 the Pontotoc territory was organized into twelve.[6]

Mississippi was experiencing a short-lived economic boom when Nichols arrived in Jackson in 1836. The Economic Panic of 1837 greatly inhibited his architectural practice for the next ten years. Nevertheless, he persevered in building at least twenty-two buildings or additions during his seventeen years in Mississippi, three of which—the Old Mississippi Capitol, the Mississippi Governor's Mansion, and the Lyceum at the University of Mississippi—would be his most noteworthy works of Greek Revival architecture. Each of these buildings would become iconic symbols for the state of Mississippi as well as the antebellum South.

The Mississippi Capitol

Named after Andrew Jackson, who was much loved in Mississippi, the town of Jackson was established in 1822 as the state's capital. Built on high ground near a trading post called LeFleur's Bluff (named after the Frenchman who established it, Louis LeFleur), the new settlement was located near the Pearl River, which provided river transport. The town itself was laid out in a checkerboard plan originally suggested by Thomas Jefferson to W. C. C. Claiborne when he was territorial governor of Louisiana as a way to expand the city of New Orleans. His proposal was based on the idea of a chessboard; the town would have a layout in which the black squares were developed as building lots and the white squares remained as open green spaces or parks.[7]

The town of Jackson was originally platted by Peter Vandorn, clerk of the Mississippi House of Representatives, in 1822. Vandorn designed an area bounded on the west by State Street, on the north by Amite Street, and on the south by Pearl Street, which he called the "Capitol Green." Beyond the east of the Capitol Green, Vandorn labeled public lands as the "Commons." North of the Commons, Vandorn proposed a "College Green" as a future college site; he also proposed fourteen squares or parks that were interspersed with the developed blocks. Only one of the open squares remains undeveloped; it is now known as Smith Park and is located north of the Governor's Mansion. Neither the College Green nor the Commons was ever built, and the other green squares were sold to finance the construction of the new state capitol.[8] The large Capitol Green that Vandorn designed in the Jackson town plan would later become the site of Nichols's new capitol building.[9]

The first permanent state legislature building was a twenty-four-hundred-square-foot brick house, located at the northeast corner of Capitol and President streets, one block to the west of the Capitol Green. Up to that point, the Mississippi legislature had met in de France's tavern in Washington, then in Natchez, followed by a session held in Columbia before locating in Jackson. The fledgling town of Jackson had a difficult time retaining the right of its existence as the state's capital. Population growth was sporadic at best and the legislature continued removing vital offices, such as the county courthouse and the land office, out of town.[10] Throughout the antebellum period of the state's history, legislators plotted to relocate the capital to their own districts but each one failed to convince their fellow legislators to buy into their proposition. Jackson's fate was secured and sealed when the Constitution of 1832 stipulated that the city would remain the state capital; also, the state's High Court of Errors and Appeals (the precursor of the Mississippi Supreme Court) was mandated to meet in Jackson instead of Natchez, creating a more pressing need to build a grander state capitol.[11] Moreover, the security in knowing that no further attempts would be made to move the capital for many years allowed the state to safely invest in more permanent buildings befitting the dignity of the state government.

By 1833, economic prosperity, fueled by land speculation, drove the cultural aspirations of Mississippians. The treasury was running a surplus and the general sentiment of the state's leaders was to build edifices that reflected permanence and prosperity, which would also downplay the rough and recent frontier history of the state. In 1833, the Mississippi legislature proposed allocating ninety-five thousand dollars for the erection of a new State House and to provide additional funding for its construction through the sale of lots and open green spaces in the town of Jackson. They also proposed allocating an additional ten thousand dollars for the building of a governor's mansion. The legislature stipulated that the governor would have the authority to appoint a state architect who would execute these and other state building projects. The new state capitol building would not only house the legislature but also the High Court of Errors and Appeals and all of the high state officers. The legislature also stipulated that the new capitol building would be built with permanent materials including brick, stone, and cypress timbers. Although they allocated ninety-five thousand dollars for the project, they also limited the building contract ceiling amount to seventy-five thousand dollars with the remaining amount of twenty thousand placed in a contingency fund. In February 1833, Governor Abram Scott approved the resolution.[12]

Scott then began the search for a state architect; initially he inquired only within the state but soon found the search fruitless due to political infighting and the lack of any qualified candidates. He had at first offered the position to David Morrison of Nashville, Tennessee, who had gained acclaim remodeling The Hermitage (Andrew Jackson's home) and in designing and building the tomb of Andrew Jackson's wife, Rachel. However, due to contractual issues and scheduling, negotiations fell through. Morrison walked away and Scott resumed the search. Very soon after, Scott died of cholera.[13]

Scott's successor, Charles Lynch (1783–1853), attempted to bully Morrison into accepting the position ("repair to this place [Jackson] immediately[,]") and begin designing the capitol building. Morrison declined.[14] Faced with the possibility of not finding a satisfactory candidate for the job, Lynch consulted Tennessee governor William Carroll, who then recommended John Lawrence, an architect and carpenter from Nashville. Another candidate, Hugh Roland of Kentucky, heavily lobbied for the position, with Governor Carroll and Kentucky governor John Breathitt writing letters of recommendation for him. Apparently this failed to impress Lynch who did not respond to Roland and apparently ignored his application.[15] Despite the perception that there were no qualified candidates for the job, it was in fact a hotly contested and coveted position.

Lynch also chose to snub Nichols, who pursued the job with his usual bravado by promoting his experience designing and building state capitols, college campuses, prisons, and churches throughout North Carolina and Alabama. Nichols even requested Alabama governor John Gayle to write a letter of recommendation for him. All of this was to no avail; Lynch never responded to Nichols and instead hired John Lawrence.[16]

John Lawrence, who arrived in Jackson in October of 1833, had come with glowing recommendations from Tennessee governor William Carroll and had the hearty support of Governor Charles Lynch. The next month he presented to the Mississippi legislature a plan for a Gothic Revival State House. None of the drawings Lawrence prepared remain in the Mississippi archives; it is entirely likely that he took his drawings with him when he left Jackson. But the design must have greatly impressed the Mississippi legislature as they immediately ordered Lawrence to begin preparing contracts and begin construction of the new capitol building.

At the same time that Lawrence presented the Gothic Revival capitol design, Lynch stepped down from the governor's office as required by a new electoral process stated in the 1832 Mississippi Constitution; Hiram Runnels (1796–1857) became governor. Lawrence languished in building the capitol. His efforts to organize and mobilize tradesmen and material acquisitions proved unsuccessful. The main problem that Lawrence faced was out of his control: the lack of a consistent cash flow for the project. A significant amount of the funding was coming from the sale of lots in Jackson, which was being handled through promissory notes from investors. During this time, the Bank of the United States stopped honoring such notes and their ruling affected the local banks. The Planters' Bank of Mississippi soon after reversed its decision to accept the Jackson lot notes from the state government. Consequently, Governor Runnels suspended work on the capitol building project the day the building's cornerstone was dedicated in a Masonic ceremony, citing insufficient funds. He warned the only remedy was "early legislative action." For almost all of 1835, the legislature failed in funding the project, and Governor Runnels applied for and received a personal loan from the Planters' Bank. At first he borrowed ten thousand dollars and later twenty thousand to initiate and then sustain the project's progress.[17] Lawrence did not help his case during that year; in an act made perhaps out of desperation to support himself and his family, he began advertising in the newspapers for private clients. The perception of Lawrence devoting time to private clients and the slow progress of the capitol project became a public relations disaster for Lawrence; both the press and the legislature harshly criticized him. The editor of *The Mississippian* questioned Lawrence's credentials as an architect and stated that the work so far appeared unstable. On October 9, 1835, Runnels fired Lawrence; it is unknown whether he chose to remain in Mississippi or if he returned to Nashville. At the time of his termination, little besides the foundations and the ground floor brick walls had been built. A month later, Runnels hired William Nichols just before his term as governor ended and offered him a salary of three thousand dollars a year.[18]

When Nichols arrived in Jackson in 1836, he immediately tore down Lawrence's work and started over. As he had done in North Carolina with Rhodam Atkins's Raleigh State House in 1820 and with the Alabama Capitol Commissioners' State House design in 1827, Nichols wasted no time criticizing Lawrence's design. Talbot Hamlin incorrectly considered Lawrence as having started the building and credits him equally along with David Morrison, who rejected the position of state architect outright. Robert Mellown, Ford Peatross, and Mississippi historian John Ray Skates accurately document the fact that Nichols solely designed the state capitol. Nichols had strong ideas of how a capitol building should look and how it should work programmatically. He did not have to convince anyone in the legislature that Lawrence's work was not worth keeping; by this time, both the press and the citizens of Jackson considered Lawrence's building project a fiasco. In the winter of 1836, the legislature put together a committee to investigate the construction and the professional competency of Lawrence. They concluded that the Lawrence Gothic Revival design was "against all architectural proportions of order, and the various compartments so bunglingly arranged, as to exhibit neither skill, convenience, nor comfort." They surmised that Lawrence did not possess capacity or skill enough to construct a state capitol and that firing him was in the best interest of the state of Mississippi. Nichols also helped

Figure 166. The Mississippi State Capitol, Jackson, MS, ca. 1900. (Courtesy of the Mississippi Department of Archives and History)

further seal the fate of Lawrence's work by stating to the Mississippi Board of Commissioners for Public Buildings that the bricks used to build the basement were inferior and the mortar was too soft.[19]

Lawrence's perceived incompetency was the perfect entry into the project for Nichols. It appears that the building committee's investigation validated Nichols by proving that passing him over three years earlier for the state architect position and selecting Lawrence was a mistake. The committee's conclusion was that Nichols was the only man suitable for the job. There was little doubt in Nichols's mind how the Mississippi State Capitol would look and work. Since 1821, beginning with the North Carolina State House in Raleigh, Nichols had been working on and evolving a design of a state capitol building; the Mississippi State Capitol would be the culmination of his essay on the design for bicameral government. After learning the latest fashion of architecture and decoration in New Orleans, he would also employ the very latest fashionable aspects of the Greek Revival style to his essay. The Mississippi capitol would be the most imposing structure of his career. Indeed, his "sabbatical" in New Orleans was beneficial to him. He arrived in Jackson a much better architect and designer than he had been previously. Nichols was well prepared to design and build his masterpiece (figure 166).

Nichols encountered many challenges while building the Mississippi State Capitol. In the early stages of construction he was faced with a chronic shortage of skilled tradesmen, similar to his problem in Alabama. Throughout the project, he was constantly advertising and trying to recruit tradesmen worthy of such an important project. He was able to count on his old colleague John Robb, who years earlier had carved the stone columns at Gerrard Hall at the University of North Carolina, the North Carolina State House, and the buildings he designed and built in Alabama. (Robb had arrived in Jackson two years earlier and had been working on Lawrence's version of the capitol.[20]) Materials such as brick were a constant struggle for Nichols to obtain. The shortage of satisfactory bricks and the political cronyism from legislators and brick vendors that led to Lawrence's downfall would also plague Nichols and result in bitter feelings between the state government (specifically with the Board of Commissioners for Public Buildings) and Nichols. The main culprit of the brick problem was Edwin Moody, the leading local brick manufacturer. Moody supplied the bricks for Lawrence's failed capitol project and the bricks he supplied helped undermine Lawrence's project and his reputation. The bricks were of poor quality. Some units were fired too much in the kiln but most units had not been fired enough to be sufficiently strong for wall construction, leading to costly delays. The Board of Commissioners for Public Buildings chose not to renew their contract with Moody when they fired Lawrence.[21]

By the time Nichols began building his capitol, the board and Governor Runnels had hired James Joplin and William Orr to supply the project with a million and a half bricks. Joplin's and Orr's bricks were also of such a poor quality that Nichols complained bitterly. Joplin retaliated by delaying delivery of new bricks, which led to yet another delay. Nichols submitted his opinion on their poor quality to the building commissioners, saying that based on his oath "to protect the interest of the state [it was] impossible for him to certify that Joplin and Orr fulfilled their contract." They were promptly fired. In an effort to expedite the project, Governor Runnels himself became a brick manufacturer for the project. This, too, proved to be equally disappointing. Finally a brick vendor and mason named Landy Lindsay agreed to produce brick for the project at nine dollars per thousand and produced three million bricks for the capitol. Nichols complained twice to the board about the poor quality, but by now the Board of Commissioners for Public Buildings would accept anything to complete the project.[22] The board then rehired Moody, who was also inconsistent in delivering suitable bricks in a timely manner but apparently he was the only brickmaking vendor left in Jackson who had not supplied the capitol project with bricks. Nichols continued to complain to the board and he would later on in the project fire Moody. The board was now growing weary of Nichols's rants and began to grow suspicious of his motives. This would later become a liability for Nichols.[23]

Cut ashlar stone would also prove to be a frustrating material for Nichols to obtain. Nichols used a very soft and fragile sandstone, Catahoula sandstone, from a resort east of Jackson known as Mississippi Springs, near Raymond. This sandstone was the only native building stone in central Mississippi; several buildings in both Raymond and Jackson were built out of it, as well as tombstones. Unfortunately, it has poor bearing strength and is prone to crumbling.[24]

Not only was the quality of the cut stone a problem for Nichols, so was the production of the stone material from the quarry at Mississippi Springs. In September 1836, Nichols informed the building commissioners that John Robb had forwarded him a letter from Alexander Baird, the contracted stonecutter, indicating that Baird "had laid down his mallet and would not resume it and go to work until he and Robb should have a settlement," presumably a payment for the work that had already been done. Nichols investigated the matter, and reported back to the Commissioners:

> I went to the Public quarry on Sept. 1st and found Mr. Baird and his workmen no longer pursuing their work for the State Capitol, as by the conditions of their contract they were bound to do, but busily engaged in preparing rock for other purposes. The ground around the Quarry is covered with head stones and foot stones, with large square tombs, covers for reservoirs, etc. whilst there remaining but one solitary unwrought piece of rock quarried for one of the columns of the basement story to indicate that the stone yard of the state bears any relation to the State Capitol. This unfortunate circumstance could not have happened more inopportunely than at the present . . .
>
> For some time past Mr. Robb has complained of the tardy manner in which he has been supplied with wrought rock. This is now more clearly accounted for by the quality of work manufactured for other places. By this means the best and most select rock has been pilfered from the State and the more indifferent stone sent for the State Capitol.[25]

It appears that Baird was busy making cistern caps and tombstones with the stone intended for the capitol. The board dismissed Baird and hired Robb, who was to supply and cut the stone along with the erecting of brickwork for the basement story. The board had learned their lesson and soon after only entered short-term contracts with contractors and builders such as Robb, who entered into several short-term and specific contracts for building elements such as columns and pilasters. Nichols's handling of Baird's malfeasance demonstrates his ability to manage a complex building project during the early history of Mississippi and Alabama. Not only were materials and skilled tradesmen in short supply in Jackson but also any familiarity with building large-scale buildings such as the capitol. With his thirty-five years of experience designing and building in the South, which included designing and building important institutional buildings, Nichols proved his statement to Lynch in 1833 to be true regarding his architectural and building expertise, when he first applied for the position of state architect for Mississippi:

> . . . from the circumstance of having had more experience in the construction of State Capitols than any other individual in the Union—and from being well versed in the various prices and modes of building in the Southern Country . . . I could bring with me a fund of information which would result in producing an Edifice not surpassed for Elegance, Convenience, Stability, and Economy of Expenditure by any building of similar Character in the Union.[26]

The incident with Baird and Robb was one of several obstacles that Nichols encountered in building the capitol in Jackson. He not only had a problem finding good brick and stone; he also found it very difficult to find good masons to build the masonry walls. The first masonry subcontractor, Robert MacDonald, died shortly after accepting the commission's contract; the second subcontractor, a partnership between independent masons, John and William Gibbon, proved to be as frustrating for Nichols as the delivery of acceptable bricks.[27] Skilled brickmakers were also as rare as suitable bricks in Jackson. The brick suppliers, Landy Lindsey and Thomas Harris, traveled all the way to Cincinnati, Ohio, in search of skilled workers in the summer of 1837. Later in September, the commissioners agreed to pay for an advertisement for skilled brickmakers in the Cincinnati *Mirror*.[28]

These problems clearly illustrate the difficulty of building a monumental building in the frontier that was the "old Southwest." Nichols drew on his experience in New Orleans and soon began importing skilled carpenters and stone/wood carvers from the Crescent City, such as Robert McKee and David Daly, who were recruited during one of his trips back to New Orleans when he was trying to solve the brick quality problem. He also secured contracts from stone carver Ezra Williams of New Orleans, and records show that John Robb carved an Ionic column for the portico.[29]

On May 10, 1837, banks throughout the United States failed to make payments in specie (gold and silver coinage) to their creditors. The economic bubble, which had been created with the use of credit and no collateral in order to purchase land, led to bank foreclosures on farms and plantations. The problem was exacerbated by the economic policies of the Jackson administration, including the creation of the Specie Circular of 1836, which required that gold and silver be used for the purchase of federal land, and Jackson's refusal to renew the charter of the Bank of the United States. These two actions essentially brought to an abrupt end the boom period that began after the War of 1812 and continued through Jackson's two presidential terms. Both money and credit essentially vanished and nearly a third of the banks in the United States would shutter in 1837.[30] The Panic of 1837 would cause one of the worst economic depressions up to this point in American history, but for Nichols it would bring the capitol construction project to a halt. The Planters' Bank lost most of its assets and it would take months of reorganization and new deposits from the state and federal governments in order for the bank to resume its service. Nichols was frustrated by the credit crisis and its effect on the project; skillful tradesmen walked away and material suppliers stopped shipment. The Panic of 1837 and the depression that followed would have a lasting impact on the rest of Nichols's career.

In his book *Mississippi's Old Capitol: Biography of a Building*, John Ray Skates notes that a picture of Nichols emerges based on his business records: one of a careful and thorough manager and planner who was meticulous and demanding in his supervision of construction and resistive of any tendency to cut corners. Nichols's experience with similar buildings in Raleigh and Tuscaloosa benefited him building the Mississippi capitol. Nichols learned from his mistakes and also learned better management techniques during his brief tenure in New Orleans. He was also acutely aware of the widespread frustration of the Mississippi legislature, who believed that the progress was too slow in completing the building project and regarded the Board of Public Commissioners as too lax in their management of building contractors working on the building. They abolished the board and replaced it with a single commissioner, ex-governor Charles Lynch, in 1838.[31] This was the same Governor Lynch who had hired John Lawrence over Nichols to design and build the capitol in 1833. The lawmakers instructed Nichols to "superintend constantly" and appropriated an additional $120,000 to complete the capitol. This most likely motivated Nichols to carefully manage the building project. Moreover, Lawrence's failure to build the original design of the capitol was no doubt on Lynch's mind since he had to endure the humiliation of his original choice described by the leading Jackson town newspaper as "not to be an architect in the true sense of the word."[32] Finally, it is entirely likely that Nichols was well aware that Lynch was not supportive of him. This most likely motivated him to run a tight building project.

There was also tension throughout the project between Nichols and several contractors. One confrontation came to a head in the summer of 1836 when Edwin Moody, the brick supplier for Lawrence who was also fired by Nichols, began circulating a rumor that Nichols was

Figure 167. The Mississippi State Capitol, Jackson, MS. This photograph was taken three weeks before Hurricane Katrina hit Jackson in 2005. (Courtesy of Wendy Kapp)

in a secret partnership with John Robb and Alexander Baird. (Nichols had fired Baird because he was selling state-owned sandstone to other clients.) This would have been more probable with Robb, who had maintained a working relationship with Nichols since his early days in Fayetteville, North Carolina. Robb had followed Nichols from North Carolina to Alabama, where they parted ways. They resumed their working relationship in Mississippi when Nichols arrived in Jackson in 1836. However, Nichols had not had any previous dealings with Baird, who was not being supervised throughout 1836 when he was submitting substandard building stone for the capitol project. Baird's business of fabricating tombstones and cistern covers from the superior stone originally specified for the capitol was probably common knowledge with builders in Jackson. Nichols confronted Moody about circulating the rumor regarding these secret dealings and demanded a hearing and an investigation "for the interest of the state and my own reputation." The commission did not find anything out of the normal in the relationship among Nichols, Robb, and Baird. They declared that the rumors were in fact "false and malicious."[33]

Despite the difficulties of building the Mississippi State Capitol, it was Nichols's most ambitious and finest work. It is fortunate that, of all the capitol buildings he designed, this was the one that survived. There was little indecision in Nichols's mind what this building was going to be: a Greek Revival building designed for a bicameral government. Once it was finally completed in 1840, it would be appreciated by the legislature and admired by generations of Mississippians (figure 167).

Once again it followed the floor plan and massing of the two previous Nichols capitol buildings, but this time he designed the new capitol

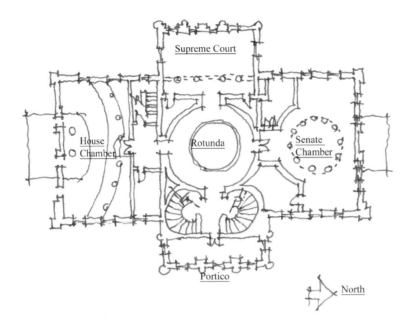

Figure 168. Alabama State Capitol, second-floor plan, Tuscaloosa, AL, 1830. (Sketch by author based on the Ruins at Capitol Park in Tuscaloosa, AL, and narratives of the interior)

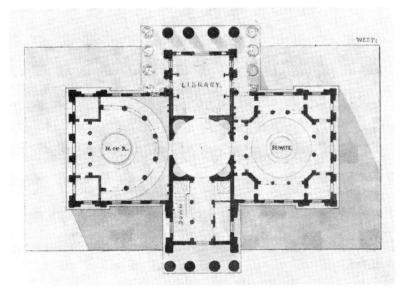

Figure 169. Second-floor plan of the North Carolina State Capitol, Raleigh, NC, by Alexander Jackson Davis, 1840. Nichols and his son, William Nichols, Jr., started the new North Carolina State Capitol after a fire destroyed the State House that Nichols designed in 1823. Originally, Davis did not want to continue to build the cruciform design that Nichols started but, due to financial constraints, he continued with the original footprint in his design. (Courtesy of the North Carolina Department of Archives and History)

by placing figurative spaces into the building so that the processional tradition of the legislature was emphasized. As he did with the capitols of Alabama and North Carolina (figures 168 and 169), Nichols designed a three-story cruciform capitol building in which the House Chamber was placed on the north side and the Senate Chamber on the south side. The House and Senate Chambers were placed on a raised primary floor, or *piano nobile*, and the actual first floor was described as a basement.[34] The west side of the building is the front façade with a shallow

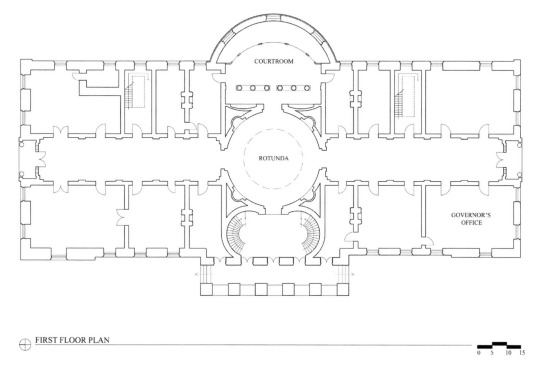

Figure 170. Main-floor plan of the Mississippi State Capitol, 1839. (Drawing by Michelle Zupancic, 2012, based on measured drawing by H. N. Austin, delineator, 1915)

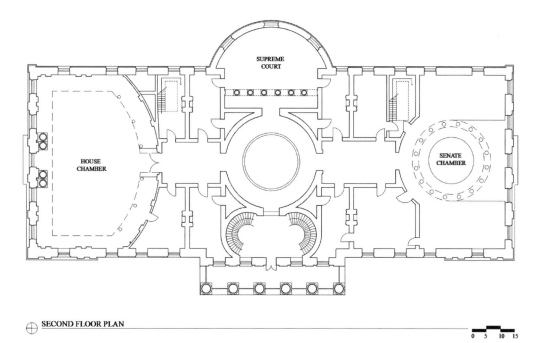

SECOND FLOOR PLAN

0 5 10 15

Figure 171. Second-floor plan, Mississippi State Capitol. (Drawing by Michelle Zupancic, 2012, based on measured drawing by H. N. Austin, 1915)

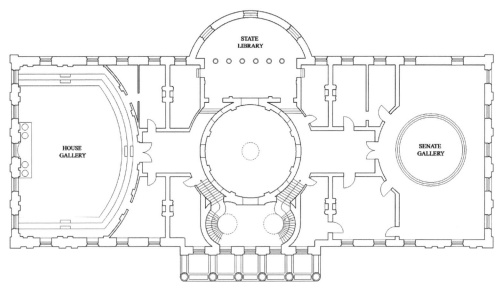

THIRD FLOOR PLAN

0   5   10   15

Figure 172. Third floor, Mississippi State Capitol. (Drawing by Michelle Zupancic, 2012, based on measured drawing by H. N. Austin, 1915)

Figure 173. Cross, west-to-east section measured drawing of the Mississippi State Capitol by H. N. Austin, delineator, 1915. (Courtesy of the Mississippi Department of Archives and History)

Figure 174. Mississippi State Capitol as seen from Capitol Street in Jackson, MS, 2005. (Courtesy of Wendy Kapp)

colossal Ionic hexastyle portico, which leads into a stair hall of two twin spiral staircases and into the Rotunda. From the Rotunda there is an east room with a semicircular apsidal space, which is repeated on the second and third floors. Here Nichols placed the Chancery Court, the Supreme Court (or High Court of Errors and Appeals, as it was originally named), and the state library. Each of these large chambers, along with the entry stairs, gives the Rotunda a powerful and dynamic sense for both occupant and visitor. Moreover, Nichols uses columns and orders in an equally dramatic way. In the middle of the rectangular Senate Chamber, he placed a circular colonnade (almost a temple) of Corinthian columns based on the Choragic Monument of Lysicrates in Athens, which defined the Senate seating area from the remainder of the rectangular space. Nichols used columns in a similar way in the High Court Room, although they were smaller and much more delicate columns based on Temple of the Winds columns. In the House Chamber, he used colossal Ionic columns to define the visitors' gallery.

Although the plan of the Mississippi State Capitol was very similar to his Alabama State Capitol in Tuscaloosa, this plan was much more sophisticated. Its detailing was strongly influenced by the ideas of Lafever. Details found in the entablatures, the columns, the doors, and the entryways clearly reflect the influence of Lafever and Dakin. Moreover, its engineering was more audacious with longer spans and taller domes, which reflected Nichols's experiences studying the new buildings being built in New Orleans in the 1830s (figures 170–174).

The play of walls and columns to define space is a completely new aspect in Nichols's work. Prior to his stay in New Orleans, he rarely used colonnades to define space or to give the illusion of grander space. Nichols's use of colonnades, especially in the High Court Chambers and the Rotunda, is similar to Gallier's and Dakin's work, specifically the Custom House, and Jacques Bussiere de Pouilly's Rotunda in the Saint Louis Hotel.

The main rooms within the apsidal east end of the building, Rotunda, and the Senate Chamber, are examples of the high level of sophistication in Nichols's design of figurative space in the Mississippi State Capitol. Nichols had indeed matured as an architect; he had begun to think more conceptually and theoretically and no longer in a utilitarian manner like a builder. His plan elegantly plays with poché space, which he developed for the figurative chambers and where he placed the more functional offices of the capitol. This suggests that Nichols learned a great deal about planning during his time observing Dakin and Gallier. While it is true that both the North Carolina and Alabama capitols also had figurative spaces and the University of Alabama even had a Jeffersonian-influenced Rotunda, it was the Mississippi capitol that was the culmination of both elegant planning and sound engineering. However, the fact that he was still learning and honing his craft is evidenced by what appears to have been the original design scheme for the Rotunda. During the recent restoration in 2008, square recesses were discovered behind the plaster between the niches on the lower part of the Rotunda. There was no evidence that the recesses had ever been finished. There is also no pictorial or descriptive evidence of the recesses. Apparently, he designed the Rotunda this way originally (similar to the Alabama capitol ten years earlier) but redesigned it without recesses before the plaster was applied. This change gives the space a more monumental feel somewhat lacking in the earlier, busier Rotunda seen at the Alabama capitol.[35]

Ornamentally, the capitol is a dramatic expression of Nichols's acceptance of Greek Revival–inspired design. Gone are the English-inspired ideas of Soane and Pain; here, Nichols fully utilizes the ideas of scale and proportion found in the works of Minard Lafever. The front portico, which dictates not only the façade of the building but also the massing, was completely based on the description of the Ionic order of the Erectheum featured in Lafever's *Guide* (figures 167 and 168). It is worth noting that James Dakin originally drew this specific plate. With the exception of the column's attic bases, which are Roman inspired, Nichols directly copies the Erectheum precedent that Lafever and Dakin describe in the *Modern Builder's Guide*. Nichols makes the tympanum flatter, no longer using the Roman pitch of six inches of

Figure 175. Mississippi State Capitol, ca. 1930. Oblique view of the main façade from North State Street. (Courtesy of the Mississippi Department of Archives and History)

Figure 176. North entry of the Mississippi State Capitol in 2005. (Courtesy of Wendy Kapp)

rise for twelve inches of run; instead, he opts for the five to twelve Greek roof pitch.[36]

The Mississippi capitol was the largest of the three capitol buildings by Nichols; he lengthened the building by one bay on each end of the longer north-south axis and widened it east-west, making the building deeper. The size and proportion of the footprint of the Mississippi capitol corresponds to the size of the footprint of the rebuilt 1832 North Carolina State Capitol (figure 169) that Nichols started. He also widened it by rounding the projecting east wing, giving it an apsidal configuration. As in his earlier capitols, Nichols constructed the walls of the lower floor out of brick and clad the exterior with local sandstone. He built the walls of the upper floors out of brick covered with stucco, which was scored and painted to resemble smooth faced ashlar stone. Sills and lintels of windows, doors, capitals, and bases of columns were carved from the local sandstone. The window lintels were replaced with decorative cast-iron ones in 1870, due to the poor quality of the original building stone. The colossal hexastyle portico, set on simple pier and beam "porch" (it was

Figure 177. Mississippi State Capitol, ca. 1940. The building was renovated in 1915 but the stucco finish that Nichols specified remained. It was, however, removed in 1957, exposing the red brick and radically changing the building's appearance. (Historic American Buildings Survey, Library of Congress, Washington, DC)

Figure 178. Front portico of the Mississippi State Capitol in 2005. Nichols based the portico design on Lafever's and Dakin's Plate of the Erechtheum. (Courtesy of Wendy Kapp)

Figure 179. The south elevation of the Mississippi State Capitol in 1915. (Courtesy of the Mississippi Department of Archives and History)

later altered to its current arcaded form in 1870 after the original stone beams failed), dominated the west or main façade (figures 170–179).

The main entrance to the capitol, located under the projecting portico on the west, led into the grand stair hall with the two circular stairways. The Rotunda's ceiling at the basement level is a gently sloped coffered cove that culminates with the circular opening for the main gallery below the dome of the Rotunda, which spans grandly above both the ground floor and the main floor. It is coffered with gilded rosettes; colossal Corinthian pilasters flank the walls of the Rotunda with a denticulated entablature supporting a row of delicate acroterions. The main gallery, located on the main floor, or *piano nobile*, has a circular classical balustrade and simple dado cornice that visually supports the pilasters. The entire space is delicately lit through the oculus and the dome's simple lantern. Between the pilasters are simple recessed panels with circular openings above them.

The ornamental composition of the Mississippi capitol is a deliberate departure from the simpler ornamentation found in the North Carolina and Alabama capitols; Nichols was inspired by James Dakin's dome in the New Orleans Merchants' Exchange where he saw firsthand the splendor of the elaborate detailing of the Greek ornament. Nichols's use of Lafever's ideas would not stop at the Rotunda or the portico; he would rely heavily on Lafever's ideas throughout the entire building. Instead of the simple openings he typically used, Nichols adapted the design of a "Parlor Door" by Lafever found on Plate 19 of *The Beauties of Modern Architecture*. The doorways that line the corridors on the ground floors were battered (the door surrounds taper toward the door) and shouldered in a distinctively "Greek" manner. The second- and third-floor corridors had rectilinear casings around each doorway.[37] Nichols used a simple bed mold to support the small rake that spans over the surround where he then embellishes an equally delicate scroll with a delicate acroterion as a centerpiece for the door. The door surrounds alone would have made the building appear opulent, but Nichols carries his elaborate ideas of ornament even further by using Lafever's Plate 31, *The Corinthian Order of Lysicrates at Athens*, for the circular colonnade in the Senate Chamber and the Temple of Winds columns in the High Court of Errors and Appeals.

Nichols also eloquently plays with ceiling planes throughout the building.[38] He gracefully uses barrel vaults in the ground floor north-south hallways and introduces a rhythm in the space with applied ribs in which anthemia are asserted. The ceiling of the House Chamber is gracefully accented with the cornice of the Ionic Temple of Illissus, a favorite of both Nichols and his longtime stone and wood carver, John Robb. The opulent interior is equally matched with the deliberate and forceful exterior, which not only features numerous Lafever-driven architectural ornaments but also Nichols's well-understood ideas about designing such a monumental building.

He then sets the colossal Ionic portico on a rusticated base, which sets the height of the entire building. The end bays of the wings slightly project, alluding to flanking pavilions. Nichols built the same façade in Alabama and influenced A. J. Davis to continue the cruciform plan of the North Carolina State Capitol that he designed in Raleigh five years earlier. Curiously and perhaps in a rare moment to save money, he uses Roman Doric[39] pilasters to help define the north and south pavilions of his composition; the pilasters are so skillfully placed that one does not notice them supporting a Greek-inspired entablature. All of the windows have Lafever-inspired curved lintels with delicate scrollwork applied across them. A simple masonry parapet goes around all of the building except on the east side; the north and south faces of the building culminate with elaborate scrolls. Nichols covered the brick with a light whitish stucco and scored the surface to make it appear to be ashlar stone.

At the ground floor entrances on the north and south sides, Nichols reuses one of his older precedent books and designs these entrances based on the Doric order of the Temple of Apollo at Delos. Unlike his Alabama capitol where he designs a projecting porch, here he designs the entrance in *antis* gracefully recessing the entrance where he designs the doors in a distinctively Lafever manner.

At the east elevation, Nichols stopped the elaborate ornamentation, giving only minor gestures to the building's features, such as the cornice of the entablature, and chose not to cover the brick walls with stucco. Clearly, Nichols regarded the east side of the capitol as the back of the house and saw no need to expend funding and energy on detailing this face of the building. The low-sloped dome emerges from the center of the building. Built out of timber ribs in an updated de L'Orme[40] tradition, it is similar in profile to Charles Bulfinch's dome for the U.S. Capitol. The lantern that terminates the entire composition is both elegant and functional; its understated design only suggests the monumental space that it is illuminating.

Shown in early lithographs and etchings of Jackson in the nineteenth century, the building commands Capitol Street and dominates the town skyline as few capitol buildings did. When the much larger Beaux-Arts "New Capitol" was built on the site of the old penitentiary, which had also been designed by Nichols and located a few blocks from the now-called "Old Capitol" in the early twentieth century, the city of Jackson lost its civic architectural order which Nichols so masterfully implemented. Even so, the Old Capitol's placement and articulation still dominate the downtown of Jackson and remain its centerpiece. It is fortunate that it survived decades of deferred maintenance by

Figure 180. Mississippi State Capitol, typical door portal (photograph taken in 1940). The details of the Mississippi State Capitol reflect the influence of the work of Minard Lafever and James Dakin on Nichols's architecture in Mississippi. (Historic American Buildings Survey, Library of Congress, Washington, DC)

Figure 181. Plate 19, "Parlor Door," from Minard Lafever's *The Beauties of Modern Architecture, Second Edition* (New York: D. Appleton & Company,1839). (Courtesy of the Ricker Art and Architecture Library, University of Illinois)

the Mississippi legislature and did not collapse due to neglect during almost all of its existence.[41]

As the first building Nichols designed and completed after his time in New Orleans, the Mississippi State Capitol shows his radical change in designing architectural ornament. Here, the influence of Lafever and Dakin is evident in nearly every facet of his detailing, especially in comparison with his work in North Carolina eleven years earlier. In 1825, Nichols designed a simple monument directly influenced by John Soane for his close colleague Archibald Henderson[42] for his grave in the Old Lutheran Cemetery in Salisbury, North Carolina. Nichols designed a stylized fluted Doric column with a capital, a simple plain acroterion, and an urn with a wreath on top.[43] In a typical doorway at the capitol, the portal composition has entasis and the acroterion applied to the lintel is articulated, ornamental and linear in form, all of which reflect the influence of Lafever's ideas found in *The Beauties of Modern Architecture* and *The Modern Builder's Guide*. After working over thirty years in

Figure 182. Plate 26, "Parlor Door Detail," from Minard Lefever's *The Beauties of Modern Architecture, Second Edition* (New York: D. Appleton & Company, 1839). (Courtesy of the Ricker Art and Architecture Library, University of Illinois)

Figure 183. Plate 46, "Frontpiece," from Minard Lafever's *The Beauties of Modern Architecture, Second Edition* (New York: D. Appleton & Company, 1839). (Courtesy of the Ricker Art and Architecture Library, University of Illinois)

Figure 184. Archibald Henderson Monument, Old Lutheran Cemetery, Salisbury, NC. Nichols designed this monument in 1825. It epitomizes his preference for using Grecian/Soane–influenced ornamentation in his architecture while working in North Carolina. (Photograph by author)

North Carolina, Alabama, and New Orleans, Nichols had updated his design ideas and was now an architect who was as contemporary in his detailing as any architect in the country (figures 180–184).

Not only did Nichols's time in New Orleans influence his ideas of architectural ornament and proportion but also practical ideas such as building security. During the planning of the latest renovation of the capitol, architectural historian Richard Cawthon uncovered evidence that the original front doors into the entry logia were double-leaf doors with glazing. These doors also had exterior shutters attached to them. The carpenters who built these shutters "are also to make frames, sash, doors, and shutters for the principal entrances under [the] portico of [the] State Capitol, the doors to be hung and fastening fitted to shutters and fixed and completed in accordance with the accompanying plan."[44]

Cawthon reinforces his argument through historic photographic evidence. In a 1901 photograph of the Old Capitol that was first published in *Art Work of Mississippi*, it is clearly apparent, through an enlargement of the photograph, that one of the front doors at the basement was a double-leaf door with glazed panels in the left-hand bay and a solid panel door leaf on the right-hand bay. He surmises that this arrangement is consistent with the prevailing method of installing commercial doors in the 1830s and 1840s in New Orleans, where there are numerous surviving examples of glazed double-leaf doors that are protected by exterior shutters. Based on the photographic and pictorial evidence that has survived, neither the 1824 North Carolina State House nor the 1831 Alabama State Capitol had exterior shutters attached to their front doors. The incorporation of exterior shutters, which was common in New Orleans but not as common in Mississippi, shows how Nichols adapted his architectural ideas and incorporated regional practices found in places where he lived and worked in his later designs.

The Mississippi capitol is not without numerous flaws in both its design and construction. These errors would annoy the building's occupants and threaten the building's longevity. One such example is the design solution to heat the building during the winter. Nichols designed twenty-eight wood-burning fireplaces throughout the capitol—twelve on the first story, eight on the second, and eight on the third. These fireplaces heated the House and Senate Chambers and offices for the governor and the high officers of the state. However, Nichols neglected to provide any source of heat for the three apsidal rooms on the east side: the Chancery Court Room on the first story, the High Court Chamber on the second, and the original state library on the third. Shortly after occupying the building, the House of Representatives concurred with the Senate and passed a resolution on January 11, 1842, instructing the Commissioner of Public Buildings "to furnish the Chancery Court with three dozen chairs and a stove." In April 1853, a payment was made to James Smith for installing a stove in the state library. It is entirely likely that the High Court Chamber had a stove installed in it as well at this time.[45] Another more significant architectural conceptual flaw was the roof's design. The roof, originally covered with copper and abutting the three parapets of the building and the portico on the west side, was a constant problem for the Commissioner of Public Buildings. Nichols designed internal built-in gutters, which constantly leaked. Four years after the building was completed, Nichols was hired by the legislature to fix the leaky roof. They appropriated $2,240 for the project.[46] He designed revisions to the roof drains and the parapet flashing. Nevertheless, the roof continued to leak. This would lead to structural weakness for the roof members as noted in 1860 by architect G. J. Larmour (or Larmon) in his structural conditions report made to Governor John J. Pettus for the roof:

> Having examined the capitol in reference to the nesisary [sic] repairs, commencing at the roof I find the roof in a bad condition wich [sic] has by constant leaking caused the roof timber to rot. The roof needs about twenty square of new tin and then [to be] thoroughly painted with composition roofing Paint.[47]

Pettus was probably not surprised by Larmour's report. He and everyone else were enduring problems in their offices caused by a leaking roof. In 1861, a correspondent for the *London Times*, William Howard Russell, noted that the walls and ceiling of the governor's office were "discolored by mildew."[48] As was the case with his capitol building in Tuscaloosa, which also leaked, Nichols's Mississippi capitol was plagued by a faulty roof design and improper construction.

Despite these problems, the legislature and the citizens were proud of the new capitol. Shortly after its completion, it was prominently displayed to former president Andrew Jackson, who made an official visit in 1840 to the city that was named in his honor before he was president, and he toured the newly constructed capitol. Nichols played an active role in preparing the building for Jackson's tour by hanging garlands and curtains in the legislature chambers. Jackson, who was already in poor health and in decline, was brought to Jackson by stagecoach from Vicksburg, after traveling most of the journey by train, and was greeted by an honor guard on the capitol grounds. It is probable—but not documented—that Nichols was introduced to Jackson during the former president's tour of the capitol and that Jackson most likely viewed the construction of Nichols's next project for the state of Mississippi, the Mississippi Governor's Mansion.[49]

The Mississippi capitol is William Nichols's finest work as an architect and his greatest accomplishment as a builder. It is doubtful that anyone else could unify unskilled rural workers and slave labor with highly trained urban artisans to build such an opulent and elegant building. His Mississippi capitol must have conspicuously stood out as a beacon in a struggling town that lacked either the elegance or the scale for this masterpiece. Nichols constantly faced drastic shortages in material, labor, and funding for the project; he was confronted with

Figure 185. Mississippi State Capitol, typical corridor (photograph taken in 1940). (Historic American Buildings Survey, Library of Congress, Washington, DC)

Figure 186. Interior view of the dome, Mississippi State Capitol, 2005. (Courtesy of Wendy Kapp)

Figure 187. The Mississippi State Capitol rotunda. (Historic American Buildings Survey, Library of Congress, Washington, DC)

Figure 188. The House of Representatives Chamber, Mississippi State Capitol, ca. 1903. (Courtesy of the Mississippi Department of Archives and History)

Figure 189. View of the High Court Chamber in 1915. The capitol suffered extensive damage from a hurricane in 1909. The building was not restored until 1917. (Courtesy of the Mississippi Department of Archives and History)

Figure 190. View of the Senate Chamber in 1903 from the *Official and Statistical Register of 1904*. (Courtesy of the Mississippi Department of Archives and History)

Figure 191. View of the entry of the Senate Chamber in 1903 from the *Official and Statistical Register of 1904*. (Courtesy of the Mississippi Department of Archives and History)

Figure 192. The Old Mississippi State Capitol by William Nichols, 2010. The Old Capitol underwent a comprehensive renovation after suffering damage from Hurricane Katrina in 2005. (Courtesy of the Mississippi Department of Archives and History)

constant distractions from the Mississippi legislature, and his suppliers and tradesmen threatened to stop work throughout the project. He grappled with substandard brick and stone. Yet, he persevered, because of his tremendous amount of experience and knowledge in building and, of course, his audacity.

Nichols had also mastered the "modern" architecture of his era, the "Greek" of Minard Lafever. It is important to emphasize that he employed his understanding of the Classical orders and personalized it in order to meet his own needs, taste, and sensibility. The result was highly expressive architecture, but it was uniquely his own. Buildings such as the Mississippi capitol are examples of the infinite possibilities of Classical architecture when built by the hands of a master architect such as Nichols. He proved that classically inspired buildings could be fresh and inventive. Rather than simply adapting the accepted fashionable tastes in building and ornamentation, he embraced the new Lafever-influenced Classical architecture and fully understood its power of expression. The capitol is an icon in Jackson; it is hard to imagine the city without it. It was the culmination of his understanding of state capitols and the last and most meaningful of the four capitol buildings he had designed and built. It demonstrated how skillful and expressive William Nichols had become as an architect (figures 185–192).

Nichols was later hired to design one last feature for the Mississippi State Capitol, a wrought-iron fence. On March 5, 1846, the legislature approved "A[n] Act making compensation for repairs on Publis [*sic*] Buildings" which provided five thousand dollars for "the grading and enclosing of the Capitol square in Jackson . . ." This included the design, fabrication, and erection of an iron fence around the square. Nichols designed the fence to be nearly seven hundred feet long with iron pickets atop an eighteen-inch-tall brick base wall. Once again, Nichols utilized his experience in New Orleans to design the fence. The capitol fence was very similar in size and appearance to the fence surrounding the Old United States Mint in New Orleans, which had wrought-iron pickets with attached spear points. Thicker posts were placed at eight- or nine-foot intervals supported at the back by angled brackets. The thicker posts had broader three-pointed spear tips and a crescent below them. The thicker posts conveyed a symbolic military meaning since they resembled poles called "spontoons," weapons that were carried by junior officers or sergeants to control troop formations. The fence only extended the entire length of the west side of the block facing State Street. Due perhaps to insufficient funding for the iron fence project, wooden fences were placed along the north and south sides of the Capitol Green. The east side appears not to have had any fencing at all.

There were three gates in the iron fence, all flanked by stone piers. The main center gate, located directly in front of the portico, was ten feet wide to accommodate carriages and was flanked by two smaller openings for pedestrians. Each of these gates was five feet wide. There was also a northern and southern secondary gate; both of these gates' openings were five feet wide. The main center gate had two tall tapered piers, made from local sandstone, which were decorated with wreaths and topped with gaslights in 1870. The bas-relief sculpture of the wreaths consisted of a circular wreath of two branches that are bound at the top and open at the bottom. The overall composition frames the entrance to the capitol and further refines its relationship to State Street.[50] The wrought-iron fence was reconstructed during the latest renovation of the Old Mississippi Capitol in 2008–2009.

The Mississippi capitol suffered from neglect throughout the last half of the nineteenth century. The trabeated portico base failed and was replaced with Roman arches in 1870. In 1903, the legislature vacated the building and moved into the "New" Mississippi Capitol that was designed by Theodore Link of St. Louis, Missouri.[51] Link also restored the building in 1915 and it was used as various offices for the state government. From 1959 to 1961, the "Old" Capitol, as it was now called, was thoroughly renovated and was converted into the Mississippi State History Museum. During this renovation, the stucco was removed to expose the red brick as part of a misunderstanding of early documentation regarding the exterior finishing of the building. Ironically, damage incurred from Hurricane Katrina in 2005 allowed the Mississippi Department of Archives and History to reconsider this decision concerning the red brick exterior appearance,[52] and through an overdue comprehensive restoration led by Jackson architect Robert Parker Adams and former Mississippi Department of Archives and History Chief Architectural Historian Richard J. Cawthon, Nichols's faux stone stucco finish was restored.

The Mississippi State Penitentiary and the Governor's Mansion

Even while Nichols was busy with the capitol, the Mississippi legislature assigned him two other high-profile projects—the Mississippi State Penitentiary and the Mississippi Governor's Mansion. After the legislature and state officers occupied the capitol, Nichols moved his office into one of the old state offices, located a block from the capitol near the dilapidated old 1822 State House on Capitol Street.[53] Even as Nichols was supervising the completion of the capitol and planning for Andrew Jackson's visit, he remained busy designing and building these two important buildings for the state government in Jackson.

Figure 193. Mississippi State Penitentiary, ca. 1895, Jackson, MS. (Von Seutter Photograph Collection of Jackson, Mississippi, courtesy of the Mississippi Department of Archives and History)

Figure 194. The Mississippi State Penitentiary, ca. 1900. (Courtesy of the Mississippi Department of Archives and History)

Figure 195. Interior courtyard of the Mississippi State Penitentiary, 1901. At the time that this picture was being taken, the penitentiary was being demolished to make way for the new Mississippi State Capitol. (Courtesy of the Mississippi Department of Archives and History)

During the first quarter of the nineteenth century, Mississippi was in need of a state penitentiary. Small towns throughout the state had difficulty addressing law and order and most of them did not have the means to build jails suitable for incarceration. Governor Gerard Brandon pleaded with the legislature to fund a state penitentiary in 1827 but was unsuccessful in persuading them to allocate the funding. However, in 1836 the legislature approved the establishment of a state penitentiary in Jackson. Governor Charles Lynch signed the bill.[54]

The only photographic evidence of Nichols's Mississippi penitentiary reveals its appearance after repairs from extensive damage from the Civil War. The building complex was largely rebuilt after the Civil War along the lines of Nichols's original design (figures 193 and 194). Nichols had experience in designing prisons, having built the Wake County Jail in the early 1820s. He had also had submitted a design for the North Carolina State Penitentiary, which was never built, but was mentioned in correspondence among James Johnston, John Winslow and James Iredell, Jr. Winslow described it as "elegant."[55]

The penitentiary was an enormous complex (figure 196). Begun in 1836, the same year as the capitol project, it covered four square blocks in downtown Jackson, northwest of the capitol where the current Mississippi "New Capitol" is located. True to precedents found in both the United States and England, the penitentiary was designed in a severe form of English Gothic that came to define the building typology (figures 194 and 195). Penitentiaries were relatively new concepts for penal reform; their predecessors, prisons, were specifically for incarceration, whereas the intent of penitentiaries was to rehabilitate the inmate through isolation and reflection that would lead to penitence.

At the time of the Mississippi penitentiary's construction there were two prevailing theories of penitentiaries and penal systems: one was the Pennsylvania System, the other, the Auburn System. The Pennsylvania System was developed in 1829 with the construction of Eastern State Penitentiary in Philadelphia, designed by John Haviland. The revolutionary design reflected the system's theory of isolating the inmate in a cell. There was an adjacent isolated outdoor exercise yard. Contact with the inmate was forbidden; guards would place hoods over the heads of the inmate during transfers out of the cell and all contact with other inmates was discouraged. The objective was to encourage self-reflection by the inmate of the crimes he had committed. Haviland's design consisted of an eleven-acre block with a formidable stone wall with crenulated towers and battlements; a Gothic castle–like house for administration delineated the entry into the complex. Once inside, a central hub guardhouse anchored a system of wings of cells that worked like spokes on a wheel, allowing an innovative and efficient way to monitor the inmates in the penitentiary.

The Auburn System, which was developed by the New York Department of Corrections, is also known as the New York System. It was first introduced at New York State's Auburn Prison and later in Sing-Sing. It differed from the Pennsylvania System in that prisoners were in solitary confinement at night, but during the day inmates would work together on public work and hard labor projects. Political leaders in New York believed that the Pennsylvania System lacked the opportunity to teach inmates self-discipline, respect for property, and how to work with others. Architecturally, the system would be defined not by cell blocks radiating from a central hub, but with large square

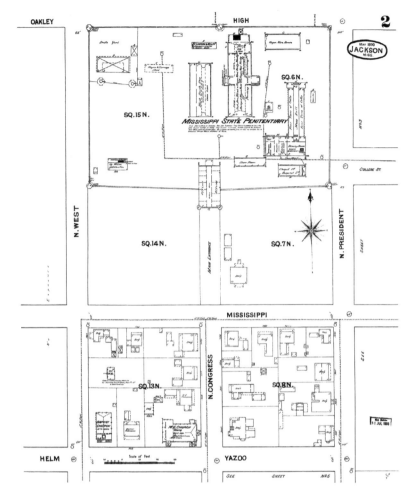

Figure 196. The 1890 Sanborn Insurance Map of the Mississippi State Penitentiary in Jackson, MS. The penitentiary covered four square blocks. The head house façade terminated the view from Congress Street. Today, the New Mississippi State Capitol lies in the former location of the penitentiary. (Courtesy of the Mississippi Department of Archives and History)

prison blocks that resembled warehouses for containing and boarding inmates. Nichols was very familiar with designing and building penitentiaries that were based on the Auburn System. In 1834–1835, he had overseen the construction of the Louisiana State Penitentiary in Baton Rouge, which was based on the Auburn System and modeled on the Wethersfield Prison in Connecticut. With such extensive experience in building penitentiaries, Nichols had little trouble designing the Mississippi penitentiary in an expedient and efficient manner.

Although both the Mississippi State Penitentiary and the Louisiana State Penitentiary were based on the Auburn System, the Mississippi building complex was visually different. John Haviland's Eastern State Penitentiary in Philadelphia, which was built in the English Gothic Revival style, ornamentally influenced Nichols. The overall composition of the complex consisted of a head house that served the administrative purposes of the penitentiary and a large prison block located to its east. A large formidable brick wall with recessed panels surrounded the compound. The head house was very similar in delineation to Haviland's in Philadelphia. It consisted of two flanking crenulated octagonal guard towers. An elaborate battered pair of towering parapets connected by crenulations and joined to the two flanking towers by crenulated parapets defined the center entry. Behind this imposing façade, the head house consisted of a one-story building that ended with the guard tower. The east prison block was "T" shaped, also being one story tall with crenulated parapets, a taller battered entry, and tall windows. Through the examination of historic photographs taken in 1899, additional details of its design can be determined. It appears there was another building north of the head house with a tower and a separate holding yard (figure 196).

The complex loomed heavily over Jackson. Obviously, this was Nichols's intent; Gothic architecture conveyed the appropriate foreboding, making it a popular choice for penitentiaries. There were significant precedents in England and the United States that he could have adapted in his design but Nichols chose to follow the standard that Haviland began with the Eastern State Penitentiary. By the time the first phase was completed in 1829, the Eastern State Penitentiary became the iconic image for incarceration.[56] Its system for corrections was adopted by at least three hundred other similar facilities worldwide; ominous and severe English Gothic would forever be associated with its function. Nichols understood this; more significantly, he understood the power of image and architecture. There is little doubt that citizens of Jackson and visitors alike clearly understood the function of the building sitting on the hill east of Capitol Street on the outskirts of town.[57]

Although Nichols was able to design the penitentiary in a short period of time, building it was another matter. Construction of the penitentiary languished in the same way the capitol did. Progress in building both construction projects suffered during the Depression of 1837. Construction would resume and then halt due to inconsistent cash flow and lack of materials and skilled tradesmen. In 1838, work resumed on both projects and by 1840, the capitol was finished enough to hold its first session of the legislature while the penitentiary housed its first 39 inmates.[58] It would eventually accommodate a total of 220 inmates during its existence, with an average of 85 incarcerated at one time.[59]

Similar to the Louisiana State Penitentiary in Baton Rouge, the main yard was used for industrial production by the inmates. This was in keeping with the ideas of the Auburn System, which promoted inmates' rehabilitation through manual labor. There were blacksmith shops, wheelwright shops, a cotton mill, and a brickyard, among others. When the Civil War began, it was converted into a munitions plant and a repair center for cannons and rifles. During the Vicksburg campaign, Sherman's army set fire to the complex and gutted the structure in May of 1863. After the Civil War, it was rebuilt in 1866 at a cost of thirty thousand dollars and was again used as a penitentiary. In 1900, the penitentiary was demolished and the "new" Mississippi capitol was built on its site.[60]

Even while working on both the penitentiary and the capitol, William Nichols was given the commission to design the Mississippi Governor's Mansion in 1838. The Governor's Mansion would prove to be one of Nichols's greatest triumphs. It is the second-oldest, continuously occupied, purpose-built governor's mansion in the United States[61] and a great source of pride for the citizens of Mississippi. Once again it was a building design by Nichols that not only defined its primary function as office of the governor but also characterized how Mississippians wanted to be perceived by the outside world. The elegance of its detailing and the setting in which Nichols placed the building on Capitol Street demonstrate an acute awareness of his audience and their main thoroughfare.[62]

None of Nichols's drawings of the design of the Governor's Mansion survive but in a letter to the legislature asking for supplemental funding, Nichols elegantly describes his design:

> The mansion house for the residence of the Governor is now being built agreeably with the plan approved by the last Legislature. The building will be 72 by 53 feet. The ground or basement story is eight feet high and is divided into servant's rooms, store room and cellar.
>
> On the principal floor, the main entrance is from a portico 28 by 12 feet into an octagon vestibule, which communicates with a drawing room 50 by 24 feet, with a dining room, which by means of folding doors, may be made of the same size, and with the great stair-case leading to the upper floor; in rear of these will be a suite of comfortable family rooms; the upper floor will contain four spacious chambers, a wardrobe and a private stair-case, communicating with the basement story.
>
> The portico on the principal front will be supported by columns of the Corinthian order. In finishing the building, it is intended to avoid a profusion of ornament, and to adhere to a plain republican simplicity, as best comporting with the dignity of the State.[63]

Nichols encountered the same headaches and setbacks in building the Governor's Mansion as he had with the capitol and the penitentiary; the legislature was again sporadic in providing funding for the project. But as he had done so many times before, he also made his own headaches; this time, the outrageous cost overruns permanently damaged his reputation and eventually led to his dismissal as state architect. Nichols's reputation for overreaching both architecturally and financially followed him wherever he went and the legislature was already wary of him working within a budget; but the fact that the state was already spending a tremendous amount of its funding on capital projects added a significant strain on both Nichols and the legislature.

The Governor's Mansion would become a major showdown between two colossal egos: William Nichols and Richard S. Graves (1814–1886?). Graves was the state treasurer and an ex-officio member of the Commission of Public Buildings; it was his job to assure sufficient funding for the project but it remained unclear whether he had final approval of all requests for payment. Nichols naturally assumed that he was in charge of approving payments as well as representing the state as an agent in negotiating and securing contracts with tradesmen and material suppliers. Unlike the orderly management of the capitol with Lynch, working with Graves in managing the Governor's Mansion would be disastrous. The abolishment of the Commission of Public Buildings by the legislature added more confusion to the process, especially since it occurred during the final stages of the capitol and penitentiary construction projects and while the Governor's Mansion was under design. Finally, poor bookkeeping by the Commission of Public Buildings' journal of expenditures further exacerbated the problem.

The legislature approved Nichols's design of the Governor's Mansion in 1838. He procured the services of S. D. Howell and Graves (no relation to the state treasurer) to excavate the one block site of West Street and Capitol Street in September 1839. Nichols then contracted the brickwork with several contractors. He first engaged the services of S. D. Howell, who apparently started the foundation work but did not complete it; he was paid $7,600. Nichols then had the company of Walker and McLacklan complete the work for $2,000. As the building progressed, more and more of the applications for payment were not processed. Walker and McLacklan filed another invoice to the state for $4,325 in early 1840 only to be paid in the spring of 1842. Woodcarver Reuben Clark would be paid $6,500 in the spring of 1842 for work he did in the fall of 1841, but an invoice for $16,000 would remain unpaid. It is interesting to note that almost all of the tradesmen and contractors who worked on the capitol either chose not to work on the Governor's Mansion or were not retained by Nichols. The most noticeable name absent from the expenditures' journals, which were kept by Richard S. Graves, was Nichols's former stone and wood carver, John Robb. Why Robb was not hired is not known, but it is apparent that he did not produce the intricate work which Nichols demanded now that his style of ornamentation was more Greek. William Gibbon and Ezra Williams did almost all of the intricate carving in wood and stone.

Originally from New Orleans, Gibbon and Williams were two of the few craftsmen who had also worked on the capitol.[64]

Work continued in 1840 after a supplemental appropriation of $20,000 was made by the legislature for the project. It would, however, stop again due to a lack of funding in the state treasury. Nichols instructed his workmen to install temporary roofing over the incomplete mansion. It did not keep the winter rains from damaging the ornamental plasterwork on the second floor. Work resumed in the spring of 1841 but this time no supplemental funding had been allocated; only a directive was made by Governor Alexander McNutt to continue the construction project. Somehow Nichols persuaded tradesmen and contractors to work and provide materials on credit. This would later lead to disastrous results. Nichols was given the directive to have the mansion ready for occupancy for the new governor at the time of his inauguration on January 10, 1842. He worked feverishly, making deals with workmen and suppliers alike to finish the building and make six rooms habitable by Governor Tilghman Tucker's inauguration. The mansion was somewhat finished in February of 1842.

By the time it was completed, the final cost for the construction of the Governor's Mansion was impossible to determine. Tradesmen and suppliers all came forth with invoices; since so few of the expenditures were documented it became impossible to know which of them were legitimate. Graves attempted to determine how much the building cost and concluded that it was approximately eighty-five thousand dollars. Five thousand dollars of it may have actually been duplicate payments. The legislature was horrified to learn that the mansion cost so much and demanded an explanation from Nichols.

Nichols angrily responded that Graves's report was "calculated to mislead the public mind and place the subject in the worst possible light." Nichols then countered that $11,000 of the amount Graves stated had already been paid and that he was adding that to the $85,000 final price tag. Nichols also accused Graves of overestimating the landscaping cost by $1,500 and showed by his records that the construction of the Governor's Mansion cost $61,556, not $85,000. Although the cost of the Governor's Mansion seemed exorbitant to most of the members of the Mississippi legislature, when compared to the cost of building it in today's dollars it would be worth $1.9 million (this does not include electricity, air conditioning, or plumbing)—a considerable bargain in construction when one takes into account the opulence that the building possesses.[65] Graves responded to Nichols's accusation in a letter to the state legislature dated February 26, 1842, asking that the legislature begin an investigation and an audit of "'His Highness, the ex-State Architect's' books on the cost of Mansion." By this time Graves was able to convince the legislature that the office of state architect should be abolished "because it was a useless and wasteful expense to the state," which they did. Nichols no longer had a job while Graves pledged to "faithfully discharge the duties of his office."[66]

Ironically, the legislature did conduct an investigation on the cost overruns and they found that Graves had embezzled over $150,000 from the Mississippi treasury during his two-year term as state treasurer. Graves was immediately arrested, dismissed from office, and placed under guard. However, Graves escaped prison with the assistance of his wife, Martha Thomas Graves, in a bizarre yet creative manner. While visiting, guards allowed Graves and his wife to meet behind closed doors for privacy. Graves then dressed in his wife's clothes, walked calmly past the guards, and fled prosecution. After he escaped the guards, Graves and his wife fled to Canada.[67] The investigation into Nichols's accounting practice soon halted as Graves's reputation was ruined. Even so, the whole affair had cost Nichols his position as state architect.

The budget overruns on the project were stunning. What was originally budgeted in 1833 to cost ten thousand dollars, a considerable sum of money for that time, cost well over eighty thousand dollars nine years later on a building that was still not completely finished. Certain decisions by Nichols in the design, most notably his use of zinc sheets for roofing, brought disastrous results since the material was unsuitable for the high humidity in Mississippi and the skilled labor to install it was nonexistent. It would not be until a slate roof was installed on the building in 1852 that the building's roof finally stopped leaking. Once again, Nichols's roof designs, which may have been sophisticated in their design, were impossible to build using the technology and tradesmen that were available in the 1830s and 1840s in the upland South.[68]

Despite all the problems that plagued construction, the Mississippi Governor's Mansion is one of William Nichols's most outstanding works and one of the most beautiful and memorable homes in Mississippi. When the Mississippi Governor's Mansion was first completed in 1842, it was well received by the citizen populace of the state despite its high price tag (figure 197). In designing the building, Nichols once again was heavily influenced by Lafever's *The Beauties of Modern Architecture*, first published in 1839. The design is truly a lavish celebration of the Greek Revival architecture of the antebellum era. It also shows how Nichols adjusted his design sensibilities to the lifestyle of Victorian America, most notably with the use of connected parlors, commonly found in cities such as Natchez (figure 198). In plan, it is by far his most ambitious domestic design (figure 199). The building is cubic in overall form, as are most of his residential designs; its façade is defined by a semicircular colossal portico based on Lafever's Choragic Monument of Lysicrates, which sets up the classical portion

Figure 197. The Mississippi Governor's Mansion, Jackson, MS, 1842. (Historic American Buildings Survey, Library of Congress, Washington, DC)

Figure 198. The Mississippi Governor's Mansion. (Courtesy of Wendy Kapp)

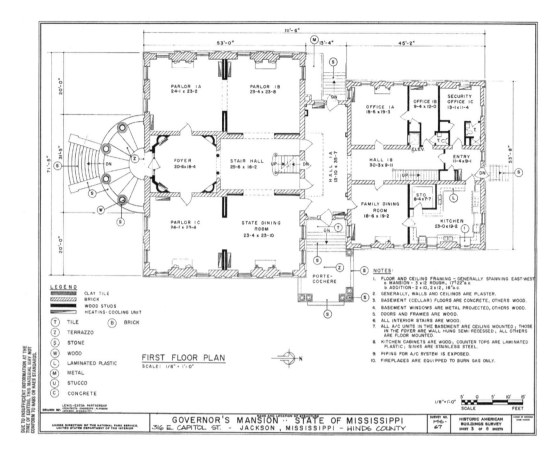

NOTES:
1. FLOOR AND CEILING FRAMING – GENERALLY SPANNING EAST-WEST
   a. MANSION – 3 x 12 ROUGH, 17½-22"o.c.
   b. ADDITION – 2 x 10, 2 x 12, 16"o.c.
2. GENERALLY, WALLS AND CEILINGS ARE PLASTER.
3. BASEMENT (CELLAR) FLOORS ARE CONCRETE, OTHERS WOOD.
4. BASEMENT WINDOWS ARE METAL PROJECTED, OTHERS WOOD.
5. DOORS AND FRAMES ARE WOOD.
6. ALL INTERIOR STAIRS ARE WOOD.
7. ALL A/C UNITS IN THE BASEMENT ARE CEILING MOUNTED; THOSE
   IN THE FOYER ARE WALL HUNG SEMI-RECESSED, ALL OTHERS
   ARE FLOOR MOUNTED.
8. KITCHEN CABINETS ARE WOOD; COUNTER TOPS ARE LAMINATED
   PLASTIC; SINKS ARE STAINLESS STEEL.
9. PIPING FOR A/C SYSTEM IS EXPOSED.
10. FIREPLACES ARE EQUIPPED TO BURN GAS ONLY.

LEGEND
- CLAY TILE
- BRICK
- WOOD STUDS
- HEATING-COOLING UNIT

(T) TILE   (B) BRICK
(Z) TERRAZZO
(S) STONE
(W) WOOD
(L) LAMINATED PLASTIC
(M) METAL
(U) STUCCO
(C) CONCRETE

FIRST FLOOR PLAN
SCALE: 1/8" = 1'-0"

GOVERNOR'S MANSION · STATE OF MISSISSIPPI
316 E. CAPITOL ST. - JACKSON, MISSISSIPPI - HINDS COUNTY

Figure 199. First-floor plan of the Mississippi Mansion, Jackson, MS. (Historic American Buildings Survey, Library of Congress, Washington, DC)

and overall height of the building. The layout of the building is composed of an octagonal-shaped foyer where Nichols used a considerable amount of poché and placed four recessed niches for sculpture. The north wall of the foyer is defined by a large cased opening with a Corinthian ordered entablature supported by two Corinthian columns and two pilasters (figures 200 and 201). Beyond the foyer is a grand staircase.[69] Flanking the center foyer and staircase are three parlors (the Front Rose, Back Rose, and the Gold Parlor),

Figure 200. Column of the front portico of the Mississippi Governor's Mansion. (Photograph by author)

Figure 201. Balcony detail of the Mississippi Governor's Mansion (photograph taken in 1936). (Historic American Buildings Survey, Library of Congress, Washington, DC)

Figure 202. Entry rotunda, Mississippi Governor's Mansion (photograph taken in 1936). (Historic American Buildings Survey, Library of Congress, Washington, DC)

and the State Dining Room. The two rose parlors are connected by a large set of pocket doors, a new influence not seen before in Nichols's work. Also, the Gold Parlor and State Dining Room are connected by large folding doors[70] (figure 202). It is also interesting to note that the State Dining Room and the Back Rose Parlor have secondary exits into the stair hall that enabled better service. The original Nichols design included a rear "cottage" or small wing.[71] The second-floor plan reflects the same layout as the first floor; above the foyer is a second floor sitting hall and four bedrooms that flank the sitting and stair halls and the green, cream, gold, and pumpkin bedrooms.

The ornamentation throughout the building shows the remarkable skill of ornamental plasterer William Gibbon.[72] For the entire major door surrounds, Nichols designed them following architrave entries described by Lafever in *The Beauties of Modern Architecture*. Similar to the entryways found in the capitol, these entries are lavish with delicate acroterions mounted on top of the rakes, which sit on battered and pronounced door casings (figures 203–205). The columns also show Lafever's influence with lavish and lush acanthus leaves and plinth blocks deleted from the column allowing the torus of the base

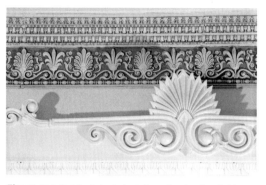

Figure 204. Detail of a typical antefix and anthemion, Gold Parlor, Mississippi Governor's Mansion. (Historic American Buildings Survey, Library of Congress, Washington, DC)

Figure 203. View from the Gold Parlor to the State Dining Room, Mississippi Governor's Mansion (photograph taken in 1936). (Historic American Buildings Survey, Library of Congress, Washington, DC)

Figure 205. Typical parlor cornice, Mississippi Governor's Mansion. (Historic American Buildings Survey, Library of Congress, Washington, DC)

to rest directly on the floor. The original cornices also show the Lafever influence with rich plaster leaves and deep moldings. The earthtone colors of the rooms celebrate the height of the Greek-inspired movement.

For the exterior, Nichols used stylized Corinthian pilasters into which he sets the large double-hung windows. The entablature is large and dominates the entire composition with its deep architraves and cornices with tall dentils. The entire entablature hides the low-pitch hipped roof of the building. A Greek-inspired door surround with a low-pitch Grecian tympanum, all of which highlights a delicately designed doorway with flanking sidelights, defines the center entry. Above the doorway is an elegant balcony supported by scrolled brackets and anthemia.[73] Another entablature and portal entryway is set behind the balcony, which has a geometric Chippendale-influenced railing (figure 201). The Mississippi Governor's Mansion was the last significant building Nichols designed during his tenure as state architect.

The legislature abolished Nichols's position of State Architect of Mississippi shortly after the completion of the capitol in the spring of 1842. He had served as state architect for the states of North Carolina, Alabama, Louisiana, and Mississippi for twenty-two years. But now William Nichols would face uncertainty for the rest of his years. His public bickering with Richard Graves was the final blow and although Graves's reputation was ruined so was Nichols's. Without the prospect of retirement or the support of his two sons (both of whom remained in North Carolina), William Nichols would have to find work wherever he could.[74]

The Governor's Mansion, the capitol, and the state penitentiary were the key buildings that justified the existence of Jackson. All of these buildings were the result of the Mississippi Constitution of 1832, which greatly expanded the powers of the state government and defined and restricted the role of the executive branch in the state. These three buildings expanded the services and infrastructure of the state government; interestingly enough, the constitution stipulated that the location of the state government would be conditional in Jackson and subject for review again eighteen years later in 1850. At that time the legislature would revisit the site of the state capital and evaluate Jackson based on demographics as well as the inevitable shift of both population and wealth in the state. In 1832, the legislature stipulated that all public buildings in Jackson would have to be funded through the sale of town lots, a typical business plan for funding public building. Despite the fact that the location of the state government was in a state of flux, the need of permanent infrastructure had to be addressed if the state was to continue to serve all Mississippians. As the state continued to develop so did its need for permanent institutions. Mississippi needed a penitentiary, a capitol building, and an executive mansion. Prior to the building of the Governor's Mansion, Mississippi governors including Lynch and Runnels treated the office as a part-time occupation. They met sporadically with the legislature and tended to conduct business out of their own domiciles in their region of the state. This caused friction and suspicion between the citizens and the legislature with the executive branch, which suspected regional favoritism. In a state that was experiencing both dynamic population and economic growth based purely on real estate development, this became a serious political problem. The only suitable solution was a centrally located state capital where all could at least perceive neutrality. However, as political power and population continued to shift from the southwest section of the state to the northeast section, Jackson's claim as Mississippi's capital city would remain in question.[75]

Despite Nichols's impressive achievements at the capitol, the penitentiary, and the Governor's Mansion, the town of Jackson would not be perceived as successful a city as Tuscaloosa. The legislature's idea of funding capital buildings through the sale of lots in Jackson was not as successful as they had hoped; most Mississippians thought of Jackson as an outpost and not a potential city. Few of its citizens believed that Jackson was destined to be the permanent capital of the state despite the sizeable investment in buildings. The establishment of Jackson was inauspicious at best and its development failed to impress foreign visitors. In his book on the Old Mississippi Capitol, John Ray Skates alludes to this when he quotes the impressions of the town by Theresa Pulszky, a woman who accompanied Hungarian patriot Louis Kossuth on a visit to Jackson in 1852. She described her accommodations as dreadful; her hotel was a "wretched abode that showed attempts at finery, but the ceiling and the walls looked as if they could not resist a strong wind." She would also compare the plates of food to the "coloured girls that served it, untidy and neglected."[76] The sense of shabbiness and lawlessness came about from several reasons; settlers in the upland South were less concerned about the finery of high cultured living. Secondly, Jackson in the 1830s was a frontier boomtown with all the trappings of such a place; it was a somewhat lawless and rowdy town full of transient people cashing in on the land rush and booming speculative real estate market.

But the need to present a better and more sophisticated face was not lost to all of the state's citizenry; the southwest section of Mississippi, specifically Natchez, and the areas closer to the ports of New Orleans and Mobile soon realized that Jackson would need to become more sophisticated. This sentiment was perhaps motivated to rebut the opinions of northeast Mississippians who were from cities such as Columbus, Aberdeen, and Holly Springs, all of which by the late 1830s were up-and-coming communities soon to surpass Jackson in both size and refinement. Although the Natchez elite had by now lost their grip on the state government, they were not interested in seeing the capital go any farther north. Even with the tremendous amount of building investment expended on the capitol (estimated final construction cost was $300,000), the penitentiary (estimated at $150,000), and the Governor's Mansion (estimated at $85,000), there was a strong sentiment to move the state government out of Jackson. In 1850, the legislature passed a resolution by thirteen votes to keep the state capital in Jackson and not move it to Yazoo City at the edge of the Mississippi Delta.[77]

If the ruling elite wanted the finest architecture available for Jackson they had the right architect in William Nichols. As he had done in Alabama and North Carolina, he produced beautiful work and he made them pay for it. The capitol cost three times more than the original allocation in the budget; the penitentiary costs doubled, and the Governor's Mansion, originally budgeted at ten thousand dollars, would end up costing eighty-five thousand dollars. Once again Nichols overspent set budgets on public buildings.

Nichols had come to the Deep South to profit from the vision of Andrew Jackson and for thirteen years he was able to do so with mostly favorable results. The Age of Jackson was the most dynamic period of growth the South has ever witnessed. In the short period between 1815 (when Jackson won the Battle of New Orleans) and 1837 (when he left the presidency), the South was transformed from frontier territory to one of the wealthiest and most refined areas in the country. During this time, William Nichols built significant buildings that helped define this age. He would never leave the state of Mississippi but he left Jackson to "follow the money," and he designed and built the last of his buildings in his long and illustrative career. During the last ten years of his life, William Nichols continued to leave his mark by designing and building several landmark buildings, specifically the campus of the University of Mississippi.

Chapter Eight

"... Entire Master of His Profession"

O ther than his time in Edenton, North Carolina, William Nichols's ten-year stay (1836–1846) in Jackson, Mississippi, was the longest of any place he ever lived in the United States. He designed eight more churches, schools, and residences before leaving Jackson in search of work. During the last seven years of his life, Nichols worked and moved continuously, designing yet another university campus, palatial homes, modest homes, and a masterpiece of a county courthouse. His work was so exquisite that he would be called the "entire master of his profession," a final tribute to the man who brought English classicism to the American South.

When Nichols left the position of state architect he joined the ranks of architects, builders, and real estate developers who had successfully built notable architecture in Mississippi. These men were accomplished builders and designers who built exceptional buildings in Natchez, Vicksburg in the western part of the state, and Columbus in the eastern part of it. However, they were also engaged in other business ventures, either in manufacturing or real estate development, and tended to work only in their hometowns. What set Nichols apart from his building colleagues, after he was relieved of his duties as state architect, was that he only practiced as an architect and he worked in various towns throughout Mississippi. From 1842 until his death in 1853, he designed buildings in central Mississippi, from Hinds County to Madison County, and as far west as Warren County. Moreover, he designed and built in north Mississippi, specifically the University of Mississippi in Oxford.

There were at least a dozen notable builders in Mississippi during Nichols's time there. Massachusetts native Levi Weeks (1776–1819) was one of the first builders/architects who introduced classical architecture to Mississippi when the state was still a territory. Weeks arrived in Natchez about 1809 and started a cabinet and chair shop. Prior to coming to Natchez, he had worked between 1798 and 1803 for his older brother, Ezra, who was a housewright in New York. His career in New York was brought to an abrupt end when he was accused of murdering his lover, Juliana Sands, and disposing her body in a well. He was acquitted of the heinous crime and soon returned to Massachusetts. Weeks later drifted from Cincinnati, Ohio, to Lexington, Kentucky, and finally settled in Natchez.[1]

From 1809 to 1812 he designed and built the Natchez Hospital, the office for the Bank of Mississippi, and the First Presbyterian Church. Unfortunately, none of these buildings survive. The most impressive building Weeks designed and built was the home of Lyman Harding called Auburn in 1812. Auburn is considered one of the most magnificent residences in Natchez. It is a two-story brick building with a colossal portico that is composed of a tetrastyle portico with Ionic columns supporting a Corinthian entablature. As did Nichols, Weeks relied on the popular pattern books from the late eighteenth century for his architectural ideas. At Auburn, he based the portico on Abraham Swan's *Collection of Designs in Architecture* and William Pain's *British Palladio*. He was four years older than Nichols and was also emerging from the master builder tradition to become an architect; however, his creative potential was unfilled. Weeks died from yellow fever in 1819 while building the east wing of Jefferson College in Washington, Mississippi.[2]

Andrew Brown (1793–1871) was another contemporary of Nichols, who was as talented an architect as both Nichols and Weeks, but chose to concentrate his talents in building a successful sawmill and lumber business called Andrew Brown and Company. A native of Scotland, Brown supposedly studied architecture at the University of Edinburgh before immigrating to the United States. He first settled in Pittsburgh, Pennsylvania, and arrived in Natchez in the early 1820s. Brown first worked at the sawmill owned by prominent Natchez businessman Peter Little (1781–1856) and in 1823 designed and built Little's mansion, Rosalie. In 1827, Brown designed and built the Masonic Temple in Natchez. As was the case with most Masonic lodges of this period, it was a masonry building covered with stucco with engaged Ionic columns. Unfortunately, it was demolished at the end of the nineteenth century. Although highly talented, Brown never pursued architecture as a profession. Instead, he purchased Little's sawmill in 1828 and focused his efforts on expanding its operation. In 1835, he increased his capacity from three thousand board feet of production to ten thousand board feet by employing a new steam engine sawmill. By 1860

Brown's sawmill was the most prominent lumber operation in Adams County; he supplied the lumber for Haller Nutt's iconic but unfinished residence designed by Samuel Sloan, Longwood.[3]

Nichols's other contemporaries in Mississippi were mostly involved in speculative real estate ventures spurred on by the land development boom that occurred in the 1830s and most of them suffered greatly during the Panic of 1837. Developers and builders Joseph Neibert and Peter Gemmell built several important buildings in Natchez and hired Scotland native builder/architect James Hardie (1808–1889) to design them. Together, Neibert, Gemmell, and Hardie built Choctaw and D'Evereux in Natchez.[4] The economic depression that followed the 1837 panic ruined Neibert and Gemmell; both of them died the following year in a yellow fever epidemic that ravaged the city. Hardie continued designing and building but never considered himself an architect; in the 1860 census, he was listed as a carpenter.[5] Along with his work with Neibert and Gemmell, it is believed that Hardie designed Saint Mary's Catholic Cathedral in Natchez in 1841.[6] Saint Mary's Cathedral is a brick masonry Gothic-style church with a center spire announcing its entry and tall finials terminating each of the church's buttresses.[7] There were also in Natchez two other notable builders. In 1857, the iconic mansion Stanton Hall was designed and built by Thomas Rose. John Crothers built the full peripterial colonnaded mansion called Dunleith. Both Rose and Crothers worked in Natchez and did not build on the regional level in the way Nichols did. They were builders first and architects second.[8]

Natchez was not the only city that was served by accomplished builders. Vicksburg and Columbus also had outstanding designers but none of them aspired to be practicing architects like Nichols. Instead, they either designed and built buildings, or they developed construction-building enterprises. In Vicksburg, builder William Bobb designed and built the Willis-Cowan House, which later became General John C. Pemberton's headquarters during the Battle of Vicksburg. He also designed and built Cobb House and Lakemont in Vicksburg.[9] Two Irish-born brothers, George and Thomas Weldon, nearly equaled Nichols in the number of notable public buildings built in Mississippi from the late 1840s until the outbreak of the Civil War. The Weldon brothers designed and built the jail at Port Gibson, Institute Hall in Natchez, and the Hinds County Courthouse in Raymond. Their masterpiece was the Warren County Courthouse (now the Old Courthouse Museum) in Vicksburg in 1858. An African American draftsman named John Jackson assisted them.[10] Even though the Weldon brothers developed an impressive reputation designing and building significant buildings in Mississippi and in Louisiana, their primary business was their lumber mill in Rodney in Jefferson County, Mississippi.[11]

Columbus, located in east Mississippi, was another prosperous market town where impressive architecture was built during the antebellum period. Vermont-born James S. Lull (1814–1872) arrived in Columbus in 1837 and soon began his successful housewright business. Lull designed the city hall in 1846 and designed and built the courthouse in 1847. He also designed and built numerous residences in Columbus such as his own residence, Camilia Place, in 1847, and several mansions—Riverview, Leighcrest, and the Colonnade. All of these residences embodied a severe and heavy architectural expression of the Greek Revival style. Lull rarely built outside of Columbus and although he greatly influenced Columbus, he did not influence other parts of the state or the South to the extent that Nichols did.[12]

Nichols's reputation as the state architect of Mississippi distinguished him from his contemporaries. He was known and respected as an architect; this allowed him to work solely as an architect for the last eleven years of his life, 1842 to 1853. He did partake in real estate development, specifically a hotel in Jackson around 1850, and he purchased a building lot in Oxford in the late 1840s. Unlike his builder counterparts in Mississippi—Hardie, the Weldon brothers, and Lull—Nichols continued to build notable buildings and refine his architectural expression, both in composition and ornamental detailing.

While still in Jackson, Nichols designed or was engaged in four privately commissioned buildings during his tenure as state architect: the Brandon Male and Female Academy in Brandon, the Rankin County Courthouse and Jail, also in Brandon, the Jackson Methodist Episcopal Church, and the Jackson Presbyterian Church. He worked on these buildings from 1837 until 1839; perhaps he undertook these commissions during the time when the state-supported building projects were stopped due to the lack of funding resulting from the economic collapse caused by the Panic of 1837. The earliest private building design that can be attributed to Nichols during his time in Jackson was the Brandon Male and Female Academy, later known as Johnson Hall, in Rankin County, Mississippi (figures 206 and 207). Built in 1837, Johnson Hall was a two-story brick temple-form building with a tetrastyle Ionic portico. The interior consisted of one large room, one small (music) room, and a hall with the stairs therein and library on the first floor. On the second floor there was a large classroom and a small classroom and a similar hall. Each room had a large fireplace. There were two wings, one on each side of the main block, which were added later.[13] Johnson Hall was very similar in appearance to his later works, the Lyceum at the University of Mississippi and the Lexington Female Academy, which he built at the end of his career. More importantly, the portico at Johnson Hall appears to be yet another one of his Ionic porticos based on the Temple of Illissus.[14]

Figure 206. Front façade of the Brandon Male and Female Academy, Brandon, MS. (Courtesy of the Brandon Historical & Genealogical Society)

In 1838, Nichols designed the Methodist Episcopal (M.E.) Church in Jackson[15] (figure 208). He most likely received the commission to design the church through the support of S. P. Bailey, the clerk for the State Building Commission in charge of overseeing the construction of the state capitol and secretary for the church's building committee.[16] He may have also had the support, or scrutiny, of another member of the church's building committee, Edwin Moody, who had accused him of having a secret business relationship with Alexander Baird and John Robb during the building of the capitol.[17] The M.E. Church was located on the northwest corner of North Congress Street and Yazoo Street, only a block or two from the Mississippi State Penitentiary (which was beginning to be built) and faced the green space now known as Smith Park.[18] The church was a simple gable ended masonry building that was covered with stucco. The church's massing and fenestration layout resembled Christ Episcopal Church in Tuscaloosa, which he designed and built eight years earlier. However, there were two significant features of the M.E. Church which made it different from his Tuscaloosa church design. The first feature was a cupola, which marked its entry, and the second feature was the simple Roman arched openings that marked the two front entries into the church. As was the custom for churches of this era, there were two entrance doorways with fanlight windows above them flanked by doubled pilasters. Five large windows with Roman

Figure 207. Side view of the Brandon Male and Female Academy, Brandon, MS. (Courtesy of the Brandon Historical & Genealogical Society)

M. E. CHURCH, SOUTH, JACKSON, MISS.
ERECTED IN 1838.

Photographed by E. v. Skytter, Jeweler and Artist.

Figure 208. The Methodist-Episcopal (M.E.) Church, located on the corner of Yazoo and North Congress streets, Jackson, MS. (Courtesy of the Mississippi Department of Archives and History)

arches and fanlights were placed along the long side of this rectangular building. Based on a January 12, 1838, "Request for Bids" from the church that was published in the Jackson *Mississippian*, each window had twenty-four lights with panes that were twelve inches wide and sixteen inches tall. The advertisement[19] also stated that the church would have five hundred lineal feet of pews and two sets of double doors with circular tops.[20]

It appears that Nichols, as state architect, performed administrative duties such as administering the bid processes for local government building projects. Newspaper announcements verify that he designed buildings for county governments as well while he was the state architect. In 1839, he had some involvement in either the design or the administration of the building contract for the Rankin County Courthouse and Jail. No images or drawings survive that described these two buildings. An advertisement for construction bids in the December 12, 1839, *Southern Sun* in Jackson confirms Nichols's involvement with this project:

Notice—Sealed proposals will be received until the 1st March, for building a brick Court House and Jail in the town of Brandon, according to plans and specifications, which will be exhibited on application to Capt. Nichols, State Architect at Jackson, or to the undersigned, at Brandon.

Willis P. Coleman,
JNO. B. Burke, Com'rs.[21]

Figure 209. The Jackson Presbyterian Church, built 1843–1846, Jackson, MS. View is from the northwest corner of North State Street and Yazoo Street. John Robb most likely reconstructed the front façade in 1851. (Courtesy of the Mississippi Department of Archives and History)

Figure 210. The Jackson Presbyterian Church, ca. 1890. (Van Seutter Photograph Collection of Jackson, Mississippi, courtesy of the Mississippi Department of Archives and History)

The courthouse and jail was demolished in 1853 to make way for a new courthouse.[22]

The Jackson Presbyterian Church, built 1843–1846 (demolished in 1891), most likely was a collaborative design between Nichols and his old colleague, John Robb, who was a member of the church's board of trustees. H. G. O. Parker was the contractor for the brickwork, which cost $2,150.[23] It was located close to the M.E. Church on the northwest corner of North State Street and Yazoo Street[24] and was somewhat similar in appearance to the M.E. Church. It was a rectangular brick building with a pedimented front gable and cylindrical belfry. It had one simple entry, flanked by simple Doric pilasters that lacked any entasis.[25] None of the windows or the front entry were arched; instead, they were trabeated. The church had a lower pitch gable than the M.E. Church. Through the examination of the details of the Presbyterian Church in historic photographs, it appears that Nichols's involvement in the execution of the design was either peripheral or had been altered after it was originally completed. Construction began on the church project in 1843, but then the project languished during 1844 and 1845 due to a lack of funding. By February 1846, when the church was completed and held its first service, Nichols had left Jackson for Oxford to begin work on the campus of the University of Mississippi.[26] It was documented that, in 1851, the church was busy raising funds to repair and stucco the building. Apparently, the front of the building was in a state of near collapse for reasons that are unknown. The Presbyterian Church vacated the building in May of 1851 during its repairs (or renovation) and held services in the Baptist Church. In October 1851, the church began rebuilding the façade of the building. This work, along with the furnishing of the church's basement rooms, cost $2,500 and was completed in 1852.[27] The rebuilding of the façade was most likely designed by Robb,[28] who had recently completed parts of the masonry work for the Mississippi capitol[29] (figures 209 and 210).

By the late 1830s Nichols had established himself as an accomplished and known architect in Mississippi. In the years after his death, several historic buildings throughout Mississippi have been mistakenly attributed to Nichols. One such example is the First Baptist Church in Columbus, Mississippi.[30] Begun in April 1835 and completed in September 1839, this church was designed and built by James S. Lull.[31] It was a two-story rectangular temple-form building with an Ionic ordered portico and four columns that appears to have been based on the Temple of Illissus and bears a strong resemblance to the Lyceum at the University of Mississippi and Johnson Hall. However, the Baptist Church featured elements that Nichols never designed in his public buildings. It was surmounted by a very tall steeple composed of five octagonal drums resembling the steeple designed by Sir Christopher Wren for St. Bride's Church in London. As was Nichols, Lull was influenced by the pattern books of Lafever.[32] But Nichols never designed a steeple or any structure of significant height during his entire career. All of the churches that have been verified or attributed to Nichols were much smaller, consisting of one single story in height. Furthermore, he never used the Illissus Ionic portico in any of the churches he designed. Instead, as found in Christ Episcopal Church in Tuscaloosa and the M.E. Church in Jackson, he tended to design churches that were compact, cubic in form, and used either arches for openings or columns in antis for the main entry. After the completion of the Baptist Church, Lull continued to have a successful building career in Columbus.[33]

From 1842 until 1846, Nichols solicited privately commissioned work and continued to undertake small projects and consulting work for the Mississippi state government in Jackson, specifically the new iron fence that fronted the capitol and a project to repair the capitol's leaking roof. As late as 1850, he advertised in the Jackson newspaper, *The Mississippian*, his work to "furnish designs for residences in every style of Architecture, accompanied with plans, details, specimens, and directions, with a careful and accurate estimate of the cost."[34] In this period of his work, he continued to evolve his architecture based on the ideas he learned in New Orleans, specifically the design ideas of Minard Lafever. He also reinterpreted designs of residences he had built earlier in his career. The buildings that either survived or were photographed before demolition show these facets of his designs.

From 1842 until he left Jackson in 1846, Nichols engaged in work for private clients in central Mississippi who had limited means and built less ambitious buildings. It appears that he needed to continue working in order to support both himself and his wife, Lydia. He relied on business relationships developed through his work in Jackson and North Carolina to obtain this work. During this brief period of his career, he designed three modest but sophisticated residences, one in Jackson, another in Vicksburg, and a third in Madison County, thirty miles northeast of Jackson. He also designed a building for a small women's college in Madison County.

The Jackson house, known as the John J. Poindexter House (figure 211), was built between ca. 1845 and late 1849 or early 1850; it was located on West Capitol Street. Perry Cohea, one of the state building commissioners during Nichols's state architect tenure, introduced Poindexter to Nichols.[35] Cohea most likely commissioned Nichols to design and build the house for Poindexter and his daughter, Mary Ann, as a wedding present.[36] It was a two-story wood-frame residence; its prominent feature was the monumental tetrastyle Ionic order portico based on the Stuart and Revett plate of the Temple of Illissus. When originally built, it was a temple-form building with the monumental portico placed on the gable end. Later, additional wings were added that featured crude simple framed two-story porches. The architrave of the portico stopped at the massing of the house; the frieze and cornice were carried around the entire roofline. The wood carved Ionic columns were refined and featured detailed scrolls and egg and dart ornamentation. The column shafts were fluted and the bases were

based on Lafever's design. Three doors opened onto the portico, one at the center of each bay. Despite the fact that later wing additions were added to each side of the original temple form, the Poindexter House retained the elegance of proportion and Greek-inspired design that defined Nichols's architectural work.[37] It would be the last building Nichols would design following the Gerrard Hall model he developed in Chapel Hill in 1822.

Nichols was most likely introduced to Charles Kimball Marshall, a prominent Methodist minister from Vicksburg, Mississippi, through his relationship with S. P. Bailey, whom he met while working on both the State Capitol and the Methodist Church in Jackson. Marshall was a major figure in the Southron Rights Movement of the 1840s and 1850s, a movement committed to advocating the self-expression and perpetuation of southern culture and values. Marshall deeply believed that the only way this could be achieved was to establish institutions of higher education in the South that focused not only on a sound education in the classics, natural sciences, and rhetoric, but also instilling southern and moral values for future generations of southerners or, as they had begun to call themselves, Southrons.[38] In his address before the Southern Convention of 1855, Marshall pleaded his case to support and establish new colleges and universities in the South:

Figure 211. John Poindexter House, ca. 1845–1849, Jackson, MS. Originally located on West Capitol Street, the home was moved to Robinson Street in 1925. The two-story wings were added and it was converted into apartments. The building was demolished in 1960. (Courtesy of the Mississippi Department of Archives and History)

Figure 212. The front colonnaded portico, Charles Kimball Marshall House, ca. 1844, Grove Street, Vicksburg, MS (photograph taken in 1936). (Historic American Buildings Survey, Library of Congress, Washington, DC)

We are in the habit of sending our sons and daughters to the north, far from their homes and home influences, there to be exposed to those, which we believe dangerous to our interests, and damning to our peace ... It is not possible for southerners to be safely educated at the north. They cannot come back with proper feelings towards their families and their people. Our sons and daughters return to us from their teachings and influences against the institution of slavery with erroneous religious opinions on the subject, and with the idea that it is a sin to hold slaves.[39]

Through his advocacy work, Marshall met and worked with the most prominent educators in the South, one being David Lowry Swain, former governor of North Carolina and president of the University of North Carolina. Swain was not only familiar with Nichols's work in Raleigh and in Chapel Hill, he was also an admirer of it. It is entirely likely that Marshall met Nichols through his involvement in the newly built Methodist Church in Jackson, through prominent members of the church such as Bailey, or through his work in higher education advocacy where he met colleagues such as Swain.[40] Nichols's professional relationship with Marshall would allow him to obtain building commissions for the Methodist Church and individuals associated with it.

Based on historic photographs, it appears that Nichols only designed the portico and reworked the fenestration of the main façade of Marshall's modest cottage in 1843 or 1844 in Vicksburg (figure 212). Unfortunately, the Marshall house, a small one-story Greek Revival brick masonry and stucco house, was demolished in 1962.[41] The house had a hipped roof and a gable ended wing. Its most distinctive feature was its hexastyle one-story portico detailed in the Greek Ionic order based on Lafever's plates. The entablature was taller than what was typically built for Greek Ionic porticos. Adding to its dominance was a small parapet above the portico. The portico abutted the hipped roof, which clearly conveys it was an addition to the original house. The fenestration beneath the portico was grander and more refined than the windows and doors on the side elevation of the main house and the wing. Windows in the front rooms were composed of triple-hung sashes that met the floor. The window surrounds on the façade featured deep entablatures and Doric pilasters. The main entry resembled that of the Governor's Mansion, a tall transom supported by Doric-influenced pilasters. The front door was flanked by tall multilight sidelights supported by raised panels. The hexastyle portico, the elaborately detailed windows, and the front entry suggest that Nichols could have designed these features as an addition to Marshall's original residence.[17]

It is likely that Nichols was able to secure two building commissions in Madison County through his relationship with Marshall: a small office for the Sharon Female College and a small plantation manor house called Sedgewood. A significant number of Methodists in Madison County were active in the Southron Rights Movement and supported Marshall's idea for establishing colleges that would help shape the minds of future generations of southerners. First established by Presbyterians, Baptists, and Methodists in 1837 as the Sharon Female Academy in the town of Sharon, this small women's college not only offered the traditional nineteenth-century curriculum but also courses in Christianity and ornamental needlepoint specifically for the benefit of "Southron" women. In 1843, the Mississippi Methodist Conference converted it into the Sharon Female College. In 1844, Reverend E. S. Robinson became president of the college, revised the curriculum, and increased the enrollment of the school from eighty young women to one hundred. At this time, it appears that a small wood frame office was built to complement the two-building campus. The level of refined detail and composition in conjunction with its construction date suggests that Nichols designed this small office for Robinson[43] (figure 213).

Built circa 1844, the small office is another example of sophisticated detailing and proportion. It is a temple-form wooden building with a tetrastyle portico consisting of two fluted Ionic columns set in antis between two square piers. The entire building rested on brick piers. The interior of the building consisted of two simple rooms, each one flanked by windows. It appears to have never had a fireplace. The door and window surrounds with Greek-inspired trabeated detailing are very similar in appearance to the door and window detailing found at the Mississippi Governor's Mansion.[44] After the Sharon Female College went defunct, this office was moved from Sharon to a lot east of the courthouse square in Canton in the 1850s. In the early twentieth century the small building was used as a dental office.[45]

Figure 213. View of the front façade of the Sharon Female College Office, built ca. 1843. This small office was first built in Sharon, Mississippi, but it was later moved to Canton, Mississippi, where it became a dental office. (Courtesy of the Mississippi Department of Archives and History)

Nichols most likely received his next commission to design the manor house at Sedgewood Plantation near Vernon, Mississippi, through his relationship with Sharon Female College Board of Trustees president, Reverend James P. Thomas of nearby Vernon. It is likely that James P. Thomas introduced Nichols to his relative John H. Thomas, who hired Nichols to design his new plantation manor house near Sharon. John H. Thomas was an attorney and planter also from Vernon.[46] Along with James, he was a founding member of the Vernon Methodist Church and a member of the Vernon Southron Rights Committee.[47]

Sedgewood is a one-story wood–frame Greek Revival cottage with a low-sloped hip roof[48] (figure 214). Its most defining feature is a Doric tetrastyle portico in the center of the five-bay façade. The residence's plan is quite simple. It consists of four large rooms, each one approximately eighteen feet square with a twelve-foot-wide center hall. The cottage is graced with tall ceilings and rests on brick piers. Sedgewood

is notable and distinctive compared to other regional homes because
of its elegance in overall design and sophisticated detailing. With its
simple cubic form and low-sloped hipped roof, Sedgewood is similar
in appearance to one of Nichols's earliest works—the Joseph Blount
Skinner House in Edenton, North Carolina, built thirty years earlier.
The classical columns that are featured on the simple, small porches
define both residences. At the Skinner House, Nichols used the Roman
Doric order as articulated by William Pain; at Sedgewood, he used a
Greek Doric order influenced by Minard Lafever. The porch entablature
defines the cornice height at both residences. Prominent wood pilasters
mark the corners of the two residences and accentuate the clapboard
surfaces and the placement of the large double-hung sash windows.

Similar in size to the Skinner office center porch, the Doric tetrastyle porch at Sedgewood is an elegant design that includes Greek
Doric columns, a coffered ceiling, paneled soffits, and jamb panels
that flank the front door. The jamb paneling is somewhat Gothic in its
design. This detailed millwork is similar to the ceiling millwork of the
main portico at the Governor's Mansion. A feature that is both unique
and odd is the freestanding Doric columns flanking the front door. The
detailing and the proportions of the front door are also similar to those
at the Governor's Mansion (figure 215).

The detailing of the interior suggests that it is most likely not the
work of Nichols, although the builder was clearly influenced by his
design. All of the doors and windows have surrounds based on Lafever's
ideas in both form and proportion; however, all of the pediments are
capped with a Vitruvian scroll motif, an uncharacteristic feature for a
Nichols design. This detail suggests that Nichols designed and produced
the drawings but the owner, John H. Thomas, hired a local builder.

Figure 215. Detail photograph of the front portico ceiling at Sedgewood. (Courtesy of Todd Sanders)

Although these buildings were impressive, they were small, built out of wood, and designed with economy in mind. With the Poindexter House, Nichols updated his previous design ideas of the Greek temple as a residence using Lafever's ideas in its detailing and proportion. With the Charles Kendall Marshall house, Nichols began to explore current ideas of Greek Revival proportion and form; it is the first time he designed a hexastyle portico without a tympanum, an idea made popular by James Dakin in New Orleans. Finally, he refined his ideas in both form and ornamentation in Madison County with the office for the Sharon Female College and the manor house at Sedgewood Plantation. As much as each of these buildings demonstrates Nichols's sophisticated skill as an architect, they also reflect the modest means of the clients who had hired Nichols to design them, including a newlywed couple, a Methodist minister, a small women's college, and a middle-class attorney/planter. It is likely that the Great Depression of 1837 had taken its toll in Mississippi, and these projects were the only ones available to Nichols. But his luck would change. In 1846, Nichols won a large-scale architectural commission, the design and construction of the campus of the University of Mississippi in Oxford. It would be his last institutional work.

The University of Mississippi

Nichols was involved with the University of Mississippi from its initial planning and site selection to the completion of its first seven buildings. His involvement in the design was long and protracted. The creation of the state's main university was mired in both regional politics and the catastrophic loss of funding from the economic calamity of 1837. As with the struggles for placement of the state's capital, the University of Mississippi was also the subject of several bitter regional debates among state legislators, pitting southern counties against northern counties for the prize of having the state's university located in their town. Even the rationale for having a state university was debated. It would take five years to resolve these issues, making Nichols's involvement long and drawn out. However, he persevered and designed and built his most impressive college campus. It is one of the most beautiful and memorable campuses in the South.

Unlike the state of Alabama, Mississippi was slow in establishing a state institution for higher education. As early as 1798 when the U.S. Congress established Mississippi as a territory, it was stipulated that "religion, morality and knowledge being necessary to good government and the happiness of mankind, schools and the means of education shall forever be encouraged."[49] In order to accomplish this laudable goal, the ordinance also stipulated the donation of public lands, typically, two townships.[50] The state of Alabama was authorized to do the same, which they did. Through a misunderstanding (or perhaps a political arrangement), Jefferson College, a private corporation near Natchez in Washington County, received a grant of one township from Congress in 1812. Another township that was reserved for the Mississippi territory was located in what would become Alabama. When Alabama became a state, it took claim of this section of public land and used it to fund Nichols's University of Alabama campus. It would take a separate act of Congress in 1819, two years after Mississippi was admitted into the union, to authorize two new townships within the state borders to be sold as funding for the establishment of its state university.[51] In an address to the state legislature in 1821, Mississippi governor George Poindexter requested that the legislature select thirty-six sections (twenty-three thousand acres) to fund the establishment of a state university. The legislature was slow to act but land was selected in 1823. Governor Walter Leake also pleaded with the legislature to sell these lands as soon as possible. They ignored his request.[52]

During this period of Mississippi statehood, a private academy, later to become a college, was established. In 1826, Hampstead Academy was established in Clinton, Mississippi. Hampstead Academy was changed to Mississippi Academy and began receiving financial support from the legislature. In 1829, the trustees changed the name from Mississippi Academy to Mississippi College and appeared before the legislature, requesting the state's one township for education be awarded to them.[53] Governor Gerard Brandon supported the proposal, but it was denied by the legislature. Support for establishing a state university would wax and wane throughout the 1830s. However, the legislature decided to lease and sell township land with the revenue to be identified as the "Seminary Fund" and be deposited in two banks, the Union Bank of Mississippi and the Planter's Bank of Mississippi. The revenue accounts were identified as the "Seminary Fund." By 1837, the Seminary Fund had grown substantially. In his address to the legislature, Governor Charles Lynch reported that the fund was $310,000 and was earning 10 percent interest, or $30,000 annually, at the two largest banks in Mississippi.[54]

Unfortunately for the state, the two banks soon failed. They closed in 1841, another casualty of the economic crash of 1837 and the rampant land-credit speculation that caused it, a disastrous blow for the state government and the Seminary Fund. This crisis only exacerbated the political debate on whether or not Mississippi should even establish a state university. The Jacksonian Democrats favored state-supported college education, while the Henry Clay–led Whigs believed that education was a luxury, rather than a right, and should be enjoyed by only those who can afford it.[55] The Jacksonian Democrats prevailed and won the debate to establish a state university.

Throughout the years in which the finances for a state university were debated between the legislature and the governors, both the locality of the university and its overall mission were debated as well. In February 1840, Representative James Alexander Ventress[56] of Wilkinson County and chairman of the house committee on the Seminary Fund introduced a bill "to provide for the location of the State University." The House passed the bill on February 10, 1840, and Governor Alexander G. McNutt promptly signed it into law on February 20, 1840. The House appointed three commissioners, William L. Sharkey, Joshua Russell, and J. A. Van Hoesen to select a site for the state university. The House also directed Nichols to serve the commission as their consultant; he personally traveled to each city being considered by the commission and submitted reports on his findings.

In January 1841, the commissioners presented seven towns to be considered for the location of the state university: Mississippi City, Oxford, Brandon, Monroe Missionary Station, Louisville, and Kosciusko. The legislature selected Oxford over Mississippi City by a vote of fifty-eight to fifty-seven.[57] In 1844, three years after the site had been designated, Representative John Cushman of Lafayette County introduced a bill to charter the University of Mississippi. Governor Albert G. Brown signed the bill into law on February 24, 1844. The charter created a thirteen-member, self-perpetuating board of trustees and allocated $125,000 from both the Seminary Fund and the state treasury. Two senior-ranked members of the board, Ventress and John Johnston McCaughan of Hancock County,[58] worked closely with

Nichols in designing and building the original campus of the University of Mississippi.[59]

The board of trustees first met in Jackson on January 15, 1845. At that meeting the board filed for the incorporation of the university, elected officers, and requested the state to provide the monetary amount in the Seminary Fund. At the second meeting of the board of trustees on July 14, 1845, the trustees were informed that the state auditor refused to disclose any information regarding the Seminary Fund, presumably because the money had been depleted despite the allocation from the year before. (Governor Brown would later state that this money was "lost.") They did, however, receive an allocation of fifteen thousand dollars from the legislature.

The board of trustees met for the third time in Jackson on January 12, 1846, where they were informed that the legislature was reconsidering funding for the university in the state's yearly appropriation bill. Two weeks later, they learned that the money was being designated for funding the university; however, the actual amount had not been determined. Two days later, the board invited Nichols to submit "sundry plans and suggestions as to the University buildings," authorized James M. Howry, secretary and later treasurer of the board, to supervise the campus building project, and authorized the fifteen thousand dollars to be placed in the treasurer's account for building purposes (with the stipulation that the construction budget for the campus could not exceed twenty thousand dollars).[60] They also accepted two tracts of land lying immediately west of Oxford donated by James Stockard and John Martin. Lastly, they hired Nichols as the architect of the new campus. Three days later, on January 15, 1846, Nichols submitted campus designs to the board of trustees in Jackson.[61] At this meeting, they voted to engage in a two-year contract with Nichols to supervise construction of the campus buildings in Oxford for the amount of one thousand dollars per year.[62]

On the very next day, Nichols presented designs of each of the seven campus buildings to the board of trustees in Jackson.[63] Soon after, Nichols's work was approved and he was appointed to be the architect supervising the construction of the campus. The board of trustees forwarded a request for more funds to Governor Brown, along with the request to officially incorporate the university. Brown submitted his recommendations to authorize the funding of the university to the legislature, but with a stipulation as to how the campus buildings should be constructed:

> This institution (the university) has been located at Oxford, in Lafayette County, where a suitable site has been procured for the buildings. The trustees held a meeting in July 1845, and subsequently furnished me

with the printed copies of their proceeding, which I herewith transmit
to the legislature. An appropriation will be necessary to enable them to
erect their buildings. Economy should be observed to their construction;
convenience and durability being consulted, rather than beauty and ornament. I recommend that the sum set apart be limited to $50,000. The
State ought to assume the $110,000 lost in the Planters' Bank and place
at once on the same footing with the $103,287 now in the treasury. The
fund would then amount in round numbers to $250,000. Two hundred
thousand dollars of this should be retained as a permanent fund, and the
residue appropriated to the erection of college buildings in Oxford, as
heretofore suggested.[64]

Through his recommendation for funding the campus buildings at
the University of Mississippi, Brown was blunt on how the buildings
of the new university should be built, stipulating that the buildings be
built for "convenience and durability," rather than "beauty and ornament." Brown was most likely expressing his concern about Nichols's
work up to this point. After all, Nichols had been busy for the past
two years at the capitol designing repairs to the leaky roof. Limiting
the funding for the campus also could have been Brown's way to make
Nichols work within a firm budget. The cost overruns for building the
capitol, penitentiary, and Governor's Mansion were still fresh in the
minds of the governor and the members of the Mississippi legislature.
On January 26, 1846, the legislature approved Governor Brown's sup-
plementary act to incorporate the University of Mississippi; however,
they authorized twenty-five thousand dollars to be spent building the
campus in 1846 and another twenty-five thousand dollars for 1847. It is
also in this document that the fate of the Seminary Fund is disclosed.
Money for the accounts was deposited into two banks, one being the
Planter's Bank as mentioned by Brown. Both of them failed, causing
the financial loss.

Upon receiving news that he was hired as the architect and that
funding had been approved, Nichols immediately left Jackson and
moved to Oxford.[65] Nichols proposed a campus site plan, which
reflected his extensive experience in architecture and master planning.
It was elegant and efficient in its composition, a harmonious ensemble
of architecture in a natural setting. The Stockard/Martin tract was
less than a mile west of Oxford's courthouse square and described
by the Town Selection Committee as "romantically situated" on a
ridge between the Tallahatchie and the Yockony Patawfy rivers.[66] The
campus Nichols proposed consisted of seven buildings, in the shape
of an octagon, which enclosed the peak of a ridge. A road from the
town of Oxford entered the enclave from the east. Nichols utilized his
experience designing two state universities earlier in his career. This

Figure 216. The Lyceum, University of Mississippi, Oxford, MS, ca. 1860 (Courtesy of the Mississippi Department of Archives and History)

Figure 217. Map of the campus of the University of Mississippi in 1860. Research and drawing by Deborah Freeland, archivist, University of Mississippi. (Courtesy of the University of Mississippi Archives)

octagonal geometry of the campus was the result of his understanding of the rolling topography of Lafayette County. By nestling the buildings along the brow of the hill, Nichols was able to design the campus as efficiently as possible. It also resulted in making a lovely space in which groves of trees and buildings created a spatial arrangement that was both harmonious and insular.

As he did at both the universities of North Carolina and Alabama, Nichols kept the campus complex simple. He designed two three-story brick dormitories, similar in appearance to townhouses, each having six entries, low-pitch gable roofs, and simple façade designs. They resembled Nichols's Old West and the expansion of Old East at the University of North Carolina as well as the Washington, Jefferson, Franklin, and Madison dormitories that he built at the University of Alabama. As was the case at Alabama, the student dormitories at the University of Mississippi were named after heroes of the American Revolution—Jefferson, Lafayette, and Rittenhouse. At the north and south axis of the octagonal grounds, he designed two similar but somewhat smaller professors' residences. Based on the layouts shown in the 1895 Sanborn maps, the professors' residences were duplexes with a party wall extending along the north-south axis; the entries and porches for the residences were located at the east and west sides of the buildings. At the head of the octagonal ensemble was the most important building of the campus—the Lyceum (figures 216 and 217).

Nichols was directed to design the Lyceum to accommodate a large chemical theater for lectures, a laboratory (first floor), a natural history museum, four lecture halls (second floor), and finally, a library and lecture rooms (third floor). Nichols initially proposed a building incorporating a vertical composition that was similar to his Mississippi capitol design with a *piano nobile* level over an above-grade basement and capped with a third floor. This design had a central block, flanked by winged pavilions, with a colossal portico erected on a pier-based colonnade.[67] Interestingly, the board of trustees rejected the proposed design; Ventress was apparently involved in both the review and revision of the Lyceum's design. It was noted in the minutes that the design was amended, "[o]n motion from Mr. Ventress, a plan submitted by the architect was adopted, with the addition of another story, and dispensing with the foundation story."[68] Nichols revised his design for the Lyceum. After it was approved, the board of trustees awarded the construction contract to Oxford builder Daniel Grayson.[69]

The Lyceum is one of Nichols's last interpretations of one of his beloved precedents—the Temple of Illissus. It also reflects a Jeffersonian influence on Nichols, with its red brick, Ionic temple style, and white trim. The rectangular building is oriented on its gable end. The portico, which fronts the entire façade, is spanned by six colossal Ionic columns. Nichols faithfully follows the Stuart and Revett plate of proportions and details except that the pitch of the roof is flatter, set at a five to twelve pitch which is more Greek than Roman. This differs from Gerrard Hall or the old North Carolina Governor's Palace, with its six to twelve pitch. The moldings do follow the shape of his earlier work but, since the building experienced a fire in the 1920s, it is difficult to determine exactly how much original fabric remains in the building. (Upon examination of actual conditions and historic photographs, it appears the central block and the portico still embody Nichols's design intent.)[70] The columns do suggest Nichols's hand, following the precedent of the Temple of Apollo at Delos: the columns' shafts are plain for the first third of their height but become fluted up to the capitals. Nichols had experimented with the surfaces of shafts on several of his buildings, most notably at the Mordecai House in Raleigh, North Carolina, twenty years earlier, but with the Lyceum, it appears that he is more decisive in the column shaft treatment. Nichols then culminates the façade of the Lyceum with a curious Egyptian-inspired front doorway. The incongruent nature of this juxtaposition cannot be easily explained; perhaps this was a request of the administration, because it is certainly an inconsistent gesture by Nichols. It is entirely likely that the Egyptian entry was an idea from Ventress when he suggested changes to Nichols's original Lyceum design.

Despite the fact that the building underwent a fire and that two smaller flanking wings were added to the original building, the Lyceum at Ole Miss still retains what both Nichols and the university's board of trustees wanted with its creation—an iconic symbol of the university's mission. In an interesting coincidence of history, both William Nichols and Theodore Link were involved in the design of the Lyceum and what is now known as the Old Capitol. After Link designed the "New" Mississippi State Capitol, he designed the remodeling and renovation of Nichols's capitol in Jackson. He then remodeled Nichols's Lyceum and added the flanking wings in 1927.[71]

Although so much of its original fabric has been lost, the Lyceum's influence over the campus at the University of Mississippi is significant; it has become part of the university's official seal and has been the scene of many important moments in history, most notably James Meredith's entrance into the university as its first African American student in 1962.

Nichols's other known design that has survived at the University of Mississippi is a small building known as the Old Chapel,[72] later known as the Campus Y. It is now a center for international studies. Once again, it is likely that Nichols had a hand in the design but it is doubtful he had any involvement in its construction. The building was planned in 1849–1850 but was not completed until 1853, the year

Nichols died. The exterior of the building closely resembles earlier buildings that Nichols designed such as Old West at the University of North Carolina and Washington Hall and Jefferson Hall at the University of Alabama. While the outside is certainly reminiscent of Nichols with its rectangular massing, gable ends, two main doors, and simple fenestration, the interior is incongruent. It has been reconfigured as a chapel with a long aisle, pews, and a balcony, meaning the building was altered either during construction or shortly after it was completed. The original intent of this building is unknown. It would be sensible to conclude that Nichols's original intent was to design this building as a dormitory; the building resembled the Washington, Lafayette, and Rittenhouse dormitories. Moreover, the student population had increased in size in 1853. Over the years, reconfiguration of interior spaces in college buildings is as common as the changing mission of the institution. This appears to be the case with the building called the Old Chapel and Campus Y. It recently underwent a significant rehabilitation and is now called the Croft Institute for International Studies.

The first phase of the campus, which included the Lyceum, two dormitories, two professors' residences, and a steward's hall (which was very similar in design to Nichols's steward's hall, now called the Gorgas House, at the University of Alabama), was completed in the fall of 1848. Therefore, on November 6, 1848, the board of trustees terminated Nichols's services. Rather than returning to Jackson, he moved to Yazoo City to design a new courthouse for Yazoo County. Interestingly, the Mississippi legislature was debating relocating the state seat of government to Yazoo City during this time. After Nichols left Oxford, the board of trustees completed Nichols's octagonal master plan in 1857 under the leadership of Chancellor Fredrick A. P. Barnard. Barnard was familiar with Nichols's work as he was a professor at the University of Alabama in the early 1830s. He would later champion building new buildings, including an observatory and a new steward's hall, all of which were built in 1857. For practical reasons, both the observatory and the steward's hall were built away from the academic oval. Barnard's expansion of the campus was a departure from Nichols's original campus plan.

Today only the exterior center section of the Lyceum, the exterior shell of the Old Chapel–Campus Y (Croft Institute building), and the octagonal campus plan remain from the original campus Nichols designed and built (figure 218). The three dormitories, the faculty residences, and the steward's hall were all demolished and new buildings were built on their sites during the last quarter of the nineteenth century and the first decades of the twentieth century. Despite this, the essence of Nichols's master plan remains.[73] Nichols's octagonal

Figure 218. The Old Chapel/ Campus Y at the University of Mississippi, Oxford, MS. (Courtesy of the University of Mississippi Archives)

Figure 219. Jefferson, Lafayette, and Rittenhouse men's dormitories, University of Mississippi, Oxford, MS. (Courtesy of the Mississippi Department of Archives and History)

building ensemble is now commonly known as the "University Circle"[74] (figure 219).

So what happened to Nichols's original design for the Lyceum? Perhaps it was used to build the Chickasaw Female College in nearby Pontotoc County.[75] Based on the *Minutes of the Board of Trustees of the University of Mississippi*, Nichols had originally proposed the Lyceum with a vertical organization similar to his state capitol design in Jackson, a basement floor with trabeated masonry openings, a first floor at the *piano nobile* level, and a second floor. Begun in 1853 and completed in 1856, the Chickasaw Female College, also known as the Presbyterian

Figure 220. Front façade of the Chickasaw Female College, Pontotoc, MS. The façade of the Chickasaw Female College, built in 1853, bears a striking resemblance to Nichols's Mississippi State Capitol. It was demolished in 1938. (Courtesy of the Mississippi Department of Archives and History)

Female Collegiate Institution of Pontotoc, followed this description in its overall form.[76] It was a vertically organized rectangular brick masonry building with a hipped roof. A hexastyle portico with flanking pavilion-like wings projected from the center of the façade. The portico was set at the first floor, piano noble level, and the ground floor entry was defined by a six-bay trabeated entry. All of these architectural characteristics bear striking similarity to Nichols's Mississippi State Capitol (figure 220).

The floor plan of the Chickasaw Female College is noticeably similar to the original floor plan of the Lyceum (figure 221). Both buildings had hexastyle porticos and a central hall, bifurcated by a second hallway. Flanking the central hall were two small parlor-like rooms and at the end of the hall, a large room. In the Lyceum, this room was a lecture hall and chemistry laboratory. At the Chickasaw Female College, it was designed to be a chapel. The wings of the college building also had small parlor rooms; the final approved design of the Lyceum did not. Similar to the Lyceum, the Chickasaw Female College building had thick massive brick walls, which made the building "fire-proof."[77] There is, however, a significant difference between the Chickasaw Female College, the Mississippi State Capitol, and the Lyceum building: its columns. The columns used at the Chickasaw Female College were square and without entasis. Moreover, they were Doric in order

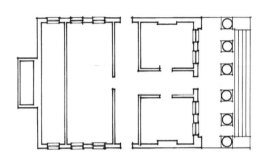
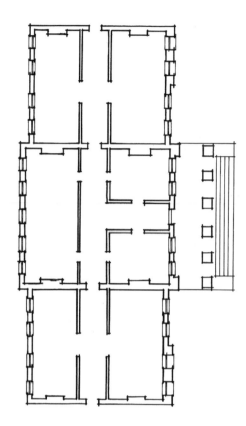

rather than Ionic, as is the case at both the Lyceum and the capitol. This would suggest that Nichols had only a minor involvement, if any, in its construction; builders in northern Mississippi constructed square columned porticos more frequently than round ones.[78]

One such builder who incorporated square columns in his portico designs was William Turner. Like Nichols, Turner had moved from North Carolina to Mississippi. He was approximately twenty-five years younger than Nichols. He is credited for building parts of the University of Mississippi campus.[79] His best-known works in Oxford are Saint Peter's Episcopal Church, built 1858–1860, and Cedar Oaks, built in 1859.[80] Cedar Oaks is a wood frame building with a central portico and colossal square columns.[81] Turner also designed and built the Sheegog House, which is similar to Cedar Oaks and would become the home of renowned novelist William Faulkner from 1930 until his death in 1962.[82]

Nichols knew Turner. On January 1, 1850, Turner purchased Nichols's house lot in Oxford for two hundred dollars.[83] One can only make a conjecture that the Chickasaw Female College is a Nichols design (specifically, his original design for the Lyceum) and that it was built by William Turner, who used Nichols's overall design composition,

Figure 221. Comparison of the floor plans of the Lyceum at the University of Mississippi and of the Chickasaw Female College. The floor plan on the left is the Lyceum; it is based on the floor plan that was included in the 1996 Lyceum Historic Structures Report by Michael Fazio. The floor plan on the right is the Chickasaw Female College; this floor plan is based on the 1920 Sanborn Insurance Map for Pontotoc, MS. (Drawings by author)

originally intended for the Lyceum, and installed his simpler detailing that is similar to what is found at Cedar Oaks. It is known that the brickmason was Billy Cooper, and his two brothers-in-law, Billy Wilkes and Willey Hubbard, did the carpentry work for the building. Turner was the master builder and oversaw the construction. As with John Robb (in North Carolina and then later in Mississippi) and John Fitch (in Alabama), it is also plausible that Turner was influenced by Nichols and designed the Chickasaw Female Academy based on his knowledge of Nichols's architectural ideas.[84] Unfortunately, the college was demolished in 1938 and records from its board of trustees no longer exist. However, based on the visual evidence from historic photographs and the Sanborn map of Pontotoc, which shows its floor plan, it is plausible that it is indeed a building originally designed or significantly influenced by Nichols.

The Yazoo County Courthouse

Yazoo City, which sits on the loam hills that divide the Mississippi Delta from the rest of the state, was second in size only to Natchez during the 1840s–1850s. Through its growth and prosperity, Yazoo City was the embodiment of the agricultural prosperity found in the extremely rich farmland of the Mississippi Delta.[85] The area was quickly becoming one of the most productive farming regions in the nation; however, it was not a place that fostered settlements. This was largely due to the fact that the region is vulnerable to flooding, malaria, and stifling heat in the summer, making it less than desirable to live in. The ruling planter class chose to live in towns along the loam hills, such as Yazoo City, bordering the Delta, and commute to their plantations. Yazoo City was becoming the southern economic hub of the Delta. Founded in 1824, it quickly rose in population and wealth. By 1849 its town fathers were ready to wrestle away the seat of state government from Jackson, its neighbor forty miles south.

Census records in 1850 identify Nichols as residing in Yazoo City.[86] He came to Yazoo City to design the Yazoo County Courthouse and once again found clients interested in showing off their prosperity with the opulence that Nichols could provide in his architectural edifices. There is very little documentation that remains from Nichols's business dealings with Yazoo County. (The city experienced occupation by Union soldiers in 1863 and a major fire in 1904.) All of the buildings that Nichols either designed or consulted on have been destroyed. The only known building that he designed in Yazoo City, the courthouse, burned in 1864. All that remains is the following description found in the local newspapers at the time it was built in 1850:

An edifice has arisen in our midst of unsurpassed beauty and convenience in the State at least—and our county may be well proud. It is an excellent specimen of Grecian style of architecture, treated with spirit and taste. It has an imposing appearance from the simplicity of design, the beautiful proportions of its parts, and perfect expression of its purpose.

The whole structure is 60 feet on Broadway, and 60 feet on Washington Street. The entrance in the centre is gained by steps to a portico of 4 massive columns, entablature etc. modeled from those of the Parthenon at Athens; the flank entrances have frontispieces in accordance with the portico. The exterior of the upper, or principal story is decorated with pilasters, the capitals of which are enriched with leaves, etc., similar to those of the Temple of the Winds at Athens, finishing with architrave, frieze, dentil cornice, and blocking course, etc. On the apex of the roof stands a cupola with a dome, etc. supported by 6 insulated Corinthian columns.

The design and execution of the building reflects the highest credit upon the architect's skill and genius . . . The perfect good taste, elegance, and simplicity, which adorn the whole, prove Captain Nichols entire master of his profession.[87]

Unlike with the campus of the University of Mississippi, Nichols was apparently given the leeway by the county government to not only design the courthouse with convenience and durability but also beauty and ornament. The building cost seventy-five thousand dollars to build in 1849–1850.[88] The citizens of Yazoo City warmly received the courthouse. The August 7, 1850, edition of the *Yazoo Democrat* expresses the general sense of pride felt in the courthouse building:

The object of most general interest however is our new Court House just now being finished, which for beauty and magnificence is second to no building of the kind in the State. Rising as it does amid the modest cottages which dot our prairie city, it presents a grand and imposing spectacle. We propose giving a minute description of the elegant structure in a subsequent number.[89]

Based on this description and Nichols's habit of rehashing his earlier designs, it appears likely that the Yazoo County Courthouse was as sophisticated in both composition and ornamentation as the state capitol in Jackson. Through this description, it can be assumed that Nichols designed yet another elegant Greek Revival building. What will never be known is whether he continued to evolve patterns and ideas based on the works of Lafever and Dakin (figure 222).

Yazoo City lost its bid to become the state capital of Mississippi in 1850 by only thirteen votes in the legislature. Part of the reasoning to keep the capital in Jackson was due to the fact that the state

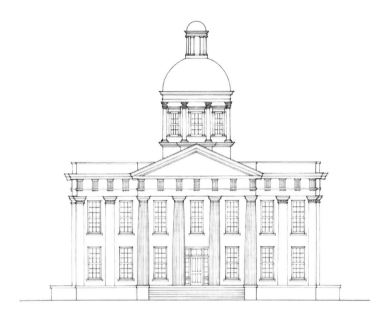

Figure 222. Main façade of the Yazoo County Courthouse, 1850. This conjectural drawing is based on a newspaper description published in the August 7, 1850, *Yazoo Democrat* and on details found in other Nichols buildings, such as Shamrock. (Drawing by author)

had invested so much money in state buildings. But another, perhaps darker, reason for the capital to remain in Jackson may have been the fear of yellow fever and malaria in Yazoo City. In 1853, three years after the vote to keep Jackson the capital, a yellow fever epidemic did hit Yazoo City, killing a significant portion of the city's population. For the rest of the nineteenth century, yellow fever would be a chronic problem for Yazoo City and the entire Delta.

The Last Designs

After 1850, Nichols and his wife, Lydia, relocated to a property in Benton, Mississippi, in eastern Yazoo County. Although it is unknown what his residence or farm looked like, the 1850 U.S. Census indicates it was valued at eight thousand dollars. Benton is approximately halfway between Yazoo City and Lexington, the county seat of Holmes County, which is northeast of Yazoo County and adajacent to it. At the sunset of his life, Nichols most likely sought a bucolic existence for himself and his wife.[90] He continued to design and build important commissions for private clients, institutions, and buildings for county governments in west-central Mississippi. His life and career as an architect would end in Lexington, Mississippi, where he is buried.

There are only three buildings that can positively be attributed to Nichols during this period, two of which, Shamrock in Vicksburg and the Hilzheim-Ledbetter House in Jackson, had features that closely resembled Nichols's Mississippi capitol and the Governor's Mansion.

The third building was the Lexington Female Academy in Lexington, which closely resembled the Lyceum at the University of Mississippi.

Based on its form, roof structure, architectural detail, and ornamentation, Shamrock can be attributed as a Nichols design for Vicksburg businessman William Porterfield in 1851.[91] Porterfield was an Irish immigrant who can best be described as a self-made and a somewhat bombastic individual; he had risen up the social and economic ladder in Warren County. After his arrival in the 1830s, he had amassed a small fortune through his investments in steamboats, wharf property, and an insurance business. After he married Jefferson Davis's adopted niece Julia, Porterfield built the most impressive and conspicuous house in Vicksburg on Oak Street, overlooking the confluence of the Yazoo and Mississippi rivers.[92] He named his residence Shamrock in honor of his native land.[93]

Shamrock was demolished in 1936; all that is known about it is through the extensive architectural documentation by the Historic American Buildings Survey in 1934 and the verbal descriptions of its interior written by Mrs. N. D. Deupree in 1902.[94] Shamrock was the culmination of William Nichols's ideas about grand residential architecture that he first explored with Hayes thirty-three years earlier. Imposing in both scale and demeanor, it was, in its day, an iconic symbol of the antebellum South. Here, Nichols reconciled the ideas of Lafever and Dakin with his own deep-rooted English sensibilities. The result was a richly detailed, elegant house that deliberately responded to the hot humid environment of Vicksburg and the Mississippi River. The house was cubic in its overall form, reminiscent of his residential designs in Alabama such as the Dearing House in Tuscaloosa and Thornhill in Forkland. It was three stories tall with two identical colossal Roman Doric hexastyle colonnades on its east side facing Oak Street and on its west side facing the Mississippi and Yazoo rivers (figure 223). Its interior layout featured a wide center hall flanked by parlors, reception rooms, and bedrooms. In planning the house, Nichols took full advantage of the hillside, making the lower level or ground floor plan as opulent as the main floor or *piano nobile* level. On the ground floor, he designed a carriage lane beneath the west colonnade. The ground floor featured a wide hall running west to east; to its north was a grand banquet hall, similar to the large banquet room he designed at Rosemount. It was twenty-four feet by forty-two feet in size with eighteen-feet-tall ceilings, a floor covered with marble of alternate blue and white blocks and two large fireplaces on its north wall. Opposite the banquet hall and south of the large hall were two reception rooms of equal size. The main floor was composed of a dining room at the northeast corner, a parlor on the northwest corner, a drawing room on the southeast corner, and a library on the southwest

Figure 223. Shamrock, Vicksburg, MS, 1851. This photograph was taken in 1934 before the building was demolished. (Historic American Buildings Survey, Library of Congress, Washington, DC)

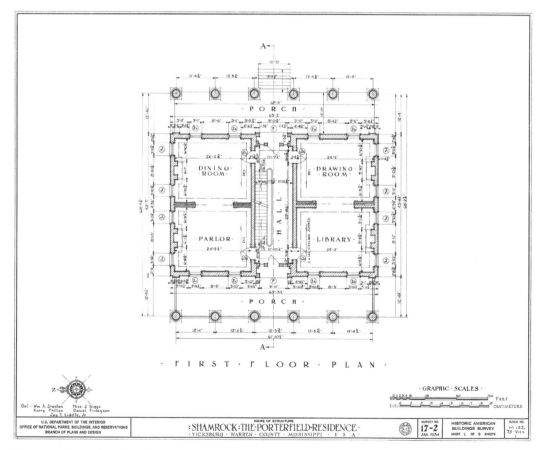

Figure 224. Shamrock, first-floor plan. (Historic American Buildings Survey, Library of Congress, Washington, DC)

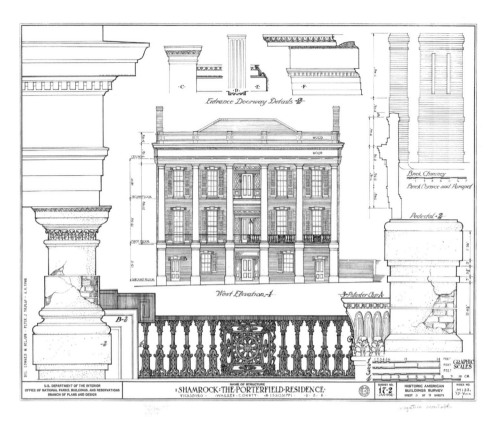

Figure 225. Shamrock, façade and details. Noted Louisiana architect A. Hays Town delineated this drawing of Shamrock when he was a young man. (Historic American Buildings Survey, Library of Congress, Washington, DC)

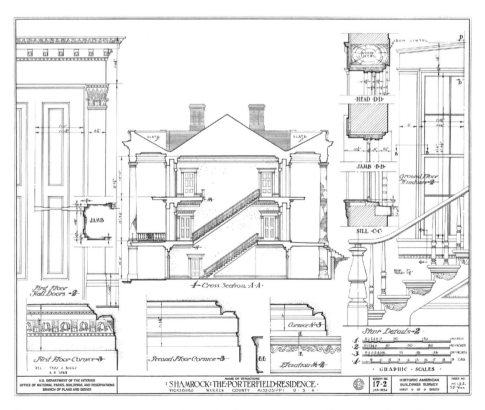

Figure 226. Shamrock, building section and interior details. (Historic American Buildings Survey, Library of Congress, Washington, DC)

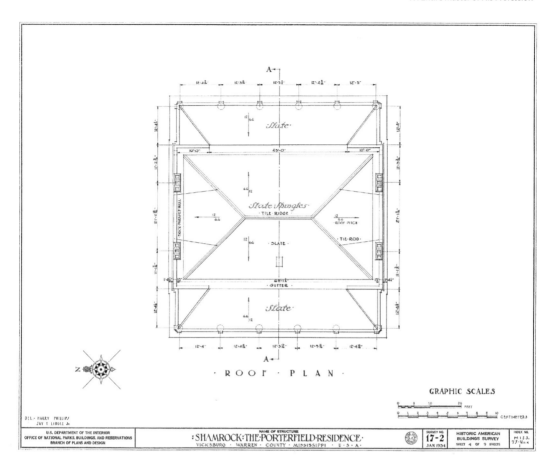

Figure 227. Shamrock, roof plan. Nichols used a roof structural system similar to that of Dakin's Merchants' Exchange in New Orleans. (Historic American Buildings Survey, Library of Congress, Washington, DC)

corner. The upper floor was composed of four equal-sized bedrooms. A heavily detailed grand staircase dominated the center hall that ran almost the entire length of the house. This suggests that the staircase was not designed by Nichols but instead ordered from a catalogue such as the Hinkle Guild Company of Cincinnati, Ohio, by Porterfield[95] (figure 224).

Shamrock had two distinct Nichols features. The first is an ornamental detail of acanthus leaves covering the necking of the Roman Doric columns (figures 225 and 226). This distinctive detail appears to be consistent with the description from a Yazoo *Sun* article describing Nichols's Yazoo County Courthouse, completed a year earlier: ". . . the capitals of which are enriched with leaves, etc., similar to those of the Temple of Winds at Athens . . ." The second feature is the sophisticated roof structure and interior gutter system, which spanned the main house and the east and west colonnaded porches. Nichols treats the entablature as a large parapet and designs the portico roofs as a shed pitched toward the center of the house, rather than away from the building as was typical during the antebellum period in Mississippi.

The shed section then abutted into a parapet where a trough gutter was placed to handle the storm water from the hip roof of the main house and the shed roofs of the colonnaded porticos. Interior storm water leaders were placed inside of the wall cavity to carry water away from the building. The roof design was bold and innovative; very few, if any, builders in nineteenth-century Mississippi would have proposed such a sophisticated roof structure but Nichols did. He first saw this type of roof system in New Orleans at Dakin and Gallier's Merchants' Exchange Building and relied heavily on it as precedent for Shamrock (as he did for the dome design of the Mississippi State Capitol). At Shamrock, Nichols used a shed roof design Dakin had originally introduced in New Orleans to give prominence to the parapet and entablature as well as to conceal the downspouts from the building. This gave the building a purity of form as well as ornament but was no doubt a maintenance problem for the owner. This design feature probably exacerbated Shamrock's decline after it had been abandoned (figure 227).

Before it was demolished, a Historic American Buildings Survey team that included a young but accomplished architect from Louisiana named A. Hays Town carefully documented Shamrock.[96] There is little doubt that Town was profoundly influenced by the ideas that Nichols portrayed at Shamrock since so many of Town's larger residential designs reflect Shamrock's proportions and its detailing, including his own residence in Baton Rouge.

The last two years of William Nichols's life are shrouded in mystery. Even though it appears that his work in Yazoo City, Oxford, and Vicksburg was warmly received, he never could develop a firm client base in any of those towns. Although he continued to advertise his designs for residences "with careful and accurate estimate of the cost," by now his reputation as an architect with expensive tastes and equally expensive fees preceded him; he was seventy years old, and it is entirely likely that his work had fallen out of fashion. However, one last residence that can be attributed to him was the Hilzheim-Ledbetter House in Jackson (figure 228). Built in 1851 in a style similar to Shamrock, it was a two-story, double-pile brick residence with a hexastyle colossal colonnade in the Greek Ionic order (not the Roman Doric as was the case at Shamrock) with a deep, elaborate entablature. The entablature suggests that it also had a roof structure with a large built-in gutter and internal leaders as at Shamrock. Centered in its façade was a small wooden balcony with an elaborate railing similar to the center balcony at the Governor's Mansion. The front doorway also bears a strong resemblance to the Governor's Mansion with a similar transom and sidelights.

Located on the corner of North State and College streets, the Hilzheim-Ledbetter House was one of the largest and grandest houses

Figure 228. The Antoinette Hilzheim House, Jackson, MS, ca. 1852. Located on the corner of North State Street and College Street, the residence had a hexastyle portico and deep entablature that resembled Shamrock and the Charles Kendall Marshall House, and its balcony resembled the balcony featured on the Mississippi Governor's Mansion. (Courtesy of the Mississippi Department of Archives and History)

built in Jackson before the Civil War. Jackson businessman William R. Miles built the residence between 1851 and 1853. Miles was a member of the Magnolia Hotel Company board of directors, a speculative development venture interested in building a high-end hotel near the train station on the west end of Jackson. Also serving on the board was former governor Charles Scott who knew Nichols through the Mississippi capitol and Governor's Mansion projects. Jackson historian William McCain alludes that Nichols was involved in this business venture as well and he also suggests that Miles knew Nichols from common business relations, most notably the building of the capitol. The hotel development project was never built.[97] Mrs. Antoinette Hilzheim acquired the residence in 1859 and resided there until her death in 1884. Her niece, Antonia Hilzheim Ledbetter, inherited the house and sold it in 1903. In 1924, it was converted into apartments and substantially altered. The building was demolished in 1960.[98]

In 1852, Nichols's pursuit of work led him to Lexington, the county seat of Holmes County, on the border of the Mississippi Delta. Socially, Lexington was very similar to Yazoo City; it resided on the loam-based bluffs bordering the Delta and attracted the wealthy planter elite. As was the case throughout his life, William Nichols followed the money to a place where people celebrated their wealth though their homes, schools, public buildings, and churches. Lexington, Mississippi, was the last town where Nichols worked.

Nichols's last design was the Lexington Female Academy (later Lexington Training School) (figure 229). Based on an old, faded, black and white photograph, the academy appears to be a rehashed design

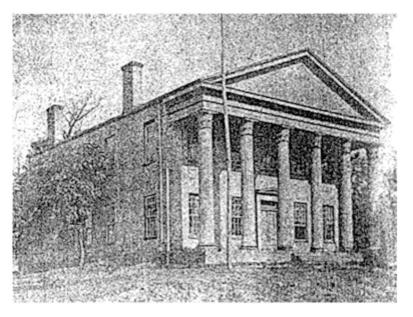

Figure 229. Lexington Female Academy, also known as the Lexington Training Institute, Lexington, MS. The Lexington Female Academy was strikingly similar to the Lyceum at the University of Mississippi. The only differences were the use of Corinthian columns for the portico and a simpler detailed entry. (Courtesy of the Mississippi Department of Archives and History)

of the Lyceum at the University of Mississippi. It was a hexastyle Greek temple with stucco-covered brick walls that was virtually the same size, shape, and fenestration as the Lyceum. The biggest difference was the columns themselves, which appear to have been Temple of the Winds columns while the entablature was in fact the Temple of Illissus. The front entry echoes the robust Greek Revival–Lafever detailing that Nichols designed for the Governor's Mansion in Jackson. The academy closed during the Civil War and reopened as Central Mississippi Normal School in the 1870s. The academy was demolished in 1904 and replaced with the Lexington public school.[99]

It is unknown if Nichols saw his last work completed. He died in Lexington in 1853 at the age of seventy-three and was buried in the local Odd Fellows Cemetery. No family, friends, or acquaintances surround him. It is both logical and fitting that the Odd Fellows Lodge of Lexington buried Nichols and erected his tombstone. They were a fraternal order of tradesmen and he was one of them. Their mission was to welcome the traveler, relieve the distressed, and bury the dead.

Nichols's tombstone features a virgin maiden weeping over a grave, a typical motif for the Victorian era.

WILLIAM NICHOLS, ARCHT.
A native of Bath England
Died
December 12, 1853
Aged 73 years

Haply thy Spirit in some higher sphere
Soars with the motions which it measured here
While thy worn frame enjoys its long repose
Freed from the cares of Life and all its woes.

It is unknown whether his third wife, Lydia Lucinda Smith, was alive at the time of her husband's death. Her whereabouts after the 1850 Census is unclear, and it is unknown where and when she died or even where she is buried. No documentation regarding the histories of sons Samuel and William, Jr., has been recovered since the charges of thievery against William, Jr., were dropped in 1841. No descendent has ever surfaced in North Carolina, Alabama, or Mississippi to claim that their ancestor designed the architectural monuments of these states. Obituary articles were published in newspapers in Raleigh, North Carolina; Montgomery, Alabama; and Jackson, Mississippi, stating his impressive achievements as an architect. His memory and his influence were discussed by the likes of David Lowry Swain, former North Carolina governor and president of the University of North Carolina, who wrote the following:

> The white framed cottage, planned and constructed for the late Moses Mordecai, was copied again and again in remote sections of the State, and various Court Houses and other public structures were designed, and in some instances erected under his immediate supervision as in Guilford and Davidson . . . He was a skillful and experienced artist and he made the public greatly his debtor for a decided impulse given to architectural improvements throughout the State in private as well as public edifices.[100]

It was indeed a remarkable journey for the carpenter-turned-architect from Bath, England, to, over fifty years later, be buried at the edge of the Mississippi Delta during the last decade of the antebellum South. William Nichols had a truly extraordinary life, and his work would help to define the aesthetics of the South for decades after his death. He had, at times, been a reckless businessman, a cad, and a knave, but he had also been an accomplished and skilled architect. He had an incredible ability to merge new ideas within the broad stream of architectural theory with practical ideas for everyday living. Moreover, his ability to bring these ideas with great skill and force to the remote and rural lands of the Deep South is truly extraordinary. William Nichols helped define an architectural aesthetic in the American South. This is his legacy.

Epilogue

Throughout the writing of this book, both Todd Sanders and I have agreed that William Nichols is a difficult, yet important, American architect to document and comprehend. His influence and impact on the American South is both obvious and obscure. One drawing, a few letters, and some ledgers are his only personal effects that survive. More of his buildings have been lost than have survived, and many of those have been altered beyond recognition. Those that survive, intact—Hayes, the Old Mississippi Capitol, the Mississippi Governor's Mansion—are the living embodiments of William Nichols the architect and his contribution to the built landscape of the American South.

Always in the background, Nichols has been inexplicably overlooked for the past hundred years. While he has been the subject of articles and featured or footnoted in books, the catalogue by Peatross and Mellown was the only overview of Nichols's work throughout his career. Until now, no one has ever published an in-depth book that holistically examines his work. We found both the man and his career fascinating. His work, ever evolving, made a profound impact on every region and town where he lived and worked. At first his style evolved gradually, then changed dramatically, like no other architect I have encountered. This book is the latest and most complete compilation of William Nichols's life and work across the South.

It is worth noting that Todd and I view Nichols as historic preservationists, not as architectural historians. Thanks to the Historic American Buildings Survey and state historic preservation offices in North Carolina (the North Carolina Department of Archives and History), Alabama (the Alabama Historical Commission), and Mississippi (the Mississippi Department of Archives and History), the history and architecture of William Nichols have been documented for posterity. These primary documents enabled us to write his story.

Both of us became fascinated with William Nichols through our work directly restoring or renovating his buildings. Todd's introduction occurred with his involvement in the architectural research for the restoration of the Old Mississippi Capitol. My professional relationship with Nichols came in 2002 when I first entered Gerrard Hall, a regal but humble small building, as the campus historic preservation manager at the University of North Carolina at Chapel Hill. While researching the reconstruction of its portico, I became fascinated with Nichols's life and work. I was surprised that the architect of one of the most significant buildings on the University of North Carolina campus was the same architect who had designed the historic buildings in Mississippi that had made such an impression on me as a young man. His story inspired me to write this book.

Tracing Nichols's built path has not been easy. Peatross and Mellown correctly surmised that "what is most remarkable about the career of William Nichols is the dogged anonymity which has attached itself to a man whose talents were widely acclaimed during his fifty years of active practice."[1] The lack of drawing documentation, a loss of records, and the destruction of his built work were the challenges that faced us in understanding, then writing, about the architect and his work. However, we have learned a great deal about Nichols's work through carefully documented archival research. These include the drawing of his proposed "remodeling" of the North Carolina State House, references of his proposed design of the campus of the University of Alabama, and Nichols's initial design for the Lyceum at the University of Mississippi. There are also accounting records from various building commissions that were extremely important in understanding how he built his most notable works. Journal and travel books written during his time by individuals describing their firsthand glimpses of his buildings have provided invaluable glimpses into his architecture, especially those no longer standing. All of these written accounts were quoted exactly throughout the book (including incorrect spelling, grammar, and syntax) in order to provide the reader the full context of crucial moments in Nichols's history.

In order to determine that Nichols was the architect of any specific building that lacked recorded documentation, a three criteria approach that we called triangulation was used: 1) Did the building embody specific and particular architectural features commonly used by Nichols throughout his career? 2) Can a compelling argument be made that the client knew or worked with Nichols in previous building projects or business ventures? 3) Was Nichols present in the building's vicinity when it was built? Using these criteria, a thorough vetting process was developed that allowed us to determine with a high degree of confidence that a building either was or was not designed by Nichols. Triangulation made clear his dominant signature style and helped us determine how he influenced the indigenous vernacular architecture of the region and other builders, including John Berry in Hillsborough, North Carolina; John J. Webster in Tuscaloosa, Alabama; and William Turner in Oxford, Mississippi.

Since Nichols chose to practice architecture predominantly in the upland sections of the Deep South, where skilled builders and architects were scarce, and since he chose to design buildings of a higher style and complexity, his work tends to stand out and be identified, especially in Alabama and Mississippi. His distinctive architecture has led many to assume that William Nichols designed any building built between 1815 and 1853 in a classical idiom style in North Carolina, Alabama, or Mississippi. This caused us to be highly critical in our examination of buildings attributed to Nichols and to base our judgment on the facts and our triangulation approach.

Indeed there are numerous buildings that have been attributed to Nichols but were, in fact, not designed by him. It does not seem plausible that Nichols designed Lochiel and Farintosh[2] in North Carolina, which were attributed as his designs by Peatross and Mellown in 1979. Catherine Bishir incorrectly cites Nichols as the architect of Cove Grove in Perquimans County in eastern North Carolina, perhaps because of its colossal tetrastyle portico and its center balcony. The builder is actually James Leigh, who built it in 1830, three years after Nichols had left for Alabama.[3] These residences did not embody any of the design characteristics found in documented Nichols buildings. There are several other buildings built early in his career that are attributed to Nichols by local tradition that cannot be proven or disproven. They are the Baptist Meeting House, the Hariss House, and the Chowan County Jail, all built in 1810 in Edenton, North Carolina.[4] Another is the State Bank in Tuscaloosa, which Mellown attributes as a Nichols design.[5] Since none of these buildings still stand and there is no other documentation that either supports or disputes that Nichols designed them, we felt that they should not be mentioned in the chronological listing of his buildings nor discussed in detail in the book.[6] We could also not verify if Nichols had designed either the Baptist or the Methodist churches in Tuscaloosa as claimed by Peatross and Mellown; no images or accounts have come to light. Research by the Alabama Historical Commission does state that both of these churches were built in 1830, when Nichols was building both the Alabama State Capitol and the University of Alabama.[7] However, there are no existing records stating that Nichols designed these churches and no images survive that depict the architecture of these churches.

New documentation has surfaced since the 1979 printing of Peat-ross and Mellown's catalogue that has corrected earlier mislabeling of buildings said to have been designed by Nichols; one such build-ing was Terry-Stone in Lexington, Mississippi. Peatross and Mellown mistakenly attributed Nichols as the architect of this Italianate-style residence built for J. M. Dryer and located north of Lexington.[8] It was indeed designed and built by a skilled architect and master builder. His name was A. Doyle. Although it was built in 1853, while Nich-ols was still alive, this A. J. Downing–influenced wood-frame high style Italianate residence shows little similarity to its neighbor a few miles away, Nichols's Lexington Female Academy, or any of the other Greek Revival architecture he designed during his seventeen-year career in Mississippi. In reality, local tradition misled their research, which confused facts that related the Lexington Female Academy with Terry-Stone.[9]

The Holmes County Courthouse in Lexington, built circa 1852, has also been attributed as a Nichols design but due to the lack of infor-mation pertaining to its appearance or his involvement it is difficult to state that this is plausible.[10] It burned in 1892 and, with no surviv-ing photographs or drawings, it is impossible to cite this building as a Nichols design. The only surviving document that depicts this build-ing is the 1892 Sanborn Map of Lexington, which only describes it as a square, cubical mass with a cupola and two one-story porches. The Sanborn map does not suggest the elaborate features of a domi-nant dome and a colossal columned portico, as the courthouse was described in the Yazoo *Mississippian*. Nichols may have been involved as a manager, an agent, or a designer, as he was in the building of the Rankin County Courthouse in 1839. However, without any primary documentation, any involvement by him is purely speculation.

Historians have connected Nichols to buildings due to his associa-tion with their prominent owners. However, after careful examination of key construction dates and Nichols's chronology, we have concluded that he did not design several buildings including Saint Andrew's Epis-copal Church in Jackson. Once again, there are no surviving images of the 1850 church, which burned in 1863.[11] Historians have attributed the building to Nichols based solely on his personal and professional relationship with the first bishop of the Mississippi Episcopal Diocese, William Mercer Green. Green had been rector of Saint Matthew's Church in Hillsborough, North Carolina, in 1825 when Nichols had designed that church so it would seem plausible that Green hired Nichols to design Saint Andrew's. However, key dates in the church's history clearly prove that if Nichols designed Saint Andrew's Church, William Mercer Green was not the client of the design. Green conse-crated the completed Saint Andrew's Church on November 24, 1850,

Figure 230. Burrwood, Holmes County, MS, built ca. 1850. Although the building has not been documented as having been designed by Nichols, the front balcony is similar in design to the balcony on the Mississippi Governor's Mansion. (Courtesy of the Mississippi Department of Archives and History)

his first service as the Episcopal bishop in Mississippi, having recently moved to Jackson from North Carolina. By the time Green arrived in Jackson, Nichols was living in Yazoo City. Furthermore, historian William McCain documented that the church's cornerstone had been laid on November 11, 1846, nearly four years before Green's arrival and ten months after Nichols had left Jackson for Oxford. Without any documentation linking the church and Nichols or any image of the building before it was destroyed, once again, a plausible argument cannot be made connecting Nichols with this church.

Photographic evidence led us to speculate that a residence in Lexington, known locally as Burrwood, may have been a Nichols design. Architectural features, specifically the front balcony, strongly resembled the Governor's Mansion balcony. But since the building was demolished and no records of it remain, it is impossible to draw a conclusion (figure 230).[12]

Local tradition and historical narratives have also confused the understanding of events in Nichols's life. In *Mississippi's Old Capitol: Biography of a Building*, John Ray Skates states that after the completion of the Governor's Mansion, Nichols owned and operated a hotel near the depot.[13] Skates most likely based this information on McCain's statement that Nichols operated a hotel in west Jackson called the Rail Road House at the Jackson depot, which he first opened for business on November 1, 1842. McCain does not indicate in which newspaper

the advertisement or announcement appeared. This information
appears to be untrue since the railroad was not built in west Jackson
until 1852 when Nichols was living in eastern Yazoo County and working in Lexington.[14] It is entirely likely that Nichols's involvement with
William R. Miles and the Magnolia Hotel Company was the basis for
this misunderstanding of Nichols's life.

Thirty-three years after Peatross and Mellown produced their
exhibit on the architecture of William Nichols, new interest and devel-
opments about Nichols and his work have arisen. The foundations of
the old University of Alabama were discovered, the portico of Gerrard
Hall has been rebuilt, and the Forks of Cypress has been designated
a National Historic Landmark. In 2001, the University of Mississippi
restored the Lyceum and in 2008 it restored the "Old Chapel" for a
new occupant; it is now the Croft Institute for International Studies.
Although the Old Mississippi Capitol was restored because of damage
incurred by Hurricane Katrina, the restoration did correct mistakes
made during its last renovation in 1959. All of these events and devel-
opments make a new, more comprehensive reassessment of Nichols's
works all the more appropriate.

Nichols and the South

Throughout the twentieth century, most architectural historians have
undervalued William Nichols; he was never considered to be in the
same company as the greatest architects of his time, such as Benjamin
Henry Latrobe, Alexander Jackson Davis, Minard Lafever, and James
Dakin. Although the buildings he designed and built were important
in their historic function, they simply became part of the backdrop of
the South. While most of them were designed with English influences,
they are deeply and uniquely southern. His preference for working
and living in the upland South away from cosmopolitan southern cities such as Richmond, Charleston, Savannah, and Mobile is partly the
reason why he is underappreciated, but his work, in Raleigh, Tuscaloosa, and Jackson is as important to these cities as works by the more
renowned architects in the port cities. Nichols was part of a trans-
formational era in American history, designing and building for the
post–Revolutionary War generation. His opportunities to build these
impressive buildings came from fortunes acquired during the Age of
Jackson—an era of inexpensive land, cheap credit, and reallocation of
political power. He was the right man at the right time in North Carolina, Alabama, and Mississippi, and all of these states share a common
architectural thread because of his work. He also helped define the
modern university campus in the American South and helped redefine

the appearance and function of the large residence in the Deep South by blending local building traditions with Grecian and, later, Greek Revival precedents. Most importantly, he helped define the "Temple of Democracy"—the state capitol. Inspired by Latrobe's work at the U.S. Capitol, he would give bicameral government its architectural form in three southern states.

Most people often overlooked Nichols's buildings. As was the case with Gerrard Hall (without its portico), his buildings were often taken for granted and accepted as good, solid buildings but nothing more. The reconstructed portico at Gerrard Hall caused people to pause, take notice, and appreciate his work. The same can be said about the Old Capitol after its stucco finish was reapplied nearly fifty years after it was removed. His buildings are best appreciated after they have been restored accurately and with features that he deliberately designed.

As both Todd and I compiled the list of his known buildings, we were struck by how many of them no longer exist. It is simply a wonder that we know anything at all about William Nichols. Buildings such as his Old Mississippi Capitol in Jackson were deemed as antiquated and cast aside for new, modern buildings, but few of these newer buildings capture the spirit of the people in the same way his work captured the Age of Andrew Jackson. When Mississippi built its new and more opulent state capitol in 1902, it embodied all the ideals of the American Renaissance, but with its Indiana limestone walls, columns, and lack of an appreciable scale, it is more of a generic state capitol rather than one that represents the culture of Mississippi. Nichols's Old Capitol is different. Its recognizable scale with its neighboring buildings and Lafever-based detailing embody the aspirations and excesses in the third and fourth decades of nineteenth-century Mississippi. Few architects can epitomize the age they lived in through their work, but William Nichols did.

Nichols was a transient individual who moved with great frequency throughout North Carolina, Alabama, and Mississippi. His fellow Americans almost his entire life considered him a foreigner. The Englishman from Bath struggled to create an aesthetic ideal in a rough frontier. His work was based on an English Palladianism that would later transform into a robust Greek Revival architecture. He left Bath, England, in 1800 and travelled to another country to reinvent himself. He was a carpenter who became a professional architect. He found success in North Carolina, but either his restless spirit or reckless business decisions led him to roam the South searching for work, sometimes for riches, sometimes for survival. As an architect, I can empathize with his trials and tribulations of designing, building, and simply making a living. He faced uncertainty and calamity throughout his life and career. He constantly argued with clients, builders, and suppliers. He rarely worked within his set budget. The roofs of all three of his capitols leaked badly. His large ego can be partly to blame for his misfortunes but the circumstances, which were beyond his control, were accountable as well, such as economic calamities at both the state and national levels. Nevertheless, he built complicated and sophisticated buildings in areas where quality materials were scarce and quality skilled tradesmen were few and far between. Moreover, he built complex spaces requiring technical solutions that had not yet been invented, such as the Rotunda Library at the University of Alabama with its disastrous acoustical qualities. It is true that Nichols's budgetary problems and arguments with clients (especially political ones) caused him to be dismissed as state architect in North Carolina and Mississippi. However, one must also consider the effect of the Great Depression of 1837 on his state work in Mississippi with the closing of the two largest banks and, with their closings, the loss of a significant amount of the state treasury; this was an event that was completely out of Nichols's control. He may have blown the budgets for building the Mississippi penitentiary and the Governor's Mansion but the state's inability to pay the invoices did not help the situation either. Moreover, although he received accolades for his work from journalists and visitors, his work was often underappreciated by powerful clients such as Mississippi governor Albert G. Brown who instructed him to build the University of Mississippi for "convenience and durability, rather than beauty and ornament." As all practicing architects know too well, the practice of architecture remains to this day an uncertain, often underappreciated, and unprofitable profession and business. Latrobe probably summed it up best: "I shall at last make cloth, steam engines or turn tailor for money, for money is honor . . ."[15]

Despite not writing any treatise or publishing a carpenter's guide or pattern book, William Nichols influenced the architecture of the Old South. It is remarkable to reflect on his work in the upland South, away from port cities that benefitted from cosmopolitan architectural ideas. Without Nichols, would white colossal Ionic columns have ever graced plantation mansions in the Alabama Black Belt or in Tuscaloosa? Would the Jeffersonian tradition ever have taken hold in the universities of Alabama and Mississippi? Would bicameral government have an architectural form in state government?

When Nichols arrived in 1800 in New Bern, he was a young man taught in the apprentice and guild tradition of carpentry and cabinetmakers of eighteenth-century Somerset, England. There were no "architects" in North Carolina. Nichols effectively used his cultured European roots and, with sheer audacity, presented himself as more than a carpenter. He was also bold enough to fraternize with the ruling elite of the state, a practice that was uncommon with builders in early nineteenth-century North Carolina. This alone allowed him to be considered part of the professional class, an equal with the doctors and lawyers of his day; obtaining the title of state architect solidified his new status. It is important to remember that becoming an architect during this age was no small feat. It required an understanding of building proportion in the Virtruvian manner, timber construction, the alchemy of mortar mixes for masonry, and superior business skills for managing a business and a building project. Nichols was one of the few men who successfully made the transition from carpenter-builder to architect. He prevailed through his unstoppable will, his considerable talent, and his outrageous sense of salesmanship. He was able to combine the talents of marketing with running a business and designing buildings, all of which are essential skills for becoming an architect and developing a successful practice. His sense of business and marketing helped to establish the idea that a professional architect should be hired in order to design important buildings for the state and the community.

Why and how William Nichols transformed his work from the restrained Grecian architecture in the John Soane and Benjamin Henry Latrobe English tradition to the rich, flamboyant, and fresh American forms expression of architecture espoused by Minard Lafever will never be truly known. However, it is clear that Nichols left Alabama for Louisiana as one architect and came to Mississippi a profoundly different one. We will never know how he made that evolution; no building can be found that shows his experimentation of new forms. This makes the transformation of his work all the more dramatic and unexpected when it is found in his creations, the Old Capitol and the Governor's Mansion in Jackson. It is here that William Nichols is fresh and different, and indeed an American architect.

While it is true that Nichols did not create a new architectural form, he did communicate new architectural forms into the interior of the rural South, which is his contribution to southern architecture. Along with architects including Kentucky's Gideon Shryock and Savannah's William Jay, he was part of a small but crucial group of regional architects that popularized the Greek Revival idiom in the South.

Nichols built in the classical tradition within the context and limitations of the region, but by combining high-styled forms with vernacular building traditions that responded to the environment, his architectural contributions enabled the South to become a distinctive and iconic place in the United States. The pragmatic nature found in his work, especially in how he responded to the climate, defined his distinctive work. With the observatories at Hayes and Eagle Lodge in North Carolina, the colossal porches and porticos at the Forks of Cypress and Rosemount in Alabama, and finally, the large windows that allowed cross ventilation at the Mississippi Governor's Mansion,

Sedgewood, and Shamrock in Mississippi, Nichols eloquently and beautifully responded to the heat and humidity of the southern summers. His understanding of passive cooling defined his work as much as his philosophical principles, which embraced the Greek Revival movement.

The fact that William Nichols was able to build refined Greek-inspired architecture in the American frontier is an extraordinary feat. It must have been amazing to drift down the Black Warrior River and suddenly see the splendor of Nichols's Alabama State Capitol, the University of Alabama, or Christ Episcopal Church, or to drift down the Pearl River in 1840 and see the classical edifice of the Mississippi State Capitol sitting on Lefleur's Bluff and rising over the marshlands. Not only did Nichols build the iconic images of culture and civility in frontier Alabama and Mississippi, he also helped to introduce urban form to both Jackson and Tuscaloosa. All of these places would have no doubt evolved into profoundly different places without the influence of William Nichols.

So, in the pantheon of the great architects of the American South, where does William Nichols fit? He did not develop a grand architectural vision that harkened back to idealized distant antiquity, as did Thomas Jefferson. He did not introduce English classicism to America as did Benjamin Henry Latrobe, and he did not further propagate it as did John Haviland or Robert Mills. He did not write about design or theory as did Davis or Lafever. But, on a regional level, Nichols should be carefully considered as one of the most influential architects of the American South. Catherine Bishir has always been fond of Nichols, referring to him as "North Carolina's Latrobe."[16] In Alabama, Robert Mellown and Robert Gamble have carefully considered his impact on the landscape of their state. Richard Cawthon painstakingly documented his work on the Old Capitol in 2008. Yet, he is not an architect whose work is studied in the field of architectural history in academia. This has occurred in large part due to architectural historians at state historic preservation offices focusing on Nichols's impact in their respective states and working with his story in the professional world of historic preservation rather than the academic world of architectural and art history for the past thirty years. Professional architectural historians working in state historic preservation offices focus on the building, while the academic tends to focus on the ideas associated with the building, both architectural and cultural.

As he was a regional architect, it is quaint to refer to him as "our Latrobe," and on a superficial level there are obvious similarities. However, it is more accurate to compare him to Isaiah Rogers of Massachusetts, a builder who became an architect, or Gideon Shryock of Kentucky, who apprenticed under William Strickland for one year in

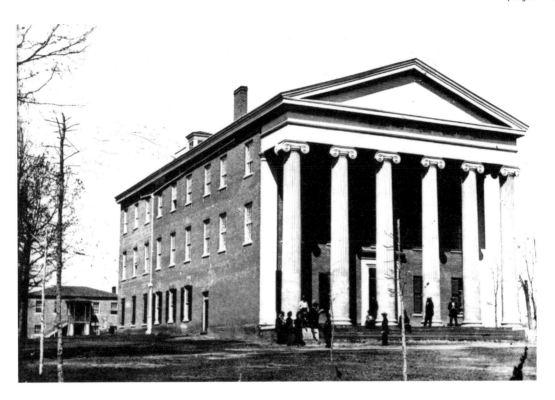

Figure 231. The Lyceum at the University of Mississippi. (Courtesy of the Mississippi Department of Archives and History)

Philadelphia as a draftsman but later returned to Lexington to practice architecture. Both of these architects assimilated the prevailing design theories of their age and made them their own. Through the work of Nichols, Rogers, and Shryock, it is apparent that classicism was not and is not a dead idiom of architecture; rather, it is a highly inventive, spontaneous, and personal architectural expression that can react to the particular climate where it is employed.

Winston Churchill was famous for saying that "[w]e shape our buildings; thereafter they shape us."[17] If this is indeed true then William Nichols profoundly influenced not only the architecture of the South, but also its culture. Would James Meredith's entry into Ole Miss in 1962 have been less powerful had he not walked past the imposing Ionic columns to the front door of the Lyceum? Nichols's influence in developing the primary structure of the campus plan in Chapel Hill, especially in the continued master plan of the campus of the University of North Carolina, is still felt to this day and will continue to be as long as there is a campus in Chapel Hill. By articulating the Grecian idiom of early nineteenth-century America in the South, Nichols helped define what it meant for homes and buildings to look "southern" and be "southern" to the generations of people who have inhabited the region and lived and worked in his creations (figure 231).

Figure 232. Mississippi Governor's Mansion. (Historic American Buildings Survey, Library of Congress, Washington, DC)

And what of those he influenced in architectural design? He certainly influenced his contemporaries John Berry and Henry Richards in Hillsborough and William Turner in Oxford. Eight decades later he would play a considerable role in shaping the ideas of a young Louisiana architect named A. Hays Town who, as an old man at the end of his career, single-handedly resurrected vernacular Greek Revival residential architecture by designing beautiful contemporary residences using historic precedents. Scholars attribute Town's work to the Creole-Cajun influence of Louisiana, but as a young man in the Great Depression he elegantly recorded the details and elevations of Nichols's Shamrock in Vicksburg, Mississippi. Although it is true that Town was influenced by the Creole architecture of his native state, his classical, Greek Revival refinement in both detail and composition obviously reflects the influence of Nichols. New residential architecture in Jackson and Baton Rouge aspires to convey Town's spirit of the place, and so, Nichols's legacy in the Deep South lives on.

To some of us, Nichols's work was more of a stage backdrop in our lives than object d'art. Living as a teenager in Jackson, Mississippi, I heard Eudora Welty read a passage from her book *Delta Wedding* in the old House Chamber of Nichols's Old Mississippi Capitol. Looking back, I cannot imagine being in another place for such an occasion.

That building, shaped by the vision of William Nichols in 1840, also shaped me as a young man. I toured it during history classes in high school. I passed by it on weekend walks whenever I was in downtown Jackson. This book, filled with freehand sketches I made while retracing the path of William Nichols and images I uncovered in archives at the universities of North Carolina, Alabama, Mississippi, the Historic New Orleans Collection, and the historic photographs discovered by Todd in the Mississippi Department of Archives and History, is our small contribution to reestablishing his extraordinary legacy in the American South (figure 232).

William Nichols's fifty-three-year career was indeed an odyssey that led him from the inner coastal sounds of North Carolina to the rolling loam hills of Mississippi. Along the way, he created the architecture that would help define the Deep South as a society. I found his tombstone on a hot August day on the edge of the Mississippi Delta. After years of researching and retracing Nichols and his career, it ended here, in Lexington's Odd Fellows Cemetery. His tombstone looked like the others except in one regard. Ascribed next to his name was his profession—"architect." Through his buildings I was able to know William Nichols and the life he lived. The arc of his life, which he always wanted to improve, was simply astounding.

Notes

Introduction

1. Karen Moon, "UNC–CH To Host Preview of Robin Williams Movie: Patch Adams," *Daily Tar Heel* (University of North Carolina at Chapel Hill), December 4, 1998. A scene from the movie *Patch Adams*, starring Robin Williams, was filmed in several locations, one of which was the University of North Carolina at Chapel Hill. The scene of Adams defending his methods to a board of jurists was filmed inside of Gerrard Hall.

2. Talbot Hamlin, *Greek Revival Architecture in America* (Oxford: Oxford University Press, 1944), 27. L'Enfant imprinted the planning concepts of his native Versailles on his landmark design of Washington, D. C.

3. C. Ford Peatross Photography Collection, North Carolina Collection, Louis Round Wilson Library, University of North Carolina at Chapel Hill. C. Ford Peatross never submitted a completed doctoral dissertation to the University of North Carolina at Chapel Hill. He did donate his photograph collection on Nichols to the North Carolina Collection, Wilson Library at the University of North Carolina at Chapel Hill.

4. C. Ford Peatross and Robert O. Mellown, *William Nichols, Architect* (Tuscaloosa, Ala.: University of Alabama Art Gallery, 1979). The exhibit also travelled to the Old Mississippi State Capitol Museum and the North Carolina Museum of History that same year.

Chapter One

1. William S. Powell, *Dictionary of North Carolina Biography* (Chapel Hill, N. C.: University of North Carolina Press, 1996), 586. Samuel Johnston was the father of James Johnston, one of the first two senators from North Carolina and the first owner of Hayes Plantation in Chowan County, North Carolina, which Nichols designed.

2. William S. Powell, *North Carolina Through Four Centuries* (Chapel Hill, N. C.: University of North Carolina Press, 1989), 10–105.

3. Nichols's entry in the 1850 U.S. Federal Census (Yazoo County, Miss.) states that he was born "abt 1776" in Bath, England. However, inscribed on his tombstone is the death date of "December 12, 1853 / Aged 73 years." Nichols's age at death would make his birth year 1780, which is the date I have used as the basis of calculations throughout the text. These two records are the only evidence related to his birth date.

4. John Sanders, interview by the author, June 14, 2005. It is believed that Samuel, who also operated a cabinetmaking warehouse, was the father of William Nichols. Sanders proposes this idea because William names one of his sons Samuel.

5. English Heritage Building ID: 268064. Samuel Nichols is listed as a "Carpenter and a Builder" from 1800–1812 in the Bath directories. He is also credited as the architect/builder of Dinder House, which was built in 1802.

6. Catherine Bishir, Charlotte Brown, Carl R. Lounsbury, and Ernest H. Wood III, *Architects and Builders in North Carolina: A History of the Practice of Building* (Chapel Hill, N. C.: University of North Carolina Press, 1990), 125–128. Bishir describes the sophisticated design proposal by Nichols for the interior renovation and steeple addition at Saint Paul's Episcopal Church in Edenton, North Carolina.

7. Peatross and Mellown analyzed Nichols's work and compared it to the guidebooks by William Pain and *The Antiquities of Athens* by Stuart and Revett, which was a common source for architectural inspiration by many notable architect-builders during the first decades of the nineteenth century. Upon my careful examination of Nichols's early work, I concur with their synopsis. Peatross and Mellown, *William Nichols, Architect*, 5, 6.

8. William S. Powell, *North Carolina Through Four Centuries*, 102.

9. Catherine Bishir, Charlotte Brown, Carl R. Lounsbury, and Ernest H. Wood III, *Architects and Builders in North Carolina: A History of the Practice of Building*, 127.

10. John Jones Papers, Athenaeum of Philadelphia, Philadelphia, Pa. Jones was a carpenter-builder who studied architecture at the Franklin Institute of Philadelphia and had aspirations to make the transition to the title of "architect." He entered several competitions but never won any commissions, and settled back into the builder profession. He would later help build the Philadelphia Opera House. Notes that he took while attending lectures by the famous Philadelphia architect Thomas U. Walter present the commonly believed knowledge base that was necessary to master to be considered an architect in the first half of the nineteenth century.

11. Michael W. Fazio and Patrick A. Snaden, *The Domestic Architecture of Benjamin Henry Latrobe* (Baltimore: Johns Hopkins University Press, 2006), 3–16. Benjamin Henry Latrobe, a Nichols contemporary and fellow countryman, had the opportunity to learn architectural and engineering principles and theories under respected London engineer John Smeaton and London architect Samuel Pepys Cockerell. His "architectural tour" of Europe had a great influence on his work, most notably the United States Capitol in Washington, D.C.

12. Adamesque is an eighteenth-century architectural neoclassical style of interior and exterior architecture popularized in Great Britain by two of the best-known Adam brothers from Scotland—Robert Adam (1728–1792) and James Adam (1732–1794). The style was influenced by Roman archaeological motifs discovered during the eighteenth century.

13. John Summerson, *The Life and Work of John Nash, Volume I* (Berkeley, Calif.: University of California Press, 1980), 3–19. John Nash (1752–1835) was an English architect best known for converting Buckingham House into Buckingham Palace. He was one of the leading proponents of British Palladianism.

14. William H. Pierson, Jr., *American Buildings and Their Architects, Volume 1: The Colonial and Neoclassical Styles* (Oxford: Oxford University Press: 1970), 388–390. Pierson discusses the only fireproof building in the American South in the early nineteenth century, the Fireproof Building in Charleston, S. C., designed by Robert Mills and built in 1827. Each room had a masonry ceiling constructed out of single groin vaults that held up the floor above, thus eliminating the need for any timber to be used in the building.

15. Frank Cousins and Philip Madison Riley, *The Woodcarver from Salem: Samuel McIntire, His Life and Work* (Boston: Little, Brown and Company, 1916). Samuel McIntire (1757–1811) was a carpenter/builder/architect from Salem, Massachusetts. He is best known for the Derby Summer House and the Benjamin Hawkes House.

16. Banister Fletcher and J. C. Palmes, *Sir Banister Fletcher's A History of Architecture* (London: Taylor and Francis, 1996 [reprint]), 815–833. The ancient city of Pompeii was discovered in 1738 and its artifacts became a source of fascination first in Europe and then later in America.

17. Talbot Hamlin, *Greek Revival Architecture in America*, 12–15.

18. Catherine Bishir, *North Carolina Architects and Builders: A Biographical Dictionary*, North Carolina State University Libraries, http://ncarchitects.lib.ncsu.edu, accessed June 9, 2012. Uriah Sandy (b. circa 1790) was a leading carpenter and builder in New Bern. He designed and built First Presbyterian Church from 1819 to 1822. Asa King (circa 1782–1843) was a highly skilled carpenter who built well-crafted porches such as the front porch on the Eli Smallwood House in New Bern.

19. Bishir et al., *Architects and Builders*, 57–95.

20. John Wood the Elder (1704–1754) designed and built the Royal Crescent in Bath. His son, John Wood the Younger, completed it in 1764. John Wood the Younger (1728–1782) designed the Royal Crescent in Bath and the Bath Assembly Rooms.

21. U.S. Census Records, Craven County, North Carolina 1800–1820. Census records document that a majority of white immigrants came from England. Benjamin Henry Latrobe came to Norfolk, Virginia, five years earlier. With his impressive education, which helped him attract the attention of George Washington and Thomas Jefferson, he easily rose to the top of the nation's fledgling architectural profession.

22. Carville Earle, "Pioneers of Providence: The Anglo-American Experience, 1492–1792," in the *Annals of the Association of American Geographers*, Vol. 82, No. 3 (Sept. 1992), 478–499.

23. Powell, *North Carolina Through Four Centuries*, 143–146.

24. Bishir et al., *Architects and Builders*, 95.

25. Peatross and Mellown, *William Nichols, Architect*, 6.

26. Mills Lane, *Architecture of the Old South: North Carolina* (New York: Abbeville Press, 1985), 121.

27. Talbot Hamlin, *Greek Revival Architecture in America*, 133. Isaiah Rogers (1800–1869) was a builder-architect from Massachusetts. He designed and built the Merchants' Exchange in Boston and was the last superintendent for building the Ohio Statehouse in 1861.

28. Mills Lane, *Architecture of the Old South: North Carolina*, 43. The main section of Tryon Palace was burned in a fire in 1798.

29. Catherine Bishir, *North Carolina Architecture*, 55–58.

30. Hawks was influenced by the work of William Chambers and Abraham Swan's book *British Architect and Designs in Architecture*.

31. Bishir et al., *Architects and Builders*, 93. Bishir discussed the brief period in which artisans came from Philadelphia to work on Tryon Palace in the late 1760s and how these artisans helped give New Bern refined architecture.

32. Thomas Tileston Waterman and Frances Benjamin Johnston, *The Early Architecture of North Carolina* (Chapel Hill, N.C.: University of North Carolina Press, 1941), 81.

33. North Carolina County Marriage Records 02–258, North Carolina Department of Archives and History. William Nichols married Mary Rew on 20 October 1805 in New Bern, Craven County, North Carolina.

34. North Carolina County Marriage Indexes 0259317–0259319, North Carolina Department of Archives and History. William Nichols married Sarah Simons on 18 November 1815 in Edenton, Chowan County, North Carolina.

35. North Carolina Grand Lodge of Ancient Free & Accepted Masons Records, St. John's Lodge, No. 3. Records state that Nichols joined in 1806 but there was no record of his status since 1807 and there were no returns of his record status from 1807 to 1846. Lynda Vestal Herzog, "The Early Architecture of New Bern, North Carolina, 1750–1850" (Ph.D. diss., University of California at Los Angeles, 1977), 323, 324.

36. Banister Fletcher and J. C. Palmes, *Sir Banister Fletcher's A History of Architecture*, 1044–1069. William Chambers (1723–1796) published the Treatise of Civil Architecture in 1759. He designed Somerset House in London and was appointed royal architect by George III.

37. Talbot Hamlin, *Greek Revival Architecture in America*, 10. Abraham Swan (ca.1720–ca.1768) wrote *The British Architect or the Builder's Treasury of Staircases* in London in 1745. An etcher, John Norman, produced etchings of Swan's drawings and published *The British Architect* along with Robert Bell in 1774. It was the first architecture book published in America.

38. Lynda Vestal Herzog, "The Early Architecture of New Bern, North Carolina, 1750–1850," 98.

39. Frances Benjamin Johnston and Thomas Tileston Waterman, *The Early Architecture of North Carolina, A Pictorial Survey with Architectural History* (Chapel Hill, N. C.: University of North Carolina Press, 1941), 32–33, 249. Both Tryon Palace and the Chowan County Courthouse, which are attributed to John Hawks, did not have porticos at their entries. Like the New Bern Academy, these buildings were cubic massed brick buildings.

40. Peatross and Mellown compare Soane's Sydney Lodge to the New Bern Academy. Peatross and Mellown, *William Nichols, Architect*, 10, English Heritage Building ID: 354989.

41. Hamlin, *Greek Revival Architecture in America*, 12. Hamlin establishes early American builders' reliance on William Pain, especially in New England where builders such as McIntire and Isaiah Rodgers practiced architecture and building arts.

42. Talbot Hamlin, "The Birth of American Architecture," in *Parnassus*, Vol. 10, No. 6 (Nov., 1938), 8–12.

43. Bishir, Peatross, and Sanders, "William Nichols (1780–1853)," *North Carolina Architects: A Biographical Dictionary*, N. C. State University Libraries, retrieved 11 July 2009, http://ncarchitects.lib.ncsu.edu.

44. James H. Craig, *The Arts and Crafts in North Carolina 1699–1840* (Winston-Salem, N. C.: Museum of Early Southern Decorative Arts, 1965), 321, 323, 327.

45. North Carolina Grand Lodge of Ancient Free and Accepted Masons Records, Unanimity Lodge, No. 7. Chris Reid [creid@msfreemason.org] "Re: Information about William Nichols, Architect of the Old Capitol," e-mail message to author, November 19, 2012. There is no record of William Nichols being a member of the Mississippi Grand Lodge of Free & Accepted Masons from 1836 until 1853.

46. Saint Paul's Episcopal Church records state that the vestry first met in the building in 1760 when the building still did not have windows or doors. It was not until 1767, when the vestry installed windows and doors, that the brick shell was fully enclosed.

47. Carl R. Lounsbury, "Anglican Church Design in the Chesapeake: English Inheritances and Regional Interpretations," *Perspectives in Vernacular Architecture, Vol. 9, Constructing Image and Place* (2003), 22–38.

48. Saint Paul's Episcopal Church National Register of Historic Places (1972).

49. Bishir et al., *Architects and Builders*, 127.

50. William S. Powell, *Dictionary of North Carolina History*, 487. Calvin Jones (1775–1846) was a physician, member of the N. C. House of Commons and one of the first members of the University of North Carolina Board of Trustees. He also helped establish the North Carolina Medical Society.

51. Catherine Bishir, "Severe Survitude to House Building," in *Southern Built: American Architecture, Regional Practice* (Charlottesville, Va.: University of Virginia Press, 2006), 152. Bishir cites correspondence between Nichols and Josiah Collins, who represented the Saint Paul's Church Restoration Committee, from January until May of 1806. The correspondence was found in the Saint Paul's Church Records. They were transcribed by Elizabeth V. Moore and provided to Bishir.

52. William S. Powell, *Correspondence of William Tryon* (Chapel Hill, N. C.: University of North Carolina Press, 1987), 2:835. Joseph Caldwell, *The Numbers of Carlton* (New York: G. Lang, 1828), 5. Caldwell's involvement with Nichols led him to echo a long-standing sentiment of the time that was first stated in one of "Atticus's complaints about William Tryon."

53. Saint Paul's Episcopal Church experienced a fire in 1949 that damaged the spire. The spire was repaired but the urns that Nichols designed and fabricated were not replaced. The urns are shown in the HABS drawings from 1934. Saint Paul's Episcopal Church Records.

54. James Iredell House National Register of Historic Places Nomination, NR No. 360771, February 26, 1970.

55. Chowan County Courthouse National Register Nomination (1972).

56. Hager Smith Design, PA Raleigh, North Carolina, "Old Chowan County Courthouse, Edenton, N. C. Field Notes." Unpublished. Hager Smith Design was the architectural firm that designed the renovation of the Chowan County Courthouse in 2000, verifying what had been designed and built by Nichols in the building.

57. John Summerson, *The Life and Work of John Nash, Architect* (Berkeley, Calif.: University of California Press, 1980), 23–33.

58. Bishir, Peatross, and Sanders, "William Nichols (1780–1853)," *North Carolina Architects: A Biographical Dictionary*, N.C. State University Libraries, retrieved 11 July 2009, http://ncarchitects.lib.ncsu.edu.

Chapter Two

1. Powell, *Dictionary of North Carolina Biography*, 78. Claude Joseph Sauthier (1736–1802) was a native of Strasbourg, France. He was trained as a surveyor, a cartographer, an engineer, and a landscape gardener. He went to North Carolina in 1767 at the request of Royal Governor William Tryon (1729–1788) for whom he produced maps of all of the notable towns in North Carolina at that time, including Edenton. When Tryon was appointed royal governor of New York in 1771, Sauthier

followed him to New York. Tryon appointed Sauthier royal surveyor of New York. He returned to France in 1777 and lived there for the rest of his life.

2. North Carolina Collection, Wilson Library, University of North Carolina at Chapel Hill, Chapel Hill, N. C. Aside from the Sauthier map and the family map, no other known record of the first house at Hayes Plantation exists.

3. Mills Lane, *Architecture of the Old South: North Carolina* (New York: Abbeville Press, 1985), 148.

4. William S. Powell, *Dictionary of North Carolina Biography Vol.2, H–K*, 302–303.

5. Lane, *Architecture of the Old South: North Carolina*,146–152.

6. Samuel Johnston to James C. Johnston, November 14, 1814 (letter), Hayes Collection, North Carolina Collection, Wilson Library, University of North Carolina at Chapel Hill, Chapel Hill, N. C.

7. "William Nichols to James Johnston, May, 1814," Hayes Collection, North Carolina Collection, Wilson Library, University of North Carolina at Chapel Hill, Chapel Hill, N. C.

8. Receipt of Bricks from James Cunningham, March, 1815, Hayes Collection, North Carolina Collection, University of North Carolina Library, Chapel Hill, N. C.

9. Hayes Manor, Chowan County, N. C., Historic American Buildings Survey, Washington, D. C.

10. William Nichols to James C. Johnston May 1, 1817 (letter), Hayes Collection, North Carolina Collection, University of North Carolina at Chapel Hill Library, Chapel Hill, N. C.

11. John Sanders, interview by the author, April 18, 2006.

12. John G. Zehmer, Jr., "Hayes: An Architectural Analysis," 1–5, unpublished. Zehmer links Hayes with the Skinner Office and the work done at Iredell House to Nichols based on the details such as the Greek key motif found at all three buildings. He reinforces Peatross's argument that Nichols designed and built these buildings and continues to identify details that Nichols used throughout his career in North Carolina.

13. Horace Walpole, *A description of the villa of Horace Walpole, youngest son of Sir Robert Walpole Earl of Oxford, at Strawberry-Hill, near Twickenham: With an inventory of the furniture, pictures and curiosities* (printed by Thomas Kingate, 174). Peatross and Mellown, *William Nichols, Architect*, 8, 9.

14. Catherine Bishir, "Severe Servitude to House Building" in *Southern Built: American Architecture, Regional Practice*, 148.

15. William S. Powell, *Dictionary of North Carolina Biography, H–K, Vol. 2*, 254. James Iredell, Jr. (1788–1853) was a first cousin of James Johnston (Johnston's aunt married James Iredell, Sr., and was Junior's mother). He was a prominent figure in North Carolina politics and served as governor 1827–1828.

16. James C. Johnston to James Iredell, Jr., December 10, 1816, Johnston Papers, Hayes Collection, North Carolina Collection, Wilson Library, University of North Carolina at Chapel Hill, Chapel Hill, N. C.

17. John Sanders, interview by the author, November 12, 2006.

18. Max R. Williams, "Clash of Titans: The Johnston Will Case, Volume 1 and 2" in *The North Carolina Historical Review*, April 1990, and William S. Powell, *Dictionary of North Carolina Biography*, 303.

19. Max R. Williams, *The North Carolina Historical Review, April 1990*, "The Johnston Will Case: A Clash of Titans, Part 1 and 2," the Hayes Collection, Hayes Library Collection, and Eileen McGrath Papers. James Johnston survived the Civil War and died at the end of the war, a frail and frightened elderly man. James Johnston, Jr., nephew of James Johnston, contested James Johnston's will after James

had removed him as the inheritor of the estate, which included at least three siz-able plantations, Hayes being one of them. The elder Johnston became enraged when his nephew fled Hayes for his wife's home in Lynchburg, Virginia, when the Union army occupied Edenton and Hayes and promptly changed his will, leaving two of his plantations to his overseers and Hayes to Edward Wood, an Edenton lawyer. The younger Johnston and his cousins contested the will and hired former governor Zebulon Vance (among other notable North Carolinians) who introduced the "insanity basis" idea for the first time in North Carolina, citing that the elder Johnston was insane when he rewrote his will. The North Carolina Supreme Court did not overturn the will and Wood became the owner of Hayes. His descendants sold an original copy of the Declaration of Independence that was owned by Samuel Johnston in 1981 for several million dollars.

20. The current owners, John and Susan Wood, completed a meticulous paint-ing project in 2005 in which noted architectural conservator George Fore deter-mined that the original paint scheme of the house was a soft peach with white trim and dark green shutters.

Chapter Three

1. U.S. Census 1820, Cumberland County, North Carolina, Fayetteville, 4:204.

2. John MacRae Map of Fayetteville, North Carolina, 1825, North Carolina Map Collection, North Carolina Collection, Wilson Library, University of North Carolina at Chapel Hill, Chapel Hill, N.C.

3. F. Rachel Long and Karen Copeland, "The Building Notes of the University of North Carolina at Chapel Hill." University of North Carolina at Chapel Hill Facilities Planning and Design Department, unpublished, 1993. Archibald Debow Murphey was an early graduate and professor at the University of North Carolina, a prominent lawyer in Hillsborough, North Carolina, and an important North Caro-lina state senator representing Orange County from 1812 until 1818. He was a strong advocate for public education and financing public infrastructure and road projects throughout North Carolina.

4. John G. Zehmer, Jr., to John L. Sanders, "Memorandum: William Nichols—Miscellaneous Notes," April 3, 1974.

5. James C. Johnston to James Iredell, Jr., December 10, 1816, Johnston Papers, Hayes Collection, North Carolina Collection, Wilson Library, University of North Carolina at Chapel Hill, Chapel Hill, N. C.

6. North Carolina House of Commons, *Report on the State of the Public Buildings and Resolutions of the General Assembly on that Subject.* N.C. Legisla-tive Papers, 1824–1825, 369, North Carolina Department of Archives and History, Raleigh, N. C.

7. John G. Zehmer, Jr., to John Sanders, "Memorandum: William Nichols—Miscellaneous Notes," April 3, 1979.

8. Hamlin, *Greek Revival Architecture in America*, 39, 40.

9. Paul Venable Turner, "Joseph-Jacques Ramee's First Career," *The Art Bul-letin*, Vol. 67, No. 2 (June 1985), 259–277. Joseph-Jacques Ramée (1764–1842) was a French architect trained in the French tradition of classical architecture by Belangier. He was forced to flee to Hamburg, Germany, to escape the terror of the French Revolution in 1793. In 1813, he designed the campus at Union College in Schenectady, New York; the revolutionary design featured a lawn and rotunda three years before Jefferson designed the University of Virginia.

10. Hamlin, *Greek Revival Architecture in America*, 38–42.

11. Ibid., 43.

12. *North Carolina Standard* (Raleigh, N. C.), February 8, 1854. Remarks by David Lowry Swain after William Nichols's death.

13. William S. Powell, *North Carolina through Four Centuries*, 98–109.

14. It is also known as the McLeran/Adam/Sandford House.

15. James Iredell, Jr., letter to James C. Johnston, 15 September 1817, North Carolina Collection, Wilson Library, University of North Carolina at Chapel Hill, Chapel Hill, N. C.

16. The date when the Oval Ballroom was moved is not known.

17. Hamlin, *Greek Revival Architecture in America*, 196.

18. Fayetteville Women's Club of Fayetteville, North Carolina, owns and operates both the Oval Ballroom and the McLeran/Adam/Sandford House. Heritage Square is located on Dick Street, a few blocks away from the city's Market House.

19. Mills Lane, *Architecture of the Old South: North Carolina*, 150.

20. John Sanders, "William Nichols in North Carolina," unpublished, 1983.

21. The North Carolina General Assembly of 1820, *Chapter LIV of the Session Laws*, CR 29.001, Laws of 1820, c.54, North Carolina Department of Archives and History, Raleigh, N.C.

22. Cumberland County Book of Deeds, Book 40, p. 54–55, August 22, 1821, North Carolina Department of Archives and History, Raleigh, N.C.

23. Cumberland County Book of Deeds, Book 34, p. 427, June 15, 1822, North Carolina Department of Archives and History, Raleigh, N.C.

24. John Alexander Oates, *The Story of Fayetteville and the Upper Cape Fear* (Fayetteville, N. C.: Dowd Press, 1951), 35–45.

25. John MacRae, "Map of Fayetteville, North Carolina, 1825," North Carolina Map Collection, North Carolina Collection, Wilson Library, University of North Carolina at Chapel Hill, Chapel Hill, N. C.

26. Linda Jasperse, "Historic Resources of Fayetteville, North Carolina, Architectural and Historic Resources Multiple Register Listing," National Register of Historic Places, April 28, 1983.

27. Archibald Henderson, *The Campus of the First State University* (Chapel Hill, N. C.: University of North Carolina Press, 1949), 5–17.

28. F. Rachel Long and Karen Copeland, "The Building Notes of the University of North Carolina at Chapel Hill." University of North Carolina at Chapel Hill Facilities Planning and Design Department, unpublished, 1993.William Richardson Davie was the quartermaster general for General Nathaniel Greene's Southern Continental Army during the American Revolution and a governor of North Carolina. He is widely considered the "Father of the University of North Carolina." Samuel E. McCorkle and James Hogg were two of the first members of the UNC Board of Trustees. Joseph Caldwell was the first president of the University of North Carolina in 1795. Davie, McCorkle, and Caldwell graduated from the College of New Jersey, now known as Princeton University, which was a Presbyterian college before the American Revolution. Interestingly, Davie was a Freemason and led a Masonic cornerstone setting ceremony at Old East on October 12, 1793.

29. Josiah Quincy, *A History of Harvard University, Vol.1* (Boston: Crosby, Nichols, Lee & Co., 1860), 1–15. The first buildings built for Harvard College were also described as "built for business and nothing else." Like the early Carolina buildings, Harvard's original campus consisted of several plain brick buildings.

30. Mary N. Woods, "Thomas Jefferson and the University of Virginia: Planning the Academical Village," *Journal of the Society of Architectural Historians* 44 (Oct. 1985), 282–283.

31. F. Rachel Long and Karen Copeland, "The Building Notes of the University of North Carolina at Chapel Hill," University of North Carolina at Chapel Hill Facilities Planning and Design Department, unpublished, 1993. Freemasons believed that the practice of orienting buildings toward the southeast was necessary to gain the maximum morning sunlight and also follow the precedent set by King Solomon when he built his temple in Jerusalem. Freemasons refer to this practice as orientalization.

32. North Carolina Geological Survey, interview by the author, February 8, 2006. George Fore, Architectural Conservator, interview with the author, March, 2006.

33. John V. Allcott, *The Campus at Chapel Hill: Two Hundred Years of Architecture* (Chapel Hill: Chapel Hill Historical Society, 1986), 24–25.

34. F. Rachel Long and Karen Copeland, "The Building Notes of the University of North Carolina at Chapel Hill," University of North Carolina at Chapel Hill Facilities Planning and Design, unpublished, 1993.

35. Walter Edgar, ed., *The South Carolina Encyclopedia* (Columbia, S. C.: University of South Carolina Press, 2006), 637–638. Robert Mills (1781–1855) has been called America's first native-born architect. Along with the University of South Carolina, Mills designed the Washington Monument in Washington, D. C.

36. The Athenaeum of Philadelphia. Thomas U. Walter (1804–1887) was a prominent Philadelphia architect who would be best known for his design of the U.S. Capitol dome.

37. Amelia Peck, *Alexander Jackson Davis, American Architect 1803–1892*, (New York: Rizzoli, 1992). Alexander Jackson Davis (1803–1892) was considered the leading architect in the United States in the first half of the nineteenth century. He and his partner, Ithiel Town, would complete Nichols's design of a new state capitol in Raleigh, North Carolina. From 1842 to 1850, Davis would expand Old East and Old West and build Smith Hall, commonly known as Playmaker's Theater.

38. Kemp Battle, *History of the University of North Carolina, From its Beginning to the Death of President Swain* (Raleigh, N. C.: Edwards and Broughton Publishers, 1907), 29–33.

39. John V. Allcott, *The Campus at Chapel Hill: Two Hundred Years of Architecture*, 25.

40. Archibald Henderson, *The Campus of the First State University*, 86–89. Henderson states that Elisha Mitchell, the noted geology professor at the University of North Carolina, first proposed the "southern yard" of the Carolina campus. He reveals that the Chapel Hill town merchants, along with the waggoners who engaged in cross-country trade, began a "quiet" campaign of opposition against this campus plan on the grounds that it would impair commerce on Franklin Street and lead to the building of a new avenue for business and trade in Chapel Hill. Henderson erroneously credits Alexander Jackson Davis for the design of the south portico at Gerrard, but Davis's own drawings of Gerrard in which he proposed a new west-facing portico and a low pitch dome clearly show Nichols's portico as an existing condition of the building.

41. University of North Carolina Engineering Information Services, Plan Room Archives. In 1917, Milburn and Heister Architects of Washington, D. C., proposed a radical alteration of Gerrard in which the entire building would be transformed from Ionic to Roman denticular Doric and would have a colossal Doric portico built facing east toward the South Building. The design, although extensively detailed, never was pursued by the university and the building was simply structurally retrofitted in 1930. The base of the old south-facing portico was still in place in 1917 and may have been removed at this time.

42. Nancy Sultan, Professor of Classics, Illinois Wesleyan University, "Re: Temple of Illissus," e-mail message to author, November 8, 2011. The Temple of

Illissus was located along the Illissus River in Athens, Greece. The Ottoman Turks destroyed it in the late nineteenth century. The temple was dedicated to Artemis, according to Pausanias. Today, the modern city of Athens is built on its site. See *Pausanias's Description* of Greece 1.19.6.

43. Talbot Hamlin, *Greek Revival in America*, 55; Archibald Henderson, *The Campus of the First State University*, 82–86.

44. Kemp Plummer Battle, *History of the University of North Carolina, Volume I* (Raleigh, N. C.: Edwards and Broughton Company, 1907–1912), 178–179, 595–596.

45. The Gerrard Hall Rehabilitation Design Team included Ann Beha Architects of Boston, Massachusetts; George Fore, Architectural Conservator; Pierce, Brinkley, Cease and Lee Architects of Raleigh, North Carolina; and Paul Hardin Kapp, Campus Historic Preservation Manager for the University of North Carolina at Chapel Hill. The Gerrard Hall Rehabilitation began in the fall of 2003 and was completed in the fall of 2007.

46. Robb would become one of several craftsmen who would develop a long-term business relationship with Nichols and would eventually follow him to the Deep South where together they would build the capitols of Alabama and Mississippi and the campus of the University of Alabama.

47. "Accounts for Disbursements by William Nichols, September 1, 1826." Board of Trustees Records, North Carolina Collection, University of North Carolina at Chapel Hill, Chapel Hill, N.C.

48. Henderson, *The Campus of the First State University*, 32–42. Archibald Henderson states that Elisha Mitchell was superintendent of buildings and grounds from 1830 to 1850, but it has never been substantiated that he initiated a painting program on the Chapel Hill campus.

49. David L. Swain to James K. Polk, April 24, 1847, David Lowry Swain Papers, North Carolina Collection, University of North Carolina. George Fore, Architectural Conservator, "Gerrard Hall Exterior Historic Finishes Analysis," July 21, 2005.

50. Archibald Henderson, *The Campus of the First State University*, 87.

51. Ibid., 90. F. Rachel Long, "Building Notes of the University of North Carolina at Chapel Hill," Facilities Planning and Design Department, University of North Carolina at Chapel Hill, 1993, 215.

52. Mills Lane, *Architecture of the Old South: North Carolina*, 152. Catherine Bishir, *North Carolina Architecture*, 102.

53. Eagle Lodge No. 19, A. F. & A. M. "A Brief History of Eagle Lodge, Hillsborough, North Carolina." R. B. Studebaker, "The History of Eagle Lodge No.19 A. F. & A. M." Freemasons. Eagle Lodge No. 19 (Hillsborough, N. C.) Records, North Carolina Collection, Wilson Library, University of North Carolina at Chapel Hill.

54. Freemason. Eagle Lodge No. 19 (Hillsborough, N.C.) Records, Folder 10, North Carolina Collection, Wilson Library, University of North Carolina at Chapel Hill.

55. Ibid. Unfortunately, the lodge's financial records are missing. The lottery records for funding the construction of the building do exist and are in the North Carolina Collection in Wilson Library at the University of North Carolina at Chapel Hill.

56. R .B. Studebaker, "The History of Eagle Lodge No. 19, A. F. & A. M."

57. Ibid.

58. Barbara Church, architectural historian, interview by the author, November 10, 2006.

59. James H. Craig, *The Arts and Crafts in North Carolina, 1699–1840*, 343.

60. James Dinsmore and John Neilson were Irish carpenters who originally worked in Philadelphia and then came to work for Thomas Jefferson in the early

nineteenth century. They are credited for building the later designs of Monticello, the University of Virginia, and James Madison's remodeling of Montpelier.

61. Guilford and Alamance counties are located directly west of Hillsborough and Orange County.

62. According to local tradition, in 1805, John Berry, who was sixteen years old, helped brick mason and contractor Samuel Hancock build a small brick dwelling that is one block west of the Hassel-Nash House on Queen Street in Hillsborough. It was built as a residence for both Berry and his mother. It still exists.

63. David Lowry Swain, *Early Times in Raleigh* (Raleigh, N. C.: Walters, Hughes & Co., 1867), 8, 9.

64. John Sanders, "Nichols Chronology," unpublished, 1979.

65. *Raleigh Register and North Carolina Gazette*, November 1, 1826, Vol. XX, No. 1014, 77.

Chapter Four

1. James H. Craig, *The Arts and Crafts in North Carolina, 1699–1840*, 365.

2. Bishir et al., *Builders and Architects*, 127.

3. William Nichols to "Committee appointed to confer with the superintendent of public buildings as the disposal of the Statue of Washington," 3 September 1821, L.P. 367, 1818–1825, Legislative Papers, North Carolina Department of Archives and History, Raleigh, N. C.

4. William Nichols, "Report to Committee on Public Buildings, 1819, L.P. 370, Legislative Papers, 1818–1825, North Carolina Department of Archives and History, Raleigh, N. C.

5. The North Carolina General Assembly of 1818, "*Report of the Committee on the State of the Public Buildings and Resolutions of the General Assembly on that Subject*," December 25, 1818, L.P. 369, Legislative Papers, 1818–1825, North Carolina Department of Archives and History, Raleigh, N. C.

6. The North Carolina General Assembly of 1818, *Specifications for Remodeling of the State House by William Nichols*, December 25, 1818, L.P. 309, Legislative Papers, 1818–1825, North Carolina Department of Archives and History, Raleigh, N. C.

7. William Nichols to Governor John Branch, "Estimate for the Remodeling of the State House," December 1, 1820, L.P. 327, Legislative Papers, 1819–1820, North Carolina Department of Archives and History, Raleigh, N. C.

8. Report of Committee on Public Buildings, 1819, Capital Building Papers, Treasurer's and Comptroller's Papers, L.P. 327, Legislative Papers, 1819–1820, North Carolina Department of Archives and History, Raleigh, N. C.

9. Nichols's drawings of the remodeling of the State House no longer exist.

10. The North Carolina General Assembly of 1819, *House of Commons Recommendations to Remodel the State House by Alfred Moore*, December 7, 1819, L. P. 317, Legislative Papers, 1819–1820, North Carolina Department of Archives and History, Raleigh, N. C.

11. The North Carolina General Assembly of 1819, *Senate Approval for Financing the Remodeling of the State House*, December 31, 1819, L. P. 317, Legislative Papers, 1818–1819, North Carolina Department of Archives and History, Raleigh, N. C., and *Raleigh Register and North Carolina Gazette*, December 31, 1819, Vol. XXI, No. 1058, p. 3.

12. The North Carolina General Assembly of 1819, *Authorization for Public Lands to be Sold to Fund the State House Remodeling*, December 18, 1819, L. P. 10,11,

Legislative Papers, 1818–1819, North Carolina Department of Archives and History, Raleigh, N. C.

13. The North Carolina General Assembly of 1820, *Senate Approval for Creating the Position of State Architect*, December 25, 1820, L. P. 369, Legislative Papers, 1820–1821, North Carolina Department of Archives and History, Raleigh, N. C.

14. William Nichols to Jesse Franklin, April 6, 1821, L. P. 369, Legislative Papers, 1821–1823, The North Carolina General Assembly of 1821, and *Recommended Salary for the State Architect*, April 10, 1821, L. P. 369, Legislative Papers 1821–1823, North Carolina Department of Archives and History, Raleigh, N. C.

15. The Maison Carrée, an ancient Roman temple in Nîmes, southern France, inspired the architecture of the Virginia State Capitol. It was built circa 16 B. C. when the Roman Empire stretched throughout current-day Europe, Africa, and the Middle East. Jefferson visited the Maison Carrée when he was ambassador to France, 1785–1789.

16. Latrobe's design was based on an original design by Dr. William Thornton.

17. Thomas U. Walter Papers, Athenaeum of Philadelphia. Charles Bulfinch completed Latrobe's dome, it was replaced with the current dome, designed by Thomas U. Walter, during the Civil War.

18. William H. Pierson, Jr., *American Buildings and Their Architects, Volume 1*, 399–403.

19. *Raleigh Register and North Carolina Gazette*, October 19, 1821, p. 3. This is the most complete description of the North Carolina State House building after Nichols renovated it.

20. Edward T. Davis and John Sanders, *A Romantic Architect in Antebellum North Carolina: The Works of Alexander Jackson Davis* (Raleigh, N. C.: The Historic Preservation Foundation of North Carolina, 2002), 39.

21. Report of Committee on Public Buildings, 1821, Capitol Building Papers, North Carolina Department of Archives and History, Raleigh, N. C.

22. The North Carolina General Assembly of 1822, *Termination of the Position of State Architect*, December 6, 1822, L.P. 98, Legislative Papers, 1821–1823, North Carolina Department of Archives and History, Raleigh, N. C.

23. James H. Craig, *The Arts and Crafts in North Carolina, 1699–1840*, 365.

24. Catherine Bishir, *North Carolina Architecture*, 97–98. Cecil D. Elliot, "The North Carolina State Capitol," *Southern Architect*, Vol. V, No. 6, 23–26.

25. Gabriel Holmes Address to the North Carolina General Assembly, November 18, 1822, L.P. 371, Legislative Papers, 1821–1823, North Carolina Department of Archives and History, Raleigh, N. C.

26. Anne Newport Royall, *The Black Book; or, A Continuation of Travels in the United States* (Washington: Printed for the Author, 1828–1829), 137, 138.

27. Ibid., 134–136.

28. Henry Russell Hitchcock and William Seale, *Temples of Democracy: The State Capitols of the U. S. A.* (New York: Harcourt Brace Jovanovich, 1976), 127.

29. Rexford Newcomb, *Architecture in Old Kentucky* (Urbana, Ill.: University of Illinois Press, 1953), 45–48. Gideon Shryock's Old State Capitol in Frankfort, Kentucky, was built in 1830 six years after Nichols built the State House in Raleigh.

30. William Seale, "Second Federal Design Assembly: The Design Reality," *Design Quarterly*, No. 94/95 (1975), 14–15.

31. John Sanders to John G. Zehmer, Jr., "Memorandum: William Nichols—Miscellaneous Notes," April 3, 1974.

32. John Sanders Papers, "Nichols Chronology," unpublished, 1979.

33. Wake County, North Carolina Book of Deeds Book 7, Page 321, June 2, 1825, North Carolina Department of Archives and History, Raleigh, N. C.

34. Wake County, North Carolina Book of Deeds Book 11, Page 379, June 1, 1826, North Carolina Department of Archives and History, Raleigh, N. C.

35. Wake County, North Carolina Book of Deeds Book 7, Page 383, January 22, 1827, North Carolina Department of Archives and History, Raleigh, N. C.

36. Wake County, North Carolina Book of Deeds Book 7, Page 393, April 23, 1827, North Carolina Department of Archives and History, Raleigh, N. C.

37. Elizabeth Reid to John Sanders Correspondence, April 20, 1979.

38. Peatross and Mellown, *William Nichols, Architect*, 15.

39. Ibid., 10–13. Nichols remodeled and added a new piazza to the George E. Badger house in 1827. This residence was located on West Edenton Street near Dawson Street in Raleigh. It is no longer standing.

40. *Raleigh Register* (semiweekly), April 7, 1829, Page 3, Column 4, North Carolina Collection, University of North Carolina at Chapel Hill Library, Chapel Hill, N. C.

41. John Sanders to John G. Zehmer, Jr., "Memorandum: William Nichols—Fayetteville Water Works," April 3, 1974.

42. John Sanders, "William Nichols in Raleigh," unpublished, November 1983, 15.

43. William Nichols, Jr., to David Lowry Swain, December 22, 1833, Epistolary Correspondence, David L. Swain Papers, University Archives, University of North Carolina at Chapel Hill.

44. Edward T. Davis and John Sanders, *A Romantic Architect in Antebellum North Carolina: The Works of Alexander Jackson Davis*, 2–35. The General Assembly hired Ithiel Town and Alexander Jackson Davis of New York. Town had a business of building lattice truss bridges up and down the eastern seaboard and even had a business office in Fayetteville, where he became acquainted with Nichols's work and perhaps even Nichols himself. Town also had political connections to North Carolina since William Gaston, a prominent North Carolina legislator, was his personal lawyer.

45. Cumberland County Miscellaneous Papers Box C. R. 29.916.6, March 19, 1831, North Carolina Department of Archives and History, Raleigh, N.C.

46. William Nichols, Jr., to George W. Haywood, March 24, 1841, North Carolina Department of Archives and History, Raleigh, N. C.

47. Marriage certificate between William Nichols, Jr., and Nancy Dunn, January 21, 1839, Wake County, North Carolina. North Carolina Department of Archives and History, Raleigh, N.C.

48. John Sanders to Elizabeth Reid Correspondence, April 30, 1979.

49. Wake County, North Carolina, Court Records 99.311.3, North Carolina Department of Archives and History, Raleigh, N. C.

50. William Nichols, Jr., to Governor John Motley Morehead, March 14, 1841. North Carolina Department of Archives and History, Raleigh, N. C.

51. William Nichols, Jr., to George W. Haywood, March 24, 1841.North Carolina Department of Archives and History, Raleigh, N. C.

52. William Powell, *Dictionary of North Carolina History*, 393. Weston R. Gales was secretary pro tem of the Whig Party at the Whig Political Party Convention of 1842.

53. Weston R. Gales to W. W. Birth, July 26, 1841, North Carolina Collection, Wilson Library, University of North Carolina at Chapel Hill, Chapel Hill, N. C.

54. Wake County, North Carolina, Court Records 99.311.3, North Carolina Department of Archives and History, Raleigh, N. C.

55. Wake County, North Carolina, Court Minutes 99.301.16, North Carolina Department of Archives and History, Raleigh, N. C.

56. Wake County, North Carolina, Court Records 99.311.3, North Carolina Department of Archives and History, Raleigh, N. C.

Chapter Five

1. The Alabama Territory achieved statehood on December 14, 1819, as the twenty-second state admitted to the Union.

2. *Encyclopedia of Alabama* (Auburn, Ala.: Draughon Library Publications, 2011), s.v. "Alabama Fever." "Alabama fever" was an expression commonly used by 1817 that described the frenzied land rush into the area formerly known as West Florida or East Mississippi by settlers from North Carolina, Virginia, and Georgia.

3. The term "Virginia dynasty" refers to the succession of four United States presidents from Virginia since the inception of the presidency: George Washington (1789–1797), Thomas Jefferson (1801–1809), James Madison (1809–1817), and James Monroe (1817–1825); the succession is interrupted by John Adams from Massachusetts, second U.S. president (1797–1801).

4. William E. Weeks, *John Quincy Adams and American Global Empire* (Lexington, Ky.: University Press of Kentucky, 2002), 170–175. The Adams-Onis Treaty of 1819 between the United States and Spain was named after John Quincy Adams, then secretary of state under President James Monroe, and Louis de Onis, foreign minister for King Ferdinand VIII of Spain. Contrary to popular belief, the United States did not purchase Florida in this treaty; rather, the U.S. paid residents' claims against the Spanish government for approximately five million dollars, after which Florida was ceded to the United States, which took possession of it in 1821. In exchange, the United States renounced any claims it had to Texas and other Spanish territories in the Southwest.

5. Gary R. Mormino, "Cuba Libre Florida, and the Spanish American War," *Theodore Roosevelt Association Journal*, Winter/Spring 2010, Vol. 31, Issue 1/2 (New York: Theodore Roosevelt Association), 43–54.

6. Richard E. Ellis, *The Union at Risk: Jacksonian Democracy, States' Rights and the Nullification Crisis* (New York: Random House, 1989), 253–286.

7. Historic American Buildings Survey: HABS No. Ala-35, "Cathedral of Immaculate Conception, Mobile, Ala., Photographs and Written Historic Description Data No. 16," 1–3, Historic American Buildings Survey, Library of Congress. Claude Beroujon (1797–1875) designed the Cathedral Basilica of the Immaculate Conception in Mobile, Alabama, in 1833. It is designed in the Roman basilica revival style.

8. Robert Gamble, *The Alabama Catalog: Historic American BuildingsSurvey: A Guide to the Early Architecture of the State* (Tuscaloosa, Ala.: University of Alabama Press, 1987), 50.

9. John Morin Gallalee, *The University of Alabama: A Short History* (New York: Newcomer Society in North America, 1953), 3–27.

10. Robert O. Mellown, "Alabama's Fourth Capital: The Construction of the State House in Tuscaloosa," *The Alabama Review*, October 1987 (Montgomery, Ala.: Alabama Historical Society), 261.

11. Harry L. Watson, "The Age of Jackson," *Wilson Quarterly*, Autumn 1985 (Washington, D.C.: Smithsonian Institution), 101–107.

12. Robert V. Remini, *Andrew Jackson and the Course of American Democracy, 1833–1845* (New York: Harper, 1984) 5–127.

13. Archibald Henderson, *The Campus of the First State University* (Chapel Hill: UNC Press, 1949), 173.

14. Robert O. Mellown, "Alabama's Fourth Capital: The Construction of the State House in Tuscaloosa," 259–262.

15. Ibid., 262.

16. Ibid., 262–264.

17. U.S. General Land Records, 1797–1830, AL0760.178.

18. *Journal of the Alabama Senate* (Tuscaloosa, 1828), 69–70.

19. Robert O. Mellown, "Alabama's Fourth Capital," 262.

20. Philibert de l'Orme (1510–1570) was a French-born architect who developed an innovative timber frame dome system.

21. John Sanders Photographic Collection on William Nichols.

22. Robert Mellown, "Alabama's Fourth Capital," 266.

23. *Journal of the Alabama Senate* (Tuscaloosa, Ala., 1828), 69–70.

24. *Alabama State Intelligencer* (Tuscaloosa, Ala.), November 12, 1831.

25. Kentucky separated from Virginia and became the fifteenth state in the Union in 1792.

26. Henry Russell Hitchcock and William Seale, *Temples of Democracy: The State Capitols of the U.S.A.* (New York: Harcourt Brace Jovanovich, 1976), 30–75.

27. Ibid., 90.

28. Ibid., 58.

29. Robert Mellown, "Alabama's Fourth Capital: The Construction of the State House in Tuscaloosa," 271–274.

30. Ibid. Like Nichols, Fitch also aspired to become an architect; he designed a courthouse in a nearby county and built a house for his family near the capitol grounds.

31. Ibid., 273.

32. John G. Zehmer to John Sanders, "Memorandum: William Nichols—Miscellaneous Notes, April 3, 1974." This is the first instance of William Nichols being referred to as captain, an honorific title his southern contemporaries bestowed upon him.

33. Ibid., 275.

34. *Alabama State Intelligencer* (Tuscaloosa, Ala.), November 12, 1831, *State Rights Expositor* (Tuscaloosa, Ala.), October 17, 1835.

35. Robert Mellown, "Alabama's Fourth Capital: The Construction of the State House in Tuscaloosa," 275–277.

36. Edward T. Davis and John Sanders, *A Romantic Architect in Antebellum North Carolina: The Works of Alexander Jackson Davis*, 38–42. David Paton was a Scots-born architect and builder who had worked for John Soane in London before working for Town and Davis. Historians credit him for the success of the Davis design of the North Carolina State Capitol.

37. Ibid., 44.

38. William H. Pierson, Jr., *American Buildings and Their Architects, Volume 1*, 339–360. Thomas Jefferson's design of the University of Virginia (begun 1817) shares striking similarities with that of Union College in Schenectady, New York, designed by the French architect Joseph-Jacques Ramée (1813–1814) a few years earlier. Architectural historians have speculated that Jefferson may have been influenced by Ramée's French-inspired neoclassical mall design with a rotunda centerpiece.

39. Alabama Department of Archives and History Database, Montgomery, Ala.

40. Paul V. Turner, *Campus: An American Planning Tradition* (Cambridge, Mass.: MIT Press, 1984). It was not uncommon for strangers to write the Sage of Monticello requesting advice. For example, in 1810, Jefferson was asked to design the new East Tennessee College, later to be the University of Tennessee. In a letter dated 6 May 1810, Thomas Jefferson made recommendations to the board of trustees of East Tennessee College stating that it was infinitely better to erect small detached lodgings for professors and classrooms and connecting barracks for students than building one large building.

41. G. Ward Hubbs, "Dissipating the Clouds of Ignorance: The First University of Alabama Library, 1831–1865," *Libraries & Culture*, Vol. 27, No.1 (1992): 20–35.

42. James B. Sellers, *History of the University of Alabama, Vol. I* (Tuscaloosa, Ala.: University of Alabama Press, 1953), 4–29.

43. Ibid., 30.

44. Committee members included Jack Shackelford, George Phillips, N. E. Benson, Quinn Morton, and Samuel W. Oliver.

45. C. Ford Peatross and Robert O. Mellown, "Architect of a Region: William Nichols," *Society for the Fine Arts Review*, Vol. IV (Summer 1982), 6–10.

46. James B. Sellers, *History of the University of Alabama, Vol. I*, 27.

47. Robert O. Mellown, *The University of Alabama: A Guide to the Campus Historic Architecture* (Tuscaloosa, Ala: University of Alabama Press, 1988), 4–35.

48. James B. Sellers, *History of the University of Alabama, Vol. 1*, 30. University of Alabama historian James B. Sellers speculated that either the buildings and grounds committee or Nichols had traveled to Charlottesville, Virginia, to experience firsthand Jefferson's University of Virginia. However, this has never been verified.

49. Ibid., 34.

50. Josiah John Morin Gallalee, *The University of Alabama: A Short History* (New York: Newcomer Society in North America, 1953). Gorgas was chief of ordinances for the Confederate States of America during the Civil War. He became vice-chancellor of the University of the South in Sewanee, Tennessee, after the war and then the president of the University of Alabama in 1879; he was forced to retire from the presidency due to poor health soon after he arrived in Tuscaloosa. He died in 1883.

51. Richard Thigpen, "The Four Public Buildings of the University of Alabama to Survive the Civil War," *The Alabama Review*, Vol. XXXIV, No. 1 (January 1981): 50–58.

52. James B. Sellers, *History of the University of Alabama, Vol. I*, 28–32.

53. *Southern Advocate* (Huntsville, Ala.), October 9, 1830.

54. The Rotunda at the University of Virginia was last restored between 1973 and 1976; Fredrick Doveton Nichols was an advisor. The architectural firm of Ballou and Justice of Richmond, Virginia, designed an interior restoration to its Jefferson appearance and repaired and restored Stanford White's exterior, with one notable exception: the dome roof. The roof was restored to what was believed to have been what Jefferson intended. Richard Guy Wilson and Sara Butler, *The Campus Guide: University of Virginia* (New York: Princeton Architectural Press, 1999), 45.

55. James B. Sellers, *History of the University of Alabama, Vol. I*, 28–32.

56. G. Ward Hubbs, "Dissipating the Clouds of Ignorance: The First University of Alabama Library, 1831–1865," 23.

57. Robert O. Mellown, *The University of Alabama: A Guide to the Campus Historic Architecture*, 11.

58. James B. Sellers, *History of the University of Alabama, Vol. I*, 31.

59. Wallace Clement Sabine, a physics professor at Harvard University, founded the field of architectural acoustics in 1895 when he began improving the acoustical performance of the newly built Fogg Lecture Hall.

60. *Southern Advocate* (Huntsville, Ala.), October 9, 1830.

61. Richard Thigpen, "The Four Public Buildings of the University of Alabama to Survive the Civil War," 53, Alabama Department of Archives and History, Montgomery, Ala.

62. Basil Manly to the University of Alabama Board of Trustees, November 25, 1841.

63. Robert Gamble, *Historic Architecture in Alabama: A Guide to Styles and Types, 1810–1930* (Tuscaloosa, Ala.: University of Alabama Press, 1990), 45–49.

64. Peatross and Mellown, *William Nichols, Architect*,18. Peatross and Mellown mention several possible client connections such as James Hunt Dearing, a building commissioner for the Alabama State Capitol.

65. Robert Gamble, architectural historian, Alabama Historical Commission, interview by the author, June 15, 2005.

66. "Lauderdale County, Alabama: History of the Shoals," *Florence Times-Daily*, September 21, 2008.

67. Robert Gamble, interview with the author, June 15, 2005.

68. Robert Gamble, *The Alabama Catalog*, 50.

69. U.S. Census of Tuscaloosa, Alabama, of 1830.

70. Talbot Hamlin, *Greek Revival Architecture in America*, 70. It predates Nicholas Biddle's and Thomas U. Walter's Andalusia conversion by five years. Mississippi Department of Archives and History Database, Jackson, Miss. Only one residence in the Deep South, The Forest, had been built in the Greek temple form before Forks of Cypress. It was located near Natchez, Mississippi, and completed in 1816. Three builders, Elisha Roundtree, Jacob Baker, and Issac Hence built it. It is unknown who actually designed it.

71. Thomas McAdory Owen, *History of Alabama and Dictionary of Alabama Biography* (Spartanburg, S. C.: The Reprint Company Publishers, 1978), Volume IV, 1670.

72. Marl was a term to describe calcareous manure that was used by farmers and planters in the Deep South to help rejuvenate the soil. Edmund Ruffin in his "Essay on Calcareous Manure," which was published in 1832, first proposed its use.

73. Michael Bailey, "Thornhill," National Register of Historic Places Nomination Form, February 1984, Alabama Historical Commission.

74. Ralph Hammond, *Ante-Bellum Mansions of Alabama* (New York: Bonanza Books, 1951), 109–110.

75. Ibid., 110.

76. Michael Bailey, "Thornhill," National Register Form, 1984.

77. Peatross and Mellown, *William Nichols, Architect*,18.

78. W. Warner Floyd, "Rosemount," National Register of Historic Places Nomination Form, October 21, 1970, Alabama Historical Commission.

79. Robert Gamble, *Historic Architecture in Alabama: A Guide to Styles and Types, 1810–1930*, 178.

80. Historic American Buildings Survey, Field Report, Ala 32. Fork.VI.

81. Robert Gamble, *Historic Architecture in Alabama: A Guide to Styles and Types, 1810–1930*, 57.

82. Peatross and Mellown, *William Nichols, Architect*, 12–14. Peatross and Mellown mention that Nichols designed the State Bank in Tuscaloosa, but this attribution cannot be verified.

83. Historic American Buildings Survey, "Addendum to the Dearing-Bagby House (Doctor Deal House), (Governor's Mansion), (University Club)," HABS No. AL-230, HABS ALA 63-Tuslo, 16.

84. University of Alabama University Club website, http://www.universityclub.ua.edu/pages/history.html, retrieved April 12, 2012. University of Alabama students abducted Dearing's woman servant and brought her back to the campus. Dearing then searched on the campus for her, which resulted in a near riot. The students retaliated by attacking the Dearing residence, destroying the front gate, and then raiding Dearing's hen house. Dearing exchanged gunfire with the students, injuring a son of a close friend of his. After the incident, Dearing sold the house to Richard H. Lewis for $14,500 and built a residence south of Tuscaloosa away from both the town and university in Hale County.

85. Ibid.

86. Robert Gamble, *Historic Architecture in Alabama: A Guide to Styles and Types, 1810–1930*, 52. Historic American Buildings Survey, "President's Home," HABS No. ALA 207, HABS ALA 63-Tuslo-3 B.

87. Gamble, *The Alabama Catalog*, 78, 79, 353.

88. Examples of Robb's Ionic columns include Pilgrim's Rest and Eagle Lodge in Hillsborough, North Carolina, and the columns that support the south-facing portico on Gerrard Hall at the University of North Carolina.

89. Mississippi Department of Archives and History with John Ray Skates, "Mississippi State Capitol, Old," National Register of Historic Places Nomination Form, July 13, 1990, Mississippi Department of Archives and History.

90. Peatross and Mellown, *William Nichols, Architect*, 22.

91. Letter from William Nichols to Governor Charles Lynch, October 12, 1833, Alabama Department of Archives and History, Montgomery, Ala.

92. Isabella Margaret Elizabeth Blandin, *History of Higher Education of Women in the South* (New York and Washington, D. C.: Neale Publishing Company, 1909), 104–105.

93. Robert O. Mellown, "Alabama's Fourth Capital," 280.

94. Letter from William Nichols to Charles Lynch, October 12, 1833. Mississippi Department of Archives and History, Jackson, Miss.

95. John Zehmer to John Sanders Correspondence, April 12, 1974.

Chapter Six

1. John Zehmer to John Sanders Correspondence, April 12, 1974.

2. Wake County, North Carolina, Deed Book 11, 00383-00386, October 22–23, 1834. North Carolina Department of Archives and History, Raleigh, N. C.

3. Wake County, North Carolina, Deed Book 12, 00046, June 25, 1835. North Carolina Department of Archives and History, Raleigh, N. C.

4. James H. Craig, *The Arts and Crafts in North Carolina*, 160–165.

5. Peatross and Mellown, *William Nichols, Architect*, 26.

6. Arthur J. Scully, Jr., *James Dakin, Architect: His Career in New York and the South* (Baton Rouge, La.: Louisiana State University Press, 1973), 4–10.

7. Talbot Hamlin, *Greek Revival Architecture in America*, 60.

8. John Sanders and Catherine Bishir, "Paton, David (1801–1882)," *North Carolina Architects & Builders, A Biographical Dictionary*, North Carolina State University Library, 000021, http://ncarchitects.lib.ncsu.edu (accessed April 28, 2012).

9. Arthur Scully, *James Dakin, Architect*, 56.

10. It was assumed for several decades that Gideon Shryock designed the Bank of Louisville. Shryock supervised its construction. Rexford Newcomb, *Architecture in Old Kentucky* (Urbana, Ill.: University of Illinois Press, 1953), 114–120.

11. Ibid., 51–66.

12. Jacob Landy, *The Architecture of Minard Lafever* (New York: Columbia University Press, 1976), 280–285.

13. Hamlin, *Greek Revival Architecture in America*, 222–225.

14. Mills Lane, *The Architecture of the Old South: Louisiana* (New York: Abbeville Press, 1985), 57.

15. John Ray Skates, "Mississippi State Capitol, Old," National Register of Historic Places Nomination Form.

16. Mark T. Carleton, *Politics and Punishment: The History of the Louisiana Penal System* (Baton Rouge, La.: Louisiana State University Press, 1971), 3–31. Mark Carleton credits Edward Livingston for proposing that the Wethersfield, Connecticut, Prison be used as a model for the Louisiana State Penitentiary in Baton Rouge. Livingston, a New York lawyer who moved to Louisiana in 1830, was an advocate for the humane treatment of convicted prisoners.

17. Leon Stout, "Origins and Early History of the Louisiana Penitentiary" (M.A. thesis, Louisiana State University, 1934), 3–57.

18. John Magill, curator, Williams Collection, "Re: Inquiry about William Nichols in New Orleans," e-mail message to author, December 22, 2011.

19. Melissa Stein, architectural historian, Louisiana Office of Cultural Development, Division of Historic Preservation, "Re: William Nichols in New Orleans," e-mail message to author, January 6, 2012.

20. Samuel Wilson, Jr., ed., *Impressions Respecting New Orleans by Benjamin Henry Boneval Latrobe, Diary and Sketches, 1818–1820* (New York: Columbia University Press, 1951), xi–xxii.

21. Charles F. Zimpel, *Topographical Map of New Orleans and its Vicinity, Embracing twelve miles up, and eight and three quarters miles down the Mississippi River and Part of Lake Pontchartrain, representing all Public Improvements existing and projected, and important Establishments,* The Historic New Orleans Collection, Williams Research Center, New Orleans, La.

22. John Salvaggio, *New Orleans' Charity Hospital: A Story of Physicians, Politics, and Poverty* (Baton Rouge, La.: Louisiana State University Press, 1992), 60–68.

23. Building Contract between the State of Louisiana and Owen Evans, Contractor, June 25, 1834, Louisiana State Archives, Baton Rouge, La.

24. Mary Louise Christovich, Roulhac Toledano, Betsy Swanson, and Pat Holden, *New Orleans Architecture: Volume II: The American Sector (Faubourg St. Mary), Howard Avenue to Iberville Street, Mississippi River to Claiborne Avenue* (Gretna, La.: Pelican Publishing Co., 1972), 14. William Seale to John Sanders, "William Nichols in New Orleans," October, 12, 1973. Noted historian William Seale uncovered this information regarding Nichols's design while researching state capitols for his book *Temples of Democracy*, coauthored with Henry-Russell Hitchcock.

25. Joseph Holt Ingraham (1809–1860) was a noted author in the United States. He was a native of Portland, Maine, spent several years at sea, and later taught languages in Mississippi from 1840 to 1851. He became an Episcopal clergyman in 1851. He wrote several books and published *Arthur's Magazine* in the 1840s. Archives and Special Collections, University of Mississippi.

26. Christovich, Toledano, Swanson, and Holden, *New Orleans Architecture: Volume II: The American Sector,* 14.

27. Arthur Scully, *James Dakin, Architect,* 121.

28. Ibid., 121.

29. Christovich, Toledano, Swanson, and Holden, *New Orleans Architecture: Volume II: The American Sector,* 14.

30. Richard Campanella, professor of geography, Tulane University, "Re: New Orleans Merchant Exchange," e-mail message to author, May 1, 2012. At the time the Merchants' Exchange was destroyed by fire, it housed a movie theater and a well-known restaurant called Glucks.

31. Richard J. Cawthon, *Comprehensive Historical Report on the Architectural History of the Old Mississippi State Capitol and the Restoration of 2005–2008,* Appendix F, 90–113, report prepared at the request of the Mississippi Department of Archives and History, 27 February 2008. In the log of tradesmen listed in the

payment ledger for the building of the Mississippi capitol, several craftsmen, such as Ezra Williams, were accomplished craftsmen from New Orleans who had worked on the Merchants' Exchange and other buildings designed by Dakin and Gallier.

Chapter Seven

1. Peatross and Mellown, *William Nichols, Architect*, 29. The U.S. Census of 1850 for Yazoo County, Mississippi, documents Lydia Lucinda Smith as being forty-six years old and born in North Carolina.

2. Mary Carol Miller, *Lost Landmarks of Mississippi* (Jackson, Miss.: University Press of Mississippi, 2002), 25. Mary Carol Miller refers to this building as the Lexington Male and Female Academy. It has also been called the Lexington Training Institute.

3. John K. Bettersworth, *Mississippi: A History* (Austin, Tex.: The Steck Company, 1959), 108–114. Spain ceded what is now southern Mississippi (including Natchez) to the United States in the Treaty of San Lorenzo in 1795. Natchez would not formerly be controlled by the United States until 1798. The lower part of West Florida remained Spanish until the rebellion of 1810.

4. Ibid., 169.

5. John Ray Skates, *Mississippi's Old Capitol: Biography of a Building* (Jackson, Miss.: Mississippi Department of Archives and History), 7.

6. Edward Mayes, *History of Education in Mississippi* (Washington, D. C.: Government Printing Office, 1899), 131–132.

7. Thomas Jefferson proposed a similar approach in planning the city of Washington, D. C., in 1791.

8. William Claiborne, a confidant of Thomas Jefferson, was instrumental in integrating the Louisiana Territory into the United States after the Louisiana Purchase in 1803.

9. William D. McCain, *The Story of Jackson [Vol.1]: A History of the Capital of Mississippi, 1821–1951* (Jackson, Miss.: J. F. Hyer Publishing Co., 1953), 140–144.

10. Curiously, to this day, Hinds County, Mississippi's capital county, has two county seats and two courthouses, one in Jackson and the other in Raymond. Hinds County is one of ten counties in Mississippi with dual county seats.

11. Mississippi Department of Archives and History.

12. John Ray Skates, *Mississippi's Old Capitol: Biography of a Building*, 21.

13. Letter from Governor Abram Scott to David Morrison, May 20, 1833, Governor's Correspondence, Mississippi Department of Archives and History.

14. Letter from Governor Charles Lynch to David Morrison, June 22, 1833, Governor's Correspondence, Mississippi Department of Archives and History.

15. John Ray Skates, *Mississippi's Old Capitol: Biography of a Building*, 22–33.

16. Ibid., 33.

17. Ibid., 25.

18. Richard J. Cawthon, *Comprehensive Historical Report on the Architectural History of the Old Mississippi State Capitol and the Restoration of 2005–2008*, Appendix F, 90–113, report prepared at the request of the Mississippi Department of Archives and History, 27 February 2008. Building records show that William Nichols was paid a quarterly salary of $750 from February 29, 1836, until October 23, 1840. His annual salary was $3,000 for the design and building of the Mississippi capitol.

19. Proceedings of the Mississippi Board of Commissioners of Public Buildings, 1836–1841, March 3, 1836, Mississippi Department of Archives and History.

20. Richard J. Cawthon, *Comprehensive Historical Report on the Architectural History of the Old Mississippi State Capitol and the Restoration of 2005–2008*, Appendix F, 90. John Robb and Alexander Baird were paid five thousand dollars for masonry work on the first design of the Mississippi State Capitol on November 21, 1834.

21. John Ray Skates, *Mississippi's Old Capitol: Biography of a Building*, 38.

22. Ibid., 39.

23. Ibid., 40.

24. Richard J. Cawthon, *Comprehensive Historical Report on the Architectural History of the Old Mississippi State Capitol and the Restoration of 2005–2008*, C-1.2. Due to the poor quality and lack of structural strength of the original building stone, numerous areas of the Old Capitol had the original stonework replaced with cast-iron lintels and limestone during the building's first renovation in 1870–1871 designed by Joseph Willis. All of the original stone was replaced with Indiana limestone during the 1959–1960 renovation, which was designed by Overstreet, Ware and Ware. Cawthon, *Comprehensive Historical Report on the Architectural History of the Old Mississippi State Capitol and the Restoration of 2005–2008*, C-2.1. In his comprehensive architectural history report, Richard Cawthon quotes Dr. David Dockery of the Office of Geology, Mississippi Department of Environmental Quality, who produced summation of the building stone used for the Mississippi State Capitol for the Mississippi Department of Archives and History. Robert O. Mellown, interview by the author, June 3, 2005. Robert Mellown stated that William Nichols always wanted to build with ashlar stone but unfortunately never lived or worked in states that possessed suitable native building stone.

25. William Nichols's report to the Commissioners of Public Buildings, September 3, 1836, as recorded in Proceedings of the Commissioners of Public Buildings, 1836–1840, entry for September 5, 1836.

26. William Nichols to Governor Charles Lynch, October 12, 1833, Governor's Correspondence, vol. 18, Mississippi Department of Archives and History.

27. John Ray Skates, *Mississippi's Old Capitol: Biography of a Building*, 41. Nichols visited New Orleans to examine a newly invented brickmaking machine in 1837; he reported that the machine was impractical.

28. Ibid., 41. "Proceedings of the Commissioners of Public Buildings, 1836–1840," entries for September 25 and December 18,1837.

29. "Proceedings," July 1836.

30. Jon Meacham, *American Lion: Andrew Jackson in the White House* (New York: Random House, 2008), 127–343.

31. John Ray Skates, *Mississippi's Old Capitol: Biography of a Building*, 42.

32. Ibid., 25.

33. "Proceedings," June 9, 1837.

34. The first story was originally referred to as the basement in the European sense of the word throughout the "Proceedings of the Commissioners of Public Buildings, 1836–1840." In Italian Renaissance architecture, the *piano nobile* is the first elevated story and is typically where all of the prominent rooms are located.

35. Todd Sanders, architectural historian, Mississippi Department of Archives and History, interview by the author, March 19, 2011. The four recesses were uncovered during the 2006–2008 renovation of the Old Capitol after Hurricane Katrina damaged it in 2005.

36. Richard J. Cawthon, *Comprehensive Historical Report on the Architectural History of the Old Mississippi State Capitol and the Restoration of 2005–2008*, C-1.2. Nichols designed the face of the tympanum to be plain. In 1847, a clock was installed in it. It was a gift from the Jackson municipal government. H. B. Evans

installed it for seventy-five dollars. No images of the clock exist and by 1916, when the capitol was first renovated, "the plate of rust" was removed and a circular window was installed in its place.

37. The 1916 measured drawings that were delineated by H. N. Austin state how each of the doorways in the corridors of the Mississippi State Capitol were detailed.

38. Ibid., E-5.4. A gas light reflector added in 1870 and documented in early twentieth-century photographs was mistakenly identified as a skylight in the mid-twentieth-century restoration. It appears that the faux dome is Nichols's original design.

39. Edward T. Davis and John Sanders, *A Romantic Architect in Antebellum North Carolina: The Works of Alexander Jackson Davis*, 45. In his description of the revisions of Nichols's second North Carolina capitol, Sanders refers to Nichols's tendency to design engaged Ionic columns. In fact, neither the Mississippi nor the Alabama capitols had engaged Ionic columns. The Mississippi capitol had Roman Doric-inspired pilasters.

40. Philibert de L'Orme (1514–1570) was a French architect who is credited for helping to establish classicism in French architecture. He was an innovative engineer who devised a method for fabricating curved timber ribs, which formed a lightweight dome. During his stay in France in the late eighteenth century, Thomas Jefferson was very impressed with de L'Orme's structural designs and built the first de L'Orme dome in America at his home, Monticello. James Stevens Curl, "Orme, Philibert de L." *Dictionary of Architecture and Landscape Architecture* (London: Encyclopedia Britannia, 2000).

41. *New York Herald*, March 1861. In an article about the secession of the state of Mississippi from the Union, the following was used to describe the Mississippi State Capitol: "The Mississippi State House, upon a shaded square in front of my window, is a faded, sober edifice, of the style in vogue fifty years ago." The Greek Revival style of architecture stayed popular in the Deep South long after it was supplanted by the Italianate style, which was first made popular by Alexander Jackson Davis, Renaissance Revival, and Second Empire Style, all of which flourished in the Northeast during the mid-to-late nineteenth century.

42. William S. Powell, *Dictionary of North Carolina Biography*, 98. Archibald Henderson (1768–1822) was a prominent lawyer in Salisbury, North Carolina, and a representative in the U. S. Congress from the Federalist Party. He served in Congress from 1798 until 1802. He then represented Rowan County in the North Carolina General Assembly from 1807 until 1820. John Marshall considered Henderson one of the ablest lawyers of his time.

43. Catherine W. Bishir, "Nichols, William (1780–1853)," *North Carolina Architects and Builders: A Biographical Dictionary* (2009), http://ncarchitects.lib.ncsu.edu (accessed March 19, 2012).

44. Richard J. Cawthon, *Comprehensive Historical Report on the Architectural History of the Old Mississippi State Capitol and the Restoration of 2005–2008*, Part C—Building Exterior, C-6.2. Richard Cawthon notes that there are very few antebellum institutional and commercial buildings with relatively unchanged first-story façades, making it difficult to judge how commonly exterior shutters were used in Mississippi. He notes two examples of buildings of this period with exterior shutters: the Bank of Port Gibson in Port Gibson, erected in 1840, and the Trinity Episcopal Church in Natchez, which received a Greek Revival façade in 1838. He also notes that the practice was common in Mobile, Alabama; commercial buildings, such as the Lafayette Hotel from the 1840s, had exterior shutters attached to the front door.

45. Ibid., Part D—Building Interior, D-5.1.

46. "Proceedings," February 6 and 13, 1845.

47. Richard J. Cawthon, *Comprehensive Historical Report on the Architectural History of the Old Mississippi State Capitol and the Restoration of 2005–2008*, Part C—The Roof, the Dome and the Lantern, C-7.2.

48. Ibid., Part E—Building Interior—specific rooms, E-4.2.

49. John Ray Skates, *Mississippi's Old Capitol: Biography of a Building*, 55. The real motive of Jackson's visit was to ask Governor Alexander McNutt to forgive an outstanding debt that Jackson's adopted son, Andrew, Jr., owed McNutt. Apparently the visit was successful for Jackson; McNutt forgave the loan owed by Andrew, Jr.

50. Richard J. Cawthon, *Comprehensive Historical Report on the Architectural History of the Old Mississippi State Capitol and the Restoration of 2005–2008,*, Part B—Site and Landscape, B-6.3 and B-6.4.

51. Elbert Hillard, "Mississippi Capitol National Register Nomination," Mississippi Department of Archives and History, October 11, 1969. The "New Capitol" cost over one million dollars to build, which came from back taxes owed by the Illinois Central Railroad.

52. Todd Sanders, interviews by the author, March 19, 2011, and June 11, 2011. The Historic Preservation Division staff at the Mississippi Department of Archives and History had wanted Nichols's stucco finish restored on the main elevations of the capitol. The Hurricane Katrina emergency restoration project expedited this project, which had been proposed several years earlier.

53. "Proceedings," March 5, 1840, 229.

54. Mary Carol Miller, *Lost Landmarks of Mississippi*, 115.

55. Letter from James Iredell to James Johnston, May 18, 1817, Johnston Papers, North Carolina Collection, Wilson Library, University of North Carolina at Chapel Hill.

56. Marianna Thomas, ed., *Eastern State Penitentiary: Historic Structures Report*, Philadelphia, Philadelphia Historical Commission, 2 vol., 1994. Eastern State Penitentiary would continue to have cellblock buildings added to it until 1956. Due to its poor building condition, the Commonwealth of Pennsylvania closed it in 1971.

57. Mississippi Legislature, Joint Committee on Public Buildings. "Report from the Committee on Public Buildings" (1840).

58. E. Bruce Thompson, "Reforms in the Penal System of Mississippi, 1820–1850," in *The Journal of Mississippi History* 7:2 (April 1945).

59. Ibid.

60. Mary Carol Miller, *Lost Landmarks of Mississippi*, 115–118.

61. The Virginia Executive Mansion, built in 1813 in Richmond, is the oldest continuously used governor's residence in the United States.

62. Mary Lohrenz, curator of the Mississippi Governor's Mansion, interview by the author, July 30, 2005.

63. William Nichols's Special Report to the Mississippi Legislature, April 1840, Volume 22, Mississippi Legislature Records.

64. Ibid.

65. Lawrence H. Officer and Samuel H. Williamson, *Purchasing Power of Money in the United States from 1774–2010* (New York: MeasuringWorth, 2011), 5–18.

66. John Ray Skates, *Mississippi's Old Capitol: Biography of a Building*, 156.

67. James B. Lloyd, *Lives of Mississippi Authors, 1817–1967* (Jackson, Miss.: University Press of Mississippi, 2009), 202–203. After Richard Graves escaped Mississippi and fled to Canada, he wrote a short pamphlet attempting to justify his actions to the state of Mississippi. His wife, Martha Thomas Graves, whom he had just married before the embezzlement scandal, returned much of the money to the state government, though about $44,000 of the original $150,000 that was stolen was

never recovered. She then joined her husband in Canada. It is presumed that Graves and his wife died in Canada sometime after 1886.

68. David G. Sansing and Carroll Waller, *A History of the Mississippi Governor's Mansion* (Jackson, Miss.: University Press of Mississippi, 1977), 3–16.

69. William R. Mitchell, *Edward Vason Jones, 1909–1980, Architect, Connoisseur, and Collector* (Athens, Ga.: Martin–St. Martin Press, 1995), 178. During the Governor's Mansion Renovation Project in 1975, which was designed by Charles Peterson and Edward Vason Jones, the grand staircase was reconstructed based on physical evidence. The original was removed during a remodeling in 1908. There was also a service stair, which apparently went from the basement to the attic, located between the main stair hall and the state dining room. It was removed in 1908.

70. Mississippi Department of Archives and History, Jackson, Miss. Pocket doors were installed between the entry hall and the parlors in the 1850s.

71. This small wing was replaced with the current wing facing West Street during the 1975 renovation.

72. Mary Lohrenz, curator of the Mississippi Governor's Mansion, interview by the author, July 30, 2005. Most of the plasterwork in the Governor's Mansion is not original. Significant sections were altered in the 1850s when gas lighting was installed and again in the early twentieth century. During the 1975 restoration, Charles Peterson and Edward Vason Jones added new plaster ornament in the parlors of the mansion, all of which is conjectural. The foyer columns are original. Most of the decorative woodwork appears to be original.

73. William R. Mitchell, *Edward Vason Jones, 1909–1980, Architect, Connoisseur, and Collector*, 179. Edward Vason Jones designed the current front door in 1975.

74. Richard J. Cawthon, "Re: William Nichols Questions," e-mail to Todd Sanders, 2 November 2011: lines 1–8.

75. John Ray Skates, *Mississippi's State Capitol: Biography of a Building*, 63.

76. Ibid.

77. Martha Boman, " A City of the Old South: Jackson, Mississippi, 1850–1860," *The Journal of Mississippi History*, XV (January, 1953), 6–8. Boman states that in 1850 there was discussion about moving the capital to three Mississippi cities or towns, Yazoo City, Vicksburg, and Raymond, but it was determined that Jackson would remain the state capital of Mississippi. Clay Williams, "Re: William Nichols' Land," e-mail to Todd Sanders, 26 March 2011: lines 1–14. Williams states that McCain's history of Jackson discusses the 1832 Constitution. Not only did it say Jackson would be capital until 1850, but any change of seat of government had to be done during the first session in 1850 or Jackson would be the permanent seat of government. It would not be up for debate year after year. The House and Senate Journals of 1850 does mention a bill about locating the seat of government, but it does not mention where the seat of state government would be relocated. The bill failed and Jackson remained the state capital of Mississippi.

Chapter Eight

1. Mills Lane, *Architecture of the Old South: Mississippi and Alabama*, 21–27. Todd Sanders, e-mail to author, November 21, 2012.

2. Ibid. At the time of his death, Weeks's estate included a chest of tools, two T–squares, drawings, and the following architectural pattern books: Thomas Malton's *Complete Treatise on Perspective* (London, 1776), William Halfpenny's *Art*

of Sound Building (London, 1728), and Owen Biddle's *Young Carpenter's Assistant* (Philadelphia, 1805), along with books by Swan and Pain.

3. John Hebron Moore, *The Emergence of the Cotton Kingdom in the Old Southwest: Mississippi, 1770–1860* (Baton Rouge, La.: Louisiana State University Press, 1988), 209–215.

4. Patti Carr Black, *Art in Mississippi, 1720–1980* (Oxford, Miss.: Mississippi Historical Society, 1998), 55–62.

5. Todd Sanders, e-mail to author, February 6, 2013.

6. G. E. Kidder Smith, *Source Book of American Architecture: 500 Notable Buildings from the 10th Century to the Present* (New York: Princeton Architectural Press, 1998), 195. Saint Mary was designated a minor basilica in 1999.

7. Historic American Buildings Survey, HABS MISS, 1–NATCH, 14–, St. Mary's Cathedral, Natchez, Miss.

8. Historic American Buildings Survey, HABS MISS, 1–NATCH, 21–Stanton Hall, Natchez, Miss. HABSMISS, 1–NATCH, 8–, Dunleith, Natchez, Miss.

9. Mississippi Department of Archives and History Database, accessed 16 February 2013.

10. Patti Carr Black, *Art in Mississippi, 1720–1980*, 60.

11. Todd Sanders, e-mail to author, November 21, 2012.

12. Patti Carr Black, *Art in Mississippi, 1720–1980*, 60.

13. *The Brandon News*, "Johnson Hall," April 26, 1923, Brandon, Mississippi, Public Library.

14. Mississippi Department of Archives and History, Rankin County Historical and Genealogical Society, *A History of Rankin County, MS—Vol. 1*, 135–136. Johnson Hall was demolished in 1923.

15. Mississippi Department of Archives and History Database, accessed on November 10, 2011.

16. Mississippi Department of Archives and History, Historic Preservation Division, Vertical File on S. P. Bailey. Richard J. Cawthon, *Comprehensive Historical Report on the Architectural History of the Old Mississippi State Capitol and the Restoration of 2005–2008*, Appendix F, 91.

17. William D. McCain, *The Story of Jackson, Vol. 2*, 151.

18. Richard J. Cawthon, *Lost Churches of Mississippi* (Jackson, Miss.: University Press of Mississippi, 2010), 93.

19. *Jackson Mississippian*, January 12, 1838, Mississippi Department of Archives and History.

20. Richard J. Cawthon, *Lost Churches of Mississippi*, 93 and 105. The Methodist Episcopal Church was demolished about 1882 and was replaced with the First Methodist Episcopal Church, South, which was built in 1882–1883. It was demolished to allow for the present Galloway United Methodist Church in 1913.

21. *The Southern Sun* (Jackson), "Notice—Sealed Proposals for Rankin County Courthouse," December 12, 1839, Mississippi Department of Archives and History.

22. Mississippi Department of Archives and History Database, accessed on March 17, 2012.

23. William D. McCain, *The Story of Jackson, Vol. 2*, 154.

24. 1880 Sanborn Map of Jackson, Mississippi, Mississippi Department of Archives and History.

25. Richard J. Cawthon, *Lost Churches of Mississippi*, 94–95.

26. Ibid., 95.

27. William D. McCain, *The Story of Jackson, Vol. 2*, 154–155.

28. Ibid., 155.

29. Richard J. Cawthon, *Lost Churches of Mississippi*, 94. The First Presbyterian Church was demolished in 1891.

30. Ibid., 44–46.

31. James S. Lull, letter to William Royal Roberts, 29 February 1840. Roberts is a colleague of Lull's living in Sharon, Vermont. Lull tells Roberts the following: "I have built one of the best churches in the Southern states erected at the expense of 27,000 dollars. I commenced it April 1835 and completed it last Sept."

32. Mills Lane, *Architecture of the Old South: Mississippi and Alabama*, 135, 139. James S. Lull (c. 1814–1872) designed and built the Lowndes County Courthouse in 1847 and is attributed to have designed the Riverview Mansion in Lowndes County, Mississippi.

33. Richard J. Cawthon, *Lost Churches of Mississippi*, 46. Cawthon states the following about Nichols's possible involvement in the building of the Columbus First Baptist Church: "[T]he old First Baptist Church was similar in appearance to the Lyceum at the University of Mississippi (1846–1848) and the Male and Female Academy at Lexington (ca. 1850), both designed by William Nichols, the architect of the Old Capitol. The similarity to those buildings and the fact that Nichols was one of the very few architects in the state with sufficient skill to design such a building suggest that William Nichols could have been the architect." The First Baptist Church of Columbus, Mississippi, was demolished in 1905.

34. Peatross and Mellown, *William Nichols, Architect*, 29.

35. Richard J. Cawthon, *Comprehensive Historical Report on the Architectural History of the Old Mississippi State Capitol and the Restoration of 2005–2008*, Appendix F, 93.

36. Hinds County Deed Record Book, Vol. 13, p. 475. Perry Cohea takes a loan for four hundred dollars and purchases two acres for a large town lot on West Capitol Street in Jackson where the Poindexter House is built on February 13, 1840. Hinds County Record Book, Vol. 14, p. 757, September 13, 1841. Perry Cohea sells Mary Ann Poindexter (his daughter) the two-acre lot for two dollars.

37. Mississippi Department of Archives and History, Historic Preservation Division Database, Jackson, Miss., accessed March 5, 2012. The John J. Poindexter House was originally located at what is now Poindexter Park on West Capitol Street in Jackson. It was moved ca. 1925 to a lot approximately a block to the east on Robinson Street and subdivided into apartments. The house was demolished in order to build Poindexter Elementary School in 1960.

38. *Webster's Ninth Dictionary* states that "Southron" is a variant on the word "Southerner" from early Scots and English dialects from the fifteenth century. It was popularized by Jane Porter's *Scottish Chiefs* (1810) and adopted in the United States by many in the South before the Civil War.

39. John Hope Franklin, *A Southern Odyssey: Travelers in the Antebellum North* (Baton Rouge, La.: Louisiana State University Press, 1976),70–76.

40. Isabella Margaret Elizabeth Blandin, *History of Higher Education of Women in the South* (Washington, D. C.: Neale Publishing, 1909), 192–193.

41. Mississippi Department of Archives and History, Historic Preservation Division Database, Jackson, Miss., accessed March 5, 2012.

42. Historic American Buildings Survey, C. K. Marshall House, Vicksburg, Miss., HABS: MS-130 (1936).

43. Edward Mayes, *History of Education in Mississippi*, 54–56.

44. Catherine O. Wohner (edited by Brenda Rubah, MDAH), Kirkpatrick Dental Office, Madison County, Mississippi, National Register of Historic Places Nomination, March 1991, Mississippi Department of Archives and History, Jackson, Miss.

45. Catherine O. Wohner, Kirkpatrick Dental Office, Canton, Miss., National Register of Historic Places Nomination, March 1991.

46. Elmore Graves, Vernon, Missisippi, Cemetery Record, compiled August 1979, Mississippi Department of Archives and History, Jackson, Miss.

47. William P. Howard, "Re: Book on Nichols," e-mail to Todd Sanders, February 17, 2012: lines 15–18. Marika Caroline Pieneda, James Lindsay Andrews and Related Families (Kearney/Girault/Thomas/Green), Madison County, Mississippi, 1830–1865, unpublished manuscript, June 12, 2003.

48. William P. Howard, Sedgewood Plantation, National Register of Historic Places Nomination, March 27, 2000.

49. Edward Mayes, *History of Education in Mississippi*, 127.

50. A township is legally thirty-six square miles (or sections) of land.

51. Allen Cabaniss, *The University of Mississippi: Its First Hundred Years* (Hattiesburg, Miss.: University and College Press of Mississippi, 1971), 3.

52. Ibid., 4.

53. Mississippi College is affiliated with the Mississippi Baptist Convention.

54. David G. Sansing, *The University of Mississippi: A Sesquicentennial History* (Jackson, Miss.: University Press of Mississippi, 1999), 2–46.

55. Allen Cabaniss, *The University of Mississippi: Its First Hundred Years*, 23.

56. David G. Sansing, *The University of Mississippi: A Sesquicentennial History*, 28–29. James Alexander Ventress (1805–1867) was born in Wilkinson County, Mississippi. He was considered one of the leading intellectuals of the planter class in Mississippi. From 1825 until 1833, Ventress studied at Oxford University, the University of Edinburgh, the Sorbonne in Paris, and the University of Berlin. He became acquainted with the leading European intellectuals of the early nineteenth century and published literary and scientific articles. He even wrote novels. He was an advocate of nonsectarian influences in the first curriculum of the University of Mississippi. In 1938, the Mississippi legislature designated James Alexander Ventress "Father of the University of Mississippi."

57. David G.Sansing, *The University of Mississippi: A Sesquicentennial History*, 22.

58. Allen Cabaniss, *The University of Mississippi: Its First Hundred Years*, 25.

59. Lynda Lasswell Crist, "Re: James Alexander Ventress," e-mail to author, November 7, 2011: lines 3–11. There has been speculation by Sansing that Ventress had designed the campus master plan for the University of Mississippi and that Nichols only executed it. In her Ph.D. dissertation, Lynda Crist confirms that Ventress was only an active member of the board of trustees and an engaged client for the university. He did not actually design the campus. See Lynda Lasswell Crist, "Useful in His Day: James Alexander Ventress (1805–1867)" (Ph.D. dissertation, University of Tennessee, 1980).

60. Edward Mayes, *History of Education in Mississippi*, 130.

61. Michael W. Fazio, "Historic Structures Report for the Lyceum Building at the University of Mississippi, Oxford, Mississippi," 29 October 1996, 1.

62. Florence E. Campbell, "Journal of the Minutes of the Board of Trustees of the University of Mississippi" (M.A. thesis, University of Mississippi, 1939), 8.

63. David G. Sansing, *The University of Mississippi: A Sesquicentennial History*, 46.

64. Edward Mayes, *History of Education in Mississippi*, 130.

65. Ibid., 135. Mayes cites the Mississippi Senate Journal, 1846, pp. 13, 14, and 23–25.

66. David G. Sansing, *The University of Mississippi: A Sesquicentennial History*, 23.

67. Michael W. Fazio, "Historic Structures Report for the Lyceum Building at the University of Mississippi, Oxford, Mississippi," 29 October 1996, 1–5.

68. David G. Sansing, *The University of Mississippi: A Sesquicentennial History*, 46.

69. Florence E. Campbell, "Journal of the Minutes of the Board of Trustees of the University of Mississippi," 24.

70. Michael W. Fazio, "Historic Structures Report for the Lyceum Building at the University of Mississippi, Oxford, Mississippi," 29 October 1996. The Lyceum had several expansions after Nichols completed it in 1848. Chancellor Fredrick A. P. Barnard first expanded three bays on its western end in 1856. Wings were added on both the north and south elevations in 1905. They were designed by Theodore Link, who was also completing building Mississippi's new state capitol. In 1916, a fire damaged the interior of the Lyceum. It was renovated, and a portico that matched Nichols's original one was added to its west facing or rear elevation in 1927. As with the capitol, Nichols originally intended the tympanum to be plain. A clock was added to it during the 1927 renovation. The interior of the Lyceum was completely renovated in 2001, and it now houses only the university's administration.

71. Ibid., 2.

72. Mary Carol Miller, *Lost Landmarks of Mississippi*, 7.

73. Sanborn Insurance Maps, "Oxford, Miss—University of Mississippi," 1890, 1900, 1910, and 1920, Mississippi Department of Archives and History, Jackson, Miss.

74. Gene Ford, "Lyceum—The Circle Historic District, University of Mississippi," National Historic Landmark Nomination, January 23, 2007, Mississippi Department of Archives and History, Jackson, Miss. Lyceum—The Circle Historic District was designated a National Historic Landmark District in 2008. Its listing as a National Historic Landmark was based on the enrollment of prominent civil rights advocate James Meredith at the University of Mississippi in 1962.

75. Pontotoc, Mississippi, the county seat of Pontotoc County, is located thirty-four miles southeast of Oxford, Mississippi.

76. Edward Mayes, *History of Education in Mississippi*, 67. Chickasaw College, the Presbyterian Female Collegiate Institution of Pontotoc, was begun in 1853 after the Chickasaw Presbytery agreed to take over the earlier Female Academy from the town of Pontotoc. The institution was officially chartered on October 14, 1852. On April 28, 1853, the town deeded the site where the building was constructed as well as all the buildings on the site to the institution with the understanding that the Presbytery would spend up to five thousand dollars on building, upkeep, and academic needs within five years from that date. The building was occupied for use in 1855 and completed in 1856.

77. Callie B. Young, *From These Hills: A History of Pontotoc County* (Pontotoc, Miss.: Pontotoc Women's Club, 1953), 96. The construction of Chickasaw College involved the use of 225,000 hard bricks burned on site.

78. Todd Sanders, interview by the author, March 19, 2011. See also Mary Carol Miller, *Lost Mansions of Mississippi*.

79. Megan Emily Davis, "William Turner: A Builder's Legacy in Oxford, Mississippi" (M.A. thesis, University of Mississippi, 2001), 98.

80. Mills Lane, *Architecture of the Old South: Mississippi and Alabama*, 146, 152.

81. Mississippi Department of Archives and History Database, accessed November 14, 2011.

82. William Nathaniel Banks, "William Faulkner's Oxford" in *Antiques: The Magazine*, March/April 2012, 130–139. Thomas S. Hines, *William Faulkner and the Tangible Past: The Architecture of Yoknapatawpha* (Berkeley, Calif.: University of California Press), 55–58.

83. Lafayette County, Mississippi, Deed Book E, 525. Historian Thomas Hines suggests that the Avant-Stone House in Oxford, Mississippi, may have been designed by Nichols and built by William Turner but this cannot be verified. Thomas S. Hines, *William Faulkner and the Tangible Past: The Architecture of Yoknapatawpha*, 59.

84. Callie B. Young, *From These Hills: A History of Pontotoc County*, 96.

85. Mary Carol Miller, *Lost Landmarks of Mississippi*, 26.

86. U.S. Census of Yazoo County, Miss., 1850.

87. *Yazoo City Mississippian*, October 5, 1850.

88. W. H. Lambeth, "Recollections of Old Yazoo," *Yazoo Sentinel*, October 24, 1912, Ricks Memorial Library, Yazoo City, Mississippi.

89. *Yazoo Democrat*, August 7, 1850, 1, Ricks Memorial Library, Yazoo City, Mississippi. This reference is courtesy of John E. Ellzey, reference and local history librarian, Ricks Memorial Library.

90. John E. Ellzey, "Re: William Nichols' Land," e-mail to Todd Sanders, 7 March 2011, lines 1–14.

91. Peatross and Mellown, *William Nichols, Architect*, 31.

92. Mary Carol Miller, *Lost Mansions of Mississippi*, 37–38. During the siege of Vicksburg in 1863, Union gunboat gunners mistakenly assumed that Shamrock was the headquarters of Confederate General John C. Pemberton. One artillery shell hit the residence; it went through the parlor, exited through the back doorway and clipped a chunk of stucco and brick off one of the columns. This damage was documented in the HABS drawings.

93. Mary Carol Miller, *Lost Mansions of Mississippi*, 36–38.

94. Ibid., 284. Mary Carol Miller documents that the verbal description of Shamrock was written in "Historic Homes of Mississippi," publication of the Mississippi Historical Society 6 (1902): 245–264.

95. Todd Sanders notes that the Hinkle Guild Company had an active business furnishing fine woodwork down the Mississippi River to numerous residential clients before the Civil War.

96. A. Hays Town (1903–2005), known as the "Premier Architect of the South," developed an extraordinary residential architectural practice that helped continue the rich tradition of Creole and English traditional vernacular architecture into the twenty-first century. Cyril E. Vetter and Phillip Gould, *The Louisiana Houses of A. Hays Town* (Baton Rouge, La.: Louisiana State University Press, 1999), iii–iv.

97. William D. McCain, *The Story of Jackson, Vol. 2*, 70.

98. Todd Sanders, *Images of America: Jackson's North State Street* (Charleston, S.C.: Arcadia Publishing, 2009), 22.

99. Mississippi Department of Archives and History Database, accessed March 15, 2012. Mary Carol Miller, *Lost Landmarks of Mississippi*, 26.

100. Raleigh, *North Carolina Standard*, February 8, 1854, obituary statement written by former North Carolina governor and University of North Carolina President David Lowry Swain.

Epilogue

1. Peatross and Mellown, *William Nichols, Architect*, 3.

2. Catherine Bishir, *North Carolina Architecture*, 473. Bishir speculates that Nichols could have designed the Roman Doric one-story portico at Farintosh but this has never been verified.

3. Ibid., 201.

4. Bishir, Peatross, and Sanders, "William Nichols" in *North Carolina Architects: A Biographical Dictionary*, N. C. State University Libraries, retrieved 25 May 2012, http://ncarchitects.lib.ncsu.edu/people/P000106.

5. Robert O. Mellown, "Variations on a Capitol Plan" in *Alabama Heritage*, Summer 2005, Issue 77, 14.

6. John Sanders Papers.

7. Alabama Historical Commission Database, accessed on March 9, 2012.

8. Peatross and Mellown, *William Nichols, Architect*, 31. Peatross and Mellown based this attribution solely on local tradition.

9. Mississippi Department of Archives and History Database, accessed March 15, 2012. The academy relocated to Terry-Stone after a fire destroyed their Nichols-designed building in 1904. Over time, the Nichols attribution as its architect was transferred from the Female Academy to Terry-Stone. Terry-Stone would suffer the same fate as the Lexington Female Academy; it was destroyed by fire in 1917.

10. Richard J. Cawthon, interview by the author, July 22, 2005.

11. Richard J. Cawthon, *Lost Churches of Mississippi*, 99–100. Saint Andrew's Episcopal Church was rebuilt in 1867. This church was superseded by a new church, located a block to the west, in 1903. The old church was demolished about 1904–1905 to allow construction of the Jones-Kensington Department Store (now the Heritage Building) at that location.

12. Mississippi Department of Archives and History Database, accessed on March 9, 2012.

13. John Ray Skates, *Mississippi's Old Capitol: Biography of a Building*, 46.

14. William D. McCain, *The Story of Jackson*, Vol. 2, 67. Mississippi Department of Archives and History Database, accessed on March 19, 2012.

15. Talbot Hamlin, *Greek Revival Architecture in America*, 29.

16. Catherine Bishir, interview with author, October 11, 2009.

17. Sir Winston Churchill, "House of Commons Rebuilding," *Commons Sitting HC Deb Hansard 1803–2005, Vol. 28, October 1943, Vol. 393, cc403–73* (UK Parliament Archives, 1943). http://hansard.milkbanksystems.com/commons/1943/oct/28/house-of-commons-rebuilding, accessed May 16, 2012. In context, Churchill stated: "On the night of 10th May, 1941, with one of the last bombs of the last serious raid, our House of Commons was destroyed by the violence of the enemy, and we have now to consider whether we should build it up again, and how, and when. We shape our buildings and afterwards our buildings shape us. Having dwelt and served for more than 40 years in the late Chamber, and having derived fiery great pleasure and advantages therefrom, I, naturally, would like to see it restored in all essentials to its old form, convenience and dignity. I believe that will be the opinion of the great majority of its Members. It is certainly the opinion of His Majesty's Government and we propose to support this resolution to the best of our ability."

Bibliography

Manuscripts and Archival Material

Baton Rouge, Louisiana

Louisiana Division of Historic Preservation, Office of Cultural Development
    National Register of Historic Places—Louisiana
Louisiana State University Library
    Hill Memorial Library, Special Collections
Louisiana State Library
Louisiana State Archives

Brandon, Mississippi

Brandon, Mississippi, Public Library

Chapel Hill, North Carolina

University of North Carolina Facilities Planning, Engineering Information
Services
    Plan Room and Archives
University of North Carolina Louis Round Wilson Library
    University Archives
        Minutes, Board of Trustees
    Southern Historical Collection
    North Carolina Collection
        North Carolina Grand Lodge of Free and Accepted Masons, Eagle
            Lodge, No. 19, Hillsborough, N.C.
        C. Ford Peatross Photographic Collection
        Eileen L. McGrath Papers
        John Hawks Papers
        Hayes Collection
        Mordecai Family Papers

North Carolina Map Collection, Claude J. Sauthier Map Collection File
David L. Swain Papers
University of North Carolina Papers, University Archives, University
    Papers
Chapel Hill National Historic District Nomination

Hillsborough, North Carolina

Town of Hillsborough: Hillsborough National Historic District Nomination
Little, Ruth: Hillsborough National Historic District Inventory Update

Jackson, Mississippi

Mississippi Department of Archives and History
    Database
    Doyle File
    Governor's Correspondences, Volumes 16 and 18
    House of Representatives Journals, 1835, 1842, 1844
    Jackson, Mississippi, Sanborn Maps
    J. L. Power Papers
    Lexington, Mississippi, Sanborn Maps
    Mississippi Cemetery File
    National Register of Historic Places, Mississippi Records
    Old Capitol Subject File
    Proceedings of the Mississippi Board of Commissioners of Public Buildings
        RG 43, Volume 14
    William Nichols Subject File
    Hinds County Deed Books
    Lafayette County Deed Books
    S. P. Bailey File

Madison, Wisconsin

The University of Wisconsin Library, Digital Collections
Pain, William. *Practical House Carpenter*. London: I. and J. Taylor, 1788
http://digicoll.library.wisc.edu/cgi-bin/DLDecArts/DLDecArts-idx?id=DLDec
    Arts.PainPaBritPall

Montgomery, Alabama

Alabama Historical Commission
    National Register of Historic Places—Alabama

Oxford, Mississippi

University Papers, University Archives, University of Mississippi Library
Facilities Management Archives and Records

New Orleans, Louisiana

Louisiana State Museum, Historical Center Archives
Williams Research Center, The Historic New Orleans Collection

Philadelphia, Pennsylvania

The Athenaeum of Philadelphia
John Jones Papers
Thomas U. Walter Papers

Raleigh, North Carolina

North Carolina Grand Lodge of Free and Accepted Masons
Archives
North Carolina Division of Archives and History
Church Records, Edenton, Saint Paul's Church
National Register of Historic Places—North Carolina
North Carolina Capitol Papers
Wake County Deed Books
North Carolina State University Library
Bishir, Catherine W. "Nichols, William (1780–1853)" in *North Carolina Architects and Builders: A Biographical Dictionary.* http://ncarchitects. lib.ncsu.edu/people/P000026 (accessed March 21, 2012).
NCSU Libraries Special Collections Research Center. *The Built Heritage of North Carolina: Historic Architecture in the Old North State.* http:// images.lib.ncsu.edu:8180/luna/servlet/view/search?sort=Division+Se quence+Number%2CPageSequenceNumber%2CFilename%2CTitle& search=Search&q=Orange+County&QuickSearchA=QuickSearchA &os=450 (accessed March 21, 2012).

Tuscaloosa, Alabama

W. S. Hoole Special Collections Library, University of Alabama
University Papers, Board of Trustees Minutes

Urbana, Illinois

University of Illinois Library, Rare Book Library
Ricker Art and Architecture Library

Washington, D. C.

Library of Congress: Historic American Buildings Survey
http://memory.loc.gov/ammem/collections/habs_haer/
United States Census
http://www.rootsweb.com/~nccumber/fayettecensus.htm

Winston-Salem, North Carolina

Museum of Early Southern Decorative Arts
Research Files

Yazoo City, Mississippi

B. S. Ricks Memorial Library

Private Collections

Ann Beha Architects, Boston, Massachusetts, "Gerrard Hall Feasibility Study," 2004
George Fore, Raleigh, North Carolina, "Gerrard Hall Paint Analysis," 2004
John L. Sanders, "William Nichols Papers," Chapel Hill, North Carolina, 1950–1983
Mary Lohrenz, Jackson, Mississippi, "Mississippi Governor's Mansion Docent
    Manual," 2003
Robert Parker Adams, Jackson, Mississippi, "Historic Structures Report, The Old
    Mississippi Capitol," 2005

Newspapers and Periodicals

Alabama

Huntsville *Advocate*
Tuscaloosa *State Intelligencer*
Tuscaloosa *News and Times-Gazette*
Tuscaloosa *Independent Monitor*
State Rights Expositor

Mississippi

Jackson *Clarion-Ledger*
Jackson *Mississippian*
Jackson *Southron*
Jackson *Southern Sun*
Yazoo City *Democrat*
Yazoo City *Mississippian*
Yazoo City *Sentinel*

North Carolina

Edenton *Gazette*
Fayetteville *Gazette*
Fayetteville *Intelligencer*
Raleigh *Star*
Raleigh *Register*

Interviews

Notes are in possession of author

Robert Parker Adams, August, 2005
Catherine W. Bishir, May, 2006 (e-mail)
Charles Brownell, January, 2012 (e-mail)
Richard Campanella, December, 2011 (e-mail)
Richard Cawthon, August, 2005
Barbara Church, November, 2006

James H. Craig, May, 2005
Linda Laswell Crist, November, 2011
John Ellzey, February, 2012 (e-mail)
R. Neil Fulghum, July, 2007
Robert Gamble, June, November, 2005
Brooks Gardner, April, 2006
Pamela Hawkes, April, 2005–August, 2007 (various interviews)
Greg Lambousy, December, 2011 (e-mail)
Mary Lohrenz, August, 2005
John Magill, January, 2012 (e-mail)
Robert Mellown, June, 2005
C. Ford Peatross, June, 2005
John L. Sanders, April, 2005–August, 2008 (various interviews)
Todd Sanders, November 2010–June 2012 (various interviews)
William Seale, June–August, 2011 (e-mail)
Melissa Stein, January, 2012 (e-mail)
F. Mitchner Wilds, June, 2007
John Wood, March, 2006
Susan Wood, March, 2006

Books, Articles and Unpublished Sources

Abernethy, Thomas Perkins. *From Frontier to Plantation in Tennessee: A Study of Frontier Democracy.* Chapel Hill, N. C.: University of North Carolina Press, 1932.

Allcott, John V. *The Campus at Chapel Hill: Two Hundred Years of Architecture.* Chapel Hill: Chapel Hill Historical Society, 1986.

Banks, William Nathaniel. "William Faulkner's Oxford." *Antiques: The Magazine* (March/April 2012): 130–139.

Battle, Kemp. *History of the University of North Carolina.* Raleigh: Edwards and Broughton, 1907, 1912.

Benjamin, Asher. *The Practical House Carpenter.* Boston: R. P. and C. Williams, Annin and Smith, 1830.

Bettersworth, John K. *Mississippi: A History.* Austin, Tex.: The Steck Company, 1959.

Bishir, Catherine W., Charlotte V. Brown, Carl R. Lounsbury, and Ernest H. Wood III. *Architects and Builders in North Carolina: A History of the Practice of Building.* Chapel Hill: University of North Carolina Press, 1990.

Bishir, Catherine W. *North Carolina Architecture.* Chapel Hill: University of North Carolina Press, 1990.

———. *Southern Built: American Architecture, Regional Practice.* Charlottesville, Va.: University of Virginia Press, 2006.

Black, Patti Carr. *Art in Mississippi, 1720–1980.* Oxford, Miss.: Mississippi Historical Society, 1998.

Blandin, Isabella Margaret Elizabeth. *History of Higher Education of Women in the South.* Washington, D. C.: Neale Publishing, 1909.

Bowsher, Alice Meriwether, and M. Lewis Kennedy, Jr. *Alabama Architecture: Looking at Building and Place.* Tuscaloosa, Ala.: University of Alabama Press, 2001.

Brantley, William H. *Three Capitals: A Book about the First Three Capitals of Alabama, St. Stephens, Huntsville and Cahawba.* Tuscaloosa, Ala.: University of Alabama Press, 1947.

Buchanan, Paul E. "The Eighteenth-Century Frame House of Tidewater Virginia." In *Building Early America*, edited by Charles E. Peterson, 54–73. Radnor, Pa.: Chilton Book Co. for the Carpenter's Company of Pennsylvania, 1976.

Cabaniss, Allen. *The University of Mississippi: Its First Hundred Years*. Hattiesburg, Miss.: University and College Press of Mississippi, 1971.

Cain, Helen, and Anne D. Czarniecki. *An Illustrated Guide to the Mississippi Governor's Mansion*. Jackson, Miss.: University Press of Mississippi, 1984.

Campbell, Florence E. "Journal of the Minutes of the Board of Trustees of the University of Mississippi." M.A. thesis, University of Mississippi, 1939.

Carleton, Mark T. *Politics and Punishment: The History of the Louisiana Penal System*. Baton Rouge, La.: Louisiana State University Press, 1971.

Carter, Edward C., II. *Benjamin Henry Latrobe and Public Works: Professionalism, Private Interest, and Public Policy in the Age of Jefferson*. Essays in Public Works, no.3. Washington, D. C.: Public Works Historical Society, 1976.

Cawthon, Richard J. "Comprehensive Historical Report on the Architectural History of the Old Mississippi State Capitol and the Restoration of 2005–2008, Part I Architectural History." Unpublished report, Mississippi Department of Archives and History, 2009.

———. *Lost Churches of Mississippi*. Jackson, Miss.: University Press of Mississippi, 2010.

Christovich, Mary Louise, Rouhlac Toledano, Betty Swanson, and Pat Holden. *New Orleans Architecture: Volume II: The American Sector (Faubourg St. Mary), Howard Avenue to Iberville Street, Mississippi River to Claiborne Avenue*. Gretna, La.: Pelican Publishing Co., 1972.

Clark, Clifford Edward, Jr. *The American Family Home 1800–1860*. Chapel Hill, N. C.: University of North Carolina Press, 1986.

Cohen, Jeffrey A., and Charles E. Brownell. *The Architectural Drawings of Benjamin Henry Latrobe*. New Haven, Conn.: Published for the Maryland Historical Society and the American Philosophical Society by Yale University Press, 1994.

Craig, James H. *The Arts and Crafts in North Carolina, 1699–1840*. Winston-Salem, N. C.: Museum of Early Southern Decorative Arts, 1965.

Crist, Linda Laswell. "Useful in His Day: James Alexander Ventress (1805–1867)." Ph.D. diss., University of Tennessee, 1980.

Crocker, Mary Wallace. *Historic Architecture in Mississippi*. Jackson, Miss.: University Press of Mississippi, Second Edition, 1982.

———. "Asher Benjamin: The Influence of His Handbooks on Mississippi Buildings."*Journal of the Society of Architectural Historians*, Vol. 38 (October 1979): 266–270.

Curtis, James C. "Andrew Jackson: Symbol for What Age?"*Review in American History 8* (June 1980): 194–199.

Dangerfield, George. *The Awakening of American Nationalism, 1815–1828*. The New American Nation Series: New York: Harper and Row, 1965.

Davis, Edward T., and John L. Sanders. *A Romantic Architect in Antebellum North Carolina: The Works of Alexander Jackson Davis*. Raleigh: Historic Preservation Foundation of North Carolina and the State Capitol Foundation, 2000.

Davis, Megan Emily. "William Turner: A Builder's Legacy in Oxford, Mississippi," M.A. thesis: University of Mississippi, 2001.

Elliot, Cecil D. "The North Carolina State Capitol." *The Southern Architect* 5, No. 5 (May 1958): 19–22.

Ellis, Richard E. *The Union at Risk: Jacksonian Democracy, States' Rights, and the Nullification Crisis*. New York: Random House, 1989.

Fazio, Michael W. "Historic Structures Report for the Lyceum Building at the University of Mississippi, Oxford, Mississippi." Unpublished report prepared for the University of Mississippi Facilities Management Office, October 29, 1996.

Fazio, Michael W., and Patrick A. Snadon. *The Domestic Architecture of Benjamin Henry Latrobe.* Baltimore, Md.: Johns Hopkins University Press, 2006.

Federal Writers' Project of the Works Progress Administration. *Mississippi: The WPA Guide to the Magnolia State.* Jackson, Miss.: University Press of Mississippi, 1988.

Feller, Daniel. *The Jacksonian Promise: America, 1815–1840.* The American Moment. Baltimore, Md.: Johns Hopkins University Press, 1995.

Fletcher, Banister, and J. C. Palmes. *Sir Banister Fletcher's A History of Architecture.* New York: Charles Scribner and Sons, 1975.

Franklin, John Hope. *A Southern Odyssey: Travelers in the Antebellum North.* Baton Rouge, La.: Louisiana State University Press, 1976.

Gallahee, John Morin. *The University of Alabama: A Short History.* New York: Newcomer Society in America, 1953.

Gamble, Robert S. *Historic Architecture in Alabama: A Guide to Style and Types, 1810–1930.* Tuscaloosa, Ala.: University of Alabama Press, 2001.

———. *The Alabama Catalog: Historic American Buildings Survey: A Guide to the Early Architecture of the State.* Tuscaloosa, Ala.: University of Alabama Press, 1987.

Gatling, Eva Ingersoll. "John Berry of Hillsboro, North Carolina." *Journal of the Society of Architectural Historians,* 10, No. 1 (March 1951): 18–22.

Gilchrist, Agnes Addison. *William Strickland, Architect and Engineer, 1788–1854.* Philadelphia: University of Pennsylvania Press, 1950.

Grief, Constance M. *John Notman, Architect.* Philadelphia: The Athenaeum of Philadelphia, 1979.

Hamlin, Talbot. *Greek Revival Architecture in America.* London: Oxford University Press, 1944.

———. *Benjamin Henry Latrobe.* New York: Oxford University Press, 1955.

Hammond, Ralph. *Ante-Bellum Mansions of Alabama.* New York: Bonanza Books, 1951.

Harris, Cyril M. *Illustrated Dictionary of Historic Architecture.* New York: Dover Publications, Inc., 1977.

Henderson, Archibald. *The Campus of the First University.* Chapel Hill: University of North Carolina Press, 1949.

Herzog, Lynda Vestal. "The Early Architecture of New Bern, North Carolina, 1750–1850." Ph.D. diss., University of California at Los Angeles, 1977.

Hines, Thomas S. *William Faulkner and the Tangible Past: The Architecture of Yoknapatawpha.* Berkeley, Calif.: University of California Press, 1996.

Hitchcock, Henry Russell, and William Seale. *Temples of Democracy: The State Capitols of the U.S.A.* New York: Harcourt Brace Jovanovich, 1976.

Holcomb, Gene. "The Mississippi Governor's Mansion." *Journal of Mississippi History, II.* January 1940.

Johnston, Francis Benjamin, and Thomas Tileston Waterman. *The Early Architecture of North Carolina.* Chapel Hill, N. C.: University of North Carolina Press, 1947.

Jones, H. G. *North Carolina Illustrated, 1524–1984.* Chapel Hill, N. C.: University of North Carolina Press, 1983.

Lafever, Minard. *The Architectural Instructor.* New York: George P. Putnam, 1856.

———. *The Beauties of Modern Architecture.* New York: George P. Putnam, 1856.

———. *The Modern Builder's Guide.* New York: George P. Putnam, 1856.

Landy, Jacob. *The Architecture of Minard Lafever.* New York: Columbia University Press, 1970.

Lane, Mills. *Architecture of the Old South: North Carolina.* Savannah, Ga.: Beehive Press, 1985.

———. *Architecture of the Old South: Mississippi–Alabama.* Savannah, Ga.: Beehive Press, 1985.

———. *Architecture of the Old South: Virginia.* Savannah, Ga.: Beehive Press, 1985.

Little, M. Ruth. *The Town and Gown Architecture of Chapel Hill, North Carolina.* Chapel Hill, N. C.: Preservation Society of Chapel Hill, 2006.

Lloyd, James B. *Lives of Mississippi Authors, 1817–1967.* Jackson, Miss.: University Press of Mississippi, 2009.

Lounsbury, Carl. *An Illustrated Glossary of Early Southern Architecture and Landscape.* Charlottesville, Va.: University of Virginia Press, 1999.

Mayes, Edward. *History of Education in Mississippi.* Washington, D. C.: Government Printing Office, 1899.

McCain, William D. *The Story of Jackson.* 2 Vols. Jackson, Miss.: J. F. Hyer Publishing Co., 1953.

Meacham, Jon. *American Lion: Andrew Jackson in the White House.* New York: Random House: 2008.

Mellown, Robert O. "Variations on the Capitol Plan." In *Alabama Heritage* (Summer 2005): 8–17.

———. *The University of Alabama: A Guide to the Campus Historic Architecture.* Tuscaloosa, Ala.: University of Alabama Press, 1988.

———. "Alabama's Fourth Capital: The Construction of the State House in Tuscaloosa." *The Alabama Review.* Montgomery, Ala.: Alabama Historical Society (October 1987): 259–282.

Miller, Mary Carol. *Lost Mansions of Mississippi: Volume I.* Jackson, Miss.: University Press of Mississippi, 1996.

———. *Lost Landmarks of Mississippi.* Jackson, Miss.: University Press of Mississippi, 2002.

———. *Lost Mansions of Mississippi: Volume II.* Jackson, Miss.: University Press of Mississippi, 2010.

Mitchell, William R. *Edward Vason Jones, 1909–1980, Architect, Connoisseur, and Collector.* Athens, Ga.: Martin–St. Martin Press, 1995.

Moore, John Hebron. *The Emergence of the Cotton Kingdom in the Old Southwest: Mississippi, 1770–1860.* Baton Rouge, La.: Louisiana State University Press, 1988.

Mormino, Gary R. "Cuba Libre Florida, and the Spanish American War." *Theodore Roosevelt Association Journal* (Winter/Spring 2010), Vol. 31, Issue 1/2. New York: Theodore Roosevelt Association, 2010.

Newcomb, Rexford. *Architecture in Old Kentucky.* Urbana, Ill.: University of Illinois Press, 1953.

Nicholson, Peter. *Architectural Dictionary.* London: J. Barfield, 1819.

Peatross, C. Ford, and Robert O. Mellown. *William Nichols, Architect.* Tuscaloosa, Ala.: University of Alabama Art Gallery, 1979.

———. "Architect of a Region: William Nichols." *Society for the Fine Arts Review,* Vol. IV (Summer 1982): 6–10.

Pesson, Edward. *Jacksonian America: Society, Personality, and Politics.* Urbana, Ill.: University of Illinois Press, 1985.

Pierson, William H. *American Buildings and Their Architects. Vol. I, The Colonial and Neoclassical Styles.* New York: Oxford University Press, 1970.

Powell, William S. *The First State University: A Pictorial History of the University of North Carolina*. Chapel Hill, N. C.: University of North Carolina Press, 1972, 1979, 1992.

———. *Dictionary of North Carolina Biography*. 4 vols to date. Chapel Hill, N. C.: University of North Carolina Press, 1979–.

Remni, Robert V. *Andrew Jackson and the Course of American Democracy, 1833–1845*. New York: Harper Publishing, 1985.

Richardson, George. *New Vitruvius Britannicus*. London: J. Taylor, 1802.

Royall, Anne Newport. *The Black Book; or, A Continuation of Travels in the United States*. Washington, D. C.: Printed for the author, 1828–1829.

Sandbeck, Peter B. *The Historic Architecture of New Bern and Craven County, North Carolina*. New Bern: Tryon Palace Commission, 1988.

Sansing, David G., and Carroll Waller. *A History of the Mississippi Governor's Mansion*. Jackson, Miss.: University Press of Mississippi, 1977.

Sansing, David G. *The University of Mississippi: A Sesquicentennial History*. Jackson, Miss.: University Press of Mississippi, 1999.

Sanders, John L. "The North Carolina State House and Capitol, 1792–1872." Research report, 1972, copy in Restoration Branch, Archives and History, Raleigh, N. C.

———. " The North Carolina State Capitol of 1840." *The Magazine Antiques* (Sept. 1985): 474–84.

———. "This Political Temple, The Capitol of North Carolina." *Popular Government* 43, No. 2 (Fall 1977): 1–10.

Sanders, Todd. *Images of America: Jackson's North State Street*. Charleston, S. C.: Arcadia Publishing, 2009.

Scott, Pamela. *Temple of Liberty: Building the Capitol for a New Nation*. New York: Oxford University Press, 1995.

Scully, Arthur, Jr. *James Dakin, Architect: His Career in New York and the South*. Baton Rouge, La.: Louisiana State University Press, 1973.

Seale, William. "Symbol as Architecture." *Design Quarterly, No. 94/95, Second Federal Design Assembly: The Design Reality*. Walker Art Center (1975): 14–15.

Sellers, James B. *History of the University of Alabama*. Tuscaloosa, Ala.: University of Alabama Press, 1953.

Skates, John Ray. *Mississippi's Old Capitol: Biography of a Building*. Jackson, Miss.: Mississippi Department of Archives and History, 1990.

Smith, G. E. Kidder. *Source Book of American Architecture: 500 Notable Buildings from the 10th Century to the Present*. New York: Princeton University Press, 1998.

Stout, Leon. "Origins and Early History of the Louisiana Penitentiary." M.A. thesis, Louisiana State University, 1934.

Stuart, James, and Nicholas Revett. *The Antiquities of Athens*. Leicester: T. Combe and Company, 1762–1794.

Thigpen, Richard. "The Four Public Buildings of the University of Alabama to Survive the Civil War." *The Alabama Review*, Vol. XXXIV, No. 1 (January 1981).

University of Mississippi. *Historical Catalogue of the University of Mississippi, 1849–1909*. Nashville, Tenn.: Marshall and Bruce Company, 1910.

Vetter, Cyril E. *The Louisiana Houses of A. Hays Town*. Baton Rouge, La.: Louisiana State University Press, 1999.

Watson, Harry L. "Old Hickory's Democracy." *Wilson Quarterly* 9 (Autumn 1985): 101–33.

———. *An Independent People: The Way We Lived in North Carolina, 1770–1820*. Series edited by Sydney Nathans. Chapel Hill: University of North Carolina Press, 1983.

Waugh, Elizabeth Culbertson. *North Carolina's Capital, Raleigh.* Chapel Hill, N. C.: University of North Carolina Press, 1967.

Wilson, Samuel, Jr., ed. *Impressions Respecting New Orleans by Benjamin Henry Boneval Latrobe, Diary and Sketches 1818–1820.* New York: Columbia University Press, 1951.

Wolfe, Suzanne Rau. *The University of Alabama: A Pictorial History.* Tuscaloosa, Ala.: University of Alabama Press, 1983.

Young, Callie B. *From These Hills: A History of Pontotoc County.* Pontotoc, Miss.: Pontotoc Women's Club, 1953.

Young, David Nathaniel. *History of the Construction of State Buildings in Jackson, Mississippi, 1822–1860.* M.A. thesis, Mississippi College, 1954. Microfilm copy of typewritten manuscript (MDAH Microfilm Roll 3338).

Index

3-15

ML